Build a Robo-Advisor with Python (From Scratch)

Build a Robo-Advisor with Python (From Scratch)

ROB REIDER
ALEXANDER MICHALKA

MANNING
SHELTER ISLAND

For online information and ordering of this and other Manning books, please visit
www.manning.com. The publisher offers discounts on this book when ordered in quantity.
For more information, please contact

    Special Sales Department
    Manning Publications Co.
    20 Baldwin Road
    PO Box 761
    Shelter Island, NY 11964
    Email: orders@manning.com

Manning Publications Co.
20 Baldwin Road
PO Box 761
Shelter Island, NY 11964

Development editor:	Doug Rudder
Technical editor:	Marcus Young
Review editor:	Aleksandar Dragosavljević
Production editor:	Deirdre Hiam
Copy editor:	Tiffany Taylor
Proofreader:	Mike Beady
Typesetter:	Ammar Taha Mohamedy
Cover designer:	Marija Tudor

ISBN 9781633439672
Printed in the United States of America

brief contents

contents

CONTENTS xi

preface

We hope readers will learn about both finance and Python by reading the book. It isn't intended to teach either of those topics from the ground up—we expect that readers will have a basic understanding of probability and statistics, financial concepts, and Python programming—but accessibility is important to us.

The balance of theory and implementation varies by chapter. Some chapters are very financially focused, and the Python content is limited to showing how a few functions from existing libraries can be used to perform certain calculations or accomplish desired tasks. In other chapters, there aren't any existing Python libraries we can use. These chapters are much more code-heavy, and we essentially build new Python libraries implementing the concepts they cover. We know reading code isn't always easy, so we show example usages of new code whenever possible to aid understanding.

Much of the content related to laws or regulations, specific financial products, or types of retirement accounts is United States–focused. We've spent our careers in the United States, and the specifics we cover are what we know. However, the concepts we discuss should apply no matter where you live. Often there are non-US equivalents of topics we discuss—for example, a self-invested pension plan (SIPP) is essentially the United Kingdom's version of a self-directed IRA in the United States.

Your feedback is essential, and we invite you to send us an email at pythonroboadvisor@gmail.com or leave comments in the LiveBook discussion forum. Also, Rob plans to periodically write blog posts on the intersection of finance and Python on his website, pynancial.com. He looks forward to seeing comments and questions, sharing ideas, and collaborating there as well. We appreciate your interest and have done our best to produce the best book possible for you.

acknowledgments

Writing this book was far more difficult and time-consuming than either of us expected. We each have many people to thank.

Alex thanks Rob for conceiving the book and asking him to coauthor it, Kyle for her understanding while he spent his nights and weekends at his desk, and his Wealthfront colleagues for their support initially and along the way.

Rob thanks Jonathan Larkin (and many others at Quantopian) for igniting his interest in Python, Scott Feier for scrutinizing the manuscript and catching numerous errors, and Marty Reider for helping him set up and maintain the GitHub repository.

We both thank the entire Manning team, especially Doug Rudder for his incredible patience and helpful suggestions. Thank you also to our project manager Deirdre Hiam, our copy editor Tiffany Taylor, our proofreader Mike Beady, and Marcus Young for his technical proofing.

We would also like to thank all of our reviewers: Ashutosh Sanzgiri, Christopher Kottmyer, Claudiu Schiller, Dan Sheikh, David Cronkite, David Patschke, Eli Mayost, Keerthi Shetty, Krzysztof Kamyczek, Laud Bentil, Laurens Meulman, Marco Carnini, Marco Seguri, Marcus H. Young, Maxim Volgin, Mohana Krishna, Oliver Korten, Oren Zeev-Ben-Mordehai, Philip Patterson, Rani Sharim, Richard Vaughan, Salil Athalye, Seung-jin Kim, Simone Sguazza, Sriram Macharla, and Vatsal Desai, your suggestions helped to make this a better book.

about this book

In *Build a Robo-Advisor with Python (From Scratch)*, you'll design and develop a working financial advisor that can manage a real investing strategy. You'll add new features to your advisor chapter by chapter, including determining the optimal weight of cryptocurrency in your portfolio, rebalancing to keep your investments on target while minimizing taxes, and using reinforcement learning to find a "glide path" that can maximize how long your money will last in retirement. Best of all, the skills you learn in reinforcement learning, convex optimization, and Monte Carlo methods can be applied to numerous lucrative fields beyond the domain of finance.

WHO SHOULD READ THIS BOOK

Our target audience is anyone who is interested in finance and investments, who has some familiarity with Python, and who is interested in learning about how Python can be used to automate investment processes. You may be looking to apply the tools you'll learn for your own finances or professionally, whether you're interested in jobs in this area or you're a financial advisor who wants to automate parts of your business.

HOW THIS BOOK IS ORGANIZED: A ROADMAP

The book is organized into four parts.

- **Part One: Basic Tools and Building Blocks** starts in chapter 1 by covering the robo-advisory landscape and what robo-advisors do. We then introduce some of the basic tools and concepts used in the financial industry: plots of risk versus (expected) reward and the efficient frontier (chapter 2); methods for estimating expected future returns, volatilities, and correlations (chapter 3); and evaluating the exchange-traded funds that are typically used to construct a portfolio of assets (chapter 4).

- **Part Two: Financial Planning Tools** shows how to automate some of the financial planning services offered by advisors. Chapter 5 introduces Monte Carlo simulations and how to model various sources of risk to estimate the probability of running out of money in retirement. In chapter 6, we describe reinforcement learning and demonstrate, through several examples, how it can be applied to solving financial planning problems. Next, chapter 7 cover various methods for measuring returns when there are inflows and outflows and how to use risk-adjusted returns to evaluate the performance of investment managers. Chapters 8 and 9 discuss methods to reduce taxes. The first, asset location, involves strategically placing different types of assets in specific types of accounts to optimize tax efficiency. The second method analyzes various strategies for sequencing withdrawals during the decumulation phase of retirement when investors must draw down their savings to pay for expenses.

- **Part Three: Portfolio Construction** teaches methods for determining portfolio weights. In chapter 10, we show how to use inputs like expected returns, volatilities, and correlations, as well as constraints or other considerations, to build "optimal" portfolios. We also highlight some of the pitfalls associated with using optimization to build portfolios. Then we discuss two methodologies designed to address these pitfalls: risk parity (chapter 11) and the Black–Litterman model (chapter 12).

- **Part Four: Portfolio Management** discusses how to manage a real portfolio over time after the target weights have been determined. Chapter 13 details several approaches to portfolio rebalancing (making trades to bring a portfolio's weights in line with their targets), ranging from very simple to (somewhat) complex. Finally, in chapter 14, we discuss tax-loss harvesting, a way for investors to lower their taxes by opportunistically selling assets that have declined in value.

Parts 2–4 can be read in any order, but we recommend starting with part 1.

ABOUT THE CODE

This book contains many examples of source code both in numbered listings and inline with normal text. In both cases, source code is formatted in a `fixed-width font like this` to separate it from ordinary text. Sometimes code is also **`in bold`** to highlight code that has changed from previous steps in the chapter, such as when a new feature adds to an existing line of code.

In many cases, the original source code has been reformatted; we've added line breaks and reworked indentation to accommodate the available page space in the book. In rare cases, even this was not enough, and listings include line-continuation markers (➥). Additionally, comments in the source code have often been removed from the listings when the code is described in the text. Code annotations accompany many of the listings, highlighting important concepts.

All the chapters contain examples in Python, and many include function and class definitions. These can be found on the book's website (www.manning.com/books/build-a-robo-advisor-with-python-from-scratch) and the GitHub repository for this book (https://github.com/robreider/robo-advisor-with-python). Filenames correspond to chapter numbers.

In each chapter, later code builds on earlier code. For example, a code section in the middle of a chapter may rely on a function defined earlier or a package imported earlier. Additionally, class definitions with many methods may be broken into multiple code sections. We recommend copying or importing the code from the website or GitHub rather than straight from the text if you are working in Python while reading an electronic version of the book.

You can get executable snippets of code from the liveBook (online) version of this book at https://livebook.manning.com/book/build-a-robo-advisor-with-python-from-scratch. The complete code for the examples in the book is available for download from the Manning website at https://www.manning.com/books/build-a-robo-advisor-with-python-from-scratch.

LIVEBOOK DISCUSSION FORUM

Purchase of *Build a Robo-Advisor with Python (From Scratch)* includes free access to liveBook, Manning's online reading platform. Using liveBook's exclusive discussion features, you can attach comments to the book globally or to specific sections or paragraphs. It's a snap to make notes for yourself, ask and answer technical questions, and receive help from the author and other users. To access the forum, go to https://livebook.manning.com/book/build-a-robo-advisor-with-python-from-scratch/discussion. You can also learn more about Manning's forums and the rules of conduct at https://livebook.manning.com/discussion.

Manning's commitment to our readers is to provide a venue where a meaningful dialogue between individual readers and between readers and the authors can take place. It is not a commitment to any specific amount of participation on the part of the authors, whose contributions to the forum remain voluntary (and unpaid). We suggest you try asking the authors some challenging questions lest their interest stray! The forum and the archives of previous discussions will be accessible from the publisher's website as long as the book is in print.

about the authors

 **ROB REIDER** has been a quantitative hedge fund portfolio manager for over 15 years. He holds a PhD in finance from The Wharton School and is an adjunct professor at NYU, where he teaches a graduate course in the Math-Finance department called "Time series analysis and statistical arbitrage." He has built asset-allocation models, financial planning tools, and optimal tax strategies for a robo-advisor. Rob has given numerous lectures that combine Python with finance and has developed an online course entitled "Time series analysis in Python." As a hedge fund manager, Rob has been involved in all aspects of the investment process, from discovering new trading strategies to backtesting, executing, and managing risk.

 **ALEX MICHALKA** has worked in finance and technology since 2006. He began his career developing weather derivative pricing models at Weatherbill, spent six years conducting research on quantitative equity portfolio construction at AQR Capital Management, and currently leads the investments research group at Wealthfront. He holds a BA in applied mathematics from UC Berkeley and a PhD in operations research from Columbia University.

about the cover illustration

The figure on the cover of *Build a Robo-Advisor with Python (From Scratch)* is "Homme de schevelingen pres de la haye" or "Schevelingen man near the Hague," taken from a nineteenth-century edition of Sylvain Maréchal's four-volume compendium, Costumes Civils Actuels de Tous les Peuples Connus. Each illustration is finely drawn and colored by hand.

In those days, it was easy to identify where people lived and what their trade or station in life was just by their dress. Manning celebrates the inventiveness and initiative of the computer business with book covers based on the rich diversity of regional culture centuries ago, brought back to life by pictures from collections such as this one.

Part 1

Basic tools and building blocks

Our book begins with a discussion of what robo-advisors do, both generally and through a comparison of some of the best-known robo-advisors in the market. We also outline some of the advantages of robo-advising, including low fees, tax savings, and avoiding behavioral biases.

Chapter 2 explains some of the basic tools and concepts used in the financial industry. We show how to construct a portfolio of assets and how some asset allocations can give higher expected returns for the same amount of risk, which leads to the concept of the *efficient frontier*. The chapter ends by showing some of the questions robo-advisors use to help guide their clients into an appropriate portfolio.

Chapter 3 discusses how to estimate some important quantities: the expected returns and volatilities of individual assets and the correlations between pairs of assets. These are essential for calculating the expected return and volatility of a portfolio and for building portfolios using mathematical optimization.

Chapter 4 covers exchange-traded funds (ETFs). We'll discuss how ETFs work, why they're widely preferred over mutual funds by robo-advisors, and how to evaluate multiple ETFs competing in the same market segment.

The rise of robo-advisors

1.1 What are robo-advisors?

Robo-advisors have become a popular alternative to human financial advisors. Historically, financial advisors met with clients, discussed their goals, created a financial plan, and then managed their clients' money over time. In exchange for this personal attention, they charged clients fees, often in excess of 1% per year of their assets under management. Numerous companies have been trying to disrupt this business through online platforms that provide automated, algorithmic investment services similar to those of a financial advisor. Some of these automated systems "advise" clients through algorithmic implementations of modern portfolio theory, based on the Nobel Prize–winning work of Harry Markowitz in the 1950s, and others use optimization techniques borrowed from other disciplines. These companies have collectively become known as *robo-advisors*.

3

In this book, we show how anyone with a basic understanding of Python can build their own robo-advisor. We hope this will be useful for anyone who wants to work in this area, apply these algorithms to their own portfolio, or advise others.

1.1.1   Key features of robo-advisors

The most basic feature provided by robo-advisors is personalized asset allocation: a portfolio of investments designed to match the level of riskiness suitable for the client. The core asset allocations offered by different robo-advisors vary in their choice of asset classes but usually contain a diversified mix of stocks and bonds. Some advisors may choose to include more non-US assets in their allocations or an allocation that's more heavily weighted to growth or value stocks, but, in essentially all cases, the instruments that robo-advisors invest in are liquid and traded on exchanges and not things like venture capital, private equity, or real estate.

Aside from the core asset allocation, robo-advisors provide a handful of features. We will cover most of these in more detail later in the book; here we only provide a high-level description of each one:

- *Rebalancing*—A client's portfolio starts with weights close to the target allocation at the time of the initial investment, but differences in returns will cause the portfolio to drift away from the target over time. Rebalancing may be *drift-based*, meaning the portfolio is rebalanced whenever it deviates from the targets by a prespecified amount, or *time-based*, meaning rebalancing occurs on a fixed schedule. Additionally, rebalancing may or may not be tax-aware. In tax-aware rebalancing, some appreciated positions may not be sold if doing so would involve a high expected tax cost. In some cases, the robo-advisor may be able to keep the portfolio "on track" simply by intelligently directing dividends and deposits toward assets that have drifted below their target weights.

- *Financial projections*—A key question for most individual investors is "When can I retire?" Robo-advisors may offer tools that show projections of the client's net worth over time based on assumptions for income, spending, inflation, and investment returns. By varying these assumptions, clients can assess the feasibility of retirement at different ages.

- *Tax-loss harvesting*—The basic idea of tax-loss harvesting is to reduce the investor's current tax burden by opportunistically realizing losses in assets that have declined in value. The realized losses can be used to offset realized gains or some income. Tax-loss harvesting is a common feature offered by robo-advisors but is tricky to understand properly. We will discuss the true economic benefit and the implementation of tax-loss harvesting strategies later.

- *Glide paths*—As clients age and approach retirement, the amount of risk that they should take in their investments decreases. A glide path is a series of portfolios or asset allocations that gradually decrease riskiness over time. By the time a client reaches retirement and gives up their employment income, the glide path will assign a low-risk portfolio. Although some robo-advisors use glide paths in their investment process, others let the client control how much risk they are willing to take throughout the lifetime of their investments.

Aside from these important features, robo-advisors vary in two additional dimensions: their management fee and the minimum account size. Although there is some dispersion in these values, both are usually low compared to traditional investment advisors, making most robo-advisors accessible to clients in the earliest stages of their careers.

1.1.2 Comparison of robo-advisors

As of 2020, there were over 200 robo-advisors based in the United States alone. Table 1.1 compares the feature sets of some of the largest and best-known. Many of the advisors in this sample offer varying levels of service—for example, access to a human advisor for an additional fee. For simplicity, we show pricing for the most basic levels of service.

Table 1.1 Features of various robo-advisors

Name	Advisory fee	Minimum account size	Tax-aware rebalancing	Tax-loss harvesting
SoFi	None	$1	No	No
M1	None	$100	No	No
Acorns	$3 to $9 monthly	$0	No	No
Ellevest	0.25%	$0	No	No
E*Trade	0.30%	$500	No	No
Vanguard	0.20% to 0.25%	$3,000	No	Yes
Betterment	0.25%	$10	Yes	Yes
Ally Invest	0.30%	$100	No	No
Wealthfront	0.25%	$500	Yes	Yes
Charles Schwab	None	$5,000	Yes	Yes [a]
Fidelity	0.35% [b]	$0	No	No

[a] For accounts over $50,000.

[b] No fee for accounts below $25,000.

1.1.3 Things robo-advisors don't do

Software is useful for performing simple, repeatable tasks very quickly. Even the most complex-looking algorithms are just sequences of straightforward conditions and steps. The examples given so far are naturally suited to be accomplished using software. However, traditional advisors perform some services that software can't replicate. These are generally infrequent or one-time events that may require detailed personal information. Examples of services that are (for now) best accomplished by human advisors include estate planning, management of nontraditional assets like art and real estate, and specialized tax advice for things like stock options.

This is not to say that robo-advisors can't expand into areas that have traditionally been the domain of human advisors. For example, financial advisors are often called on to help retirees with defined-benefit pension plans decide whether to take a lump sum or monthly payments for life. The same Python programs used to analyze Social Security can be adapted to analyze pensions. Of course, there are some things that robo-advisors will never be able to do—software will never get you basketball tickets (no matter how large your account is) or treat you to dinner.

1.2   Advantages of robo-advisors

Using a robo-advisor offers several advantages over either using a human advisor or do-it-yourself investing. We highlight three of those advantages here.

1.2.1   Low fees

Surveys show that about 30% of Americans use a financial advisor of some kind. Fee-based financial advisors charge fees based on a percentage of assets under management (AUM), an annual retainer, or an hourly charge, and sometimes a combination of these. In addition to fee-based financial advisors, some advisors follow a commission-based model, where they are compensated by charging commissions on financial transactions and products like life insurance or annuities. For those that charge an AUM fee, which is the largest category, the average fee is about 1% per year. Robo-advisor fees are a fraction of that (see table 1.1). In addition, robo-advisors usually have much lower minimum account sizes than financial advisors. Even small savings, when accumulated over decades, can make a big difference. A 1% annual fee charged by a traditional human advisor may not seem like much, but the cost compounds over time. Imagine starting with a $100,000 investment, which earns a 7% return each year before fees. The 1% fee charged by a traditional advisor reduces the return to 6% annually. This means after 30 years, the $100,000 investment would grow to about $570,000. Not bad, but let's compare this to a typical robo-advisor charging 0.25% per year. With the robo-advisor, the investment would grow to about $710,000—almost 25% more!

1.2.2   Tax savings

In several chapters, we describe various tax-saving strategies that could be automated by a robo-advisor. How much money can people save through tax strategies with robo-advisors? It's difficult to give an exact number because it's different for each individual, depending on their circumstances. For example, someone who has only taxable accounts and no retirement accounts like an IRA or 401(k) will not benefit from several of the automated robo-advisor functions we talk about. But with the tools covered in this book, you will be able to estimate, through Monte Carlo simulations, the amount of savings for a specific set of circumstances. And the savings can be significant.

To give one example, consider a topic we will cover in detail in chapter 9: the optimal sequencing of withdrawals. As a brief introduction—we will cover this in detail later in the book—during the retirement stage of life, when people are "decumulating" assets instead of accumulating, numerous options are available for withdrawing assets. For example, you can take money out of your taxable accounts first, and when those are depleted, start taking money out of retirement assets (*taxable first*). You can also switch the order and take money from retirement accounts first (*IRA first*). A third strategy is to take money out of retirement accounts each year up to the top of the nearest tax bracket so that future IRA withdrawals don't push you into a higher tax bracket (*IRA fill bracket*). Finally, the fourth strategy is similar to the third, but you convert your IRA distribution into a Roth IRA (*Roth conversion*).

To illustrate how consequential those decisions can be and how much you can save by employing the best strategy for a given set of circumstances, figure 1.1 shows how long your money will last with those four strategies. The specific set of assumptions and the details of the strategy will be covered later, but the point is that it makes a big difference. The optimal strategy can extend your assets by many years.

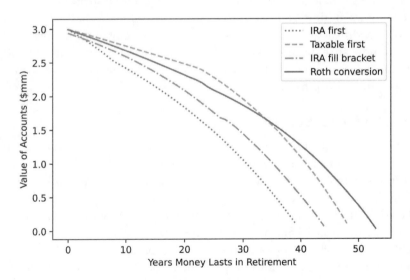

Figure 1.1 Decumulating tax-efficiently can make your money last longer.

1.2.3 *Avoiding behavioral biases*

It is well-documented that investors are subject to numerous behavioral biases, many of which can be avoided by algorithm-based automated trading:

- *Disposition effect*—Studies have shown that investors tend to hold onto losing stocks, hoping to get back to break-even. However, robo-advisors realize it's often useful to sell losing stocks to harvest tax losses.
- *Herd behavior*—Investors tend to be influenced by others, which explains why they dive into stocks during bubbles and panic during crashes. Herding might have conferred benefits when fleeing predators in prehistoric times, but it is not a great investment strategy. Robo-advisors, on the other hand, unemotionally rebalance gradually toward stocks during crashes and away from stocks during bubbles.
- *Overtrading*—Several studies on overtrading have all reached the same conclusion: the more active a retail investor tends to be, the less money they make. Individual investors may incorrectly assume that if they are not paying brokerage commissions, there is no cost to frequent trading. However, commissions are only one cost. The bid/ask spread, the difference between the price for which you can buy a stock and sell a stock on an exchange, is a significant component of trading costs. Also, frequent trading leads to short-term capital gains, which is not tax-efficient. Robo-advisors methodically factor these costs into account when they make trades.

1.2.4   Saving time

By automating simple tasks associated with investing, a robo-advisor can save investors huge amounts of time compared to a "do it yourself" approach. Monitoring the portfolio for drift away from its targets or tax-loss harvesting opportunities and placing trades to rebalance, harvest losses, or invest deposits isn't especially difficult, but it isn't especially fun, either. Robo-advisors automate these tasks, leaving investors time for more enjoyable pursuits.

1.3   Example: Social Security benefits

One thing that gets us excited about this topic is that robo-advising is still in its infancy. Consider one example: the important decision of when to claim Social Security benefits. For many Americans, their Social Security check can be considered among their most valuable assets, in many cases worth more than half a million dollars on a present-value basis. People must elect when they want to start receiving or claiming their Social Security payments, which can be anytime between ages 62 and 70, and the longer you wait, the larger your payment will be. It is one of many important retirement decisions that are consequential and mostly irreversible. So what kind of advice exists about when to claim Social Security? If you do a Google search on this topic, you'll find numerous calculators that mostly do the same thing. They usually do a simple break-even analysis like that shown in figure 1.2. (You can see a similar one, offered by Charles Schwab, at https://mng.bz/2yJN.)

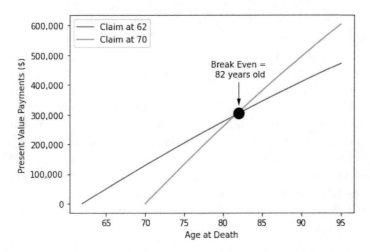

Figure 1.2   Break-even analysis on the age to start claiming Social Security

In this break-even analysis, the *x* axis represents the age you expect to die, and the *y* axis represents the present value of your Social Security payments until death. As you can see from the graph in this simple analysis that compares claiming at 62 versus 70, if you expect to live past 82, you are better off waiting until 70 to claim Social Security, and if you expect to die before 82, you are better off claiming at 62. As the chart shows, if you live to 90 and claim at 70, the present value of all payments is about $500,000.

What is this analysis missing, and how can Python be used to improve it? First, the analysis becomes exponentially more complicated when spouses are considered, and the Social Security rules can be very complicated. Although the break-even analysis in figure 1.2 can be done in a spreadsheet, taking into account couples and all the Social Security rules would overwhelm a spreadsheet and must be coded in a computer language like Python.

To accurately predict Social Security benefits, an estimate must be made for the trajectory of future income up to retirement. Python has several libraries for forecasting a time series like income. An accurate forecast requires an earnings history for the investor, which can be downloaded from the Social Security website; then, Python can be used to scrape the file.

Our example break-even analysis is not customized in any way, and Python can help here, too. Because Social Security benefits are similar to an asset like a bond, they should be incorporated into an investor's asset allocation—larger Social Security payments would mean even a conservative investor could hold fewer bonds. The break-even analysis also ignores taxes on Social Security income, as well as Social Security benefits that may be withheld when someone's income exceeds a threshold while collecting benefits. The analysis can therefore be extended to include an investor's particular tax situation.

An important and often-overlooked shortcoming of the break-even approach is that *it doesn't take risk into account.* In this case, the risk is longevity risk—the chance that you survive beyond your life expectancy and outlive your money. Social Security benefits, as well as defined-benefit pension plans and annuities, reduce that risk by guaranteeing lifetime benefits. In chapter 6 on AI, we show how to take risk into account with examples in Python.

Throughout the book, we aim to not only explain what robo-advisors currently do but also introduce various tools that few, if any, advisors currently use. We already mentioned the chapter on using AI to solve financial planning problems. We also have a chapter on asset location, which involves strategically distributing different types of assets among existing taxable, tax-deferred, and tax-exempt accounts to minimize taxes. Whereas asset allocation involves tradeoffs between risk and reward, asset location is close to a free lunch. However, the strategy can be complex, perhaps explaining why it has not been widely adopted.

1.4   *Python and robo-advising*

The designers of Python intended the language to be fast, powerful, and fun. We think they succeeded. Python is easy to start with—the classic "Hello World" program is not much harder than just typing the words "Hello World"—and easy to learn. Python's documentation is extensive, and its wide adoption means it's usually possible to find solutions to tricky problems—chances are, someone has run into them already. Finally, Python is flexible—although it supports some more sophisticated features of lower-level languages like Java, Python doesn't require them. If you want to use Python in an object-oriented way, you can—but you don't have to. Likewise, you can add "hints" for data types in Python functions, but they aren't required. Python lets you choose.

These qualities make Python easy to learn and work with for any programmer. But what makes Python a good language for robo-advising? As Python's popularity has grown, the number of mathematical and statistical packages has grown as well. Applications in this book will lean heavily on preexisting packages, including these:

- numpy—A general-purpose package for numerical computing that provides tools ranging from the basics (basic vector and matrix operations and least-squares solutions to linear systems) to the complex (such as random number generation and matrix factorizations). The numpy package achieves high speed by implementing many numerical subroutines in C.
- scipy—Provides algorithms for numerical problems, including optimization, integration, and root-finding. Also includes a large library of statistical functions. Like numpy, scipy uses subroutines written in low-level languages like Fortran and C to improve speed.
- pandas—Adds a level of abstraction on top of arrays and matrices to make data manipulation effortless. Developed at AQR Capital Management starting in 2008 and made open source in 2009.

- cvxpy—A mathematical modeling language allowing users to formulate and solve convex optimization problems using a natural and easy-to-read syntax.
- statsmodels—One of several libraries in Python that can perform a linear regression with just a few lines of code.

We should also talk about what Python isn't. Python's interpreted nature means it will never be as fast as low-level compiled languages like C and Fortran. If your application requires top speed, a compiled language may be a better choice. This also means bugs only appear when code is run and won't be found during compilation. Overall, we still think that despite these limitations, Python is a great choice for this book. Robo-advising doesn't require lightning speed, and we think the ease of use and extensive libraries and documentation outweigh any disadvantages in execution speed.

This book does not assume that readers are Python experts but will assume a basic familiarity with Python. For an introduction to programming in Python, we recommend Naomi Ceder's *The Quick Python Book.*

All the chapters after this one contain examples in Python, and many include function and class definitions. These can be found on the book's website (www.manning .com/books/build-a-robo-advisor-with-python-from-scratch) and the GitHub page for this book (https://github.com/robreider/robo-advisor-with-python). Filenames correspond to chapter numbers. Within each chapter, later code builds on earlier code. For example, a code section in the middle of a chapter may rely on a function defined earlier or a package imported earlier. Additionally, class definitions with many methods may be broken into multiple code sections. We recommend copying or importing code from the book's website or GitHub rather than straight from the text if you are working in Python while reading an electronic version of the book.

In some chapters, we have moved the longer, complicated code online, and the shorter code that relies on simplifying assumptions is placed in the body of the chapter. Also, we have a section on the website and GitHub for "extras" that don't fit easily into any chapter. For example, in the "extras" section, you will find the code for scraping the earnings history from a Social Security statement using the Python library BeautifulSoup. This code can be expanded into a full Social Security calculator in Python and incorporated into several other chapters on wealth planning.

1.5 *Who might be interested in learning about robo-advising?*

Several groups of people might be interested in the topics covered in this book:

- *You want to better understand personal finance to help you with your own finances.* There is no shortage of books on personal finance for do-it-yourself investors, but this book focuses on topics that can save you money and goes into them in depth. You won't see chapters found in other personal finance books, like "Live within your means" or "Don't buy complex financial products." Even if you have no interest in applying these techniques in Python, the book is written so that you can skip the Python examples and still understand the principles behind what the algorithms do.

- *You are interested in working for a financial advisor or wealth manager.* As we mentioned, the number of robo-advisors is growing, and the incumbents are also getting into robo-advising. Traditional wealth managers are using the same techniques for their clients. A quick search on indeed.com for jobs as a "financial advisor" currently lists over 20,000. This book provides relevant skills that are used in the industry.
- *You are a financial advisor and would like to provide your clients with a larger set of tools.* According to the Bureau of Labor Statistics, as of 2022, there were 283,000 financial advisors in the United States. The financial advisory business is obviously very competitive, and providing sophisticated services gives a firm a competitive advantage. Advisors can differentiate themselves in this crowded field and create a competitive advantage by offering more advanced tools like those described in this book. A financial advisor who can automate guidance can service many more clients while still providing customized advice.
- *You are interested in useful, practical applications of Python.* There is no better way to learn Python than by applying it to interesting, practical problems and observing intuitive results. This book will use numerous Python libraries to solve wealth management problems. We will use a convex optimization library and a hierarchical tree-clustering library to perform asset allocation, a statistical and random number library for Monte Carlo simulations, and a root-finding library for measuring portfolio performance. If you're interested in learning about AI, chapter 6 provides several fully worked examples, from start to finish, of how you can apply AI to solve financial planning problems.

Throughout the book, you may find that certain rules, regulations, investment vehicles, or account types are specific to investors in the United States. In most cases, however, the concepts discussed should apply to investors outside of the United States, even if the specifics of some rules or assumptions need to be modified.

Summary

- Robo-advisors use algorithms to automate some of the functions of human financial advisors.
- Robo-advisors have several advantages over human advisors: they have lower fees, they can save a considerable amount of money using tax strategies, and they can help investors avoid some well-documented behavioral biases that detract from performance.
- Python, with its extensive libraries, can be used to implement many of the functions of a robo-advisor, from asset allocation to tax loss optimization to Monte Carlo simulations for financial planning.

An introduction to portfolio construction

This chapter covers

- Creating risk–reward plots
- Using matrix operations to compute portfolio returns and volatilities
- Calculating, plotting, and deriving the math behind the efficient frontier
- A risk-free asset and the capital allocation line

One of the primary functions of a robo-advisor is to construct a well-diversified portfolio of assets. This chapter will provide the theoretical foundation for portfolio construction and some building blocks we will use later. We will also start using Python in our examples. Later in the book, we will delve deeper into the topic of portfolio construction, including some problems with the traditional methods that are covered in this chapter.

2.1   *A simple example with three assets*

Let's start with a simple example with only three assets: First Energy (FE), Walmart (WMT), and Apple (AAPL). The analysis that follows can always be generalized to include as many assets as you would like. In this example, the assets are individual stocks, but they could easily be bonds, exchange-traded funds (ETFs), commodities, cryptocurrencies, or even hedge funds. The problem we want to address is this: What are the optimal weights to assign to these three assets? We will begin by taking the approach of the Nobel Prize–winning work of Harry Markowitz. The Markowitz approach recognizes that investors have two conflicting objectives: they want high returns, but they also want low risk. In the last section of this chapter, we discuss how to balance these competing objectives.

Suppose we knew these three assets' expected returns, variances, and correlations to each other. Of course, we do not know things like the expected return of a stock, but for now, let's suspend disbelief for the purposes of this discussion. Let's say the annual expected returns for FE, WMT, and AAPL are 4%, 9%, and 12%, respectively. We can represent this as a vector:

$$\mu = \begin{bmatrix} 0.04 \\ 0.09 \\ 0.12 \end{bmatrix}$$

Let's say the annual *standard deviation* of returns, or *volatility* of returns (we will use these two terms interchangeably), for FE, WMT, and AAPL are 15%, 20%, and 35%, respectively. We can also represent this as a vector:

$$\sigma = \begin{bmatrix} 0.15 \\ 0.20 \\ 0.35 \end{bmatrix}$$

We can plot these three stocks in mean–standard deviation space, which some call a *risk–reward* plot, using the following code.

Listing 2.1   **Plotting points in mean–standard deviation space**

```
import pandas as pd
import numpy as np
import matplotlib.pyplot as plt

stocks = ['FE', 'WMT', 'AAPL']
mu = [0.04, 0.09, 0.12]
sigma = [0.15, 0.20, 0.35]

def plot_points(mu, sigma, stocks):
    plt.figure(figsize=(8,6))
```

```
plt.scatter(sigma, mu, c='black')   ◀─── Generates a scatter plot
plt.xlim(0,0.45)
plt.ylim(0,0.25)
plt.ylabel('Mean')
plt.xlabel('Standard Deviation')
for i, stock in enumerate(stocks):
    plt.annotate(stock, (sigma[i], mu[i]), ha='center',
                 va='bottom', weight='bold')   ◀─┐ Places ticker
                                                 │ symbol labels
plot_points(mu, sigma, stocks)                   │ above the points
plt.show()
```

Figure 2.1 shows the risk–reward plot when we run the code in listing 2.1.

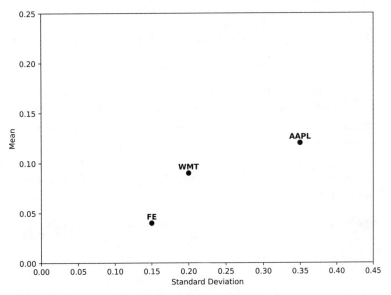

Figure 2.1   Example of the risk–reward plot for three stocks

2.2   *Computing a portfolio's expected return and standard deviation*

Our goal is to find the most efficient way to weight these assets by constructing portfolios with the highest expected return for a given standard deviation. We will see in this section that calculating the mean and standard deviation of a portfolio of assets involves summations and double summations. We will introduce matrix multiplication to perform these operations, which is preferred to using for loops in terms of computational efficiency, readability, and availability of libraries. For those who are not familiar with the field of linear algebra, don't worry: you only need to be aware that there are efficient, one-line commands in Python to perform these matrix operations, which we will demonstrate in the listings.

Suppose we represent the weights for FE, WMT, and AAPL as w_1, w_2, and w_3, respectively. In that case, we can again write this in vector notation:

$$w = \begin{bmatrix} w_1 \\ w_2 \\ w_3 \end{bmatrix}$$

The return on this portfolio, r_p, is

$$r_p = w_1 r_1 + w_2 r_2 + w_3 r_3$$

and the expected return on the portfolio is just the weighted average of the expected returns on the three assets that make up the portfolio:

$$\mu_p = E\left[r_P\right] = w_1 E\left[r_1\right] + w_2 E\left[r_2\right] + w_3 E\left[r_3\right]$$

We can write this in vector notation as the dot product of vectors w and μ:

$$\mu_p = w \cdot \mu = w^T \mu = \mu^T w$$

There are several ways to do this calculation using Python and NumPy (see the sidebar "Delving into some finer points of matrix multiplication in Python"). In this and the following chapters, we'll use the matrix multiplication operator @, which has a clear and concise syntax that makes the code more readable. The next listing demonstrates how to use the operator @ to compute the expected returns of a portfolio given the weights and expected returns of each asset. If you run this listing, the portfolio's expected return is 9.5%.

Listing 2.2   Computing expected portfolio returns

```
w = np.array([0.2, 0.3, 0.5])
mu_p = mu @ w.T
print('Expected portfolio return: ', mu_p)
```

Delving into some finer points of matrix multiplication in Python

The second line of code in listing 2.2 is all you really need to know about performing matrix multiplication using the @ operator, but in case you're interested in getting deeper in the weeds, a few additional remarks are in order:

- In listing 2.2, we transpose the second vector of weights, not the first vector of means. Whereas in mathematics, we assume vectors are column vectors, in Python, when you create a list or a one-dimensional NumPy array, it is assumed to be a row vector. Also note that to take the transpose of a vector, it has to be a NumPy array and not a list, so you would have to create the vector of weights using, for example, `w = np.array([0.2, 0.3, 0.5])` rather than using a list, such as `w = [0.2, 0.3, 0.5]`.

- When using the `@` operator for matrix multiplication, the NumPy library automatically applies broadcasting rules, which makes it unnecessary in many cases to transpose one of the arrays. In other words, you can simplify the dot product in listing 2.2 by using `mu_p = mu @ w` instead of `mu_p = mu @ w.T`. But if you do that, be careful that the broadcasting rules are working the way you think they should be working.
- The operator `*`, when applied to arrays, does element-by-element multiplication rather than matrix multiplication (multiplying entire rows in the first matrix by entire columns in the second matrix). If we used the element-by-element multiplication `mu * w` instead of the matrix multiplication `w @ mu` in listing 2.2, it would return not the weighted sum of expected returns for the three stocks, which is a scalar, but rather a one-dimensional array with three elements.
- To make things even more complicated, NumPy has a data structure called a NumPy matrix, which differs from a NumPy array. If you convert the NumPy arrays to NumPy matrices, the `*` operator does true matrix multiplication, not element-by-element multiplication.
- The NumPy function `np.dot()` is equivalent to the matrix multiplication operator `@` for 1D and 2D arrays and can be used interchangeably with `@`. However, `@` is preferred for readability.

Unfortunately, the standard deviation of the portfolio is not simply the weighted average of the individual stock standard deviations. The pairwise correlations between the assets play an important role. To illustrate with just two assets, the standard deviation of the portfolio is

$$\sigma_p = \left(w_1^2 \sigma_1^2 + w_2^2 \sigma_2^2 + 2 w_1 w_2 \sigma_1 \sigma_2 \mathrm{Corr}(r_1, r_2) \right)^{1/2}$$

Instead of working with the correlations and individual stock volatilities, it is often more convenient to deal with covariances, which combine correlations and volatilities. The covariance between assets i and j is

$$\mathrm{Cov}(r_i, r_j) = \sigma_i \sigma_j \mathrm{Corr}(r_i, r_j)$$

and if i and j are the same, it's just the variance of the asset:

$$\mathrm{Cov}(r_i, r_i) = \sigma_i \sigma_i \mathrm{Corr}(r_i, r_i)$$
$$= \sigma_i^2$$
$$= \mathrm{Var}(r_i)$$

The following listing converts a correlation matrix and a vector of individual volatilities into a covariance matrix using the previous formula. We need to convert the vector of volatilities into a diagonal matrix to scale the correlations by the corresponding volatilities.

Listing 2.3   Computing the covariance matrix from volatilities and correlations

```
Corr = [[ 1.  ,  0.1 ,  0.17],
        [ 0.1 ,  1.  ,  0.26],
        [ 0.17,  0.26,  1.  ]]

Cov = np.diag(sigma) @ Corr @ np.diag(sigma)
print('Covariance matrix: \n', Cov)
```

> **np.diag(sigma) converts the vector of volatilities into a diagonal matrix.**

This will output

```
    Covariance matrix:
     [[0.0225    0.003    0.008925]
      [0.003     0.04     0.0182  ]
      [0.008925 0.0182    0.1225  ]]
```

For N assets instead of two, and writing each term in terms of covariances, we can generalize the volatility of a portfolio as a double summation

$$\sigma_p = \left(\sum_{i=1}^{N} \sum_{j=1}^{N} w_i w_j \mathrm{Cov}(r_i, r_j) \right)^{1/2}$$

or using matrix notation

$$\sigma_p = \left(w^T \Sigma w \right)^{1/2}$$

where Σ is called the *variance-covariance matrix*, or covariance matrix for short. The covariance matrix is a square, symmetrical matrix with the variances along the diagonal and covariances on the off-diagonal elements. The next listing computes a portfolio's standard deviation from the assets' weights and the covariance matrix. If you run this listing, the portfolio's volatility is 20.7%.

Listing 2.4   Computing the standard deviation of a portfolio

```
sigma_p = (w @ Cov @ w.T) ** 0.5
print('Portfolio standard deviation: ', sigma_p)
```

Now that we have gone through the code for finding the mean and standard deviation of a portfolio, we can use Python to gain some further intuition about the portfolio construction process.

2.3   *An illustration with random weights*

In later chapters, we will show how to use a Python library to perform numerous optimizations to find the best weights under various assumptions, objectives, and constraints. But just to illustrate how some weights are better than others, we can generate many completely random weights in Python and plot the results. We will eventually compare these random weights with optimal ones. The function in listing 2.5 uses NumPy's standardized normal random number generator to generate random weights for each asset. We then normalize the weights by dividing by their sum, guaranteeing that the normalized weights sum to 1. For now, the random weights can be negative (in practice, a negative position is referred to as a *short*). Later, we will constrain all the weights to be positive.

Listing 2.5   Generating random portfolio weights

```
def random_weights(n_assets):
    k = np.random.randn(n_assets)
    return k / sum(k)
print(random_weights(3))
```

Our output is as follows. Your output will differ with a different set of random numbers, but your weights should sum to 1 like these do:

```
[ 0.45991849 -0.0659656    0.60604711 ]
```

The next function takes a vector of weights as well as the means and covariance matrix as arguments and returns the expected return of the portfolio, μ_p, and the standard deviation of the portfolio, σ_p, using the earlier equations.

Listing 2.6   Computing portfolio mean and standard deviation from weights

```
def mu_sigma_portfolio(weights, means, Cov):
    mu_p = np.dot(weights, means)
    sigma_p = (weights @ Cov @ weights) ** 0.5
    return mu_p, sigma_p
```

With these functions to compute random weights and then taking those random weights and computing the mean and standard deviation of the portfolio associated with the random weights, we are ready to add random portfolios to the risk–reward plot, as shown in the following listing.

Listing 2.7   Risk–reward plots using random portfolio weights

```
def plot_random_portfolios(mu, Cov, n_simulations):
    n_assets = len(mu)
    mu_p_sims = []
    sigma_p_sims = []                        Uses the function in
    for i in range(n_simulations):           listing 2.5 to generate
        w = random_weights(n_assets)    ◄──┘ random weights
        mu_p, sigma_p = mu_sigma_portfolio(w, mu, Cov)  ◄─┐ Uses the function
        mu_p_sims.append(mu_p)                             in listing 2.6 to
        sigma_p_sims.append(sigma_p)                       compute the mean
    plt.scatter(sigma_p_sims, mu_p_sims, s=12)             and standard deviation
                                                           of the portfolio
plot_points(mu, sigma, stocks)

n_simulations = 1000
```

```
plot_random_portfolios(mu, Cov, n_simulations)
plt.show();
```

Figure 2.2 shows the risk–reward plot when we run the code in listing 2.7 for 1,000 randomly weighted portfolios. From this plot, it is apparent that there is a pattern to the lowest possible portfolio volatility for a given level of portfolio expected return. It turns out that in the simple example we have described so far, there is a mathematical formula for the set of optimal portfolios called the *minimum-variance frontier*.

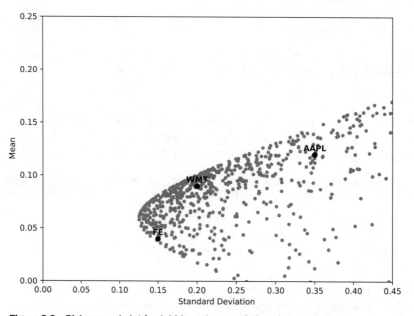

Figure 2.2   Risk–reward plot for 1,000 random portfolios of three stocks

The next listing adds the minimum-variance frontier to the risk–reward plot. (For those interested in the math, the mathematical formula is derived in the chapter's appendix, but it is not necessary to understand the derivation for anything we do later.)

Listing 2.8   Adding minimum-variance frontier to risk–reward plot

The formulas used in this function are derived in the appendix.

```
def plot_min_var_frontier(mu, Cov):
    A,B,C = compute_ABC(mu, Cov)
    y = np.linspace(0,B/A,100)
    x = np.sqrt((A*y*y-2*B*y+C)/(A*C-B*B))
    plt.plot(x,y, color='black', lw=2.5, linestyle='-')

    y = np.linspace(B/A,.45,100)
    x = np.sqrt((A*y*y-2*B*y+C)/(A*C-B*B))
    plt.plot(x,y, color='black', lw=2.5, label='Efficient Frontier')
```

Plots the bottom half of the minimum variance frontier (dashed line)

Plots the top half of the minimum variance frontier (solid line)

```
        plt.legend()

def compute_ABC(mu, Cov):   ←——
    Cov_inv = np.linalg.inv(Cov)
    ones = np.ones(n_assets)
    A = ones @ Cov_inv @ ones
    B = ones @ Cov_inv @ mu
    C = mu @ Cov_inv @ mu
    return A,B,C

plot_points(mu, sigma, stocks)
plot_random_portfolios(mu, Cov, n_simulations)
plot_min_var_frontier(mu, Cov)
plt.show()
```

> **Computes constants A,B,C (derived in the appendix) that are needed to plot the minimum-variance frontier**

Figure 2.3 shows the risk–reward plot when we run the code in listing 2.8, which now superimposes the minimum-variance frontier. The top half of the curve (the solid line) is referred to as the *efficient frontier*. Any portfolio on the lower portion of the minimum-variance frontier (the dashed line) is inefficient because there is a portfolio with the same volatility but a higher expected return on the upper side of the curve.

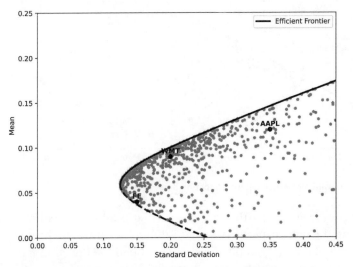

Figure 2.3   Risk–reward plot with minimum-variance frontier

In the next section, we will see how the portfolio problem changes when we add a risk-free asset.

2.4   *Introducing a risk-free asset*

Suppose we introduce one more asset, which is a risk-free asset. To be precise, the risk-free asset is not simply any government bond that is free of credit risk; the maturity of the bond exactly matches the investment horizon, and there are no intermediate coupons that might introduce reinvestment risk. For example, if you have a one-month horizon, a one-month government bond (known as a *one-month Treasury Bill*, or *T-Bill* for short) is a risk-free asset. You know the exact amount you will be receiving in a month. Therefore, this risk-free asset has zero volatility, and on the mean–standard deviation plot, it is located on the *y*-axis with a mean return of the risk-free rate. In contrast, if you buy a 10-year government bond and sell it in a month, there could be capital gains or losses, which introduces some volatility.

With a risk-free asset, we can actually do better than the previous efficient frontier. As figure 2.4 shows, the line that connects the risk-free asset to a *tangent portfolio* represents any feasible portfolio and lies above the efficient frontier. The line that goes from the risk-free rate to the tangent portfolio is sometimes referred to as the *capital allocation line*.

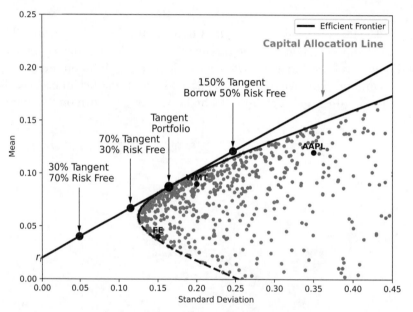

Figure 2.4   Risk–reward plot with a capital allocation line

Economists take this a step further and argue that if all investors have the same information and the same expectations, they will hold securities in the same weights, and in equilibrium, the tangent portfolio will be the market portfolio. In this case, the line that goes from the risk-free rate to the market portfolio is referred to as the *capital market line* rather than the capital allocation line. These assumptions are rather unrealistic, and, for generality, we will continue to use the term *capital allocation line* and not assume the tangent portfolio is necessarily the market portfolio.

Any point between the risk-free rate and the tangent point can be achieved by a combination of the two assets: the tangent portfolio and the risk-free asset. A portfolio that consists of 70% of the tangent portfolio and 30% of the risk-free asset lies 70% toward the tangent portfolio. A more risk-averse investor might want 70% of the risk-free asset and 30% of the tangent portfolio.

An investor can achieve points beyond the tangent portfolio using leverage. For example, an investor with $1 million in assets can borrow $500,000 and invest $1.5 million in the tangent portfolio. We assume, for simplicity, that an investor can borrow at the risk-free rate, although that assumption can easily be relaxed. If the borrowing cost were higher than the risk-free rate, the capital allocation line would be kinked at the tangent point.

The code that generates the capital allocation line in figure 2.4 is shown in the following listing. The mathematical derivation for the capital allocation line can be found in the appendix if you're interested in the math, but it is only included for completeness and is not necessary for understanding the portfolio construction process.

Listing 2.9 Plotting the capital allocation line

```
def plot_Capital_Allocation_Line(rf, mu, Cov):      ← The formulas used in this
    A,B,C = compute_ABC(mu, Cov)                       function are derived
    x = np.linspace(0,.45,100)                         in the appendix.
    y = rf + x*(C-2*B*rf+A*rf**2)**0.5
    plt.plot(x,y, color='black', lw=2.5)

plot_points(mu, sigma, stocks)
plot_random_portfolios(mu, Cov, n_simulations)
plot_min_var_frontier(mu, Cov)

rf = 0.02
plot_Capital_Allocation_Line(rf, mu, Cov)
plt.show()
```

As this section illustrates, we can separate the portfolio construction process into two steps:

1 Select the optimal composition of risky assets that lies on the tangent of the efficient frontier.
2 Decide how much to invest in the tangent portfolio versus the risk-free asset.

The first step involves only math once the expected returns and covariance matrices have been estimated. We will talk more about estimating the parameters used in the first step in chapter 3. The second step, which arguably has a much larger effect on investment returns, depends on an investor's personal preferences about the tradeoff between risk and returns, which is the topic in the next section.

2.5 Risk tolerance

People inherently have different tolerances for risk, and part of the task of a robo-advisor is to figure out where along the risk–reward curve an investor should be. Robo-advisors usually ask a series of about 6–12 questions to gauge an investor's tolerance for risk and then map those answers into a stock–bond portfolio. Many of these questionnaires can be found on the internet, and they all ask similar types of questions.

As an example, consider a few of the 13 questions from the risk-tolerance scale developed, tested, and published by Grable and Lytton, which is widely used by financial advisors (the full questionnaire can be found at www.kitces.com/wp-content/uploads/2019/11/Grable-Lytton-Risk-Assessment.pdf):

1 In general, how would your best friend describe you as a risk taker?

   a) A real gambler

   b) Willing to take risks after completing adequate research

   c) Cautious

   d) A real risk avoider

2 You are on a TV game show and can choose one of the following; which would you take?

   a) $1,000 in cash

   b) A 50% chance at winning $5,000

   c) A 25% chance at winning $10,000

   d) A 5% chance at winning $100,000

3 You have just finished saving for a "once-in-a-lifetime" vacation. Three weeks before you plan to leave, you lose your job. You would:

   a) Cancel the vacation

   b) Take a much more modest vacation

   c) Go as scheduled, reasoning that you need the time to prepare for a job search

   d) Extend your vacation, because this might be your last chance to go first-class

4 If you unexpectedly received $20,000 to invest, what would you do?

   a) Deposit it in a bank account, money market account, or insured CD

   b) Invest it in safe high-quality bonds or bond mutual funds

   c) Invest it in stocks or stock mutual funds

5 In terms of experience, how comfortable are you investing in stocks or stock mutual funds?

   a) Not at all comfortable

   b) Somewhat comfortable

   c) Very comfortable

Points are assigned to each question, and the investor is placed into one of five risk-tolerance categories (high, above average, average, below average, low) based on the aggregate score.

Some questionnaires ask the same type of question in different ways to gauge consistency. Some questionnaires ask risk-capacity questions, in contrast to risk-tolerance questions. These are questions about an investor's time horizon (an investor with a longer time horizon has a higher capacity for risk), any other asset holdings like pensions, and the need for cash. Sometimes, questions about investment experience are included in risk-tolerance questionnaires (see the last question in the previous list);

this may seem unrelated to risk tolerance, but investors who have more experience are less likely to get flustered during market drops if they have been through similar drops in the past.

Some online risk-tolerance tools use sliders and charts to help investors visualize the risks. For example, one 401(k) provider shows a simulated path of the market value of an investor's portfolio, and the investor can see the larger drops as well as the higher average returns associated with riskier portfolios, to help gauge their risk tolerance.

Python provides several widgets for making interactive graphs with sliders. Let's look at a simple example of what you can do in a few lines of Python code. Figure 2.5 shows the 95% worst-case loss and the average gain over a one-year horizon for a $1 million portfolio. The investor can move the slider at the top of the figure from 0% stocks to 100% stocks to gauge the level of risk they are comfortable with. We show the 95% worst-case loss because investors have a tendency to focus on losses (behavioral economists refer to this as *loss aversion*). We also show gains and losses in terms of dollars rather than percentages because that is sometimes easier for investors to comprehend.

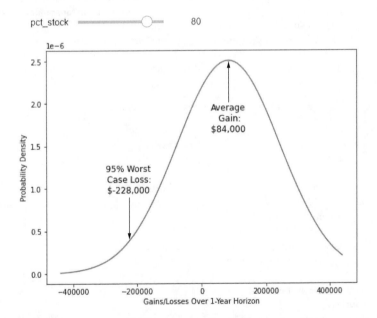

Figure 2.5 A slider used to visualize the effects of changing the stock–bond mix

The code used to generate figure 2.5 is shown in listing 2.10. The last line of the code implements the slider. Every time the user moves the slider, the `update()` function is called, and the chart is redrawn. You can set the minimum, maximum, and step size of the slider and assign the value to a variable, which we call `pct_stock`, which represents the percentage of the portfolio in stocks as opposed to bonds. The chart shows a normal distribution with the help of the `norm` function, which is part of the SciPy library. In the interactive plot, the mean value of the normal distribution is highlighted: it will go up as the percentage of stocks increases. But the maximum loss also goes up. We define the maximum loss as the 95% worst-case loss, which is 1.96 standard deviations away from the average.

> **NOTE**   Throughout the book, we will be using libraries that are not preinstalled with Python, like the `scipy` and `ipywidgets` libraries in listing 2.10. These packages, as well as any other missing packages throughout the book, can be installed with `pip install`.

Listing 2.10   Using a slider to visualize worst-case losses and gains

```
from scipy.stats import norm          ◄──┐ These are the first libraries
from ipywidgets import *                  │ you may need to pip install.

def update(pct_stock):
    wealth = 1000000
    mu = np.array([0.02, 0.10]) * wealth    ◄── Assumption for means
    sigma = np.array([0.05, 0.20]) * wealth  ◄ Assumption for standard deviations
    w = np.array([1-pct_stock/100, pct_stock/100])
    Corr = [[ 1. ,-0.1],    ◄── Assumption for the correlation matrix
            [-0.1, 1. ]]
    Cov = np.diag(sigma) @ Corr @ np.diag(sigma)
    mu_p, sigma_p = mu_sigma_portfolio(w, mu, Cov)

    x = np.linspace(-2.2*sigma[1], +2.2*sigma[1], 100)

    arrowprops = dict(arrowstyle='simple', color='k')
    xp = -1.96*sigma_p + mu_p    ◄── Worst-case loss
    xp = round(xp,-3)
    yp = norm.pdf(xp, mu_p, sigma_p)
    plt.figure(figsize=(8,6))
    plt.annotate('95% Worst\n Case Loss:\n${:,.0f}'.format(xp), xy=(xp,yp),
            xycoords='data',
            xytext=(xp,yp*2.5),
            ha='center', va='bottom', size=12,
            arrowprops=arrowprops,
            )
    xp = mu_p    ◄── Average gain
    xp = round(xp,-3)
    yp = norm.pdf(xp, mu_p, sigma_p)
    plt.annotate('Average\n Gain:\n${:,.0f}'.format(mu_p), xy=(xp,yp),
            xycoords='data',
            xytext=(xp,yp*.8),
            ha='center', va='top', size=12,
            arrowprops=arrowprops,
            )
    plt.plot(x, norm.pdf(x, mu_p, sigma_p))
```

```
    plt.xlabel('Gains/Losses Over 1-Year Horizon')
    plt.ylabel('Probability Density')
    plt.show()
interact(
    update,                                                    Creates
    pct_stock=widgets.IntSlider(value=50, min=0, max=100, step=10)    the
                                                               slider
)
```

In the slider example, as well as all the other examples in this chapter, we make assumptions about expected returns, standard deviations, and correlations for the various assets, which are inputs to our calculations. In chapter 3, we look at multiple ways to estimate those inputs.

Appendix

For those who are interested, we derive the equations for the minimum-variance frontier when there is no risk-free rate and the capital market line when we introduce a risk-free rate. This section is only for the mathematically inclined who are looking for a deeper understanding of the formulas presented earlier. If you prefer to skip it, you will still be able to understand the rest of the book.

No risk-free rate

The problem of finding the optimal weights can be described mathematically as the solution to the following problem:

$$\min_{w} \quad \tfrac{1}{2} w^T \Sigma w$$
$$\text{subject to} \quad \mu^T w = \mu_p$$
$$1^T w = 1$$

In this problem, we have not introduced the risk-free asset or imposed short-sale constraints of the form $w_i > 0$.

We can use the method of Lagrangian multipliers to find the minimum of a function subject to equality constraints. The Lagrangian equation is then

$$L = w^T \Sigma w / 2 + \lambda (1 - 1^T w) + \gamma (\mu_p - \mu^T w)$$

where λ and γ are Lagrange multipliers.

Taking the partial first derivatives of the Lagrangian with respect to the weights and setting the equations to zero gives

$$\frac{\partial L}{\partial w} = \Sigma w - \lambda 1 - \gamma \mu = 0$$

and we can solve for the optimal weights, w^*, by premultiplying this equation by Σ^{-1}:

$$w^* = \lambda \Sigma^{-1} 1 + \gamma \Sigma^{-1} \mu$$

To find the Lagrange multipliers λ and γ, we premultiply the optimal weights by $\mathbf{1}^T$ and by $\boldsymbol{\mu}^T$ and, using the two constraints of the problem, get

$$\underbrace{\mathbf{1}^T \boldsymbol{w}^*}_{1} = \lambda \underbrace{\mathbf{1}^T \boldsymbol{\Sigma}^{-1} \mathbf{1}}_{A} + \gamma \underbrace{\mathbf{1}^T \boldsymbol{\Sigma}^{-1} \boldsymbol{\mu}}_{B}$$

$$\underbrace{\boldsymbol{\mu}^T \boldsymbol{w}^*}_{\mu_p} = \lambda \underbrace{\boldsymbol{\mu}^T \boldsymbol{\Sigma}^{-1} \mathbf{1}}_{B} + \gamma \underbrace{\boldsymbol{\mu}^T \boldsymbol{\Sigma}^{-1} \boldsymbol{\mu}}_{C}$$

Solving these two equations for the two unknowns, the Lagrange multipliers are

$$\lambda = \frac{C - B\mu_p}{AC - B^2}$$

$$\gamma = \frac{\mu_p A - B}{AC - B^2}$$

where for notational simplicity, we define

$$A = \mathbf{1}^T \boldsymbol{\Sigma}^{-1} \mathbf{1}$$

$$B = \mathbf{1}^T \boldsymbol{\Sigma}^{-1} \boldsymbol{\mu}$$

$$C = \boldsymbol{\mu}^T \boldsymbol{\Sigma}^{-1} \boldsymbol{\mu}$$

Finally, the equation that relates the standard deviation of a portfolio to its mean using the optimal weights, which is the equation of the minimum-variance frontier, is

$$\begin{aligned}
\sigma_p^2 &= \boldsymbol{w}^{*T} \boldsymbol{\Sigma} \boldsymbol{w}^* \\
&= \boldsymbol{w}^{*T} \boldsymbol{\Sigma} (\lambda \boldsymbol{\Sigma}^{-1} \mathbf{1} + \gamma \boldsymbol{\Sigma}^{-1} \boldsymbol{\mu}) \\
&= \lambda \boldsymbol{w}^{*T} \mathbf{1} + \gamma \boldsymbol{w}^{*T} \boldsymbol{\mu} \\
&= \frac{A\mu_p^2 - 2B\mu_p + C}{AC - B^2}
\end{aligned}$$

and

$$\sigma_p = \sqrt{\frac{A\mu_p^2 - 2B\mu_p + C}{AC - B^2}}$$

which is a sideways parabola in mean–variance space and a hyperbola in mean–standard deviation space. The equation for the hyperbola is used in listing 2.8 to plot the minimum-variance frontier. The point on the minimum-variance frontier with the lowest variance (the leftmost point on the hyperbola or sideways parabola) is called the *global minimum variance portfolio*. Figure 2.3 depicts the top part of the minimum-variance frontier above the global minimum variance (the efficient frontier) with a solid line and the bottom part with a dashed line. To compute the location of the global minimum-variance portfolio, find the point where the slope of the parabola is zero:

$$\frac{d\sigma_p^2}{d\mu_p} = \frac{2A\mu_p - 2B}{AC - B^2} = 0$$

Solving for μ_p, the global minimum-variance portfolio has an expected return of B/A and, substituting that expected return into the equation for the parabola, a variance of $1/A$.

Adding a risk-free rate

We take a very similar approach when we add a risk-free rate. Let R_f be the return on the risk-free asset, and let w_0 be the weight of the risk-free asset. The optimization problem is only slightly modified from earlier:

$$\min_{w, w_0} \quad \tfrac{1}{2} w^T \Sigma w$$
$$\text{subject to} \quad \mu^T w + R_f w_0 = \mu_p$$
$$1^T w + w_0 = 1$$

We can eliminate w_0 from the second constraint

$$w_0 = 1 - 1^T w$$

and then substitute into the first constraint:

$$\mu^T w + R_f (1 - 1^T w) = \mu_p$$
$$(\mu^T - R_f 1^T) w = \mu_p - R_f$$

The Lagrangian equation is

$$L = w^T \Sigma w / 2 + \gamma \left(\mu_p - R_f - (\mu^T - R_f 1^T) w \right)$$

where γ is the Lagrange multiplier.

Taking the partial first derivatives of the Lagrangian with respect to the weights and setting the equations to zero gives

$$\frac{\partial L}{\partial w} = \Sigma w - \gamma (\mu - R_f 1) = 0$$

and we can solve for the optimal weights by premultiplying this equation by Σ^{-1}:

$$w^* = \gamma \Sigma^{-1} (\mu - R_f 1)$$

Now we can solve for γ:

$$(\mu - R_f 1)^T w^* = \gamma (\mu - R_f 1)^T \Sigma^{-1} (\mu - R_f 1)$$
$$\mu_p - R_f = \gamma (\mu^T \Sigma^{-1} \mu - 2R_f \mu^T \Sigma^{-1} 1 + R_f^2 1^T \Sigma^{-1} 1)$$
$$= \gamma (C - 2R_f B + R_f^2 A)$$

and

$$\gamma = \frac{\mu_p - R_f}{C - 2R_f B + R_f^2 A}$$

The equation for the standard deviation of a portfolio using the optimal weights is

$$
\begin{aligned}
\sigma_p^2 &= w^{*T} \Sigma w^* \\
&= w^{*T} \Sigma \gamma \Sigma^{-1} (\mu - R_f \mathbf{1}) \\
&= \gamma w^{*T} (\mu - R_f \mathbf{1}) \\
&= \gamma (\mu_p - R_f) \\
&= \frac{(\mu_p - R_r)^2}{C - 2R_f B + R_f^2 A}
\end{aligned}
$$

and

$$\sigma_p = \frac{\mu_p - R_f}{\sqrt{(C - 2R_f B + R_f^2 A)}}$$

The equation for the tangent line, which is plotted in listing 2.9, is

$$\mu_p = R_f + \sigma_p \underbrace{\sqrt{(C - 2R_f B + R_f^2 A)}}_{\text{slope}}$$

Summary

- Computing the expected return and standard deviation of a portfolio involves summations and double summations.
- Matrix multiplication is preferred over using `for` loops for computational efficiency, readability, and prevalence in libraries.
- The minimum-variance frontier is a curve that represents the minimum variance achievable for a given level of expected return.
- Generating random portfolio weights is an intuitive way to visualize the minimum-variance frontier.
- The mathematical formula for the minimum-variance frontier is a hyperbola in mean–standard deviation space (and a sideways parabola in mean–variance space).
- The portfolio construction process can be divided into two steps: choosing a mix between a portfolio of risky assets and a risk-free asset based on an investor's risk tolerance, and computing the optimal weights for the portfolio of risky assets.
- Questionnaires are often used to gauge risk tolerance, where answers are assigned points and those points are mapped to an appropriate mix of stocks and bonds.
- With a single line of code, a slider can be added to help investors visualize the effects of changing the allocation between stocks and bonds.

Estimating expected returns and covariances

This chapter covers

- Computing means, standard deviations, and correlations from historical data
- Adjusting historical returns for changes in valuation
- Estimating expected returns using the capital asset pricing model
- Using a GARCH model to estimate volatilities
- Testing for valid correlation matrices

With the Markowitz approach to portfolio construction, investors evaluate alternative portfolios based on their expected returns and volatilities. In chapter 2, we left open the question of how to form these estimates. The two types of inputs needed are

1. The expected returns of the individual assets
2. The variances of the individual assets and the pairwise correlations between assets

Together, these are sometimes referred to as *capital market assumptions*. We will tackle expected returns in the first section and variances and correlations in the following section.

3.1 Estimating expected returns

Expected returns are probably the most important input for portfolio construction and also the input that is the most difficult to estimate. Statistically, simply sampling historical returns more frequently can provide more accurate estimates of variances and correlations, but that doesn't help for means. Indeed, to estimate historical average returns, you only need the first and last prices, so accuracy can be obtained only with a longer time series. In this section, we consider several ways to estimate expected returns.

3.1.1 Historical averages

The most obvious way to estimate expected returns is to use average historical returns (also referred to as *realized returns*). Python makes it quick and easy to download historical prices. There are several free data providers, including Yahoo! Finance, Quandl, and Alpha Vantage. Some require free registration to get an API key. We will use Yahoo! and a Python library called `yfinance` that reads in the Yahoo! data.

We will estimate the historical returns for the three stocks in chapter 2—Apple (AAPL), First Energy (FE), and Walmart (WMT)—but of course, historical returns can be computed for any asset, as long as the data is available. The following listing shows how to download historical data for Apple stock using a single line of code, and the last five rows of the DataFrame that stores the data are shown in table 3.1.

> **Listing 3.1   Downloading historical stock prices**

```
import yfinance as yf

df = yf.download('AAPL', start='2000-01-03', end='2023-12-30')
df.tail()
```

Table 3.1   Last five rows of the DataFrame of Apple stock prices

	Open	High	Low	Close	Adj Close	Volume
Date						
2023-12-22	195.18	195.41	192.97	193.60	193.60	37122800
2023-12-26	193.61	193.89	192.83	193.05	193.05	28919300
2023-12-27	192.49	193.50	191.09	193.15	193.15	48087700
2023-12-28	194.14	194.66	193.17	193.58	193.58	34049900
2023-12-29	193.90	194.40	191.73	192.53	192.53	42628800

We are interested in the `Adj Close` column, which adjusts past prices for dividends and corporate actions like stock splits. We can download adjusted closing prices for several tickers at the same time with just one line of code. First, we store all the tickers in a list that we call stocks:

```
stocks = ['AAPL', 'FE', 'WMT']
```

Instead of downloading all fields for one ticker, we download just the Adj Close field for all tickers:

```
stock_prices = yf.download(stocks, start='2000-01-03',
                           end='2023-12-30')['Adj Close']
```

The first five rows of this DataFrame are shown in table 3.2. Note that if you are trying this at home, you may get slightly different numbers: whenever there's a new dividend or split, Yahoo back-adjusts all the prior adjusted closing values.

Table 3.2   First five rows of adjusted closing prices for three stocks

	AAPL	FE	WMT
Date			
2000-01-03	0.847207	7.525705	43.555920
2000-01-04	0.775779	7.525705	41.926163
2000-01-05	0.787131	7.802859	41.070534
2000-01-06	0.719014	7.824178	41.518715
2000-01-07	0.753073	7.866814	44.656036

To get returns, we take the percentage change of prices:

```
stock_returns = stock_prices.pct_change()
```

The first five rows of returns are shown in table 3.3. We need the previous day's prices to compute returns, so the first row is all "NaN" (Not a Number). When we compute means next, it will ignore the NaNs; but for calculations we do later in this chapter, we will have to use the dropna() method to delete the NaNs.

Table 3.3   First five rows of returns of the three stocks

	AAPL	FE	WMT
Date			
2000-01-03	NaN	NaN	NaN
2000-01-04	-0.084310	0.000000	-0.037418
2000-01-05	0.014633	0.036827	-0.020408
2000-01-06	-0.086538	0.002732	0.010913
2000-01-07	0.047369	0.005450	0.075564

Our final step is to use the pandas method `mean()` to compute the mean returns and multiply by 252 (the approximate number of trading days in a year) to get an estimate of the annualized returns:

```
stock_returns.mean()*252
```

The historical returns for the three stocks are shown in table 3.4.

Table 3.4   Average historical returns of the three stocks

AAPL	0.306962
FE	0.099765
WMT	0.081381

Unfortunately, using historical returns as an estimate of expected future returns is problematic. First of all, we will show later that the asset allocation weights from an optimization are extremely sensitive to the expected returns. Even small differences in expected returns can lead to placing oversized weights on stocks with higher expected returns. And, as the famous disclaimer goes, past performance may not be indicative of future results. Just because a stock had good returns in the historical period does not necessarily mean it is expected to outperform by the same amount in the future. And the choice of which historical period to use may have an outsized influence on historical returns. For example, growth stocks have historically outperformed value stocks over the last decade, but if you look back over several decades, the opposite is true. For those reasons, this method is not used in practice.

3.1.2   CAPM

The capital asset pricing model (CAPM) is another method for computing forecasted expected returns. The CAPM predicts that expected returns depend on three things:

1 The current risk-free rate
2 The expected return of the entire stock market
3 The sensitivity of the stock to the market, referred to as the stock's *beta*

The following equation shows the CAPM formula for the expected return of a particular stock, where r_f represents the risk-free rate, r_m represents the market return, and β is the stock's beta:

$$E[r] = r_f + \beta (E[r_m] - r_f)$$

The beta of the market itself is 1, but the betas of individual stocks vary. Some companies, like utilities and producers of household staples, aren't very sensitive to the market and have betas less than 1. Other stocks, like luxury goods, are more sensitive and have betas greater than 1.

In this section, we will go through the step-by-step procedure for calculating expected returns based on the CAPM equation, starting with computing the beta for each stock. First, we need to download the risk-free rate. We will use 3-month

Treasury Bill (T-Bill) rates as a proxy for the short-term risk-free rate. This data is available from Federal Reserve Economic Data (FRED) and can be downloaded using the `pandas-datareader` library. In the following listing, we download about 20 years' worth of 3-month T-Bill rates, and table 3.5 shows the first five rows. The code for 3-month T-Bill rates is `TB3MS`.

Listing 3.2   Downloading T-Bill data from the Federal Reserve

```
import pandas_datareader as pdr

rf = pdr.DataReader('TB3MS', 'fred', start='2000-01-01', end='2023-12-30')
rf.head()
```

Table 3.5   First five rows of 3-month T-Bill rates

Date	TB3MS
2000-01-01	5.32
2000-02-01	5.55
2000-03-01	5.69
2000-04-01	5.66
2000-05-01	5.79

The rate is an annual yield, and when we inspect the first rows of the data in table 3.5, we can see that it is represented in percentage terms. So, we have to divide by 100 (in other words, 5% is represented as 5 instead of 0.05).

We also need to download market returns to compute beta. We will use the `yfinance` library to download historical prices, as we did before to download the prices of AAPL, FE, and WMT; but now we will download the prices of the Standard and Poor's 500 (S&P 500) exchange-traded funds (ETF), ticker symbol SPY, which will be used as a proxy for the market:

```
mkt_prices = yf.download('SPY', start='2000-01-03', end='2023-12-30')
➥ ['Adj Close']
```

We are now ready to perform regressions to estimate the CAPM beta. In listing 3.3, we estimate the beta for AAPL stock. First, we import the `statsmodels` library to perform the regression. We also need to manipulate the data a little before we perform the regression. The T-Bill data we downloaded from FRED (see table 3.5) has a monthly frequency, and the stock price data is daily, so we downsample the daily stock prices to a monthly frequency using the pandas method `resample()`. The first argument, `'MS'`, returns the start-of-month value, which matches the T-Bill data. Then we compute monthly returns from monthly prices. To perform the regression, we describe the regression model by defining the data used for the dependent variable on the left side of the regression, y, and the independent variable(s) on the right side, x. Note that we have to divide the risk-free rate by 100 and then by 12 to convert it from an annual percentage to a monthly decimal value. Then we fit the regression model. Finally, we print out a summary of the regression results.

Listing 3.3   Regressing stock returns on market returns to get beta

```
import statsmodels.api as sm                      Resamples daily
                                                  stock prices to monthly
stock_prices_monthly = stock_prices.resample('MS').first()  ←
mkt_prices_monthly = mkt_prices.resample('MS').first()
aapl_returns_monthly = stock_prices_monthly['AAPL'].pct_change()  ←

                                      Computes monthly stock returns
                                      from monthly stock prices

mkt_returns_monthly = mkt_prices_monthly.pct_change()
y = (aapl_returns_monthly - rf['TB3MS']/100/12).dropna()  ← Dependent variable
X = (mkt_returns_monthly - rf['TB3MS']/100/12).dropna()  ←
model = sm.OLS(y,X)   ←— Describes the regression model       Independent
results = model.fit()   ←— Fits the regression                variable
print(results.summary())   ←— Prints out the results
```

The full output of the regression is shown in figure 3.1, with the beta highlighted. You can also extract individual attributes from the regression results of figure 3.1. For example, you can extract the beta of 1.3187 directly using the following:

```
print(results.params)
```

This will output:

```
    x1    1.3187
```

Note that because there is no intercept in this regression, there is only one regression coefficient and no constant coefficient.

Finally, the two other pieces of information we need to estimate expected returns according to the CAPM are the current risk-free rate and the expected return on the market. This line

```
print('The current risk-free rate is', rf['TB3MS'].iloc[-1],'%')
```

outputs

```
    The current risk-free rate is 5.27 %
```

And this line

```
print('The avg annualized market return is',
      mkt_returns_monthly.mean()*12*100, '%')
```

outputs

```
    The avg annualized market return is 8.0741 %
```

```
                      OLS Regression Results
==========================================================================
Dep. Variable:                      y   R-squared (uncentered):       0.304
Model:                            OLS   Adj. R-squared (uncentered):  0.302
Method:                 Least Squares   F-statistic:                  124.7
Date:                Sat, 30 Dec 2023   Prob (F-statistic):        2.94e-24
Time:                        20:13:44   Log-Likelihood:              260.62
No. Observations:                 286   AIC:                         -519.2
Df Residuals:                     285   BIC:                         -515.6
Df Model:                           1
Covariance Type:            nonrobust
==========================================================================
                 coef    std err          t      P>|t|     [0.025     0.975]
--------------------------------------------------------------------------
x1             1.3187      0.118     11.167      0.000      1.086      1.551
==========================================================================
Omnibus:                       47.774   Durbin-Watson:                2.022
Prob(Omnibus):                  0.000   Jarque-Bera (JB):           287.926
Skew:                          -0.457   Prob(JB):                   3.00e-63
Kurtosis:                       7.830   Cond. No.                      1.00
==========================================================================
```

Figure 3.1   Regression results including the beta for AAPL

Plugging everything into the CAPM equation, we get an expected return for AAPL stock of 8.96%:

$$E\left[r\right] = \underbrace{r_f}_{5.27\%} + \underbrace{\beta}_{1.3187} \; \underbrace{(E\left[r_m\right]}_{8.07\%} - \underbrace{r_f}_{5.27\%})$$
$$= 8.96\%$$

Table 3.6 shows the betas and expected returns when we repeat this procedure for FE and WMT in addition to AAPL. For comparison, we compare the CAPM expected returns with the historical average returns we computed from table 3.4.

Table 3.6   Betas and expected returns for three stocks using the CAPM

Stock	Beta	CAPM expected ret	Historical expected ret
AAPL	1.3187	8.96%	30.70%
FE	0.2958	6.10%	9.98%
WMT	0.4907	6.64%	8.14%

As table 3.6 shows, the expected returns from the CAPM model are quite different from those in table 3.4 using historical averages. For example, the expected return for AAPL goes from 30.70% to 8.96%. The historical returns assume that Apple's recent outstanding performance is repeatable, whereas the CAPM doesn't use historical-average returns.

One of the key implications of the CAPM model is that the alpha of any fund or portfolio is zero (see chapter 7 for a discussion of alpha). The efficiency of the market portfolio is a reasonable approximation because thousands of mutual funds, ETFs, and hedge funds have tried to generate positive alpha, and history shows that it's not easy to beat the market consistently. However, many empirical tests on the validity of the CAPM model fail. For example, several studies show that low-beta stocks tend to have higher average returns than CAPM predicts, and high-beta stocks have lower average returns than CAPM predicts. Studies have also shown that value stocks, relative to growth stocks, have positive alpha. And hundreds of other studies purport to show that some portfolios of stocks outperform others. There is considerable debate about the source of all these alphas that result in deviations from the CAPM:

- One view is that alphas represent mispricing and irrationality by the market. To use value stocks as an example, behavioral economists have identified a phenomenon called *recency bias*, where investors place too much emphasis on recent events. Consequently, investors may undervalue value stocks that have had recent challenges and overvalue growth stocks that are often characterized by recent strong performance.

Humorous quip about recency bias

"Honestly, survivorship bias used to be my favorite kind of bias—then I found out about recency bias, and I don't think anything could top that."

—James Medlock on X (formerly Twitter)

- An alternative view is that the outperformance of certain stocks may not be an irrational market inefficiency but rather a rational response to risk factors not captured by the CAPM beta. Again, using value stocks as an example, they typically have greater amounts of tangible capital than growth stocks, so value stocks may be more vulnerable during an economic downturn because those companies can't cut expenses as easily. According to this theory, value stocks offer higher expected returns to compensate for additional business cycle risk.

We should also point out that the anomalies may be the result of data mining. If you examine historical stock returns over and over again across many possible factors, it will appear by chance that you have discovered some mispricing. And academic researchers have an incentive to publish these findings. Indeed, many of the anomalies do not hold up in the years after they are reported in the literature. For example, value stocks have underperformed growth stocks in the last 15 years.

Another limitation of CAPM is that it is primarily used to estimate expected returns for stocks and generally is not applied to bonds. Bonds have a different set of risk factors than stocks. A corporate bond fund and a Treasury bond fund may have low betas to the stock market, but that doesn't mean their expected returns are the same and equal to the short-term risk-free rate.

So where does that leave us with the important task of estimating expected returns? CAPM has several limitations because it ignores alpha from historical returns and assumes only one source of risk. On the other hand, using realized returns as an estimate of expected returns assumes past outperformance will persist in the future. For example, suppose energy stocks significantly beat the market over some period when oil prices steadily rose. In that case, historical returns are not necessarily the best estimate of future expected returns because they assume the rise in oil prices will continue indefinitely. If oil prices remain flat or, worse, revert lower from current elevated levels, expected future returns will be lower than historical returns. The next section describes a technique that adjusts historical returns to account for valuation changes to better estimate expected future returns.

3.1.3 *Adjusting historical returns for changes in valuation*

Allocating assets based on historical returns can lead to *performance chasing*, or placing large weights on assets that have performed well in the past and assuming those superior returns will continue in the future. However, part of the outperformance may be due to valuation changes that are not repeatable. A more accurate estimate of expected returns can be obtained by using regressions to strip out the portion of historical returns that resulted from valuation changes. A good case for making these adjustments can be found in the paper "The Long Run is Lying to You" by Cliff Asness (www.aqr.com/Insights/Perspectives/The-Long-Run-Is-Lying-to-You).

Each asset class has its own valuation measures, so stripping out valuation changes will vary depending on the asset or portfolio under consideration. Let's go through a few examples to illustrate how historical returns are adjusted. A good example to start with is estimating the expected returns of bonds. Bonds have been in a secular bull market for the last 40 years, as the yield on 10-year Treasury securities has dropped from over 13% in the mid-1980s to under 1% in the early 2020s (see figure 3.2). As a result, most bond funds have had exceptionally strong results over that period, but those historical returns are not necessarily repeatable. In the example, we will look at the performance of a corporate bond index before and after stripping out the effects of the drop in yields. In particular, we will look at the BofA Merrill Lynch US Corporate 15+ Year Total Return Index, which can be downloaded from FRED using the rather long symbol BAMLCC8A015PYTRIV. It is important to use a total return index that assumes all cash flows, such as bond coupons, are reinvested. All the corporate bonds in the index are investment grade, meaning they have a credit rating that indicates a low risk of default, and all the bonds in the index have maturities over 15 years. We could perform a similar analysis for Treasury securities, junk bonds (bonds with lower credit ratings), or bonds with shorter maturities.

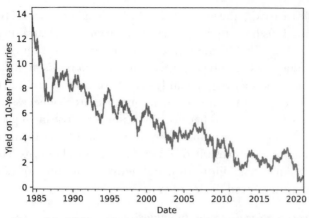

Figure 3.2   Yield on 10-year Treasury securities from the mid-1980s to 2021

In listing 3.4, we download from FRED the data on the corporate bond index, short-term risk-free interest rates, and the yields on 10-year Treasury securities, which we need for our analysis. We resample all the data from a daily to a monthly frequency. The start and end dates of the data were intentionally chosen to coincide with the peak and trough of 10-year yields to emphasize the effects of changes in yields. The code also calculates the historical average returns of corporate bonds over this period. As you would expect, this was a very good period for corporate bonds: the average annual raw returns were 9.67%. We will focus on the returns in excess of the short-term risk-free rate, or *excess returns* for short. The historical excess returns were 6.36%.

Listing 3.4   Downloading bond data and computing historical returns

```
start = '1984-06-29'
end = '2020-12-31'
symbol = 'BAMLCC8A015PYTRIV'                    Downloads corporate
                                                       bond data
bond = pdr.DataReader(symbol, 'fred', start=start, end=end)  ◄─┘
bond_monthly = bond.resample('M').last()
bond_returns_monthly = bond_monthly.pct_change()

TenYr = pdr.DataReader('DGS10', 'fred', start='1984-06-29',
    end='2020-12-31')    ◄──── Downloads Treasury yield data
TenYr_monthly = TenYr.resample('M').last()
TenYr_change_monthly = TenYr_monthly.diff().dropna()/100.
TenYr_change_monthly.rename(columns={'DGS10': 'Change 10Yr Yield'},
    inplace=True)
                                                   Downloads short-term
                                                     risk-free rate data
rf = pdr.DataReader('DTB3', 'fred', start='1984-06-29', end='2020-12-31')  ◄─┘
rf_monthly = rf.resample('M').last()/100

TenYr.plot(xlabel='Date', ylabel='Yield on 10-Year Treasuries',
    legend=False)    ◄──── Plot of Treasury yields displayed in figure 3.2
```

```
print('raw bond average returns ', bond_returns_monthly[symbol].mean()*12)
print('excess bond average returns ', (bond_returns_monthly[symbol] -
                        rf_monthly['DTB3'].shift()/12).mean()*12)
```

The output is

```
raw bond average returns   0.09673030238651532
excess bond average returns   0.06364354439564762
```

Now, let's run a regression to adjust historical returns for changes in yield. As listing 3.5 shows, the left side of the regression is the monthly excess returns of the corporate bond index. On the right side are the contemporaneous changes in the 10-year yield on Treasury securities. Therefore, the constant in the regression shows the average historical returns after accounting for changes in the 10-year yield. Of course, falling yields can explain only a portion of the excess returns of corporate bonds. Two other components of corporate bond returns are the compensation for credit risk that bondholders receive and the carry from holding longer-maturity bonds over short-term cash when the term structure of interest rates is upward-sloping.

> **Listing 3.5   Regressing corporate bond returns on changes in Treasury yields**

```
y = (bond_returns_monthly[symbol] - rf_monthly['DTB3'].shift()/12).dropna()
X = TenYr_change_monthly
X = sm.add_constant(X)
common_dates = X.index.intersection(y.index)
X = X.loc[common_dates]
model = sm.OLS(y,X)
results = model.fit()
print(results.summary())
```

The regression output is shown in figure 3.3. We highlight the two regression coefficients: the constant, which is the monthly return after accounting for changes in yields, and the coefficient on the changes in the 10-year yield, which measures the sensitivity of corporate bonds to changes in yields. To get the expected excess return for these corporate bonds after accounting for changes in yield, we just multiply the constant in the regression by 12 to annualize the monthly returns

```
print('The expected return after stripping out yield changes is ',
        results.params[0]*12)
```

which gives the output

```
The expected return after stripping out yield changes is   0.04261614539
```

So the expected excess return on corporate bonds goes from 6.36% using historical returns to 4.26% after stripping out changes in yield, for a 2.1% difference, or about a third lower. This example illustrates that even using a long time period to compute historical returns does not immunize you from the valuation effects we just described if the time period overlaps with secular trends in valuation measures. However, if we had gone back a few decades earlier when yields were lower, the adjusted returns would be very similar to the historical returns. The adjustment makes a difference only when there is a net change in yields over the estimation period.

```
                            OLS Regression Results
==============================================================================
Dep. Variable:                      y   R-squared:                       0.455
Model:                            OLS   Adj. R-squared:                  0.454
Method:                 Least Squares   F-statistic:                     364.4
Date:                Fri, 08 Dec 2023   Prob (F-statistic):           1.72e-59
Time:                        03:15:29   Log-Likelihood:                 1123.3
No. Observations:                 438   AIC:                            -2243.
Df Residuals:                     436   BIC:                            -2234.
Df Model:                           1
Covariance Type:            nonrobust
==============================================================================
                   coef    std err          t      P>|t|      [0.025      0.975]
------------------------------------------------------------------------------
const            0.0036      0.001      3.962      0.000       0.002       0.005
Change 10Yr Yield -5.9450    0.311    -19.090      0.000      -6.557      -5.333
==============================================================================
Omnibus:                      156.992   Durbin-Watson:                   1.760
Prob(Omnibus):                  0.000   Jarque-Bera (JB):             3031.811
Skew:                          -1.021   Prob(JB):                         0.00
Kurtosis:                      15.726   Cond. No.                         349.
==============================================================================
```

Figure 3.3   **Output from regressing corporate bond returns on changes in 10-year yields**

Now let's do a similar analysis for stocks, where we adjust historical returns for changes in valuations. For stocks, however, we need to use a different measure of valuation changes than the changes in yield that we used for bonds. There are several choices for stock valuation measures, like the book-to-market ratio and the price-to-earnings (P/E) ratio. We will use Robert Shiller's popular *cyclically adjusted price-to-earnings ratio*, commonly referred to as the CAPE ratio. The CAPE ratio differs from the standard P/E ratio in two ways. Whereas the P/E ratio uses the most recent earnings in its calculation, the CAPE ratio averages earnings over the prior 10 years to smooth out earnings fluctuations over business cycles. In addition, the CAPE ratio adjusts earnings for inflation.

Our goal is to estimate the expected returns of the S&P 500 by adjusting historical returns for valuation changes. Unfortunately, the S&P 500 index is not a total-return index that includes dividends, and the history of the SPY ETF that tracks the S&P 500 is not long enough. Instead, we use the historical returns of the Vanguard mutual fund that tracks the S&P 500, which has the ticker symbol VFINX.

In listing 3.6, we download all the data we need for stocks, just like we did in listing 3.4 for bonds. CAPE ratio data can be downloaded into an Excel spreadsheet from Robert Shiller's website: www.econ.yale.edu/~shiller/data.htm. This listing assumes the spreadsheet has been downloaded and is in the same directory as the code. The pandas function `read_excel()` reads the Excel file into a DataFrame. You must supply not only the name of the Excel spreadsheet but also (if the workbook contains more than one sheet) the name of the sheet. The date column in the CAPE file is in a less-standard format, where Oct 2023 would be represented by the float 2023.10, so we need a few lines of code to convert that format into a `datetime` index. Because the CAPE data has a seasonality competent, we resample the monthly data to an annual frequency. The output shows that the average annual raw returns were 12.60%, and the excess returns were 9.10%.

Listing 3.6   Downloading stock data and computing historical returns

```
start = '1983-01-01'
end = '2023-01-01'

stock = yf.download('VFINX', start=start, end=end)
stock_annual = stock.resample('AS').first()
stock_returns_annual = stock_annual['Adj Close'].pct_change()

CAPE = pd.read_excel('ie_data.xls', sheet_name='Data',        ⟵ Reads the Excel file
            usecols=['Date', 'CAPE'], skiprows=7)   ⟵         with the CAPE data
CAPE = CAPE.dropna()
CAPE['Year'] =  CAPE['Date'].astype(int)    ⟵ The year is the integer part of the date.
CAPE['Month'] = round(100*(CAPE['Date']-CAPE['Year'])).astype(int)  ⟵
CAPE['Year'] =  CAPE['Year'].astype(str)                   The month is the
CAPE['Month'] = CAPE['Month'].astype(str)          decimal part of the date.
CAPE['Date'] = CAPE['Year']+'-'+CAPE['Month']+'-'+'01'
CAPE = CAPE.set_index('Date')
CAPE.index = pd.to_datetime(CAPE.index, format='%Y-%m-%d')
CAPE.drop(columns=['Year', 'Month'], inplace=True)
CAPE = CAPE.resample('AS').first()
CAPE['CAPE_returns'] = CAPE['CAPE'].pct_change()

rf = pdr.DataReader('DTB3', 'fred', start=start, end=end)
rf_annual = rf.resample('AS').first()/100

print('raw stock average returns ',stock_returns_annual.mean())
print('excess stock average returns ', (stock_returns_annual -
            rf_annual['DTB3'].shift()).mean())
```

The output is

```
raw stock average returns  0.12596751587665478
excess stock average returns  0.09098290049203947
```

Similar to what we did with bonds, let's use a regression to adjust historical returns for changes in the CAPE ratio. As listing 3.7 shows, the left side of the regression is the monthly excess returns on the Vanguard mutual fund that tracks the S&P 500 index. On the right side are the contemporaneous percentage changes in the CAPE ratio. Therefore, the constant in the regression shows the historical returns after accounting for changes in the CAPE ratio.

Listing 3.7   Regressing stock returns on changes in the CAPE ratio

```
y = (stock_returns_annual - rf_annual ['DTB3'].shift() ).dropna()
X = CAPE['CAPE_returns']
X = sm.add_constant(X)
common_dates = X.index.intersection(y.index)
X = X.loc[common_dates]
model = sm.OLS(y,X)
results = model.fit()
print(results.summary())
```

The regression output is shown in figure 3.4. We highlight the two regression coefficients: the constant, which is the annual return after accounting for changes in the CAPE ratio, and the coefficient on the percent changes in the CAPE ratio. Because we are using annual data, the expected S&P 500 excess return after accounting for changes in valuation is simply the constant in the regression, which is 4.72%—a rather large adjustment compared to the historical returns of 9.10%. Keep in mind that the P/E ratio, as measured by the CAPE ratio, went from under 10 in the early 1980s to over 35 in the early 2020s, which is why a sizable portion of the S&P 500 returns over the last 40 years can be attributed to large changes in valuation that might not be repeatable.

```
                            OLS Regression Results
===============================================================================
Dep. Variable:                        y   R-squared:                     0.725
Model:                              OLS   Adj. R-squared:                0.718
Method:                   Least Squares   F-statistic:                   97.61
Date:                 Sat, 16 Dec 2023   Prob (F-statistic):         6.37e-12
Time:                         21:59:40   Log-Likelihood:               41.915
No. Observations:                    39   AIC:                          -79.83
Df Residuals:                        37   BIC:                          -76.50
Df Model:                             1
Covariance Type:              nonrobust
===============================================================================
                 coef      std err         t      P>|t|      [0.025     0.975]
-------------------------------------------------------------------------------
const          0.0472        0.014     3.304      0.002       0.018      0.076
CAPE_returns   0.8862        0.090     9.880      0.000       0.704      1.068
===============================================================================
Omnibus:                          2.176   Durbin-Watson:                 1.652
Prob(Omnibus):                    0.337   Jarque-Bera (JB):              1.219
Skew:                            -0.041   Prob(JB):                      0.544
Kurtosis:                         3.862   Cond. No.                      6.62
===============================================================================
```

Figure 3.4   Output from regressing stock returns on percent changes in the CAPE ratio

This type of analysis can be performed on other assets as well. For example, suppose we want to include foreign stocks in our portfolio, and we need to estimate the expected returns. For the last several decades, US stocks have outperformed European and Asian stocks, but part of that outperformance can be attributed to US stocks getting more expensive, which might not persist in the future. Similarly, value stocks have traditionally outperformed growth stocks, but that has not held up in the last 15 years. Much of the recent outperformance of growth stocks can be attributed to growth stocks becoming more expensive relative to value stocks.

One caveat is in order when adjusting historical returns for valuation changes. We are implicitly assuming that the portfolio has low turnover from year to year. The classic example of this assumption being violated is the momentum factor. There is some empirical evidence that momentum stocks, or stocks that have outperformed the market over the last year, continue to outperform. This portfolio has a high turnover, so if last year's momentum portfolio got expensive, it might not indicate that this year's portfolio is expensive if it is composed primarily of different stocks.

Adjusting for changes in valuation implicitly assumes that current valuation levels will persist in the future. When we looked at bonds, we stripped out the effects of yields dropping from about 15% in the 1980s to under 1% in 2020. But economists may believe that rates will rise in the years ahead. Estimates of expected returns that take other factors into account, like macroeconomic factors, are covered next.

3.1.4 *Capital market assumptions from asset managers*

Large asset managers, like JP Morgan, BlackRock, and AQR, make predictions of expected returns (as well as volatilities and correlations) for major asset classes, which are used by their own asset allocators and to assist financial advisors in portfolio construction. These estimates usually incorporate a combination of quantitative methods as well as fundamental insights.

The quantitative techniques can vary by asset class but offer an alternative to using historical returns. For equities, a dividend discount model has been used. The model may take the form $E[r] = (\text{div yield}) + (\text{EPS growth})$. For bonds, the expected return is typically the current yield plus the roll-down return, which is the expected capital gains if the term structure of interest rates remains unchanged and future yields equal the forward yields implied by the term structure.

Next, we tackle the problem of estimating the other main input needed for portfolio construction: the covariance matrix of the assets.

3.2 *Estimating variances and covariances*

As with expected returns, multiple ways exist to estimate variances and covariances.

3.2.1 *Using historical returns*

Using Python, it is easy to estimate volatilities and correlations from a time series of returns. Here are the volatilities for FE, WMT, and AAPL. We annualize daily volatility by multiplying by $\sqrt{252}$:

```
stock_returns.std() * (252**0.5)
```

The output is

```
AAPL    0.392659
FE      0.258756
WMT     0.235451
```

To get the correlation matrix from a time series of returns in a pandas DataFrame, we need one line of code:

```
stock_returns.corr()
```

The correlation matrix is shown in table 3.7.

Table 3.7   Correlation matrix of three assets

	AAPL	FE	WMT
AAPL	1.000000	0.209247	0.261399
FE	0.209247	1.000000	0.265760
WMT	0.261399	0.265760	1.000000

Alternatively, to compute the covariance matrix in pandas rather than the correlation matrix and volatilities, we can use this line of code (for variances and covariances, we annualize by multiplying the daily numbers by 252):

```
stock_returns.cov() * 252
```

The covariance matrix is shown in table 3.8.

Table 3.8   Covariance matrix of three assets

	AAPL	FE	WMT
AAPL	0.154181	0.021260	0.024167
FE	0.021260	0.066955	0.016191
WMT	0.024167	0.016191	0.055437

Using historical returns to estimate the covariance matrix is straightforward, but it turns out that it's not feasible if you want to estimate the covariance matrix for a large number of securities. For example, if you wanted to estimate the covariance matrix for the 3,000 stocks in the Russell 3000, you would need 3,000 historical returns for each stock. Multifactor models can be used to reduce the number of correlations that have to be estimated. In fact, many Wall Street firms subscribe to Barra, a company that built covariance matrices and risk models based on a multi-factor methodology. In the book's code on the website and GitHub (https://www.manning.com/books/build-a-robo-advisor-with-python-from-scratch

or https://github.com/robreider/robo-advisor-with-python/blob/main/chapter_03.ipynb), we describe how these multifactor models work.

The volatility estimates in this section do not take into account that volatility often changes over time, sometimes in predictable ways. Next, we will consider some more sophisticated methods to estimate volatility.

3.2.2 GARCH models

There is strong empirical evidence that volatility tends to "cluster." Periods of high volatility are more likely to be followed by high volatility, and quiet periods of low volatility are more likely to be followed by low volatility. Anecdotally, a nice example of this phenomenon is the volatility after the 1987 stock market crash. You can download the historical S&P 500 data using the code at the beginning of the chapter. As table 3.9 shows, the S&P 500 dropped by 20% on October 19, 1987. Even though daily volatility in the stock market has been about 1%/day for data going back almost 100 years, in the days following the crash, the daily moves on most days continued to be much higher than average, both positive and negative. In the five days following the crash, as table 3.9 shows, the returns were approximately +5%, +9%, −4%, 0%, and −8%.

To show a little more rigorously rather than anecdotally that large changes tend to be followed by large changes (of either sign) and small changes tend to be followed by small changes, consider the autocorrelation of squared returns, $\mathrm{Corr}(r_{t-1}^2, r_t^2)$. If there were no volatility clustering, then yesterday's squared return would not help us forecast today's squared return, and the autocorrelation would be close to zero. But in listing 3.8, we compute the autocorrelation for the S&P 500, and it is significantly positive. The autocorrelation of squared returns is 0.22, which is significantly different from zero. If returns were independent and identically distributed, and therefore there was no volatility clustering, the standard error on the autocorrelation, with $N = 8910$ data points, would be $\sqrt{1/N} \approx 0.01$; so any autocorrelation outside ±0.02 is statistically significantly different from zero.

Listing 3.8   Computing the autocorrelation of squared returns

```
SP500 = yf.download('^GSPC', start='1987-01-01', end='2022-05-10')    ←┐
                                           Downloads S&P 500 prices,
                                              Yahoo ticker ^GSPC
SP500['Ret'] = SP500['Close'].pct_change()
SP500['Sq Ret'] = SP500['Ret']**2   ← Adds a column of squared returns
AutoCorr = SP500['Sq Ret'].autocorr()  ← Computes autocorrelation of squared returns
se = 1/(len(SP500)**0.5)   ← Computes the standard error, 1/sqrt(N)
t_stat = AutoCorr/se   ← Computes the t-stat

print('The autocorrelation of squared returns is', AutoCorr)
print('The standard error is', se)
print('The t-stat is', t_stat)
```

Table 3.9   S&P500 returns around the stock market crash of 1987

Date	Close	% Change
1987-10-08	314.160004	-1.375025
1987-10-09	311.070007	-0.983574
1987-10-12	309.390015	-0.540069
1987-10-13	314.519989	1.658093
1987-10-14	305.230011	-2.9537
1987-10-15	298.079987	-2.342504
1987-10-16	282.700012	-5.15968
1987-10-19	224.839996	-20.466931
1987-10-20	236.830002	5.332684
1987-10-21	258.380005	9.099355
1987-10-22	248.250000	-3.920584
1987-10-23	248.220001	-0.012084
1987-10-26	227.669998	-8.278947
1987-10-27	233.190002	2.424564
1987-10-28	233.279999	0.038594
1987-10-29	244.770004	4.925414
1987-10-30	251.789993	2.867994

The output is as follows:

```
The autocorrelation of squared returns is 0.2228
The standard error is 0.0106
The t-stat is 21.03
```

Another empirical observation is that not only does volatility spike up during a crisis, but it also eventually drops back to approximately the same level of volatility as before the crisis. Over the decades, there have been periodic spikes in equity volatility due to crises that caused large market drops, such as the Great Depression, 9/11, the 2008 financial crisis, and the Covid pandemic. In all these cases, volatility spiked up but eventually reverted to precrisis levels. In figure 3.5, we graph the behavior of the CBOE Volatility Index (VIX) in the aftermath of the financial crisis in 2008. At the peak of the crisis, implied volatility hit a high of 80%; it gradually reverted over the following year to 21%:

```
VIX = yf.download('^VIX', start='2008-07-01', end='2009-10-16')['Close']
VIX.plot()
```

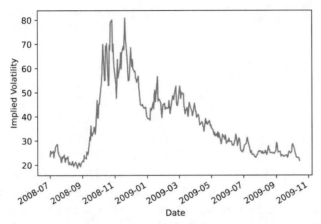

Figure 3.5 **VIX implied volatility around the financial crisis of 2008**

A class of statistical models called autoregressive conditional heteroskedasticity (ARCH) models, or the more generalized (GARCH) models, can be used to forecast volatility in the presence of volatility clustering and volatility mean reversion. There are dozens of varieties of these models, and we will only consider one of the more basic varieties. Listing 3.9 provides an example of forecasting AAPL's volatility using a GARCH model. First, we import the `arch_model` in the `arch` package. We download AAPL stock prices, as we have previously done in this chapter.

> **TIP** Notice that we scale the returns by 100 when we compute returns. The documentation for the ARCH library recommends scaling returns to ensure that the optimization converges. Sometimes optimizers have trouble when the scales of the parameters are orders of magnitude different from each other.

We also use the `dropna()` method because the optimization returns an error if the first row of returns is `NaN`. In this example, we construct a simple model, but other parameters, described in the library's documentation, explain how to build more complex models. Then we fit the model and set a forecast horizon of 63 trading days corresponding to three months.

Listing 3.9 Using a GARCH model to forecast volatility

```
from arch import arch_model

AAPL_prices = yf.download('AAPL', start='2000-01-03', end='2022-05-24')['Adj
Close']
returns = 100 * AAPL_prices.pct_change().dropna()    ←┐ Computes AAPL returns,
                                                       │ scales by 100, and drops NaNs
horizon = 63   ← Forecast horizon is 63 days, or 3 months.
```

```
am = arch_model(returns)    ←── Describes the model
res = am.fit()   ←── Fits the model
forecasts = res.forecast(horizon=horizon)    ←── Forecasts future variance
print(forecasts.residual_variance.iloc[-1,:])    ←──┐ Prints the variance forecast
                                                     └ for each of the 63 days
```

The output is

```
    h.01    9.8718
    h.02    9.8581
    h.03    9.8446
             ..
    h.61    9.2390
    h.62    9.2311
    h.63    9.2234
```

The forecast results show the one-day variance forecast at each horizon date. So h.01 is the next one-day variance forecast, h.02 is the one-day variance forecast one day in the future, etc. These one-day variances can be summed and then annualized by multiplying by 252/horizon, where horizon is the number of days in the future we are forecasting (63 in our case). Then we take the square root to convert variance into volatility, and we can divide by 100 to reverse the scaling we did on returns. Here is the code for that:

```
vol_forecast = (forecasts.residual_variance.iloc[-1,:].sum()*252/horizon)
➡ **0.5
vol_forecast = vol_forecast/100
print('Volatility forecast is ', vol_forecast)
```

This produces the output

```
    Volatility forecast is 0.4810
```

We can see that the volatility forecast, 48.1%, is considerably higher than we estimated earlier using historical volatility. Keep in mind that as the forecast horizon gets longer, the GARCH forecast converges to the historical volatility. Therefore, GARCH models provide less advantage over historical volatility for long horizons.

3.2.3   *Other approaches*

GARCH models are not the only way to get improved volatility forecasts. Some studies show that implied volatility from options prices has better forecast accuracy than GARCH models. Another alternative to using historical volatility is the exponentially weighted moving average (EWMA) estimate for volatility. Historic volatility essentially applies equal weights to all data in the past, whereas EWMA places more weight on more recent data. It turns out that EWMA can be considered a special case of a GARCH model.

3.2.4 *Subjective estimates*

Just as with estimating means, you can use capital market assumptions from large money managers or your own subjective estimates as your forecast for the correlation matrix or covariance matrix. However, one extra complication is that not all arbitrary matrices have the property that they are *positive definite*. This property is required for any optimization because it allows the matrix to be invertible.

There are a few ways to check whether a matrix is positive definite, but one that is easy to implement in Python is to check the eigenvalues of the matrix in NumPy's linear algebra library using the function `np.linalg.eigvals(matrix)`. For a symmetric matrix like a variance–covariance matrix, if all the eigenvalues are positive, the matrix is positive definite. Here are two examples that check whether all the eigenvalues are positive. This first example fails the test:

```
Corr = [[ 1. ,  0.8, -0.2],
        [ 0.8,  1. ,  0.5],
        [-0.2,  0.5,  1. ]]
eigenvalues = np.linalg.eigvals(Corr)
print(np.all(eigenvalues > 0))
```

Here's the output:

```
False
```

A small tweak of the correlation matrix passes the test. Compared to the last example, we only slightly changed the correlation between the second and third assets from 0.5 to 0.4, but now, as the output indicates, the correlation matrix is positive definite:

```
Corr = [[ 1. ,  0.8, -0.2],
        [ 0.8,  1. ,  0.4],
        [-0.2,  0.4,  1. ]]
eigenvalues = np.linalg.eigvals(Corr)
print(np.all(eigenvalues > 0))
```

Here's the output:

```
True
```

Summary

- Traditional asset allocation requires estimates of expected returns and covariance matrices.

- Expected returns can be estimated by taking averages of historical returns, but these estimates are problematic because they depend on past performance.

- An alternative approach to estimating expected returns uses the CAPM model after estimating betas.

- A third approach used by large asset managers is to form expectations based on economic and quantitative forecasts.

- Expected variances and covariances can be estimated from the sample variances and covariances.

- Sample variances and covariances do not take into account what has been referred to as volatility clustering, where high periods of volatility are often followed by high volatility.

- Any valid correlation or covariance matrix must be positive definite, which can be verified by checking whether the eigenvalues of the matrix are all positive.

ETFs: The building blocks of robo-portfolios

This chapter covers

- The basics of exchange-traded funds (ETFs)
- The advantages of ETFs in a robo-advisory strategy
- Analyzing the costs of owning and trading ETFs
- Beyond plain-vanilla indices: socially responsible investing and smart beta

As we mentioned before, there are over 200 robo-advisors in the United States alone. The features, costs, and clear investment choices vary across advisors, but nearly all share one common trait: the use of exchange-traded funds (ETFs) in implementing their investment strategies. This chapter is all about ETFs—what they are, how they work, and why they are so widely used by robo-advisors.

4.1   ETF basics

To explain what *exchange-traded fund* means, let's start with the last word first. A *fund* is just a pool of money used for some predefined purpose. In the case of an ETF, the purpose is an investment. ETFs may invest in equities (stocks), bonds, or commodities such as gold or oil. The fund's investment strategy is defined in the fund's *prospectus*: a document outlining the fund's goals and risks. The money comes from investors—these may be individual investors or institutions investing on behalf of their clients. *Exchange-traded* means exactly what it sounds like: ETFs are traded precisely like individual stocks on stock exchanges like the NYSE and the NASDAQ. Just like a stock, every ETF has a ticker symbol (like AAPL for Apple or F for Ford) and can be bought and sold during trading hours. If you have a brokerage account, you can buy and sell ETFs the same way you buy and sell stocks. The best way to think of an ETF is as a basket of stocks that can be bought and sold just like an individual stock.

4.1.1   ETF strategies

Every ETF has an investment objective and a strategy to try to achieve that objective. Here are some typical ETF objectives:

- *Growth*—Generally, this means taking more risk to earn higher returns for long-term investing.
- *Income*—A common objective for bond funds that take less risk and return money to the owner through steady dividend payments.
- *Preservation of capital*—Funds with this goal are the least risky. They are similar to cash or a savings account.

To achieve their objectives, every fund has a strategy. Most ETFs try to track or match the performance of an index: a weighted basket of stocks, bonds, or commodities intended to represent a particular market, market segment, or theme. The most famous index is probably the S&P 500; this index contains about 500 of the largest stocks in the United States, with weights set according to each company's market capitalization. Another famous index is the Dow Jones Industrial Average ("the Dow"). The Dow contains 30 stocks and is weighted according to the price of each member. Indices are defined by companies such as Standard and Poor's, MSCI, and FTSE Russell. An ETF trying to track an index buys the index members, trying to match the index's weights as closely as possible.

A minority of ETFs don't track indices; these are known as *active* ETFs. Managers of active ETFs choose a basket of stocks (or bonds or commodities) that they think will perform well. Active ETFs usually invest within a market segment or have a process for choosing which stocks to buy and in what amount. For example, an active ETF manager may try to choose stocks within the biotech sector or assign more weight to stocks that have recently outperformed (a characteristic known as *momentum*, which we will discuss later in this chapter).

4.1.2 *ETF pricing: Theory*

Regardless of whether an ETF tracks an index, we can always think of an ETF as a basket of assets—stocks, bonds, commodities, or even derivatives (ETFs may also contain a mix of different asset types). Each share of an ETF represents a slice of that basket. If the fund holds $1 billion in stocks, and there are 100 million shares of the fund outstanding, each share is "worth" $10. Now here's where things get interesting. We said before that shares of ETFs trade on exchanges just like stocks. Prices on exchanges are set by supply and demand: if a lot more people want to buy something than are willing to sell, they will have to pay more, and the price will go up.

So what happens if lots of investors want to buy shares in an ETF? Let's go back to our example where the hypothetical ETF was "worth" $10 per share. The $10 value is called the *net asset value* (NAV) of the fund's shares. This doesn't necessarily need to be the same as the price of each share of the fund. Someone could be willing to pay $10.05 or $10.25 for a share of the fund. If there are lots of eager buyers and few sellers, the price of each share could exceed its NAV. Of course, the opposite is true as well: the price of an ETF could easily fall below its NAV. The difference between the price of an ETF and its NAV is called a *premium* (when the price is higher than the NAV) or a *discount* (when the price is lower).

To prevent the price of an ETF from deviating too far from its NAV, ETFs have what's called a *create/redeem* mechanism. This mechanism allows certain traders, known as *authorized participants*, to turn a basket of stocks into shares of an ETF or vice versa. If the trader owns the right basket of stocks, they can give them to the ETF manager in exchange for ETF shares. This is the "creation" part of the mechanism because the ETF manager creates shares to give the trader in exchange for the stocks. Conversely, the trader can take shares of the ETF and give them to the ETF sponsor in exchange for the underlying stocks—the "redemption" side of the mechanism.

An example will help clarify this process. Let's imagine an ETF whose shares trade under the ticker XYZ. Table 4.1 shows the holdings of this fund.

Table 4.1 Sector weights in the market and optimized portfolios

Stock	Shares	Share price	Value
A	15,000,000	$40	$600,000,000
B	3,000,000	$100	$300,000,000
C	2,000,000	$50	$100,000,000

The XYZ fund has a total NAV of $1 billion. With 100 million shares outstanding, each share represents $10 in NAV, or 0.15 shares of stock A, 0.03 shares of B, and 0.02 shares of C. Now, what if the price per share of fund XYZ is $9.95? A trader can buy shares of XYZ at $9.95 and redeem the shares of the ETF for a basket of the underlying stocks, worth $10. Then the trader can sell these stocks for $10, making an easy $0.05 per share of XYZ.

Such a juicy opportunity would not persist for long—which is precisely the idea! If the ETF price is below the value of its holdings, traders start buying the shares to make easy profits. This buying pushes up the price of the ETF, erasing the opportunity.

The same process works in reverse. If the price of the ETF is above the value of its holdings, a trader can buy the underlying basket of stocks, give them to the ETF provider in exchange for shares of the ETF, and then sell the ETF shares for a profit. Such seemingly riskless profit opportunities are known as *arbitrage*, and the traders exploiting them are called *arbitrageurs*.

This mechanism keeps the share prices of ETFs in line with the underlying value, or NAV, that they represent—in theory. The following section will discuss what happens in practice.

4.1.3   *ETF pricing: Reality*

The actual mechanics of the create/redeem mechanism are not as friction-free as just described, for a few reasons:

- *Fees and taxes*—Creating and redeeming shares isn't free. ETF providers charge a *create/redeem fee* when a trader creates or redeems shares of the ETF in exchange for a basket of stocks. These fees depend on the ETF but can range from a few hundred to a few thousand dollars. Some exchanges (particularly outside the United States) also charge fixed fees per share traded, called *stamp taxes*, which add to the cost of trading and reduce the ability of traders to take advantage of price discrepancies.

- *Size minimums*—Creation and redemption have to be done at scale. Often, ETF providers require create/redeem trades to be done in multiples of 5,000 to 50,000 shares or millions of dollars. So an arbitrageur must be willing to buy and sell large quantities of each. Of course, doing so could move prices in the opposite direction the trader would like them to move.

- *Speed*—Trading, including the create/redeem process, isn't instantaneous. In the time it takes to make the trades necessary to take advantage of an arbitrage opportunity, prices could move adversely for the trader, erasing the opportunity or even turning the expected profit into a loss.

All these factors create friction in the creation/redemption process. Because of these frictions, ETF prices can deviate from their underlying values for extended periods. Typically, deviations are larger or persist longer for ETFs whose underlying holdings are illiquid or expensive to trade or for ETFs whose creation/redemption fees are highest.

A premium or discount isn't *necessarily* bad, if it's predictable. Paying $10.05 for something worth $10 is not terrible if you know you'll always be able to sell it for $10.05 (or, more generally, for slightly more than it's worth). The problem, of course, is that premiums and discounts can fluctuate over time. A premium of $0.05 could turn into a discount of $0.05. This adds more uncertainty to the potential return of an investment in an ETF. So, all else equal, robo-advisors (and, we would argue, most investors) prefer ETFs whose prices stay within a narrow band of their NAVs.

4.1.4   Costs of ETF investing

The past two sections have discussed the prices of ETFs. If you log on to a brokerage or financial news site, you can look up the current price of any ETF. But that doesn't mean you'll actually be able to buy or sell at that price.

At any point in time, the market for an ETF consists of a collection of orders to buy the ETF and a collection of orders to sell—just like a stock. Each trader posts an order indicating the quantity of shares they wish to transact and the price at which they are willing to transact. If a buy order and a sell order are compatible (the buyer is willing to pay at least as much as the seller wants to sell for), those two orders are filled and disappear from the market. So, we can assume that the highest price among the buy orders is lower than the lowest price among the sell orders. Prices in buy orders are called *bid* prices, and prices in sell orders are called *ask* prices. The difference between the highest bid price and the lowest ask price is called the *bid–ask spread*. The price shown on brokerage or news sites is usually halfway between the best bid price and the best ask price—a value known as the *mid* price. Figure 4.1 shows a screenshot from a brokerage platform containing numerical information at a point during the trading day for the QQQ ETF, including

- The current mid price of $285.15 and the return of the ETF from the previous day's close until this moment.
- The current best bid and ask prices of $285.14 and $285.16, respectively.
- The sizes of the best bids and asks, in shares. These quantities are 1,300 and 1,200 shares, respectively. This means there are traders willing to buy 1,300 shares of QQQ at $285.14 and willing to sell 1,200 shares at $285.16.
- The number of shares traded so far in the current trading day.

Although ETFs trade like stocks, including a bid–ask spread, a crucial difference between stocks and ETFs is that ETFs have a cost of holding, known as an *expense ratio*. The expense ratio is quoted as an annual fraction of the position's value and is the fee the ETF manager charges investors in exchange for managing the fund. For example, an investor holding an ETF with an expense ratio of 0.25% pays $0.25 for every $100 invested in the fund. The expense ratio is deducted from the fund's value each day—investors never need to write a check to the ETF management company to pay the expense ratio—and decreases the fund's total return compared to the return of the underlying holdings. Expense ratios vary from 0% (yes, a few ETFs don't charge a fee) to well over 3%, with the high end being occupied by fairly niche or specialized products.

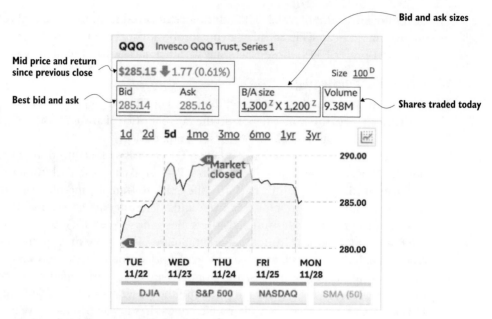

Figure 4.1   Intraday market display for the QQQ ETF

4.2   ETFs vs. mutual funds

ETFs are not the only option for investors looking for diversified exposure to stocks or bonds via a single instrument. *Mutual funds* are broadly similar to ETFs: they are pools of money coming from many investors who buy securities to pursue an investment strategy, and they charge a fee. Like ETFs, mutual funds may track an index or be actively managed. However, several key differences between mutual funds and ETFs make ETFs a more attractive choice for robo-advisors, as this section will cover in detail.

4.2.1   Tradability

Unlike ETFs, mutual funds don't trade on an exchange throughout the day. Investors can buy or sell mutual funds only once per day, at the end of the day. When they do, investors are transacting with the mutual fund provider itself rather than another investor or trader. The once-daily trading means, compared to using ETFs, it generally takes longer to get a client's money invested in mutual funds and get their money out when they request a withdrawal. Moreover, to discourage frequent trading, some mutual fund providers charge fees for selling before a minimum holding period or disallow repurchasing after buying and selling in quick succession.

Although this can create some inconvenience for investors relative to ETFs, there is an interesting advantage as a result. Because shares of mutual funds are traded directly with the provider, prices are based only on the value of the fund's holdings— meaning a mutual fund can't have a premium or discount the way an ETF can, reducing some uncertainty for investors.

4.2.2 Costs and minimums

Both ETFs and mutual funds charge management fees, as an ongoing percentage of capital invested. Mutual funds can also add more fees. Some mutual funds charge an additional ongoing fee known as a *12b-1 fee* and use the money collected to market the fund to potential new investors. These 12b-1 fees can be as high as 1% of the total investment per year.

Some mutual funds also charge one-time fees known as *sales loads* when investors buy or sell shares in the fund. Sales loads charged at the time of purchase are called *front-end loads,* and fees charged at sale are called *back-end loads.*

Unlike ETFs, mutual funds may specify a minimum investment amount, which can range from nothing to millions of dollars, creating a hurdle for small investors. To complicate things more, mutual funds can offer different share classes—basically, different versions of the same investment with different fees and minimums. A share class with a lower minimum may charge high fees and vice versa. Share classes with the lowest fees may be truly accessible only to large institutional investors such as pension funds.

4.2.3 Tax efficiency

The final key difference between ETFs and mutual funds is more subtle but nonetheless material for taxable investors. When a fund sells securities in its portfolio at a gain, it has to "pass through" that capital gain to fund holders, which can result in the investors paying capital gains taxes. Mutual funds have no way to avoid this. When a mutual fund needs to rebalance its portfolio, it has to sell some securities and buy others. ETFs have more flexibility due to the create/redeem mechanism. Rather than selling stocks, the ETF manager can give those stocks to authorized participants in exchange for other stocks that match the composition of the fund's target portfolio. Because nothing is bought or sold, there are no taxable events and no taxes due.

These types of trade are called *heartbeats.* Here's a (somewhat stylized) example to help explain how they work. Suppose an ETF is tracking a small-cap index (a basket of small-sized companies, usually below about $2 billion in market capitalization) that is being revised. Table 4.2 shows the old and new index weights.

Table 4.2   Old and new index weights

	A	B	C	D	E
Old weight	50%	30%	20%	0%	0%
New weight	0%	45%	30%	15%	10%

Stock A is being removed from the index because its market capitalization has gotten so large that it's no longer a small-cap stock, and stocks D and E are being added to the index. Table 4.3 shows the fund's portfolio, including how much it paid for each holding.

Table 4.3   Holdings and cost basis

	A	B	C	D	E
Portfolio value	$500,000	$300,000	$200,000	$0	$0
Cost basis	$300,000	$225,000	$150,000	$0	$0

To get the portfolio in line with the new index, the fund would need to sell $500,000 worth of stock A and buy stocks B, C, D, and E. This would create a realized capital gain of $200,000, which could result in taxes for the investors in the fund.

By using a heartbeat trade, the ETF can avoid this taxable event. In this example, the heartbeat trade entails the authorized participant investing $500,000 into the fund. The fund uses that money to buy $150,000 of stock B, $100,000 of stock C, $150,000 of stock D, and $100,000 of stock E. Soon after, the authorized participant asks for a $500,000 withdrawal from the ETF, which the ETF manager satisfies by giving the authorized participant its $500,000 worth of stock A. At this point, the portfolio is in line with the new index, and the ETF manager hasn't sold any stocks or created any realized gains for the fund's investors. Without the option of a heartbeat trade, a mutual fund manager would be forced to create taxable gains to accomplish the same goal. Figure 4.2 shows the portfolio at each step of this process, with dollar holdings shown in thousands.

Stock	Holdings	Weight
A	$500	50%
B	$300	30%
C	$200	20%
D	$0	0%
E	$0	0%
Total	$1,000	100%

Stock	Holdings	Weight
A	$500	33%
B	$450	30%
C	$300	20%
D	$150	10%
E	$100	7%
Total	$1,500	100%

Stock	Holdings	Weight
A	$0	0%
B	$450	45%
C	$300	30%
D	$150	15%
E	$100	10%
Total	$1,000	100%

Original portfolio   After $500,000 investment   After $500,000 withdrawal

Figure 4.2   Portfolio undergoing a heartbeat trade

4.2.4   *The verdict on mutual funds vs. ETFs*

On the dimensions we've analyzed, ETFs tend to have the advantage over mutual funds. To recap:

- ETFs can be traded intraday, compared to once per day for mutual funds.
- Mutual funds may charge more fees than ETFs and require larger minimum investments.
- ETFs can be more tax-efficient than mutual funds through the use of heartbeat trades.

The one place where mutual funds have the advantage over ETFs is in the lack of premiums or discounts—meaning when investing in a mutual fund, the investor always pays what the shares are worth. However, heavily traded ETFs tend to have very small premiums or discounts, so we can safely ignore this problem. By properly considering the choice of funds employed in an investing strategy, the potential effect of buying an ETF at a premium or selling at a discount is diminished and outweighed by the positive aspects of ETFs relative to mutual funds.

4.3 Total cost of ownership

We have now established ETFs as our investing vehicles of choice and identified the various costs associated with them. Next, we will discuss the process of selecting particular ETFs to be used in an investing strategy and how to obtain the data needed to make these selections.

4.3.1 Cost components

Let's first define the total cost of a "round trip" investment in an ETF. We can break this down into three parts:

- *Cost of trading*—This is the bid/ask spread paid when buying and selling the ETF. Specifically, the total trading cost is

$$(\text{Expected bid/Ask spread}) \times (\text{Position size in shares})$$

  Transactions may include commissions or brokerage fees as well; but for our purposes, we can ignore these since they will be the same for any ETF.

- *Cost of holding*—The amount that will be paid to the ETF provider in the form of management fees while holding the ETF:

$$(\text{Expected holding period}) \times (\text{Expense ratio}) \times (\text{Position size in dollars})$$

  This formula assumes that the holding period is known in advance, which it generally isn't. An investor may choose to withdraw their funds at any time. Even if the investor's timeline is known in advance, the holding period depends on the specifics of the investment strategy and the risk and return characteristics of the asset being considered. A position might be partially sold off to rebalance the portfolio or fully sold off as part of a tax-loss harvesting strategy. Later, when we discuss backtesting and tax-loss harvesting, we will show how an average holding period can be calculated.

- *Cost of adverse premium*—The potential loss in return if the ETF's premium or discount to NAV moves adversely from the time of purchase to the time of sale. Note that in expectation, this cost is zero: without knowing what the premium or discount will be at the time of purchase, we expect it will be unchanged at the time of sale. Additionally, the ETFs used by robo-advisors are liquid enough that the range of the premium is small. For example, the premium of Vanguard's VTI ETF ranged from −0.10% to 0.13% from January 2022 to January 2023.

Because of this, we will ignore the potential loss from adverse premiums in our calculations of the cost of ownership.

EXAMPLE: COMPARING COSTS OF OWNERSHIP

To make the previous discussion concrete, let's look at an example where we compare the costs of four different ETFs that all track the same index: the S&P 500. Table 4.4 shows all the relevant ingredients, taken from etf.com on October 3, 2021. And table 4.5 shows the size of each cost component, as well as the total, assuming a position size of $100,000 and a holding period of six months.

Table 4.4   Cost information for four ETFs

	SPY	IVV	VOO	SPLG
Share price	$434.24	$435.95	$ 399.12	$51.07
Average bid/ask spread	$0.01	$0.02	$0.02	$0.01
Expense ratio	0.09%	0.03%	0.03%	0.03%

Table 4.5   Total ownership cost breakdown

	SPY	IVV	VOO	SPLG
Trading	$2.30	$4.59	$ 5.01	$19.58
Holding	$45.00	$15.00	$15.00	$15.00
Total	$47.30	$19.59	$20.01	$34.58

From table 4.5 , we see that IVV and VOO are essentially tied as the cheapest funds out of this group. SPLG is next: because of its low share price, trading costs are higher than for the others. SPY is the most expensive of the group, owing to its high expense ratio. SPY is an extremely liquid ETF widely used for short-term trading; for longer holding periods, other options win out.

4.4   Beyond standard indices

We have already mentioned a couple of well-known indices, and you have probably heard of others as well. We mentioned that the S&P 500 is a cap-weighted index: the member stocks are weighted proportionately to their market capitalization. This is one of the more common methods of index weighting because it requires less trading to keep the portfolio's weights in line with the index's weights. There are other methods of setting the weights of an index, including the following:

- *Equal weighting*—As the name suggests, all index members are weighted equally.
- *Modified cap weighting*—This is common in indices defined over narrower sets of stocks: for example, an index that covers a particular industry such as phar-

maceuticals. A common form of modified cap weighting works like this: the index provider starts with market cap weights but then reassigns weight from the largest stocks to the smaller ones to keep the portfolio diversified. Providers of modified cap-weighted indices publish the rule set that they use in determining weights.

- *Score weighting*—Weights are assigned according to scores derived from fundamental measures. These measures can include things like market cap or whatever the index creator decides to use. Examples include valuation ratios and profitability metrics.

Index weights aren't always determined using simple rules. Some are defined using a mixture of scores and an optimization step. For example, the index weights may be set by maximizing the weighted average of scores, but with constraints keeping the weight of each industry close to the weight in a standard index.

By and large, the ETFs employed by robo-advisors track standard, cap-weighted indices. You may also see robo-advisors using ETFs tracking modified cap-weighted indices, particularly to gain exposure to individual sectors such as real estate. However, two particular families of indices—smart beta and socially responsible investing—have grown in popularity in recent years and made their way into the portfolios of robo-advisors. Because of their increasing prevalence, we want to cover these types of indices specifically.

4.4.1 Smart beta

In chapter 3, we discussed CAPM and how the expected return of a stock can be estimated using the expected return of the market and the stock's beta to the market. CAPM is a *single-factor model*; the expected return of each asset depends only on the asset's sensitivity to the overall market—the sole "factor" in the model.

Years after the CAPM was introduced, Eugene Fama and Kenneth French extended CAPM using two additional factors: value and size. They found that stocks that appeared cheap tended to perform better over time than stocks that looked expensive. The cheapness of a stock was measured using the book-to-price ratio: the per-share book value (total assets minus total liabilities) divided by the price per share. They also found that small-cap stocks tended to outperform large-cap stocks, simply using market cap to measure size.

Fama and French denoted the two new factors: HML (high minus low book-to-price ratio) and SMB (small minus big). The authors created portfolios to represent each of the two factors. The HML portfolio held the cheapest stocks long and the most expensive stocks short, whereas the SMB portfolio held the smallest stocks long and the largest stocks short. Using these new factors, Fama and French created a three-factor model to predict stock returns. The mathematical form of the model is similar to that of the CAPM, with two extra regressors for the two new factors.

Fama and French's research sparked a huge amount of research into other qualities of stocks that could help explain returns and lead to market-beating performance.

The number of factors proposed over the years extends into the hundreds, but the following few have found the most adoption in equity indices and ETF strategies:

- *Momentum*—Stocks that have higher recent returns tend to perform better than stocks with low recent returns.
- *Quality*—Stable, profitable companies tend to outperform.
- *Low beta*—Companies with low betas (from the CAPM model) tend to outperform companies with high betas relative to the performance predicted by the CAPM.

Various ETF providers offer funds that track indices that tilt toward these factors. Some also offer multifactor funds, which incorporate multiple factors into a single portfolio. The general idea of factor investing has become known as *smart beta*, with *beta* referring to the coefficients in a model like Fama and French's.

Robo-advisors have joined the smart beta trend as well. Some offer the option to use single-factor or multifactor ETFs in their portfolios, replacing or complementing ETFs tracking standard indices. Others implement smart beta themselves through direct investments in individual stocks rather than through an ETF.

4.4.2   *Socially responsible investing*

Socially responsible investing (SRI) doesn't have a single agreed-on definition, but it generally refers to the idea of considering nonfinancial factors when making investments. SRI has risen in popularity over the last decade, with several different flavors of implementation:

- *Exclusionary*—Some SRI indices simply exclude certain sets of stocks—for instance, businesses engaged in fossil fuel extraction. Aside from the exclusions, stocks are weighted according to a standard methodology, such as market cap. SPYX, which holds the stocks in the S&P 500 but excludes any company that owns fossil fuel reserves, is a good example of the exclusionary approach.
- *Narrow focus*: This refers to indices that concentrate their holdings in companies that embody a particular attribute or value. Examples include ICLN, which invests in companies involved in clean energy, and NACP, which invests in companies that promote racial and ethnic diversity in their leadership.
- *Tilted*—This type of SRI investing is sort of a middle ground between the previous two. Indices that fall into this category may exclude businesses in certain industries or business lines but try to maintain low tracking error to "standard" indices. The indices "tilt" toward stocks that score more highly on predefined measures of social responsibility. There is variation within this category, as some indices allow more tracking error to emphasize positive SRI characteristics, whereas others only allow smaller tilts.

In conjunction with SRI, another term you will hear is *environmental, social, and governance* (ESG). ESG and SRI are often used interchangeably, but you can differentiate the two by saying that ESG provides a set of metrics against which investments can be measured, with SRI products generally looking better according to these metrics.

ESG metrics are categorized into three pillars corresponding to the three letters in the abbreviation. Some examples of specific metrics in each pillar are shown in table 4.6.

Table 4.6   Examples of ESG factors

Environmental	Social	Governance
Carbon emissions	Labor management, health, and safety	Executive pay
Water and land usage	Product safety, privacy, and security	Business ethics
Toxic emissions and waste	Community relations	Tax transparency
Involvement in renewable energy		

These examples are taken from MSCI's description of its methodology. MSCI applies different metrics to various companies depending on whether the particular metric is deemed to be material to that company. For example, toxic emissions and waste are material metrics for companies involved in manufacturing but are not relevant to software companies. On the other hand, governance metrics apply to every company, regardless of its industry. Each company is scored on all applicable metrics, and the values are rolled up to an overall ESG quality score. This is the value the indices use in their optimization when trying to maximize ESG exposure subject to their tracking error limit.

MSCI is only one of several providers of ESG ratings. Other companies, including Sustainalytics, Bloomberg, FTSE Russell, S&P, and Moody's have rating methodologies. However, indices defined by MSCI have gained the most traction, with over $1 trillion in assets in funds tracking ESG-focused MSCI indices.

The ESGU ETF is a good example of an ETF following the tilted methodology. This ETF tracks an index of US stocks defined by MSCI that excludes companies involved in civilian firearms, controversial weapons, tobacco, thermal coal, and oil sands. After these exclusions, the index uses constrained optimization to maximize exposure to an overall ESG score (also defined by MSCI) while maintaining an expected tracking error target of less than 0.50% to the standard MSCI USA index.

Funds taking this last approach are usually the easiest for robo-advisors to incorporate into their investment strategies. The SRI-tilted funds have an explicit goal of low tracking error to non-SRI indices. As an example, ESGU has tracked VOO (an ETF managed by Vanguard tracking the S&P 500 index) extremely closely since its launch in 2016: figure 4.3 shows the growth of $100 invested in each of these two funds starting on January 1, 2017. The actual tracking error between the two funds was about 1.2% over this period. This is higher than the target of 0.50% but not surprising given the extreme market volatility in early 2020 with the onset of the Covid-19 pandemic. The difference in performance also captures the higher expense ratio of ESGU, which is 0.15% compared to 0.03% for VOO.

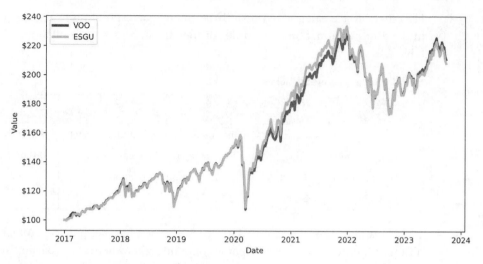

Figure 4.3   Growth of $100 invested in VOO and ESGU

Several robo-advisors offer an SRI option in their investing strategies. Typically, funds tracking standard indices are replaced by ones tracking SRI-tilted indices. Some advisors also allow the option to add focused or exclusionary ETFs to the portfolio, providing an attractive option for clients who want their choice of investments to reflect their values as well as earn a return. Later, we will show how to incorporate SRI considerations into the construction of diversified portfolios.

Summary

- ETFs are similar to mutual funds but trade like stocks. ETFs are widely employed by robo-advisors due to their intraday tradability, low fees, and tax efficiency.
- The expense ratio isn't the only cost of investing in an ETF. The data needed to calculate the total cost of ownership can be easily obtained using Python.
- The universe of ETFs is as wide as the universe of indices, which come in many flavors.
- Smart beta and SRI indices have gained popularity in recent years. Smart beta aims to improve returns by tilting the portfolio to gain exposure to nonmarket factors, and SRI aims to invest in companies whose businesses are beneficial to society.

Part 2

Financial planning tools

This part of the book shows how to automate some of the financial planning services offered by advisors. Chapter 5 introduces Monte Carlo simulations and how to model various sources of risk, including market risk, inflation risk, and longevity risk (using mortality tables), to estimate the probability of running out of money in retirement. The chapter also covers historical simulation and bootstrapping.

Chapter 6 provides several fully worked examples, from start to finish, of how you can apply reinforcement learning, a powerful branch of AI, to solving financial planning problems, including an example of when to claim Social Security that takes risk into account. The chapter also explains how to incorporate utility functions into reinforcement learning, which is a useful tool for handling financial planning decisions involving risk, but one that has not been widely adopted by financial planners.

Chapter 7 takes a detour to discuss returns: first, how to measure returns when there are inflows and outflows; and second, how to evaluate risk-adjusted returns of actively managed funds. As an example, the chapter analyzes the risk-adjusted returns of a popular environmental, social, and governance (ESG) fund.

The last two chapters cover two important methods for minimizing taxes. Chapter 8 discusses how to improve after-tax returns by intelligently assigning assets to accounts based on the tax exposure of the asset and the tax treatment given to each account—a process known as *asset location*. The optimization problem is not trivial when an investor has all three types of accounts: a taxable account, an IRA, and a Roth. Finally, chapter 9 shows how to choose an optimal strategy for sequencing withdrawals during the decumulation phase of retirement, when investors must draw down their savings to pay for expenses.

Monte Carlo simulations 5

Monte Carlo simulations have numerous applications in wealth management and financial planning. In this chapter, we will focus on a specific problem that is particularly well-suited for Monte Carlo analysis: whether you will run out of money in retirement.

In Monte Carlo simulations, random scenarios are generated and analyzed. Most people focus on the randomness of stock and bond returns, but Monte Carlo simulations can incorporate anything random, like inflation, health care expenses, life expectancy, or even future tax rates.

Why are Monte Carlo simulations necessary, rather than simply making projections based on expected outcomes? For example, if you have a 50-50 mix of stocks and bonds and expect your portfolio to have average returns of 5%/year (say, 8% for stocks and 2% for bonds), couldn't you just project how your savings are expected to evolve over time to figure out whether your money will last through retirement? This is referred to as a *straight-line* projection. There are several problems with that approach:

- *The order of returns matters.* Consider the following simple example, shown in tables 5.1 and 5.2. Suppose an investor starts with $100,000. In the first year, their investments do really well and double; in the second year, they do poorly and halve. As table 5.1 shows, the investor ends up with the same $100,000, and it makes no difference if the order of returns is switched. But now suppose the investor needs to withdraw $50,000 for expenses at the end of year 1. As table 5.2 shows, the order matters. Even though the expected returns are the same regardless of the order of returns, the outcome is different, which can be captured in a Monte Carlo simulation.

Table 5.1   Order of returns does not make a difference with no withdrawals.

	Starting wealth	Wealth at end of year 1	Wealth at end of year 2
100% return, followed by −50% return	$100,000	$200,000	$100,000
−50% return, followed by 100% return	$100,000	$50,000	$100,000

Table 5.2   Order of returns makes a difference when there are withdrawals

	Starting wealth	Wealth at end of year 1	Wealth at end of year 2
100% return, followed by −50% return	$100,000	$200,000 − $50,000 = $150,000	$75,000
−50% return, followed by 100% return	$100,000	$50,000 − $50,000 = $0	$0

- *Simulations can provide a probability distribution of outcomes.* The answer to the question of how many years your money will last in retirement is not a single number but rather a probability distribution. There are certainly rules of thumb that try to simplify the answer to a single number. The famous *4% rule* suggests that if you spend 4% of your retirement savings and adjust it for inflation every year, your savings will comfortably last for 30 years. Working backward, if you expect to spend $5,000/month, or $60,000/year, you need 25 times (= 1.0/0.04) that amount, or $1.5 million of retirement savings, to safely guarantee that your money will last. But is the probability really 100%? And what happens if you have only $1.2 million in savings, so you are forced to spend 5% of your savings rather than 4%? Monte Carlo simulations can answer questions that involve probabilities.

- *Simulations can handle more complicated situations.* Monte Carlo simulations are often used not just in finance but also in other fields like physics, when there are no closed-form solutions, or mathematical formulas, to solve a problem. Adding complications to any problem can make it impossible to solve analytically. We will discuss some of these real-world complications in this chapter, like mortality tables, multiple sources of randomness like inflation risk, and fat-tailed stock market returns.

5.1 Simulating returns in Python

By far the most common way to model stock prices is to assume they follow a lognormal distribution rather than a normal distribution. A normal distribution arises if you sum random, identically distributed price changes, and a lognormal distribution (approximately) arises if you multiply random, identically distributed returns. We will shortly see why using a lognormal distribution is much more sensible for modeling stock prices.

Let's look at a comparison of normal versus lognormal stock prices. In both cases, we assume the stock price starts at $100, and we simulate annual prices over 10 years. For the normal case, the stock price, on average, goes up by $8/year with a standard deviation of $20/year. For the lognormal case, the stock return on average is 8% with a standard deviation of 20%. We use a *seed* number, which initializes the random number generator and allows the reader to reproduce the results. Also, it is easier to compare two models when the same set of random numbers is used.

Figure 5.1 shows the first four sample paths when stock prices have a normal distribution. In this example, we would say that stock prices follow a *random walk* (with drift), and the random changes in stock prices are described as *white noise* because they are independent and identically distributed. The following listing is the code that generated the plot.

> **Listing 5.1 Simulating stock paths with a normal distribution**

```
import numpy as np
import pandas as pd
import matplotlib.pyplot as plt

np.random.seed(123)
```

```
num_years = 10
num_sims = 10000
mean = 8                                        Generates a 2D array of random
stdev = 20                                      price changes for each simulation
                                                                 run and each year
z = np.random.normal(loc=mean, scale=stdev, size=(num_sims, num_years+1))

P = np.zeros((num_sims, num_years+1))
P[:,0] = 100   ◄──── Initializes the initial stock prices in each simulation run to 100

for sim in range(num_sims):
    for year in range(1, num_years+1):
        P[sim, year] = P[sim, year-1] + z[sim, year]   ◄──  Adds a random price
                                                             change to last year's
plt.xlabel('Year')                                           stock price
plt.ylabel('Price')
plt.plot(P[0:4,:].T);
```

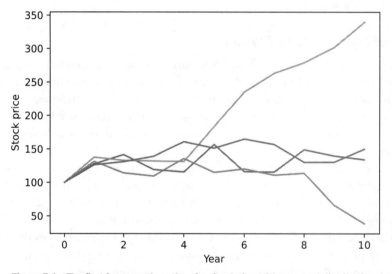

Figure 5.1   The first four sample paths of a simulation with a normal distribution

Now we use the following command to plot a histogram of final stock prices over the 10,000 simulations, which has the shape of a normal distribution (see figure 5.2):

```
plt.hist(P[:,-1], bins=50)
```

There are two problems with the normal distribution for stock prices:

- As the histogram shows, there is a small probability that stock prices can become negative.
- The *percentage* return and volatility change with the level of stock prices. In other words, when the stock starts at $100, we expect an $8 annual appreciation, or 8% return. But if the stock goes up to $200, under the normal model we still expect an $8 annual appreciation, but now it's only a 4% return. There is no reason to think returns should vary like that with the stock price.

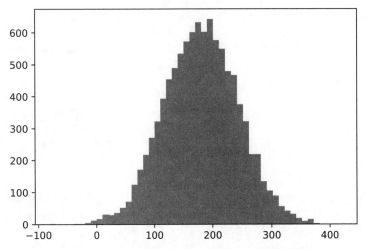

Figure 5.2   Histogram of final stock prices with a normal distribution

Therefore, we consider lognormal distributions. Figure 5.3 shows the first four sample paths when stock prices follow a lognormal distribution, generated by the code in the next listing. The seed number we used is the same one we used to generate figure 5.1, so the paths look similar but not the same.

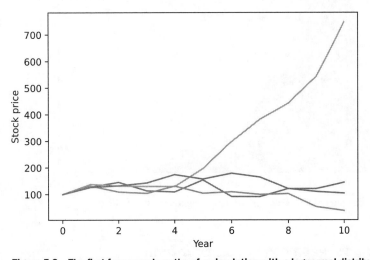

Figure 5.3   The first four sample paths of a simulation with a lognormal distribution

Listing 5.2   Simulating stock paths with a lognormal distribution

```
np.random.seed(123)

num_years = 10
num_sims = 10000
mean = 0.08
stdev = 0.20
```

```
ret = np.random.normal(loc=mean, scale=stdev, size=(num_sims, num_years+1))

P = np.zeros((num_sims, num_years+1))                          Generates normal
P[:,0] = 100                                                    random returns

for sim in range(num_sims):
    for year in range(1, num_years+1):
        P[sim, year] = P[sim, year-1]* (1 + ret[sim, year])    Multiplies the last
plt.xlabel('Year')                                             stock price by (1+r)
plt.ylabel('Price')
plt.plot(P[0:4,:].T);
```

Next, we plot a histogram of final stock prices over the 10,000 simulations, which now has the shape of a lognormal distribution. We use the same command as before, except we crop the range in the histogram because there are a few outliers with the lognormal distribution (see figure 5.4):

```
plt.hist(P[:,-1], bins=50, range=(0,800))
```

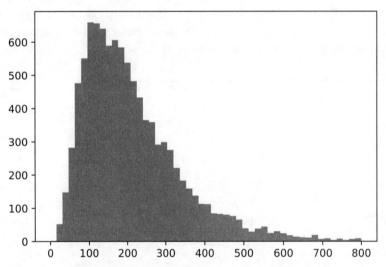

Figure 5.4   Histogram of final stock prices with a lognormal distribution

5.2   *Arithmetic vs. geometric average returns*

In the simulation, we assumed the average one-year return was 8%. But it would be a mistake to assume that the expected value of a $100 investment in 20 years would be $100 \times (1.08)^{20}$. This is an example of the concept (which comes up several times in this chapter) that the expected value of a function $f(\tilde{x})$ of a random variable $\tilde{x}$ is not generally equal to the function evaluated at the expected value of $\tilde{x}$ (unless the function is linear):

$$E[f(\tilde{x})] \neq f(E[\tilde{x}])$$

To be more specific, let's define the difference between the arithmetic average and the geometric average of a series of returns. Suppose the returns over N periods are $r_1, r_2, \ldots, r_N$. A portfolio that starts with S_0 will be worth S_N after N periods, where

$$S_N = S_0(1 + r_1)(1 + r_2) \cdots (1 + r_N)$$

The geometric average return, G, is the average growth rate that would give the same terminal portfolio value, S_N, if all the returns were identical every period:

$$S_N = S_0(1 + G)^N$$

Solving for G,

$$G = \left(\frac{S_N}{S_0}\right)^{\frac{1}{N}} - 1$$

The familiar arithmetic average return, A, is

$$A = \frac{r_1 + r_2 + \cdots + r_N}{N} = \frac{1}{N}\sum_{i=1}^{N} r_i$$

The arithmetic average, A, will always be larger than the geometric average, G. One approximation for the difference is

$$G = A - \tfrac{1}{2}\sigma^2$$

where σ^2 is the sample variance of returns defined as

$$\sigma^2 = \frac{1}{N}\sum_{i=1}^{N}(r_i - A)^2$$

so that higher levels of volatility produce a larger difference between the arithmetic average and geometric average returns. In the chapter appendix, we derive the math behind this approximation. But we can also see how well the approximation works in practice with historical stock return data. We download S&P 500 index data (the ticker symbol on Yahoo Finance is ^GSPC) using the yf package the same way we did in chapter 3. Then we downsample the daily data to annual data and compute annual returns for 50 years. Note that the S&P 500 index series does not include dividends.

Listing 5.3 Computing arithmetic and geometric average returns

```
import yfinance as yf                                          Downloads S&P daily
                                                               prices from Yahoo Finance
SP500 = yf.download('^GSPC', start='1971-12-31', end='2021-12-31')
SP500 = SP500.resample('Y').last()    ←—— Resamples daily data to annual data
SP500['ret'] = SP500['Close'].pct_change()    ←—┐ Computes annual
print('Arithmetic Average: ', SP500['ret'].mean())   │ percentage returns
print('Standard Deviation: ', SP500['ret'].std())    │ from annual prices
```

```
print('Geometric Average: ', (SP500['Close'].iloc[-1]/SP500['Close']
    .iloc[0])**(1/(len(SP500)-1))-1)
print('Geometric Average Approximation: ', SP500['ret'].mean()
    - 0.5 * (SP500['ret'].std())**2)
```

The output is as follows:

```
Arithmetic Average:  0.09400122842963611
Standard Deviation:  0.16725932009600614
Geometric Average:  0.07995730407222146
Geometric Average Approximation:  0.08001338835014699
```

We can see that over the last 50 years, the arithmetic average annual return is 9.4% (not including dividends) and the standard deviation is 16.7%. The geometric average return is 8.0%, which is almost identical to the approximation we discussed.

5.3   Simple vs. continuously compounded returns

Compounding is an additional complication and consideration when simulating returns. First, we'll discuss the difference between simple and continuously compounded interest rates, and then we'll define continuously compounded returns.

Table 5.3 illustrates the effects of compounding using a *simple annual interest rate* of 6%. The *effective annual rate*, which is defined as the percentage increase in funds invested over a one-year horizon, is higher than the simple interest rate. As the compounding frequency goes to infinity, we get *continuous compounding*, and it can be shown that a 6% simple annual rate that is continuously compounded approaches an effective annual rate of $e^{0.06} - 1 = 6.18\%$.

Table 5.3   Comparison of different compounding frequencies

	Formula	Effective annual rate
Annual compounding	$1 + 0.06$	6.00%
Semiannual compounding	$\left(1 + \frac{0.06}{2}\right)^2$	6.09%
Monthly compounding	$\left(1 + \frac{0.06}{12}\right)^{12}$	6.17%
Continuous compounding	$\lim_{m \to \infty} \left(1 + \frac{0.06}{m}\right)^m = e^{0.06}$	6.18%

A simple rate that is continuously compounded is called the *continuously compounded rate*. In general, the relationship between the effective annual rate (EAR) and the continuously compounded rate (cc) is

$$\exp(r_{cc}) = 1 + r_{EAR}$$

And to find the continuously compounded rate from the effective annual rate, we can use

$$r_{cc} = \ln(1 + r_{EAR})$$

In the same way we computed continuously compounded *interest rates*, we can also define continuously compounded *returns*, r, from simple returns, R:

$$r = \ln(1 + R) = \ln\left(\frac{P_t}{P_{t-1}}\right) = \ln(P_t) - \ln(P_{t-1})$$

In table 5.4, we compare simple returns with continuously compounded returns when a stock goes from \$100 to \$200 and back down to \$100. As the table shows, the multiperiod continuously compounded returns are simpler to work with—they are just the sum of the single-period returns. However, portfolio returns are more complicated: the average returns of a 60-40 portfolio of stocks and bonds are not simply the average of the continuously compounded returns.

Table 5.4 Comparison of simple and continuously compounded returns over two periods

	$t = 0$	$t = 1$	$t = 2$	$t = 0 \rightarrow t = 2$
Stock price	$P_0 = 100$	$P_1 = 200$	$P_2 = 100$	
Simple return		$R_1 = \frac{P_1}{P_0} - 1 = 100\%$	$R_2 = \frac{P_2}{P_1} - 1 = -50\%$	$(1 + R_1)(1 + R_2) - 1 = 0$
Continuously compounded return		$r_1 = \ln\left(\frac{P_1}{P_0}\right) = 69\%$	$r_2 = \ln\left(\frac{P_2}{P_1}\right) = -69\%$	$r_1 + r_2 = 0$

5.4 Geometric Brownian motion

We would be remiss if we did not mention another model for stock prices that is commonly used in finance and particularly in the option pricing literature. According to this model, stock prices follow a *geometric Brownian motion* (GBM) process given by the equation

$$\frac{dS}{S} = \mu\, dt + \sigma\, dz$$

which leads to the equation for the evolution of stock prices

$$S_{t+\Delta t} = S_t \exp\left((\mu - \tfrac{1}{2}\sigma^2)\Delta t + \sigma\sqrt{\Delta t}\, z\right)$$

where

$$S_t = \text{stock price at time } t$$

$$\mu = \text{instantaneous annual expected return}$$

$$\sigma = \text{instantaneous annual volatility}$$

$$\Delta t = \text{change in time, in years}$$

$$z = \text{standard normal random variable}$$

So just like our previous model, stock prices have a lognormal distribution and the continuously compounded returns have a normal distribution:

$$\ln\left(\frac{S_{t+\Delta t}}{S_t}\right) \sim N\left((\mu - \tfrac{1}{2}\sigma^2)\Delta t, \, \sigma\sqrt{\Delta t}\right)$$

This model is similar to the one we introduced at the beginning of the chapter, except we are generating random continuously compounded returns in the GBM model and we were generating random simple returns at the beginning of the chapter. The important thing to keep in mind, regardless of the model used, is that it should be consistently calibrated. For example, for the GBM model, if you are estimating volatility based on historical returns, you should use continuously compounded returns rather than simple returns.

5.5   *Estimating the probability of success*

Now that the preliminaries are out of the way, we are ready to use simulations to answer some financial planning questions. As we mentioned at the top of the chapter, a common application of Monte Carlo simulations is estimating the probability that an investor will run out of money in retirement. We'll start with a simple case and then add several bells and whistles.

In the simple base case, we assume a retiree with no income and savings of $1,200,000 initially spends $60,000/year (5% of their savings) net of any income like Social Security. We assume net spending grows at an inflation rate of 2%/year. We are ignoring any possible taxes that may be incurred when drawing down savings. To simplify things, we will perform the simulation on an annual basis rather than monthly and assume all spending occurs at the beginning of the year. We will assume the investor's blended return of stocks and bonds has a mean return of 6% and a standard deviation of 12% every year over the entire retirement period. Essentially, then, we are assuming not only that expected returns don't change over time but also that the mix of stocks and bonds doesn't change over time and that the portfolio is rebalanced once per year. We will relax many of these assumptions later in this chapter and in other chapters.

The Python code in listing 5.4 creates a two-dimensional array that tracks the path of wealth over time for each simulation, which we call `W[]`. As figure 5.5 illustrates, each row represents a different simulation and each column represents a different year of the simulation, starting with the initial wealth at year 0.

Listing 5.4   Simulating paths of wealth

```
np.random.seed(123)
num_years = 30
num_sims = 10000
mean = 0.06
stdev = 0.12
```

```
spending_0 = 60000
W0 = 1200000

inflation = 0.02

ret = np.random.normal(loc=mean, scale=stdev, size=(num_sims, num_years+1))

W = np.empty(shape=[num_sims, num_years+1])
W[:,:] = np.NaN
W[:,0] = W0      ← Every simulation starts with the initial wealth in year 0.

count_bankrupt = 0   ← Keeps a running total of how many simulations lead to bankruptcy

for sim in range(num_sims):
    spending = spending_0
    for year in range(1, num_years+1):
        # Check whether you run out of money
        next_period_wealth = (W[sim, year-1] - spending) * (1 + ret[sim, year])

        if next_period_wealth < 0:              Spending occurs at
            count_bankrupt += 1                 the beginning of the period
            break                               (subtracted before asset growth).
        else:
            W[sim, year] = next_period_wealth      Spending increases by the
        spending = spending * (1 + inflation)   ← inflation rate every year.

plt.xlabel('Year')
plt.ylabel('Wealth')
plt.plot(W[0:10,:].T);   ←——— Plots the first 10 sample paths of wealth
```

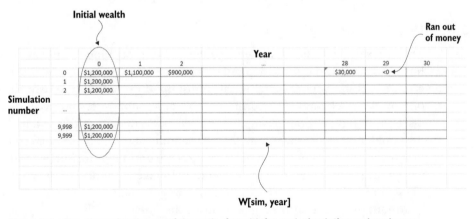

Figure 5.5 Two-dimensional array of the path of wealth for each simulation and each year

Figure 5.6 shows the plot of the first 10 sample paths of wealth from the last line of code in the listing. In only 4 of these 10 paths does the retiree's savings last for 30 years.

We can estimate the probability of going bankrupt within 30 years by dividing the number of simulations that lead to bankruptcy by the total number of simulations we ran

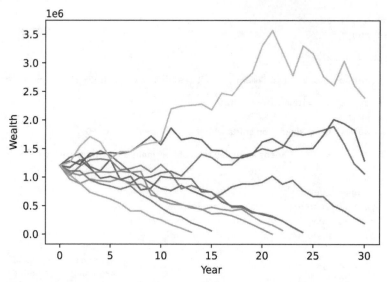

Figure 5.6   First 10 sample paths of wealth in a simulation

```
print('The probability of bankruptcy is ', count_bankrupt/num_sims)
```

which outputs

```
    The probability of bankruptcy is  0.4809
```

The probability of bankruptcy is close to 50%, which is rather high. But in the next section, we look at a spending plan that lowers spending when assets drop.

5.6   *Dynamic strategies*

The previous simulation was a *static* strategy where spending (as well as asset allocation) was fixed and did not depend on age or wealth. In reality, a *dynamic* strategy is more realistic, where spending can adjust up or down in future years depending on how the stock market performs. For example, suppose spending starts at 5% of assets, as in our previous example, but then assets decline and spending hits a 6% threshold. A dynamic strategy might cut spending at this point to avoid running out of money. On the other hand, if assets increase and spending hits a 4% threshold, a dynamic strategy might increase spending to take advantage of the good fortune. These thresholds are sometimes referred to as *guardrails* because of the way highway guardrails prevent a car from going outside its lane.

One problem with this strategy is that there is a limit to how much you can adjust spending downward. Discretionary spending like vacations can easily be cut, but essential spending, like utility bills, is much harder to reduce. So we add a twist to the standard guardrail strategy: we impose a minimum spending amount that also grows with inflation. The Bureau of Labor Statistics collects data on consumer expenditures; based on that data, we assume in listing 5.5 that essential spending is 75% of total spending (initially, $48,000/year) and grows with inflation. It is easy to implement this in Python with only a few additional lines of code that turn it into a dynamic strategy.

Listing 5.5 Simulating paths of wealth with spending guardrails

```python
np.random.seed(123)
num_years = 30
num_sims = 10000
mean = 0.06
stdev = 0.12
spending_0 = 60000
spending_min_0 = 48000    ← A new constant: minimum essential spending
W0 = 1200000

inflation = 0.02

ret = np.random.normal(loc=mean, scale=stdev, size=(num_sims, num_years+1))

W = np.empty(shape=[num_sims, num_years+1])
W[:,:] = np.NaN
W[:,0] = W0

count_bankrupt = 0

for sim in range(num_sims):
    spending = spending_0
    spending_min = spending_min_0

    for year in range(1, num_years+1):
        next_period_wealth = (W[sim, year-1] - spending) * (1 + ret[sim,year])
        if next_period_wealth < 0:    ← Checks whether you run out of money
            count_bankrupt += 1
            break
        else:
            W[sim, year] = next_period_wealth
            spending = spending * (1 + inflation)
            spending_min = spending_min * (1 + inflation)    ← Minimal essential spending grows with inflation.
            if (spending < 0.04* W[sim, year]) or (spending > 0.06* W[sim, year]):
                spending = max(0.05 * W[sim, year], spending_min)

plt.xlabel('Year')
plt.ylabel('Wealth')
plt.plot(W[0:10,:].T);
```

Checks whether spending is outside the 4% or 6% guardrails

Minimal essential spending grows with inflation.

Modifies spending if outside the guardrails, but not less than the minimum spending required

If you compare the first 10 sample paths in figure 5.7 with those without guardrails in figure 5.6 (again, we use the same seed number, and therefore the same returns, in both simulations), fewer sample paths lead to assets being depleted. On the other hand, in a few of the sample paths during bull markets, where assets grew very large, having guardrails led to fewer assets left over after 30 years, presumably because spending was ratcheted up.

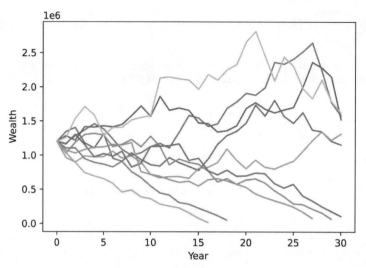

Figure 5.7   First 10 sample paths of wealth in a simulation with guardrails and minimum spending

As expected, the guardrails reduce the probability of running out of money significantly, to about 28%:

```
print('The probability of bankruptcy is ', count_bankrupt/num_sims)
```

which will output:

```
The probability of bankruptcy is  0.2804
```

This particular dynamic strategy is simple and naive. Although spending did vary depending on wealth, we chose an ad hoc rule that wasn't optimized in any way. For one thing, spending did not take age into account. Perhaps a retiree in their 80s should draw down more of their savings than a person in their 60s with many more years of spending and potential down markets ahead. Also, asset allocation was fixed and not optimized. In chapter 6, we will explore using artificial intelligence to find optimal dynamic strategies. Monte Carlo simulations will still be used to train the model, but you can specify any objective and the model will find an optimal solution.

So far, we have assumed inflation is a fixed constant throughout the life of a retiree. In the next section, we will relax that assumption and treat inflation as an additional risk.

5.7   *Inflation risk*

Inflation has been a hot topic lately. The effects of inflation could have serious consequences for how long a retiree's money will last, and inflation risk can easily be incorporated into the Monte Carlo simulation. But what is the best way to model inflation risk? Inflation rates certainly do not follow a white-noise process like stock returns, where every year is an independent draw from a normal distribution. It is closer to a random walk, where high inflation in the last period is often followed by high inflation in the next period, but it differs from a random walk in that inflation is slowly pulled toward some long-term average inflation. This is known as an *Ornstein–Uhlenback process* or, in discrete time, an *autoregressive process* (AR) with one lag (an AR(1) process). Let's estimate the parameters of that model and then implement it in our Monte Carlo simulation.

The most commonly used measure of inflation is the Consumer Price Index for All Urban Consumers (CPI-U). There are many other measures, like the CPI for Urban Wage Earners and Clerical Workers (CPI-W), which the Social Security Administration uses for cost-of-living increases, and the personal consumption expenditure price index (PCE), which is the Federal Reserve's preferred inflation gauge. We can download inflation data from FRED (Federal Reserve Economic Data). We used FRED in chapter 3 as our source for interest rate data, but FRED also maintains a database containing numerous economic time series. Listing 5.6 shows the three steps we take to download annual inflation rates. We use the `pandas-datareader` package to import the data from FRED. The symbol for Consumer Price Index for All Urban Consumers, All Items (i.e., including food and energy), Non Seasonally Adjusted is `CPIAUCNS`. We then resample the monthly index to an annual index and take percentage changes, resulting in a non-overlapping year-over-year time series of historical inflation.

Listing 5.6   Downloading inflation data

```
import pandas_datareader.data as web

start = '01-01-1947'
end = '12-30-2023'
data = web.DataReader(name='CPIAUCNS', data_source='fred', start=start,
     end=end)     ← Reads in monthly levels of CPI from FRED
data = data.resample('Y').last()     ← Resamples to annual levels of CPI
data['yoy'] = data['CPIAUCNS'].pct_change()     ┐ Takes percent changes to
data.tail()                                      │ convert from the index to
                                                 ┘ the inflation rate
```

Figure 5.8 shows the last five rows of the inflation rate DataFrame. The year-over-year inflation rate jumped from 1.4% at the end of 2020 to 7.0% at the end of 2021, back down to 6.5% at the end of 2022, and then to 3.5% at the end of 2023.

DATE	CPIAUCNS	yoy
2019-12-31	256.974	0.022851
2020-12-31	260.474	0.013620
2021-12-31	278.802	0.070364
2022-12-31	296.797	0.064544
2023-12-31	307.051	0.034549

Figure 5.8   Last five rows of the year-over-year inflation DataFrame

We model inflation as a mean-reverting process:

$$\underbrace{\inf_t - \mu}_{\substack{\text{Inflation} \\ \text{deviation} \\ \text{from mean} \\ \textbf{this} \text{ period}}} = \phi \underbrace{(\inf_{t-1} - \mu)}_{\substack{\text{Inflation} \\ \text{deviation} \\ \text{from mean} \\ \textbf{last} \text{ period}}} + \epsilon_t$$

where

$$\inf_t = \text{year-over-year inflation at year } t$$

$$\mu = \text{long-run average inflation}$$

$$\phi = \text{rate of mean reversion}$$

$$\epsilon_t = \text{Gaussian noise around the expected inflation rate}$$

Rearranging terms, we can express this as an AR(1) model

$$\inf_t = c + \phi \inf_{t-1} + \epsilon_t$$

where the constant of the regression is $c = (1 - \phi)\mu$ and therefore $\mu = \frac{c}{1-\phi}$.

Finally, we regress year-over-year inflation on its lagged value to estimate the parameters of the model, which we will use in the simulation. The following listing performs the regression using the `statsmodels` library.

Listing 5.7   Estimating inflation model parameters from a regression

```
import statsmodels.api as sm            Shifts the original data to
                                        create a column of lagged data
data['lag'] = data['yoy'].shift()  ◄───
data = data.dropna()  ◄─ Drops the first row because it contains an #NA from the shifted data
y = data['yoy']
X = data['lag']
X = sm.add_constant(X)   ◄─ Adds a column of 1s to include a constant in the regression
model = sm.OLS(y, X)
results = model.fit()
print(results.summary())
```

Figure 5.9 shows the output of the regression highlighting the section of the results that shows the coefficients of the regression. The rate of mean reversion parameter, ϕ, which is the coefficient on lagged inflation, is 0.6695, and the long-term mean parameter is $\mu = \frac{c}{1-\phi} = \frac{0.0116}{1-0.6695} = 3.51\%$.

We need to include one more parameter to simulate the Ornstein–Uhlenback process: the standard deviation of the error terms, ϵ_t. We can estimate this from the standard deviation of the residuals from the regression, which is not shown in `results.summary()` in figure 5.9 but can be found in `results.resid.std()`:

```
print('The standard deviation of residuals is ', results.resid.std())
```

```
                          OLS Regression Results
==============================================================================
Dep. Variable:                    yoy   R-squared:                       0.448
Model:                            OLS   Adj. R-squared:                  0.441
Method:                 Least Squares   F-statistic:                     59.34
Date:                Tue, 02 Jan 2024   Prob (F-statistic):           5.07e-11
Time:                        03:31:22   Log-Likelihood:                 182.68
No. Observations:                  75   AIC:                            -361.4
Df Residuals:                      73   BIC:                            -356.7
Df Model:                           1
Covariance Type:            nonrobust
==============================================================================
                 coef    std err          t      P>|t|      [0.025      0.975]
------------------------------------------------------------------------------
const          0.0116      0.004      2.958      0.004       0.004       0.019
lag            0.6695      0.087      7.704      0.000       0.496       0.843
==============================================================================
Omnibus:                       13.167   Durbin-Watson:                   1.828
Prob(Omnibus):                  0.001   Jarque-Bera (JB):               16.183
Skew:                           0.796   Prob(JB):                     0.000306
Kurtosis:                       4.626   Cond. No.                         35.1
==============================================================================
```

Figure 5.9   Output from regression of inflation on its lagged value

Here's the output:

```
The standard deviation of residuals is  0.02132
```

Now we'll modify the previous code by replacing the constant inflation with a two-dimensional array of inflation by year and by simulation. The new code is shown in listing 5.8, but again, only a few lines change, which we annotate in the code. For simplicity, we assume that inflation is uncorrelated with asset returns, although it is straightforward to incorporate a correlation between the random numbers used to generate returns and the random numbers used to generate inflation. There is empirical evidence, however, that inflation has almost zero correlation with stock returns, although it is correlated with most bond returns (except inflation-protected bonds).

Listing 5.8   Simulating paths of wealth with inflation risk

```
np.random.seed(123)
num_years = 30
num_sims = 10000
mean = 0.06
stdev = 0.12
spending_0 = 60000
spending_min_0 = 48000
W0 = 1200000
inf0 = 0.035
phi = 0.6695          Constants for the AR(1)
c = 0.0116            process for inflation
sigma_inf = 0.02132
```

```
ret = np.random.normal(loc=mean, scale=stdev,                    Generates standard
                    size=(num_sims, num_years+1))         normal random numbers
                                                                 used for inflation
z_inf = np.random.normal(loc=0, scale=1, size=(num_sims, num_years+1))  ◄┘

inflation = np.zeros(shape=(num_sims, num_years+1))  ◄┐ Initializes inflation
inflation[:,0] = inf0  ◄──────────────────────────────┘ for each simulation path

for sim in range(num_sims):                              Creates a matrix of
    for year in range(1, num_years+1):                   inflation for each year
        inflation[sim, year] = (c + phi*inflation[sim, year-1]  and each simulation
                            + sigma_inf*z_inf[sim, year])  according to the
                                                           AR(1) model
W = np.empty(shape=[num_sims, num_years+1])
W[:,:] = np.NaN
W[:,0] = W0

count_bankrupt = 0

for sim in range(num_sims):
    spending = spending_0
    spending_min = spending_min_0

    for year in range(1, num_years+1):
        next_period_wealth = (W[sim, year-1] - spending) * (1 + ret[sim,year])
        if next_period_wealth < 0:
            count_bankrupt += 1
            break                              Now spending grows
        else:                                at a random inflation rate
            W[sim, year] = next_period_wealth  rather than a constant rate.
        spending = spending * (1 + inflation[sim, year])
        spending_min = spending_min * (1 + inflation[sim, year])
        if (spending < 0.04* W[sim, year]) or (spending > 0.06* W[sim, year]):
            spending = max(0.05 * W[sim, year], spending_min)
```

The percentage of scenarios in which the retiree runs out of money increases to 51%. This is not directly comparable to the last simulation, however, because the starting inflation rate and the long-run inflation are both higher than the 2% inflation assumed in the prior simulation. If we change those two parameters and rerun the simulation to keep everything the same except inflation risk, the percentage of failed scenarios is only modestly higher.

Another point on spending in retirement is worth mentioning. Not only does spending vary in retirement due to inflation, but inflation-adjusted spending patterns also change throughout retirement. This is sometimes referred to as the retirement spending *smile*. For the first few years after retirement, retirees are active, have more free time, and typically spend more money on things like travel (the *Go-Go years*). In the middle years of retirement, empirical studies show that spending gradually declines (the *Slow-Go years*); then, toward the end of retirement, spending tends to rise again as health-related costs go up (the *No-Go years*). The spending smile could easily be incorporated into the simulation as well.

5.8   *Fat tails*

A large body of empirical evidence shows that one-period returns do not have a normal distribution: rather, they have much fatter "tails" than you would expect with a normal distribution. This is important to consider when projecting the small tail probabilities of running out of money. One strong piece of anecdotal evidence that clearly demonstrates the fat-tailed nature of stock returns is the stock market crash of 1987. On Oct 19, 1987, the stock market dropped about 20% in one day; with a daily standard deviation of about 1%/day, that drop represents a 20-standard-deviation move. If returns were truly normally distributed, we would not expect to see a single event like this in 14 billion years—the age of the universe!

A common method to quantify the degree of fat tails is to look at the *kurtosis*, or fourth standardized moment, of stock returns. If returns were independent and followed a normal distribution, the excess kurtosis should be 0 (to be fair, the independence assumption is a little unrealistic, and the GARCH effects of time-varying volatility we discussed in chapter 3 would induce fat tails even if returns were normally distributed). In the following listing, we show that the daily S&P 500 returns have had an excess kurtosis of 19, which is strongly statistically different from 0. Although daily and monthly returns exhibit excess kurtosis, annual returns have almost no excess kurtosis, so the results in this section will be more relevant when monthly returns are simulated.

Listing 5.9   Computing the excess kurtosis of S&P 500 returns

```
from scipy.stats import kurtosis

SP500 = yf.download('^GSPC', start='1971-12-31', end='2021-12-31')
SP500['ret'] = SP500['Close'].pct_change()
SP500 = SP500.dropna()
print('The excess kurtosis is: ', kurtosis(SP500['ret']))
```

The kurtosis function in scipy.stats computes the excess kurtosis of daily returns.

Here's the output:

```
The excess kurtosis is:    19.6669
```

In place of a normal distribution, we can use the generalized error distribution (GED), sometimes called the generalized normal distribution. In addition to a location and a scale parameter (similar to the mean and standard deviation for a normal distribution), the GED distribution has a parameter for the kurtosis, β. The normal distribution is a special case of the GED distribution when $\beta = 2$; but when $0 < \beta < 2$, the distribution has fatter tails than a normal distribution. To incorporate the GED distribution in our Monte Carlo simulations, we only need to modify the line of code that generates the random numbers for the simulation. We use the `gennorm.rvs` method in the `scipy.stats` module to generate the GED random numbers. We must also address one additional complication. With the normal distribution generator, the scale argument is simply the volatility. However, with the GED generator, the scale parameter must be adjusted for the kurtosis. For example, a GED random number with a scale parameter of 1 would not have a standard deviation of 1—it depends on the beta parameter. In particular, the scale should be

$$\sigma\sqrt{\frac{\Gamma(1/\beta)}{\Gamma(3/\beta)}}$$

where $\Gamma(\cdot)$ is the gamma function in mathematics, which can be computed in Python using `math.gamma()`. In the next listing, we generate GED random variables with $\beta = 1$, and we compute the standard deviation to verify that it matches the desired 12%. We also show the original code that generates normal returns, commented out for comparison.

Listing 5.10   Generating fat-tailed random returns

```
from scipy.stats import gennorm
import math

beta = 1.0   ◄── Additional GED parameter              Adjustment for
                                                        volatility for beta
scale = stdev * (math.gamma(1/beta)/math.gamma(3/beta))**0.5  ◄

#ret = np.random.normal(loc=mean, scale=stdev, size=(numb_sims, numb_years+1))
ret = gennorm.rvs(beta, loc=mean, scale=scale, size=(num_sims, num_years+1))
          ↑ Generates GED returns using
            the scipy.stats function gennorm.rvs()
print('The standard deviation is ', ret.std())
> The standard deviation is  0.1198
```

5.9   *Historical simulations and boostrapping*

Another approach to Monte Carlo simulation is to use historical returns rather than generating random returns from a normal distribution. This approach offers a few advantages:

- Time-series properties of returns can be captured, rather than assuming returns are independent from year to year as in a Monte Carlo simulation. Empirically, there has been a slight negative autocorrelation of annual stock returns: a down year in the market has been slightly more likely to be followed by an up year and vice versa. The small negative serial correlation can be captured with historical simulations.

- Non-normal distributions of returns, like fat tails and skewness, can be captured with historical simulations.

- Monte Carlo simulations assume that the correlations among assets are constant over time, which is not always the case. For example, there is some evidence that during market crises, correlations tend to increase, which can be captured with a historical simulation.

Some studies have looked at specific historical periods. For example, the period starting in 1973 can be seen as a "worst-case" scenario because it includes a bear market at the beginning as well as high inflation.

Although the historical simulation approach is easy to implement in Python (we include an example with the chapter files on the book's website and GitHub, https://www.manning.com/books/build-a-robo-advisor-with-python-from-scratch or https://github.com/robreider/robo-advisor-with-python/blob/main/chapter_05.ipynb), drawing conclusions based on a small number of overlapping years of data may be misleading. For example, in the last 50 years, there were three years when the market dropped by more than 20%; but in all three cases, the market rebounded by over 20% the following year. A historical simulation would assign zero probability of having two consecutive years of large down markets, whereas a Monte Carlo simulation would consider that as a possibility in the future.

An alternative approach is *bootstrapping*, where returns are generated by random sampling with replacement historical returns. The simulated returns have the same non-normal distribution of returns, and the correlations among assets are retained. However, by shuffling the historical returns, the time-series properties of returns like serial correlation are not preserved.

Bootstrapping is easy to implement in Python with the function `numpy.random.choice(a, size=None, replace=True)`, which can be used to generate random samples from a series of historical returns. The following listing first generates a series of annual stock market returns (this can be extended to multiple asset classes). Then we show the one line of code that replaces the original code that generated normal returns.

Listing 5.11   Sampling with replacement historical returns

```
SP500 = yf.download('^GSPC', start='1971-12-31',
    end='2021-12-31')
SP500 = SP500.resample('Y').last()                    Creates a time series
SP500['ret'] = SP500['Close'].pct_change()            of annual stock returns
SP500 = SP500.dropna()

#ret = np.random.normal(loc=mean, scale=stdev, size=(num_sims, num_years+1))
ret = np.random.choice(SP500['ret'], size=(num_sims, num_years+1))   ◄─┐
                                                  Chooses random returns, with │
                                          replacement, from the S&P500 series │
```

Technically, a total return index that includes dividends would be better to use for historical returns. The total return index on Yahoo Finance goes back to 1988, but you can also download other sources that have longer histories, such as Robert Shiller's website (www.econ.yale.edu/~shiller).

NOTE   The bootstrapping example does not preserve any time-series properties that may exist, such as autocorrelation of returns that we observe historically or any volatility-clustering GARCH effects. There are more sophisticated variations of bootstrapping that preserve some of the time-series properties of the original series of stock market returns. These techniques involve fitting a time-series model to the data and bootstrapping on the residuals of the model rather than on returns. An example of this technique is provided with the chapter files on the book's website and GitHub.

5.10 Longevity risk

So far, we have looked at the probability of a retiree running out of money over a fixed period of time: 30 years, in our examples. A more realistic estimate would factor in the probability of a retiree living longer than their life expectancy. This is referred to as *longevity risk*. Longevity risk is a consideration in a host of financial planning decisions.

We can use mortality tables to estimate the probability of dying within a year. A commonly used and publicly available mortality table was produced by the Society of Actuaries (SOA) in 2014: the RP-2014 mortality table, available at www.soa.org/resources/experience-studies/2014/research-2014-rp. According to the SOA, the mortality data was collected from private, defined-benefit pension plans, so a caveat is in order. There is a potential adverse selection problem with using pension plan data. Many pension plans offer workers a choice between a lump-sum payment and an annuity, and workers who choose an annuity are more likely to have a longer life expectancy. Their mortality rates, which do not include workers who chose the lump sum option, are lower than similar tables reported by Social Security.

In listing 5.12, we assume that you have downloaded the mortality Excel file from the SOA website and placed the file in the same directory as your Python code. We use the pandas `read_excel()` function to read the Excel file into a DataFrame. We use the Healthy Annuitant column (there is also a column on mortality data for retirees on disability), and we arbitrarily assume that our retiree is male. Figure 5.10 shows the first five rows of the mortality table.

Listing 5.12   Downloading mortality tables into a DataFrame

```
file_name = 'research-2014-rp-mort-tab-rates-exposure.xlsx'    ◄─── Mortality
sheet = 'White Collar'                                              data file
gender = 'Males'
if gender == 'Males':
    usecols = 'B,E'
elif gender == 'Females':
    usecols = 'B,I'
mort = pd.read_excel(file_name, sheet, header=3, usecols=usecols).set_
➥ index('Age')
mort.dropna(inplace=True)
mort.head()
```

Healthy Annuitant

Age	
50	0.002764
51	0.002981
52	0.003202
53	0.003429
54	0.003661

Figure 5.10   First five rows of the mortality DataFrame

Listing 5.13 modifies our original simulation to incorporate the mortality table we just downloaded. We replace the `for` loop that originally went 30 years with a `while` loop that terminates upon death or bankruptcy. For each year in each simulation, we look up the mortality probability for that age. For example, suppose the mortality probability is 2%. In that case, we generate a uniform random number between zero and one, and if it is less than 0.02, we assume the retiree dies at the end of the year. To compute mortality, we need to introduce a new variable, which is the initial age of the retiree. Instead of counting the number of bankruptcies as we did in the other examples, in this simulation we keep track of the age at which a retiree runs out of money (if they run out of money). Figure 5.11 shows a histogram of those ages.

Listing 5.13   Simulating paths of wealth using mortality tables

```
np.random.seed(123)
num_years = 50
num_sims = 10000
mean = 0.06
stdev = 0.12
spending_0 = 60000
W0 = 1200000
age_start = 60    ◀── Starting age of retiree

inflation = 0.02

ret = np.random.normal(loc=mean, scale=stdev, size=(num_sims, num_years+1))

W = np.empty(shape=[num_sims, num_years+1])
W[:,:] = np.NaN
W[:,0] = W0

age_bankruptcy = []    ◀── We will append to this list the age when money runs out.

for sim in range(num_sims):
    spending = spending_0
    year = 0
    alive = True
```

```
        bankrupt = False                          The loop ends when a retiree
        while not bankrupt and alive:   ◄───      either dies or runs out of money.
            if W[sim, year] - spending < 0:
                age_bankruptcy.append(year+age_start)    If you run out of money,
                bankrupt = True                          execute this block.
            else:
                mortality_prob = mort['Healthy Annuitant'].loc[year+age_start]  ◄──
If you live      p = np.random.uniform()   ◄─┐ A uniform (0,1)         The probability of
to the next      if p < mortality_prob:       random number that      dying, pulled from
year, execute        alive = False            will be compared        the mortality table
this block.      else:                        to the probability
                    year += 1                 of dying
                    W[sim,year] = (W[sim, year-1] - spending) * (1 + ret[sim, year])
                spending = spending * (1 + inflation)

bins = max(age_bankruptcy) - min(age_bankruptcy) + 1
plt.xlabel('Age')
plt.ylabel('Probability')
plt.hist(age_bankruptcy, bins=bins, density=True);
```

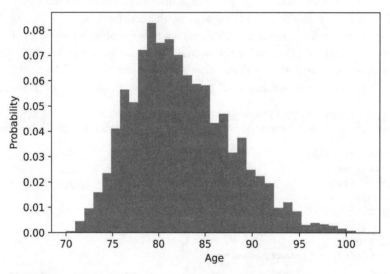

Figure 5.11   Distribution of ages when a retiree runs out of money

As before, we can calculate the probability of running out of money with longevity risk for a 60-year-old

```
print('The prob of running out of money is ',len(age_bankruptcy)/num_sims)
```

which outputs

```
    The prob of running out of money is  0.3686
```

This example cuts a few corners for simplicity. The mortality table we used represents mortality rates for different ages in 2014. Mortality rates and life expectancy tend to improve over time, but the numbers in the table show the mortality rates for all ages at one point in time. For example, a 50-year-old male has a mortality rate of 0.2764%, and an 80-year-old has a mortality rate of 3.7307%. But in 30 years, an 80-year-old will have a different mortality rate than an 80-year-old today, depending on the improvements. The SOA has a separate table, MP-2017, that projects improvements in mortality for years in the future. The chapter files on the book's website and GitHub include an example that uses both the RP-2014 mortality tables and the MP-2017 improvement ratios.

5.11 *Flexibility of Monte Carlo simulations*

Monte Carlo simulations are extremely flexible and can handle a wide variety of situations and problems. The examples in this chapter are just the tip of the iceberg of Monte Carlo's capabilities and are by no means a comprehensive list of things that can be done with a simulation. We also cut many corners to make the examples simpler and more readable. Consider using a simulation to find the optimal age to elect Social Security. We would want to include couples instead of individuals because spousal and survivor benefits are affected by the joint decisions of a couple. We should also consider taxes because Social Security benefits have special taxation rules. And we might include outside income because Social Security has an income test that can reduce benefits. An accurate Social Security calculator would perform all calculations on a monthly basis rather than annually. And our objective function would have to be modified. Rather than minimizing the probability of running out of money, we might want to use utility functions and maximize expected utility, which would take risk aversion into account. We have not seen risk aversion dealt with this way in any of the free or subscription-based Social Securities calculators, so there are clearly areas that are ripe for improvement. We are sure you can think of other features to add—consider this chapter a starting point for more complicated simulations.

Appendix

To derive the approximation $G = A - \frac{1}{2}\sigma^2$, we use the Taylor series expansion of a function $f(x)$ around $x = a$:

$$f(x) = f(a) + f'(a)(x-a) + \frac{f''(a)}{2!}(x-a)^2 + \cdots + \frac{f^{(n)}(a)}{n!}(x-a)^n + \cdots$$

For the function $f(x) = (1+x)^{\frac{1}{N}}$, the first three terms of the Taylor series expansion around $a = 0$ are

$$(1+x)^{\frac{1}{N}} \approx 1 + \frac{1}{N}x + \frac{1}{2}\frac{1-N}{N^2}x^2$$

Substituting this approximation in the formula for the geometric average,

$$G = \prod_{i=1}^{N}(1+r_i)^{\frac{1}{N}} - 1$$

$$\approx \prod_{i=1}^{N}\left(1 + \frac{1}{N}r_i + \frac{1}{2}\frac{1-N}{N^2}r_i^2\right) - 1$$

Eliminating all polynomials of third degree or higher in the product, we get

$$G \approx 1 + \frac{1}{N}\sum_{i=1}^{N}r_i + \frac{1}{2}\frac{1-N}{N^2}\sum_{i=1}^{N}r_i^2 + \frac{1}{N^2}\sum_{\substack{i=1 \\ i>j}}^{N}\sum_{j=1}^{N}r_i r_j - 1$$

$$\approx \frac{1}{N}\sum_{i=1}^{N}r_i + \frac{1}{2}\frac{1-N}{N^2}\sum_{i=1}^{N}r_i^2 + \frac{1}{2}\frac{1}{N^2}\sum_{\substack{i=1 \\ i\neq j}}^{N}\sum_{j=1}^{N}r_i r_j$$

$$\approx \underbrace{\frac{1}{N}\sum_{i=1}^{N}r_i}_{A} - \frac{1}{2}\underbrace{\left(\frac{1}{N}\sum_{i=1}^{N}r_i^2 - \frac{1}{N^2}\sum_{i=1}^{N}\sum_{j=1}^{N}r_i r_j\right)}_{\sigma^2}$$

Note that nowhere in this derivation do we make any assumptions about the distribution of returns, like normality.

Summary

- A simple financial planning analysis can give incorrect results, which is why simulations are needed.
- Arithmetic averages are higher than geometric averages and are the proper inputs for simulations.
- Once paths of wealth over time are generated, the probability of running out of money in retirement involves simply counting how many paths lead to bankruptcy.

- Inflation risk can be modeled as an AR(1) process, and the parameters can be estimated from a regression.
- Distributions of returns over shorter periods have fat tails, which can be modeled with a generalized error distribution rather than a normal distribution.
- Bootstrapping historical returns is an alternative to using normal returns and captures the non-normality of returns and correlation properties across assets.
- Mortality tables can be downloaded from the Society of Actuaries and incorporated into simulations.

Financial planning using reinforcement learning

This chapter covers

- Solving a goals-based investing problem using dynamic programming
- Solving the same goals-based problem using AI
- Using utility functions in financial planning
- Applying reinforcement learning to optimize spending using utility functions
- Extending the model to include longevity risk

When we looked at asset allocation earlier, we were essentially performing a single-period optimization. However, most financial planning decisions involve making decisions over multiple periods. And the decisions made today—not only how to allocate assets but also how much to spend, whether to claim Social Security, when to retire, what accounts to withdraw from, etc.—affect decisions in the future. These multiperiod, dynamic models, which economists sometimes call *lifecycle models*, are much more complicated to optimize.

In recent years, a branch of artificial intelligence called *reinforcement learning* has been applied to a wide range of problems involving decision-making over multiple time periods. Google famously used reinforcement learning to train a computer model to beat the best human at the game Go. Similarly, Libratus used reinforcement learning to beat some of the best poker players. And the successes are not limited to playing games. However, there is currently very little written about using reinforcement learning to solve financial planning problems. In this chapter, we will explain how reinforcement learning can be used to solve multiperiod wealth management problems. As usual, we will start with a simple example and build up to more realistic, complicated examples.

6.1 A goals-based investing example

In chapter 5, we used Monte Carlo simulations to answer the question of whether an investor will run out of money in retirement. The simple binary outcome of success or failure is an example of goals-based investing. Other examples of goals may be saving for a child's education or saving for a house.

It will be easier to understand the theory behind reinforcement learning with a concrete example in mind. Consider an investor with $1 million in assets and a goal of reaching $2 million in 10 years. For now, assume there are no savings inflows or spending outflows over the 10 years. We want to compute the optimal asset allocation over time and the probability of achieving the goal, assuming the investor follows the optimal allocation. We assume the asset allocation can change once per year.

The term *glide path* refers to how the asset allocation changes over time. Conventional wisdom says the allocation to stocks should decline over time. Indeed, target-date mutual funds are designed to automatically rebalance stock and bond funds over time according to a predetermined glide path. However, some authors have suggested an alternative view that equity exposure should increase over time. In this chapter, we will compute optimal glide paths and also show what factors affect its shape and slope.

The first example is overly simple and unrealistic on many levels. Perhaps the biggest shortcoming is that the goal is binary and does not make any distinction between achieving a final wealth of $2 million and $100 million. In reality, of course, even if someone dies after the goals are achieved, they still may derive some benefit from knowing they are giving money to charities or their children. We can modify the binary goal and use utility functions instead, which will be discussed later in the chapter. We will also discuss adding other choice variables besides asset allocation, such as how much to spend each period and when to claim Social Security benefits.

6.2 An introduction to reinforcement learning

Reinforcement learning is a branch of machine learning that involves training an agent to make decisions based on trial and error. In this approach, an agent interacts with an environment and receives feedback in the form of rewards or penalties for the actions it takes. In our example, the agent is the investor, and the environment is the stock and bond market. The goal of an agent is to learn a policy, which is a set of rules that dictate which actions to take in which situations to maximize the cumulative reward over time.

Just like the way a baby learns to walk, an agent's behavior is shaped by the rewards it receives. Positive rewards encourage the agent to take similar actions in the future, whereas negative rewards discourage it from doing so. The agent uses this feedback to adjust its policy and improve its decision-making process. The following four common features are used to describe most reinforcement learning problems:

- *State*—A state represents the relevant variables in the environment that affect an agent's actions. In our case, the state will be a tuple containing two variables: wealth, W, and discrete time steps, $t = 0, 1, 2, \ldots, T$. We will also discretize wealth into a finite set of states. We create this wealth grid in listing 6.1 and plot it in figure 6.1. A few comments are in order. Because the dispersion of potential wealth gets wider over time, our grid has a funnel shape rather than a rectangular shape. We compute a rough maximum and minimum value of wealth over time and then create an equally spaced grid in log of wealth space, which is on the right-hand side of figure 6.1. The same grid in wealth space is on the left-hand side of figure 6.1. In the figure, we use a wealth grid size of 11 points for illustrative purposes, but when training the model later in the chapter, we substantially increase the grid size.

- *Action*—An action, as the name indicates, is a decision the agent makes that changes the state. In a video game, an action can be moving a joystick to the left or right. In our example, an investor will only be able to invest in a stock fund or a risk-free bond, so an action will be the percentage of wealth invested in the stock fund; 1 minus that percentage is the percentage allocated to the bond. Just as we discretized states, we will discretize actions into 5% increments, so the action space of all possible actions is $A = 0\%, 5\%, 10\%, \ldots, 100\%$. A *policy* is a mapping from each state to the best action at that state.

- *Rewards*—A reward is a single number that represents the benefit an agent receives after taking an action. The goal of reinforcement learning is to maximize the cumulative rewards over time. A reward can be negative as well, so if the goal is to finish a task as quickly as possible, a negative reward can be assigned for every time step when the task is not completed. In our goals-based investing example, the agent receives a reward of +1 at time T if their wealth at time T exceeds the goal, and the agent receives no reward otherwise. Later in the chapter, we will look at other financial planning problems where the agent receives a reward every period when spending is taken into account.

- *Transition probabilites*—The transition probabilities define the probabilities of moving from one state at time t to another state at time $t + 1$ after taking a particular action. An implicit assumption is that only the current state at time t, and not the history of previous states before t, is relevant for computing transition probabilities. This is referred to as the *Markov property*, which is a standard assumption in reinforcement learning problems. In a game of chess, for example, the state is the positions of the pieces on the board, and the transition dynamics only depend on the current state of the board—the history of how the pieces arrived at that state is irrelevant. In the goals-based investing example, for a given wealth at time t (the state) and an asset allocation (the action), we can use the mathematics of a normal distribution to compute the transition probabilities of getting to each possible wealth state at time $t + 1$. The Python code for the transition probabilities is given in the next section.

Listing 6.1   Creating a state space grid for goals-based investing

```
import numpy as np
import matplotlib.pyplot as plt
from math import log, sqrt, exp

W0 = 1000000
T = 10
nW = 101    ◄──── Figure 6.1 uses a grid size in wealth of 11, not 101.
mu_stock = 0.08
mu_bond = 0.045
sig_stock = 0.20
sig_bond = 0.0

lnW = np.zeros((nW,T+1))
W = np.zeros((nW, T+1))

for t in range(T+1):
    lnW_min = log(W0) + (mu_stock-0.5*sig_stock**2)*t - 2.5*sig_stock*sqrt(t)
    lnW_max = log(W0) + (mu_stock-0.5*sig_stock**2)*t + 2.5*sig_stock*sqrt(t)
    lnW[:,t] = np.linspace(lnW_min, lnW_max, nW)    ◄──── Linear between min
W = np.exp(lnW)                                          and max in log space

plt.figure(figsize=(10, 6))
plt.subplot(1,2,1)
for t in range(T+1):
    plt.scatter(t*np.ones(nW), W[:,t], color='r')
plt.xlabel("time, $ t $")
plt.ylabel("Wealth, $ W $")                          Plots the state space grid
plt.subplot(1, 2, 2)
for t in range(T+1):
    plt.scatter(t*np.ones(nW), lnW[:,t], color='r')
plt.xlabel("time, $ t$")
plt.ylabel("Log of Wealth, $ \ln(W) $")
```

Now that we have described the reinforcement learning problem in terms of states, actions, rewards, and transition probabilities, the next step is to estimate the value at each state, which is referred to as the *value function*. The value function is the expected cumulative rewards starting from that state. When the value function at

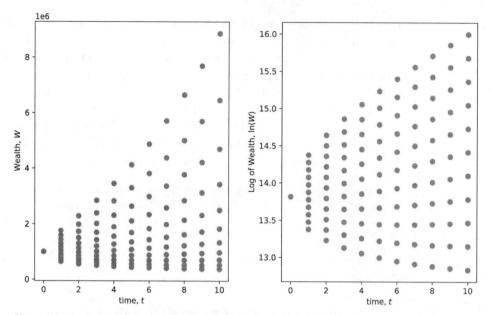

Figure 6.1   State space grid in wealth-time and log wealth-time

each state is maximized by choosing the best set of actions going forward, it is the optimal value function. In some cases, a reward today is worth more than a reward in the future, so the value function computes the present value by discounting future rewards. In our case, we only have a reward at the end, so we don't have to deal with discounting; later we will discuss other financial planning problems involving discounting.

Before we discuss the algorithms used in reinforcement learning, we will digress and discuss an older algorithm to estimate the value function. Reinforcement learning will make more sense when we explain *dynamic programming*, and it will give us a chance to highlight the method's shortcomings and why reinforcement learning has become such a powerful tool.

6.2.1   *Solution using dynamic programming*

The traditional method for solving our goals-based investment problem was to use dynamic programming (DP) with backward induction (also called backward recursion), which is a technique economists have employed for over 50 years. This method will provide a foundation for understanding reinforcement learning in the next section.

Before we can implement the DP solution, we need to compute the transition probabilities going from any wealth state at time t to possible wealth states at time $t + 1$. Listing 6.2 provides the code for estimating the transition probabilities. We start with two helper functions. The first, `compute_mu_sigma()`, is a simple function that takes an asset allocation and computes the mean and standard deviation of the portfolio. The second helper function, `compute_midpoints()`, computes the midpoints of adjacent wealth states. We will estimate the probability of transitioning to a particular discrete wealth state as the probability of wealth falling between the lower and upper midpoints of adjacent wealth states. For the extreme lowest-wealth state, the lower bound is zero wealth, and for the extreme highest-wealth state, the upper bound is infinity. We then compute the cumulative distribution function (CDF) at each midpoint: the difference between adjacent CDFs is the area under a normal curve, which corresponds to the probability of landing between the midpoints. You may notice an unusual `np.float64()` wrapper when we are computing CDF. If we are considering an allocation of 100% risk-free bonds, we will be dividing by zero volatility, which would normally produce an error, rather than +infinity or −infinity, which is what we want. Finally, note that to get the transition probabilities, this code assumes that stock returns are normally distributed, but we can easily modify the code to incorporate other distributions, like those with fat tails.

> **Listing 6.2   Computing transition probabilities**

```
from scipy.stats import norm
import warnings
warnings.filterwarnings('ignore')

def compute_mu_sigma(a):
    mu = a/(nA-1)*mu_stock + (1-a/(nA-1))*mu_bond
    sig = a/(nA-1)*sig_stock
    return mu, sig

def compute_midpoints(W):
    W_midpts = np.zeros((nW+1,T+1))
    W_midpts[0,:] = 0.000001
    W_midpts[nW,:] = np.inf
    W_midpts[1:nW,:] = (W[:nW-1,:]+W[1:nW,:])/2
    return W_midpts

def compute_transition_probs(w, t, a, W_midpts):
    mu, sig = compute_mu_sigma(a)
    W_tplus1_dist = np.zeros(nW)
    cdfs = norm.cdf(np.float64((np.log(W_midpts[:,t+1]/w)
                        - (mu-0.5*sig^2))/sig))          ◄──┐ Standardizes the return by
    W_tplus1_dist = cdfs[1:nW+1] - cdfs[0:nW]               subtracting the mean and
    return W_tplus1_dist                                    dividing by the standard
                                                            deviation and then
                                                            getting the CDF
```

Probability is the difference in adjacent CDFs.

Figure 6.2 illustrates the transition probabilities in going from the wealth state at node 54 (just under the $2 million goal) in the second-to-last period, $t = 9$, to possible wealth states at time $t = 10$, using this code.

We are now ready to use DP to compute the optimal value function. It's only a few lines of code, as shown in listing 6.3. In our goals-based investing example, we know the value function at the last time period, T. The terminal value is simply the reward

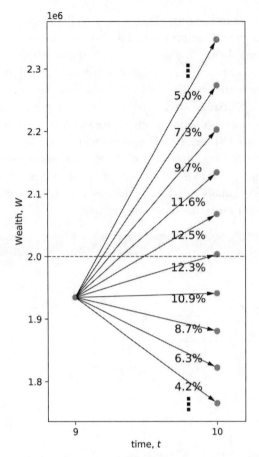

Figure 6.2   Transition probabilities from a wealth state at time $T-1$

at the end, which is +1 if we meet the goal and 0 if we don't. Going one step back in time to $T-1$, we loop through every wealth state. At each wealth state, we then loop through every possible action—or, in our case, every possible asset allocation—to find the one with the highest expected value. The expected value at a given state and choice of asset allocation is the dot product of the transition probabilities of the future state and the value at those future states. The function $V(W, t)$ is the optimal value function at each state, and we keep track of the optimal action at each state with the function $A(W, t)$. Once we find the optimal value at each possible wealth at time $T-1$, we go back one time step and keep repeating until we get to time step 0.

Listing 6.3   DP solution for goals-based investing

```
G = 2000000    ←— Dollar goal
nA = 21    ←— Number of possible actions (asset allocations)
V = np.zeros((nW, T+1))    ←— Initializes the two-dimensional optimal value function
A = np.zeros((nW, T))    ←— Initializes the two-dimensional optimal action function
```

```
EV = np.zeros(nA)   ←— Initializes the expected value as a function of possible actions
W_midpts = compute_midpoints(W)

for j in range(nW):            Computes the value function in
    if W[j, T] > G:            the last time period
        V[j, T] = 1

for t in range(T-1, -1, -1):
    for j in range(nW):
        for a in range(nA):
            W_tplus1_dist = compute_transition_probs(W[j,t], t, a,
                                                     W_midpts)
            EV[a] = np.dot(W_tplus1_dist, V[:, t+1])
        V[j,t] = EV.max()    ←— Saves the optimal value for each state
        A[j,t] = EV.argmax()   ←— Saves the optimal action for each state
```

The optimal value function at any state gives the expected cumulative rewards from that state going forward. Because the reward for success is +1 and for failure is 0, the value function represents the probability of achieving the goal at any state. For example, at the starting state at $t = 0$ and initial wealth of \$1 million, the value $V(0, 0)$ is 0.68, which means there is a 68% chance of meeting the goal if the optimal policies are followed at each state.

We can also compute the optimal glide path for this problem. Although most financial advice and target date funds assume a fixed glide path over time, it should be clear from this example that the optimal asset allocation should be not only a function of time but also a function of wealth. Therefore, it is impossible to talk about the optimal glide path without talking about the path of wealth over time. Out of the trillions of possible paths of wealth, let's consider three simple paths, which are shown in figure 6.3. In the "good" path, wealth rises by a steady 9%/year. In the "bad" path, wealth rises by a steady 6%/year. And in the "medium" path, wealth rises by 7.5%/year. This is, of course, an oversimplification, but it will illustrate how glide paths can depend on the wealth path.

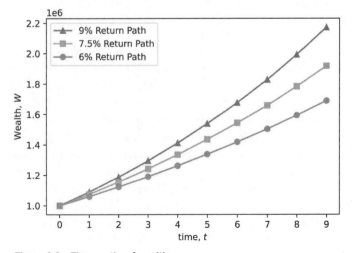

Figure 6.3 Three paths of wealth

Figure 6.4 shows the optimal allocation of stocks for the three wealth paths based on the function $A(W, t)$ that we computed when we solved the DP problem. The results should be fairly intuitive. For all three paths, we start at time 0 with a fairly high allocation to stocks of 85%, which is reasonable given our difficult goal of doubling our wealth in 10 years. In the medium return path, the allocation to stocks gradually declines. And at time period $t = 9$, the wealth is large enough that the goal can be achieved with certainty by placing all the assets in the risk-free bond; there is no reason to take any stock risk, given the reward structure of the problem. In the good-return path, the allocation to stocks declines even more rapidly, and by time period $t = 7$, the goal can be achieved by investing in the bond for the remaining time. But in the bad return path, the allocation to stocks goes up as wealth falls further and further behind in achieving the goal. By time $t = 7$, the best chance the investor has to achieve the goal is to place all assets in stocks and nothing in the bond. This "go-for-broke" risk-taking in the bad path is purely an artifact of how the rewards are specified—a more realistic objective function can lead to different behaviors, which we will see later.

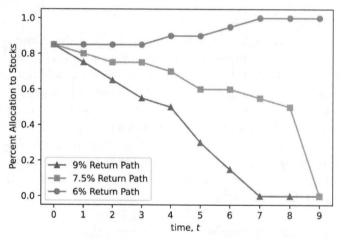

Figure 6.4   Asset allocations for the three paths of wealth

There are two main problems with the DP method. First, this method requires that we know the transition probabilities to compute expected values. In many problems, the agent does not know the exact model of the environment. Usually, in finance applications, we know the dynamics of the environment, but there are situations where it may be difficult to derive closed-form equations for the transition probabilities. However, the more serious shortcoming of DP is related to the curse of dimensionality. In our example, we have a relatively small number of states and possible actions, so the DP solution takes only a few seconds to run. However, many more realistic wealth problems involve more state variables and states and more potential actions at each state. In the DP solution, we loop through every single state and action to compute the value function. For example, we include the possibility that we can go from an extremely low wealth at time t to a very high wealth at time $t+1$ and then back to a very low wealth at time $t+2$, which is extremely unlikely. In the reinforcement learning algorithm in the next section, we go forward in time rather than backward, and we approximate the value function by simulating more likely paths rather than computing the value function exactly by looking at every possible path.

6.2.2 Solution using Q-learning

Q-learning is one of the most popular algorithms used in reinforcement learning to find optimal policies. At each time step, an agent chooses an action and tries to learn the best policy through these actions. A series of time steps from $t=0$ to $t=T$ is called an *episode*, and agents learn by running through many episodes, each time updating their estimate of the value function. With DP in the previous section, we estimated a value function for each state. In Q-learning, we estimate a function Q, which is the value at not only a state but also an action or a state-action pair. In the goals-based example, we computed $V(W, t)$. In Q-learning, we will estimate $Q(W, t, a)$, where a represents an action like an asset allocation. The function Q is initialized at the beginning, often with all zeros. But instead of starting at time $t=T$ and going backward, we go forward in time starting at $t=0$, and Q is updated according to the following equation:

$$\underbrace{Q(S_t, A_t)}_{\text{Updated } Q} \leftarrow \underbrace{Q(S_t, A_t)}_{\text{Current } Q} + \underbrace{\alpha}_{\text{Learning rate}} \left(\underbrace{R_t}_{\text{Reward}} + \underbrace{\gamma}_{\text{Discount rate}} \underbrace{\max_a Q(S_{t+1}, a)}_{\text{Optimal next } Q} - \underbrace{Q(S_t, A_t)}_{\text{Current } Q} \right)$$

To better understand this equation, let's define a few of the parameters and terms involved in the Q-learning algorithm:

- *Optimal next Q*—The term $\max_a Q(S_{t+1}, a)$ is an estimate of the maximum Q value over all possible actions at the next time step, $t+1$. It is only an estimate of the next period's value, so we are iteratively estimating this period's value based on our estimate of the next period's value.
- *Discount rate, γ*—An agent may prefer immediate rewards over future rewards, and the discount rate γ represents the rate at which future rewards are discounted ($0 \leq \gamma \leq 1$). In the extremes, if $\gamma = 1$, the agent has no preference for current rewards over future rewards, and if $\gamma = 0$, the agent is myopic and only cares about immediate rewards. Note that this discount rate can be subjective and differs from the rate of interest. For example, a smoker craving a cigarette may place a large discount on a cigarette received a year from now, and that subjective discount rate can be different from the discount rate on a bond.
- *Temporal difference (term in brackets)*—The temporal difference is the difference between the discounted value of future rewards next period and our estimate

of the value this period. If next period's estimate is above our current estimate (a positive difference), we want to increase our current estimate, and vice versa.

- *Learning rate*, α—The learning rate controls how quickly the agent updates Q based on the temporal difference.

We are now ready to implement the Q-learning algorithm in Python. We start with the same wealth–time state space grid used in the DP example. In DP, we had to compute the transition probabilities going from one wealth node at time t to all possible wealth nodes at $t + 1$. Q-learning is model-free. The agent does not need to know these probabilities—and in some problems we are interested in, these probabilities may be difficult to compute. Therefore, instead of the function in listing 6.2 that computes transition probabilities, Q-learning uses the following function, which computes a random transition from wealth at time t to a new wealth at time $t + 1$.

Listing 6.4   Generating random transition states

```
def transition(w, t, a):
    mu, sig = compute_mu_sigma(a)
    W_tplus1 = w * exp(mu-0.5*sig*sig + sig*np.random.normal())
    W_tplus1_idx = (np.abs(W[:,t+1] - W_tplus1)).argmin()   ◄─┐
    return W_tplus1_idx                    Finds the closest wealth node
                                           next period that corresponds
                                           to the next period's wealth
```

Listing 6.5 gives the code for updating Q according to the earlier equation. One fundamental feature of reinforcement learning that we have not yet addressed is the trade-off between exploration and exploitation. During the learning process, an agent must choose an action at each state. Exploitation means the agent takes an action that is expected to give the highest reward based on its current knowledge. In contrast, exploration means the agent takes random actions to learn more about the environment. Because the agent is still learning, if the agent exclusively takes "greedy" exploitative actions, it may miss out on better policies that it hasn't discovered yet. On the other hand, if the agent exclusively explored with random actions, it would be completely discarding useful knowledge, and the time to find the optimal solution would be very slow. A common strategy to balance exploration and exploitation is an *epsilon-greedy* method, where the agent explores a random action with probability ϵ and chooses the action with the highest expected cumulative reward, $Q(W, t, a)$, with a probability $1 - \epsilon$. The simple epsilon-greedy strategy is implemented in listing 6.5, although there are many more sophisticated approaches. For example, an agent can start with a higher exploration rate and gradually reduce that rate as it learns more. Or, rather than exploring by indiscriminately choosing a random action, an agent can draw an action based on a probability distribution derived from the Q values for each action, exploring actions that are more likely.

Listing 6.5   Updating Q

```
def Update_Q(w_idx, t, Q):
    if np.random.uniform() < epsilon:    ←— Explores with a probability epsilon
        a = np.random.randint(nA)
    else:
        A_array = Q[w_idx, t, :]
        a = np.where(A_array == A_array.max())[0]
        if (len(a)>1):    ←
            a = np.random.choice(a)
    W_tplus1_idx = transition(W[w_idx,t], t, a)
    Q[w_idx, t, a] += alpha*(gamma*Q[W_tplus1_idx, t+1, :].max()
                           - Q[W_idx, t, a])    ←
    return W_tplus1_idx, t+1, Q
```

If more than one action has the same Q, chooses one of them randomly

Implements the Q-learning update equation discussed in the text

The final step in reinforcement learning is to generate thousands of episodes, or paths, to learn the function Q and, consequently, the optimal actions at each state. It has been proven mathematically that if the number of episodes approaches infinity, Q-learning will converge to the optimal policy. Listing 6.6 gives the Python code for generating paths. We initialized Q the same way we initialized V in the DP section by assigning a +1 or 0 depending on whether the final wealth at time $t = T$ is greater than the goal. However, for Q-learning, this is unnecessary—we can initiate the terminal values of Q to 0, and the algorithm will learn the terminal values. Also, notice that we add a progress bar using the `tqdm` library so users can monitor the progress of the reinforcement learning algorithm and get an estimate of how long it will take to complete. Once this algorithm is finished running on thousands of episodes, it is easy to see that the optimal policies and values from reinforcement learning should come close to those from DP.

Listing 6.6   Generating episodes

```
from tqdm import tqdm

n_episodes = 1000000
epsilon = 0.5
alpha = 0.1
gamma = 1.0

Q = np.zeros((nW, T+1, nA))
for j in range(nW):
    if W[j, T]>G:
        Q[j, T, :] = 1

for i in tqdm(range(n_episodes), desc="Running..."):
    W_idx = 0
    t = 0
    while t<=(T-1):
        W_idx, t, Q = Update_Q(W_idx, t, Q)
```

We mentioned several shortcomings in the goals-based investing example. For example, because of the binary reward of success or failure, all successes and failures count the same, and the magnitude of success or failure is irrelevant. As a result, in low-wealth states, investors become extremely risk-loving and will take huge risks in a desperate attempt to achieve their goal; and in high-wealth states, investors are indifferent between having $2 million and $20 million and become extremely risk-averse once their goal can be achieved with certainty. You can argue that this is a flaw, or oversimplification, of the binary objective function we used. And other objective functions have their own flaws. For example, if the objective is to maximize final period wealth, an investor will act as if they're risk-neutral and allocate as much as possible to higher expected-return stocks, regardless of risk. A potential solution is to use utility functions in the objective function, which is the next topic.

6.3   *Utility function approach*

Economists have long used utility functions to quantify the enjoyment people derive from wealth or consumption. With a few exceptions, financial planners have not adopted utility functions in financial planning and decision-making. In this section, we will show how this area of economics can be applied to reinforcement learning, but first we will explain what utility functions are.

6.3.1   *Understanding utility functions*

Suppose we want to define a utility function that represents how much pleasure an individual derives from different levels of wealth. Let's first think about what shape this function will take. We know that people prefer more wealth to less wealth, so the function is upward-sloping. It is also reasonable to assume that the more wealth you have, the less happiness you'll derive from an additional dollar of wealth. In other words, if your wealth is $1 and you find $10 under your couch, you will be happier than if you have $1 million and find $10, just as if you are hungry, the pleasure you get from the first scoop of ice cream is greater than the pleasure you will get from an additional scoop after you've already had 10 scoops. This is the principle of diminishing marginal utility and leads to a utility function that has a concave shape; see figure 6.5.

A concave utility function also implies that the individual is risk-averse. To see that, suppose an individual wins a prize determined by a coin flip. If they guess correctly, they get $10 million, and if they guess incorrectly, they get nothing. The individual will much prefer to have a certain $5 million rather than participate in the coin flip. In fact, you can compute the *certainty equivalent* value of this prize. For the utility function in figure 6.6, the certainty equivalent amount is $2.5 million, which means the individual will be indifferent between a sure $2.5 million and the coin flip between zero and $10 million. The degree of risk aversion is related to the curvature of the utility function. An individual with a straight-line utility function is risk-neutral rather than risk-averse.

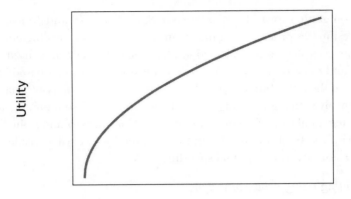

Figure 6.5 **Upward sloping concave utility function**

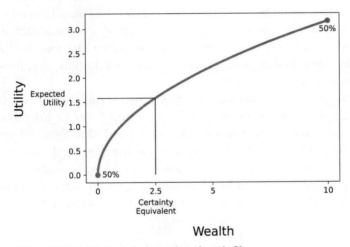

Figure 6.6 **Certainty equivalent value of a coin flip**

One utility function that is commonly used by economists is called the *power utility function*, which is given by the equation

$$U(W) = \frac{W^{1-\eta}}{1-\eta} \text{ for } \eta \geq 0, \eta \neq 1$$

The constant η is referred to as the *coefficient of constant relative risk aversion* (CRRA). When $\eta = 0$, the utility function is linear, which corresponds to risk neutrality. When $\eta \to \infty$, the utility function represents extreme risk aversion. And when $\eta = 1$, the utility function is defined as $U(W) = \ln(W)$. One of the challenges of using utility functions is estimating η, which varies by individual; the challenge is not dissimilar to that of mapping risk-tolerance surveys to an asset allocation as we discussed in chapter 2. Dozens of empirical studies in the economics literature have tried to estimate η, using lab experiments, surveys, auction behavior, labor supply behavior, insurance choices, and options prices. Several papers even try to estimate the parameters from the behavior on game shows like *Who Wants to Be a Millionaire* and *Deal or No Deal.* The range of estimates varies, and in the examples, we will use a coefficient of $\eta = 3$.

Now that we've explained utility functions, let's see how they can be used in financial planning and decision-making. A simple extension of the goals-based investing example is to replace the binary reward of +1 or 0 with the utility of final wealth, $U(W_T)$. This involves changing a single line of code: in the DP solution, the line that initializes the terminal value function, and in the Q-learning solution, the line that initializes Q with the final reward. But in the next section, we will consider a more complex extension involving optimal spending.

6.3.2 Optimal spending using utility functions

In the goals-based investing example, the only action an agent takes at each state is choosing the percentage of stock holdings. Spending, an important consideration for financial planning, is completely ignored. We touched on spending in chapter 5 on Monte Carlo simulations. But in chapter 5, when we tried to estimate how long an individual's money would last, we either assumed spending was fixed each year or adjusted it in a very simple way through guardrails, with no attempt at optimization. In this section, we will try to optimize how to choose spending each year as a function of an individual's wealth–time state to maximize expected utility, simultaneously optimizing asset allocation.

This is a classic problem in financial economics, which you can find in a Google search for "optimal consumption and portfolio choice." Later we will discuss the difference between what economists call *consumption* and what financial planners and everyone else call *spending*; but for now, assume that they are the same. Under some assumptions, there is a mathematical solution, and numerical solutions are unnecessary. However, when we add additional assumptions later, it can only be solved numerically. The mathematical description of the problem is

$$\max_{a_t,\ c_t} \quad E\left[\sum_{t=0}^{T} \gamma^t U(c_t)\right]$$

$$\text{subject to} \quad W_{t+1} = (W_t - c_t)\left(a_t \tilde{r}_t + (1-a_t)r_f\right)$$

where a_t is the allocation to stocks, c_t is consumption, W_t is wealth, $\tilde{r}_t$ is the random return on the stock portfolio, and $U(c_t)$ is the utility of consumption, all at time t, and γ is the subjective discount factor. The reward for each period is the utility of consumption, and we want to maximize the cumulative sum of discounted rewards. But we need a budget constraint that shows how wealth evolves over time and places a constraint on spending. The next period's wealth is equal to this period's wealth, net of consumption this period, plus investment income. Labor income can also be included in the budget constraint, as we'll address later in the chapter.

The code for solving this problem is very similar to the code for the goals-based investing problem. We will discuss the lines that change when we introduce utility functions and spending. As before, we start by creating a state space grid, which is shown in listing 6.7. With spending, the state space grid will be slightly different from the original listing 6.1—the lower bound must be lower to account for lower wealth states after consumption depletes wealth.

Listing 6.7 Creating a state space grid for the spending example

```
W0 = 1000000
T = 10
nW = 101
mu_stock = 0.08
mu_bond = 0.045
sig_stock = 0.20
sig_bond = 0.0

Cbar = np.zeros(T+1)
Cbar[0] = 0
for t in range(1, T+1):
    Cbar[t] = Cbar[t-1] + 1/(T-t+1)

lnW = np.zeros((nW,T+1))
W = np.zeros((nW, T+1))

for t in range(T+1):
    lnW_min = log(W0) - t*log(3)          ◄── The potential minimum wealth
                                              is lower because of consumption.
    lnW_max = log(W0) - Cbar[t] + (mu_stock-0.5*sig_stock**2)*t
                                    + 2.5*sig_stock*sqrt(t)
    lnW[:,t] = np.linspace(lnW_min, lnW_max, nW)
W = np.exp(lnW)
```

The DP code in listing 6.8 has a few key differences from the corresponding code in listing 6.3. We cannot ignore the subjective discount rate, γ, because the agent receives rewards every period from consumption. In the last period, all wealth is consumed, so we set the value function at time T equal to the utility of final wealth, $U(W_T)$. We not only have to loop through every wealth–time state and every discrete asset allocation, but now we also loop through every discrete level of consumption. In our example, consumption is expressed as a percentage of wealth, with 40 potential consumption levels ranging from 1.67% to 66.67% of wealth in 1.67% increments. When computing the transition probabilities emanating from wealth at time t, we must subtract the consumption at time t. The calculation of the expected value at a node has an extra term now: the (discounted) value next period, as before, plus the current reward, which is the utility of consumption this period.

Listing 6.8 DP solution for the spending example

```
nA = 11
nC = 40
V = np.zeros((nW, T+1))
A = np.zeros((nW, T))
C = np.zeros((nW, T))     ◄── Initializes the two-dimensional optimal consumption
```

```
EV = np.zeros((nA, nC))
W_midpts = compute_midpoints(W)

gamma = 0.95   ←— Subjective discount rate
CRRA = 3   ←— Coefficient of constant relative risk aversion
def utility(c):   ←— Power utility function
    if (CRRA == 1):
        util = log(c)
    else:
        util = (c**(1-CRRA))/(1-CRRA)
    return util

for j in range(nW):
    V[j, T] = utility(W[j,T])   ←— In the last period, all wealth is consumed.

for t in range(T-1, -1, -1):
    for j in range(nW):
        for a in range(nA):
            for c in range(nC):
                cons = (c+1)/(1.5*nC)*W[j,t]   ←— Consumption is a percentage of wealth.

                W_tplus1_dist = compute_transition_probs(W[j,t]-cons, t,
                    a W_midpts)

                EV[a,c] = np.dot(W_tplus1_dist, utility(cons)+gamma*V[:,t+1])
        V[j,t] = EV.max()
        A[j,t], C[j,t] = np.unravel_index(EV.argmax(), EV.shape)   ←—
```

Consumption is subtracted from wealth before computing the transition probabilities.

Current value is utility from consumption plus the discounted expected value next period.

Returns the row (asset allocation) and column (consumption) for the optimal solution

For the reinforcement learning solution with spending, the code in listing 6.4 that computes a random transition from wealth at time t to a new wealth at time $t + 1$ does not change because we already accounted for consumption in the starting wealth. In listing 6.9, the function that implements an epsilon-greedy strategy for updating Q is very similar to the code in listing 6.5. The code that updates Q now includes the current reward, which is the utility of current consumption.

Listing 6.9 Updating Q for the spending problem

```
def Update_Q(w_idx, t, Q):
    if np.random.uniform() < epsilon:
        a = np.random.randint(nA)
        c = np.random.randint(nC)
    else:
        AC_array = Q[w_idx,t,:,:]
        ac = np.argwhere(AC_array == AC_array.max())   ←—
        if (len(ac)>1):
            a,c = ac[np.random.choice(len(ac))]
        else:
            a,c = ac[0]
    cons = (c+1)/(1.5*nC)*W[w_idx,t]
```

Row (asset allocation) and column (consumption) of the highest Q

```
W_tplus1_idx = transition(W[w_idx,t]-cons, t, a)
```
← **Consumption is subtracted from wealth before computing the random next state.**

```
Q[w_idx,t,a,c]  += alpha*(utility(cons) +
                  gamma*Q[W_tplus1_idx,t+1,:,:].max()-Q[W_idx,t,a,c])
    return W_tplus1_idx, t+1, Q
```
← **Implements the Q-learning update equation discussed in the text, including current consumption**

Finally, generating episodes in listing 6.10 is identical to the code in listing 6.6 except that Q is initialized at $t = T$ to the utility of consuming all the wealth. We also increase the number of episodes to reflect the fact that we have a larger space of possible actions to choose, with both consumption and asset allocation.

Listing 6.10 Generating episodes for the spending problem

```
from tqdm import tqdm

n_episodes = 5000000
epsilon = 0.5
alpha = 0.1
gamma = 0.95

Q = np.zeros((nW, T+1, nA, nC))
for j in range(nW):
        Q[j,T,:,:] = utility(W[j,T])

for i in tqdm(range(n_episodes), desc="Running..."):
    W_idx = 0
    t = 0
    while t<=(T-1):
        W_idx, t, Q = Update_Q(W_idx, t, Q)
```
← **Initializes Q in the final time period to the utility of final wealth**

As you may guess from the objective function, spending is optimized when consumption is smoothed over time. It would not be wise to spend a large amount of wealth early on, giving a high reward now but a low reward in the future. For example, at the second-to-last time period, $t = T - 1$, you want to spend approximately half your wealth, saving the other half for the last time period. Also, if you adjust the parameters of the model, you can see the effects on spending:

- Higher expected returns lead to more spending today because you have higher expected wealth next period for consumption smoothing (for those interested in that relationship, you can explore the Euler equation on the book's website and GitHub: https://www.manning.com/books/build-a-robo-advisor-with-python -from-scratch and https://github.com/robreider/robo-advisor-with-python/blob /main/chapter_06.ipynb

- Higher degrees of risk aversion lead to more savings and less spending today.
- Higher subjective discount rates, which measure the preference for immediate consumption, of course, lead to more spending today.

One of the largest shortcomings of the model described in this section is that the agent knows they have exactly T years to live. For example, because of that highly unrealistic assumption, the agent can safely spend approximately half their wealth at $t = T - 1$, knowing they will have the other half for the last year. In the next section, we will extend the model to include mortality tables, allowing us to solve a richer set of financial planning problems.

6.4   Longevity risk

The uncertainty in life expectancy has an enormous effect on financial planning. Individuals face not only stock market risk but also the risk that they will outlive their assets, which is referred to as *longevity risk*. Despite the importance of longevity risk, most financial planning tools are not equipped to handle it. We mentioned in chapter 1 that a vast majority of Social Security calculators compute the present value of Social Security payments, which is essentially a risk-neutral approach. These calculators suggest claiming Social Security later if the life expectancy of an individual exceeds the break-even age.

Using lifecycle models with utility functions is a significant improvement over these other techniques for handling longevity risk. And only a few lines of code need to be changed to incorporate an uncertain date of death. We won't repeat the code, but it can be found on the book's website and GitHub.

Consider a 62-year-old individual who is deciding whether to claim Social Security right away versus waiting until 70 to take a 76% higher payout. Using the mortality tables from chapter 5, the life expectancy for a 62-year-old is about 84, which is a little above the break-even age, suggesting that it's better to delay claiming Social Security. But it's a close call, and the present value of claiming at 70 is only about $3,000 more than claiming at 62. However, when we take longevity risk into account, it's not such a close call. The utility for claiming at 70 is significantly higher than the utility for claiming at 62. But how can we translate the difference in utility to something meaningful, like dollars? We can use the concept of certainty equivalence that we discussed earlier in the chapter. For the individual who claims at 62, we can incrementally increase their starting wealth from $1 million and stop when utility equals the utility of the person who claims at 70. That number is $35,000 for someone with a coefficient of relative risk aversion of 3. To put that number in perspective, the $35,000 extra for claiming later is more than a year's worth of Social Security payments. Figure 6.7 shows the higher values for claiming Social Security at 70 for three levels of risk aversion. As you would expect, the higher the risk aversion, the greater the value of waiting to claim Social Security.

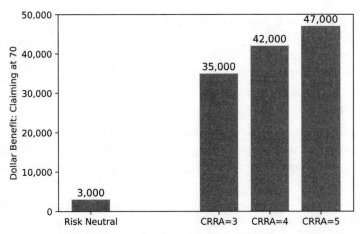

Figure 6.7 **Quantifying the benefit of claiming Social Security at 70 vs. 62**

We make several assumptions in this analysis, and the differential between claiming Social Security at 70 versus 62 will vary, depending on the assumptions. Here are a few of these critical assumptions:

- We use the mortality tables from the Society of Actuaries described in chapter 5. Of course, if life expectancies are shorter than the average life expectancy, the benefit of delaying is reduced.
- We assume a real rate of interest (the difference between the nominal rate of interest and inflation) of 2% (4.5% bond return and 2.5% inflation rate). Because Social Security payments grow with inflation, inflation rate assumptions by themselves will not necessarily affect the claiming decision, but the difference between nominal rates and inflation will. For example, if we assume a real rate lower than 2%, the benefit of delaying is even greater.
- We only consider optimization from the perspective of an individual, not a married couple. For example, if your spouse has a short earnings history, they can receive spousal and survivor benefits based on your work history. Although delaying claiming will not increase the spousal benefit, it will increase the survivor benefit if you die before your spouse, which further increases the benefit of delaying.

The same type of analysis we employed here can be used to answer other financial planning questions. For example, many employees with defined benefit pension plans must choose between taking their payout as a lump sum or as a steady stream of lifetime income. We can use the same lifecycle model to analyze this decision, with some small modifications (for example, pension payments typically don't have inflation adjustments). Another similar financial planning decision individuals face is whether to purchase annuities from an insurance company. Because of provisions in the Secure Act that were passed in 2019, many more 401(k) plans are offering annuities as an option. These annuities reduce longevity risk but often come with high fees. The types of annuities offered may also vary, ranging from annuities that begin paying income immediately to deferred annuities that delay income payments. The lifecycle models we described can be used to analyze the various options and can be customized to an individual's circumstances.

6.5   *Other extensions*

There are numerous ways to make the model even more realistic. We will leave these to you to explore, but we will give a few examples to conclude this chapter. Here are a few things to consider for extending the model (this is not meant to be an exhaustive list):

- We did not include labor income during the accumulation phase of an individual's life cycle. Empirical studies show that spending is highly correlated to labor income, and uncertainty in future labor income leads to more "precautionary savings." Similarly, we did not include medical expenses, which are also uncertain and may be treated separately from other types of consumption: usually, medical expenses are treated as necessary costs, and no utility is derived from them.

- Although taxes are discussed in other chapters, we have not incorporated them into the reinforcement learning model. For example, we have simply assumed that money for spending comes from wealth without considering the tax implications and the optimal sequence of withdrawals, which is discussed in chapter 9.

- We have assumed spending and consumption are the same thing. But economists distinguish spending on nondurable goods, which are immediately consumed, from spending on durable goods. Consider, for example, a house as a durable good. Economists argue that only a small percentage of the value of a house is "consumed" in the form of housing services, which would be the imputed rent on an owner-occupied home or, in other words, the rent paid on an equivalent house. Also, an individual can't increase their housing services by 1% if they get a little wealthier, because upgrading from a smaller house to a larger house involves significant transaction costs and can't be incrementally modified like a stock or bond holding.

- There is extensive literature on alternatives to the utility function we used. For example, prospect theory, developed by behavioral economists Kahneman and Tversky, posits that losses have a greater emotional influence than equivalent gains, leading to an asymmetric utility function around some reference point, such as current wealth or spending.

- We have ignored the bequest motive and assumed that the agent receives no reward for any money passed down to their heirs. It is straightforward to capture the bequest motive by adding an extra reward on death that is a function of the wealth that is passed down. Economists have tried to estimate a constant representing the utility a person derives from passing a dollar to heirs compared to the utility from consuming that dollar.

Summary

- Reinforcement learning, a branch of AI, has been successfully applied to many tasks and can be applied to multiperiod financial planning problems as well.
- Goals-based investing involves strategies for achieving a savings goal, such as saving a certain amount for retirement or for buying a home.
- The traditional approach to finding the optimal asset allocation over multiple periods is to use dynamic programming, working backward from the terminal state.
- The advantage of reinforcement learning over DP is that you don't need to know the probability distribution of transitioning to the next state, and DP suffers from the curse of dimensionality when there are too many states and potential actions.
- The glide path, which is the optimal allocation of stocks over time, can take many shapes depending on the wealth path.
- Using utility functions has not been widely adopted by financial planners but is a useful tool for handling financial planning decisions involving risk.
- Spending and asset allocation can be optimized simultaneously using reinforcement learning.
- The risk of outliving your assets because of uncertainty in life expectancy is referred to as *longevity risk* and generally is not properly captured with existing financial planning tools.
- Reinforcement learning that incorporates mortality tables can be used to answer financial planning questions such as when to claim Social Security, whether to choose a lump-sum pension payout, and whether to buy an annuity.
- When longevity risk is properly accounted for, the benefit of receiving payments for life is much larger than a simple break-even analysis would suggest.
- The models can easily be extended in many directions by including labor income and health expenses, taxes, housing decisions, a bequest motive, and alternate utility functions.

Measuring and evaluating returns

One of the basic functions of an advisor or a robo-advisor is to provide clients with information about their investment performance. This is particularly important if the advisor is offering actively managed investments or investments that significantly deviate from the market portfolio. Even something as seemingly simple as computing returns can be complex. We mentioned a few problems in chapter 5: the difference between arithmetic average and geometric average returns and between simple returns and continuously compounded returns. In this chapter, we focus on two other problems related to returns:

- How to compute returns when there are cash inflows and outflows
- How to measure risk-adjusted returns

7.1 Time-weighted vs. dollar-weighted returns

If there were no cash inflows or outflows, computing returns would be straightforward. You could just take the ending value of the investment divided by the starting value and annualize it based on the holding period. However, with cash inflows and outflows, there are several ways to compute returns that can give completely different answers. It is best shown with an example: see figure 7.1. Here is a quick summary of the life of this investment:

1 An investor opens an account with $10 million.
2 The manager has a good first year, with returns of 20%, so the account grows to $12 million.
3 The investor deposits an additional $10 million at the end of the first year, bringing the account up to $22 million.
4 The manager has a bad second year, with returns of −10%.
5 The account finishes the second year with $19.8 million, which is below the $20 million of inflows.

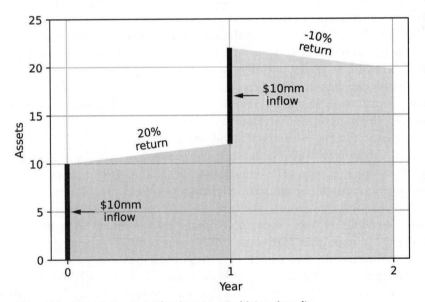

Figure 7.1   A simple example of an investment with two deposits

By one measure of returns, because the manager earns 20% returns followed by −10% returns, their geometric average return over the two years is about 4% (recall from chapter 5 that the geometric average will be lower than the arithmetic average of 5%). This is analogous to the *time-weighted return* measure. Notice, however, that the investor deposited a total of $20 million and ended with $19.8 million, so they lost money. The reason, of course, is that the good returns occurred when the investor had a smaller account, and the bad returns occurred when the investor had a larger account. The *dollar-weighted return* (also called the *money-weighted return*) weighs each period's returns based on the dollar cash flows. Next, we will go through these two alternative methods for computing returns and explain their differences and uses.

7.1.1   *Time-weighted returns*

Time-weighted returns look at the returns of the investments and strip out the effects of cash inflows and outflows. For example, the time-weighted return for the example is

$$r_{TW} = \left[(1 + 0.2)(1 - 0.1) \right]^{(1/2)} - 1 = 3.92\%$$

In general, the time-weighted return is

$$r_{TW} = \left[(1 + r_1)(1 + r_2) \cdots (1 + r_n) \right]^{(1/Y)} - 1$$

where $r_1, r_2, \ldots, r_n$ are the returns over each period, and Y is the number of years over the entire period. This formula looks like the one for geometric average returns, discussed in chapter 5, but with a difference: in chapter 5, the returns were measured over equal periods, like a year. Here, each time interval can be a different length and shorter than a year. For example, each time interval can correspond to a period with a single cash inflow or outflow at the end of the period. A simpler way to compute time-weighted returns, especially with modern computer power, is to compute daily returns regardless of whether there are inflows or outflows.

To compute the return in each period, use the market value just before each cash flow occurs. Dividends and interest are not considered inflows or outflows as long as the cash flows are reinvested. However, if an investor elects to distribute dividends and interest, they are considered withdrawals.

Notice that the time-weighted return does not use any information about the size of cash inflows or outflows. An investment manager might say this is the most appropriate measure of returns if the cash inflows and outflows are beyond the manager's control. In the previous example, an investor may have deposited additional money they inherited after year one, for example, which was not under the manager's control. However, suppose that part of the investment manager's strategy is to time the market. For example, the manager may have viewed the second year as a good time to allocate money to a particular investment, in which case the variation in assets under management should be incorporated into the measure of returns. That calculation is a little more complicated, as we will discuss next.

7.1.2   *Dollar-weighted returns*

The approach to computing dollar-weighted returns is analogous to the internal rate of return (IRR) calculation extensively used in finance to compute the rate of return from a series of cash flows. The single rate of return makes the net present value (NPV) of the discounted cash flows zero. In our simple example in figure 7.1, the

IRR is computed by solving the equation:

$$0 = 10 + \frac{10}{(1+r)} - \frac{19.8}{(1+r)^2}$$

Notice that for the last cash flow, we assume the position is liquidated on the last date (even if it is not), and the sign is opposite that of the cash deposits.

How do we solve for the IRR? In Excel, we can use the solver add-in, and in Python, we can do something similar. The SciPy library has a root-finding function called fsolve that finds the roots of an equation $f(x) = 0$. In our case, the x is the IRR we are trying to solve for. Listing 7.1 shows how we use this library. We first need to define the function f(x), which defines the cash flows and timing. In the listing, the function is based on the cash flows in the example at the beginning of the chapter. After that, a single line of code solves for the IRR. The first argument to the root-finding function fsolve is the function f(x). The only other argument we need is a starting value for the IRR to start the search. We set the starting value to 0%. When we run the code, we get a root of −0.66%, which is the IRR, or dollar-weighted return we are looking for. As we expected, the dollar-weighted rate of return is lower than the time-weighted rate because the negative returns occurred in the second year when the assets under management were larger.

Listing 7.1 Solving for a dollar-weighted return

```
from scipy.optimize import fsolve

def f(x):
    return 10+10/(1+x)-19.8/(1+x)**2
root = fsolve(f, 0)
print('The Dollar-Weighted Return is ', root.item())
```
The item() method is used to convert a numpy array of a single element to a scalar.

```
> The Dollar-Weighted Return is  -0.0066
```

The function f(x) was written specifically for the cash flows in our example. In listing 7.2, we make the function f(x) more general by passing in a list of arbitrary cash flows and a list of their corresponding dates. In this example, the dates are represented as strings with the YYYY-mm-dd format, and we use the strptime() method to convert the strings to a datetime object so they can be manipulated. We send these two new arguments to the function f using *args. Notice that because our more general function f(x, *args) requires extra parameters, the fsolve function has to be slightly modified by adding the optional argument args.

Listing 7.2 General solution for the dollar-weighted return

```
from datetime import datetime

cashflows = [10, 10, -19.8]
dates = ['2020-01-01', '2021-01-01', '2022-01-01']
```

```
dates = [datetime.strptime(dt, '%Y-%m-%d') for dt in dates]
```
Converts strings to
datetime objects

```
def f(x, *args):
    cashflows, dates = args
    sumPVs = 0
    for i in range(len(cashflows)):
        Y = (dates[i] - dates[0]).days/365
        sumPVs += cashflows[i]/(1+x)**Y
    return sumPVs
root = fsolve(f, 0, args=(cashflows, dates))
print('The Dollar-Weighted Return is ', root.item())
```

Converts days from inception into
years (note that we are ignoring
leap years for simplicity here)

The optional args argument
allows us to pass the cash
flows and dates to the
function f(x).

A word of caution is in order. It is theoretically possible to have more than one solution, or rate, that solves the problem. This is a well-known feature of IRR calculations. In some cases, for example, when you have only positive cash flows (deposits) or an initial positive cash flow is followed only by withdrawals, there is only one solution or root. But when you have more than one root, different starting values may lead to different solutions.

Once we measure returns, the next step is to evaluate whether the returns represent superior or inferior performance. But as we will demonstrate in the next section, it is overly simple to look at returns alone when evaluating investment performance.

7.2 Risk-adjusted returns

It is tempting to compare investments by simply comparing their returns. However, returns do not take risk into account. For example, returns can be magnified by employing leverage. For that reason, risk-adjusted returns are usually used. There are two main measures of risk-adjusted returns, Sharpe ratio and alpha, which we will describe next.

7.2.1 Sharpe ratio

Recall that in chapter 2, we defined the capital allocation line (CAL), which we reproduce in figure 7.2. Theoretically, the CAL represents the optimal achievable portfolios in terms of expected return and volatility. An important takeaway from figure 7.2 is that any point along the line can theoretically be achieved. So simply saying an 18% return is good or a 5% return is bad ignores the risk. In the figure, we show that the 18% return (point B) is below the CAL because the volatility is very high, and the 5% return with a very small volatility (point A) is above the CAL. Theoretically, if you wanted an 18% return, rather than choosing investment B, you could choose investment A and leverage it 4:1, achieving a higher return with a lower volatility.

The slope of the CAL is crucial for evaluating investments, and that slope is referred to as the *Sharpe ratio*. The formula for the slope is simply the vertical distance between any two points on the line divided by the horizontal distance, $\frac{\Delta y}{\Delta x}$, as in figure 7.2, which in our case is

$$SR = \frac{\mu - r_f}{\sigma}$$

Therefore, the Sharpe ratio is a measure of expected reward per unit of risk.

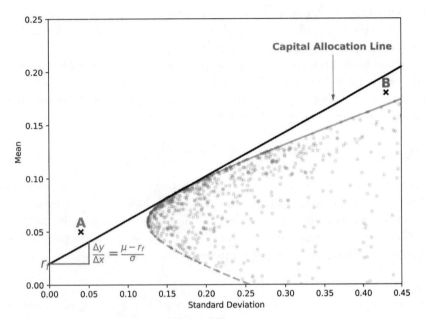

Figure 7.2   Investments above and below CAL

The Sharpe ratio offers several nice features as a measure of risk-adjusted returns:

- *Invariant to leverage*—Two investments that are identical in every way except the leverage employed have the same Sharpe ratio. Let's demonstrate this with a simple example. Suppose a client makes a $1 million investment with an expected return of 20% and a volatility of 15%, and suppose the risk-free rate is 5%. The Sharpe ratio of this investment is $(20\% - 5\%)/15\% = 1.0$. Now, suppose the client also borrows $1 million to double the investment size, thereby leveraging their investment by a factor of two. Also assume that the client can borrow the $1 million at the risk-free rate. Their expected return doubles to 40%, less the 5% the investor owes on the loan, and the volatility doubles to 30% as well, so the Sharpe ratio is $(40\% - 5\% - 5\%)/30\% = 1.0$. It remains unchanged.
- *Intuitive scale*—We have a good sense of what should be considered good and bad Sharpe ratios. For example, US stocks over the last century have had an average return, above the risk-free rate, of about 8% and an annual standard deviation of about 20%. Therefore, the US stock market has a Sharpe ratio of $SR = 0.08/0.20 = 0.4$. If a portfolio manager has a Sharpe ratio of, say, 0.3, it

raises the question "Why not just put your money in an index fund?" On the other hand, if someone claims they have achieved a Sharpe ratio of 2.0, which means their expected returns are two standard deviations above the risk-free rate, they expect to have a down year less than once every 40 years. This assumes that returns have a normal distribution; if returns have fat tails, losses may occur more frequently than that, but you get the point.

Notice that the Sharpe ratio does not take into account the length of the portfolio manager's track record. It is certainly more impressive to have achieved a Sharpe ratio of 2.0 over a 10-year period than a 1-year period.

A risk-adjusted return measure that is closely related to the Sharpe ratio is the information ratio (IR). It is defined as the expected return in excess of a benchmark (rather than the risk-free rate) relative to the tracking error of the portfolio, which is the volatility of returns around the benchmark:

$$IR = \frac{E[r - r_B]}{\sigma(r - r_B)}$$

The IR may be an appropriate measure of performance for an investment manager whose performance is compared to a benchmark. Incidentally, if a manager hedges by shorting the benchmark, the IR is equivalent to the Sharpe ratio.

There are numerous other measures of risk-adjusted returns in addition to the Sharpe ratio. However, the main alternative measure is alpha, which we discuss next.

7.2.2   Alpha

The term *alpha* is thrown around all over the place in the investment world. A search of registered SEC funds and advisors finds that more than 300 funds have the word *alpha* in their name, including funds with names like Alpha Smart, Alpha Architect, Alphadyne, and Alpha Simplex. There is even a fund named Double Alpha, which sounds twice as good. And the use of *alpha* is not confined to funds. When Google announced its name change to Alphabet, Larry Page explained the name change in a press release: "We liked the name Alphabet because it means a collection of letters that represent the language … We also like that it means alpha-bet (Alpha is investment return above benchmark), which we strive for!" So what is this seemingly ubiquitous alpha?

Suppose we plot an investment's returns, in excess of the risk-free rate, on the market's returns, also in excess of the risk-free rate. We might get a scatter plot that looks like figure 7.3. In this figure, the investment returns are highly correlated to the market because the points on the scatter plot are clustered close to a straight line. The beta of the investment is the slope of the line that best fits the data, and the alpha is the intercept of that line. The alpha represents the difference between the average return on the investment and the average return on the benchmark. A positive alpha suggests superior performance. Mathematically, the alpha comes from the following linear regression:

$$r - r_f = \alpha + \beta\,(r_m - r_f) + \epsilon$$

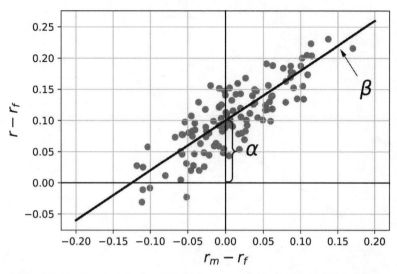

Figure 7.3 Scatter plot of returns of an investment against returns on the market

The model we just described assumes that the expected return on a stock in excess of the risk-free rate consists of two components: the alpha and a risk premium, which is the product of the risk premium offered by the market and the stock's beta to the market. This type of model is a single-factor model. There has been a search for additional factors other than the market exposure that could explain expected stock returns. Some are macroeconomic factors, and others are based on the characteristics of a firm. The most common of these multifactor models is the three-factor Fama–French model, but there are many others. On the book's website and GitHub (https://www.manning.com/books/build-a-robo-advisor-with-python-from-scratch and https://github.com/robreider/robo-advisor-with-python/blob/main/chapter_07.ipynb), we provide an example in Python of computing alpha for a multifactor model, including the code for downloading the factor return data used in the calculation. We will put some of these ideas into practice in the next section by evaluating the risk-adjusted performance of an actively managed ETF.

7.2.3 Evaluating an ESG fund's performance

As we discussed in chapter 4, environmental, social, and governance (ESG) investing has grown rapidly in popularity over the last few years: in 2021 alone, over $600 billion was poured into these funds. There is an ongoing debate about whether ESG funds outperform the market. Although proponents have argued that stocks with high ESG scores should have superior returns, there are many opposing arguments as well, so it becomes an empirical question of whether ESG stocks outperform the market. In this example, we will look at one of the largest ESG funds, which has a very long track record: the iShares MSCI USA ESG ETF (ticker symbol SUSA). This fund has been around since 2005 and currently manages about $3 billion in assets. In figure 7.4, we show a scatter plot of the returns of the fund against the returns of the market, both in excess of the risk-free rate; it looks similar to figure 7.3 but with real data.

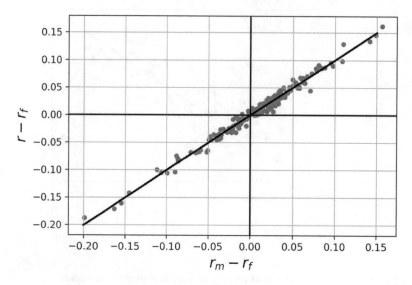

Figure 7.4   Scatter plot of returns of the SUSA ESG ETF against returns on the market

In listing 7.3, we compute the alpha of the fund. We start by downloading historical data for the ETF as well as data for 1-month T-Bills and the S&P 500, as we did in chapter 3. We resample the daily data to monthly and then compute monthly returns. Finally, we run a linear regression to estimate the fund's alpha. Note that we need to add a column of 1s to the right-hand side of the regression using the command `sm.add_constant()`. The regression coefficient on the column of 1s represents the constant or intercept of the regression, which is the alpha we are trying to compute. The output of the regression is shown in figure 7.5.

Listing 7.3   Regressing the SUSA ESG ETF returns on the market to find alpha

```
import pandas_datareader as pdr
import yfinance as yf
import statsmodels.api as sm

start='2005-02-01'
end = '2022-09-30'
rf_daily = pdr.DataReader('DGS1MO', 'fred', start=start, end=end)
ESG_prices = yf.download('SUSA', start=start, end=end)['Adj Close']
mkt_prices = yf.download('SPY', start=start, end=end)['Adj Close']
rf_monthly = rf_daily.resample('MS').first()
ESG_prices_monthly = ESG_prices.resample('MS').first()
mkt_prices_monthly = mkt_prices.resample('MS').first()
ESG_returns_monthly = ESG_prices_monthly.pct_change()
mkt_returns_monthly = mkt_prices_monthly.pct_change()
y = (ESG_returns_monthly - rf_monthly['DGS1MO']/100/12).dropna()
X = (mkt_returns_monthly - rf_monthly['DGS1MO']/100/12).dropna()
X = sm.add_constant(X)   ◄─── A column of 1s must be added to the
                              right-hand side of the regression
                              for the constant term.
```

```
model = sm.OLS(y,X)
results = model.fit()
print(results.summary())
```

OLS Regression Results

Dep. Variable:	y	R-squared:	0.981
Model:	OLS	Adj. R-squared:	0.981
Method:	Least Squares	F-statistic:	1.088e+04
Date:	Fri, 14 Oct 2022	Prob (F-statistic):	3.27e-182
Time:	01:04:09	Log-Likelihood:	751.46
No. Observations:	211	AIC:	-1499.
Df Residuals:	209	BIC:	-1492.
Df Model:	1		
Covariance Type:	nonrobust		

	coef	std err	t	P>|t|	[0.025	0.975]
const	-0.0004	0.000	-0.762	0.447	-0.001	0.001
0	1.0023	0.010	104.301	0.000	0.983	1.021

Omnibus:	4.723	Durbin-Watson:	1.975
Prob(Omnibus):	0.094	Jarque-Bera (JB):	4.506
Skew:	-0.270	Prob(JB):	0.105
Kurtosis:	3.471	Cond. No.	20.2

Figure 7.5 **Regression results from regressing SUSA ESG ETF returns on the market**

This fund has a high correlation to the S&P 500. The R-squared is 0.981, so the correlation (the square root of R-squared) is 0.99. The beta for the fund is 1.0023, which is very close to 1. And the alpha is slightly negative, −4 bp/month.

Because this fund is highly correlated to the S&P 500, let's compute the IR of the fund where we use the S&P 500 as the benchmark. The single line of code is

```
IR = (y-X[0]).mean()/(y-X[0]).std()*sqrt(12)
```

and the IR is −0.176. Note that we have to annualize the monthly IR by multiplying by $\sqrt{12}$: the monthly returns in the numerator are annualized by multiplying by 12, and the monthly volatility in the denominator is annualized by multiplying by the square root of 12, which is the same as multiplying the monthly IR by $\sqrt{12}$.

> **NOTE** A caveat to keep in mind when evaluating an investment based on its historical performance is a potential survivorship bias. The ESG fund we evaluated is a successful one. Perhaps it has gathered assets and has a long track record because it has been successful, and other ESG funds that were less successful were either shut down or merged with successful ones. By choosing this fund to analyze and not some other fund that has failed and no longer exists, we are potentially introducing a form of survivorship bias that favors ESG funds.

7.2.4   *Which is better, alpha or Sharpe ratio?*

We have presented two common methods of computing risk-adjusted returns. How are they related, and when should one be used over the other? Notice that the only risk alpha takes into account is the market risk. In figure 7.6, we show scatter plots of two hypothetical funds. The fund on the right has higher idiosyncratic or unique risk, which is the portion of risk that is not related to market moves and can be diversified away. Both have the same beta and, more importantly, the same alpha. Therefore, alpha ignores all idiosyncratic risk, whereas the Sharpe ratio includes the total risk (market risk and idiosyncratic risk) of the portfolio in the denominator of the formula. Accordingly, if the fund being evaluated is one of many assets in a portfolio and therefore the idiosyncratic risk can be diversified away, alpha may be the more appropriate measure of risk-adjusted returns. However, if this fund represents the investor's entire portfolio, the Sharpe ratio may be the more appropriate measure.

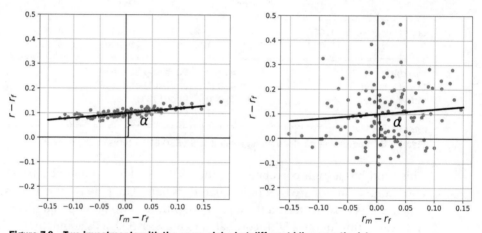

Figure 7.6   Two investments with the same alpha but different idiosyncratic risk

Summary

- Time-weighted and dollar-weighted are two different methods for computing returns when there are inflows and outflows, and these approaches can give contradictory results.
- Time-weighted returns strip out the effects of deposits and withdrawals and are a better measure of pure manager performance.
- Dollar-weighted returns weight returns each period by the dollars being managed and are a better measure of performance if the manager is attempting to time the market.
- Evaluating performance based only on returns and not factoring in risk can lead to erroneous conclusions.
- The Sharpe ratio, a widely used measure of risk-adjusted performance, is derived from the slope of the capital allocation line.

- The Sharpe ratio is the expected return on an investment in excess of the risk-free rate relative to the volatility of the investment.
- The information ratio is similar to the Sharpe ratio, but returns and volatility are measured relative to a benchmark.
- Alpha is the excess return after factoring in exposure to the market.
- Alpha incorporates market risk but ignores non-market risk, whereas the Sharpe ratio includes market risk and non-market risk.
- Alpha is a more appropriate measure of risk-adjusted returns when the investment represents only a portion of the client's assets, and the Sharpe ratio is a more appropriate measure when the investment represents the client's entire portfolio.

Asset location

This chapter covers

- Understanding asset location
- Creating Python classes to help analyze asset location strategies
- Computing the numerical tax efficiency of different types of assets
- Quantifying the benefits of tax location
- Performing an optimization to solve a three-account problem

In chapter 2, we introduced the topic of asset allocation—the optimal weighting of assets in a portfolio. But investors hold different types of accounts, ranging from taxable brokerage accounts to tax-deferred IRAs and 401(k)s to tax-exempt Roth IRAs, and we never discussed how investors should distribute their assets among these different types of accounts. This is called *asset location*. Table 8.1 lists the three main types of accounts and compares their characteristics.

Table 8.1 Comparison of taxable, tax-deferred, and tax-exempt accounts

	Taxable	Tax-deferred	Tax-exempt
Example	Brokerage	IRA, 401(k)	Roth IRA, Roth 401(k), 529, Health Savings Account
Taxation of dividends	Taxed at either ordinary-income rate or capital gains rate, depending on whether dividends are "qualified"	Taxed as ordinary income when funds are distributed	Not taxed
Taxation of capital gains	Taxed at capital gains rate when gains are realized	Taxed as ordinary income when funds are distributed	Not taxed

Whereas asset allocation involves tradeoffs between risk and return, asset location is close to a free lunch. For a given asset allocation, by choosing which types of assets are placed in taxable and tax-preferred accounts, you can increase your expected after-tax returns without taking on any additional risk. We will quantify the benefits of asset location and optimize which investments should be placed in which types of accounts. As with most of the chapters in this book, we will start with an example and build from there.

8.1 A simple example

Consider the following example to illustrate the benefits of asset location. Suppose an investor has $1 million in assets, made up of $500,000 in an IRA and $500,000 in a brokerage account. Also assume that the investor wants a 50-50 allocation between stocks and bonds. The investor could maintain a 50-50 allocation in each account. But a better strategy would be to put all the bonds ($500,000) in the IRA and all the stocks ($500,000) in the taxable account, for the following reasons:

- Capital gains on stocks are tax-deferred if the gains are not realized. In other words, IRAs allow investors to defer capital gains, but if stocks are not sold from year to year, they are already tax-deferred.
- Stocks in a taxable account are taxed at a lower capital gains rate, whereas stocks in an IRA are taxed at a higher ordinary-income tax rate when the IRA is distributed.

- Interest rates on bonds are typically higher than dividend yields on stocks, and interest is usually taxed at a higher rate than dividends. Hence, the tax-deferral feature of IRAs often helps bonds more than stocks.

Let's quantify the advantage of putting stocks in the taxable account and bonds in the IRA, compared to doing the reverse. For this simple example, we could do this calculation in Excel, and doing it in Python may seem like overkill. But you'll see that the flexibility will help us later when we add more types of investments with different characteristics.

The easiest way to do this calculation in Python is to define a class. If you're not familiar with classes, remember that Python is an object-oriented programming language, and almost everything in Python is an object. An object has attributes and contains functions that belong to those objects, which are called methods. When we create our own objects, we have to define the attributes and methods. A classic example is to define a class called `Car()` with attributes like miles per gallon (mpg) and the capacity of the gas tank in gallons. You can then define a method that multiplies the mpg by its capacity to calculate a range for a tank of gas. Once the class is defined, you can create instances of the class, like a Toyota Camry that gets 30 mpg and has a 16-gallon tank.

In our case, the objects will be different types of assets, like stocks and bonds, and each asset will have a set of attributes like expected returns, capital gains tax rates, dividend/interest rates, tax rates on the dividends/interest, cost basis, etc. If we want to add another asset, say, foreign stocks or real estate investment trusts (REITs), we only need to create a new object with different attributes. We will also define a method for projecting after-tax values for an IRA and another method for projecting after-tax values for a brokerage account.

Listing 8.1 shows how we define an `Asset()` class in Python. The class has eight attributes:

- `avg_ret`—The annual average return, including the payout. We use the geometric average because we are using a straight-line projection, as we discussed in chapter 5.
- `payout_rate`—The annual percent dividend yield for stocks or interest rate for bonds.
- `tax_rate_payout`—The tax rate on dividends or interest.
- `tax_rate_cap_gains`—The tax rate on capital gains.
- `tax_rate_ord_inc`—The tax rate on ordinary income.
- `percent_turnover`—The percent of the portfolio that is sold each year. For simplicity, we assume it is reinvested in the same asset, and for tax purposes, we use the average cost method.
- `starting_value`—The starting value of the assets.
- `cost_basis`—The initial cost basis of the assets.

Listing 8.1   Defining the `Asset()` class

```
class Asset():
    def __init__(self, avg_ret=0.08, payout_rate=0.0, tax_rate_payout=0.2,
                 tax_rate_cap_gains=0.2, tax_rate_ord_inc=0.35,
                 turnover_rate=0, starting_value=500000, cost_basis=500000):
        self.avg_ret = avg_ret
        self.payout_rate = payout_rate
        self.tax_rate_payout = tax_rate_payout
        self.tax_rate_cap_gains = tax_rate_cap_gains
        self.tax_rate_ord_inc = tax_rate_ord_inc
        self.turnover_rate = turnover_rate
        self.starting_value = starting_value
        self.cost_basis = cost_basis
    def IRA_value(self, horizon=30):
        pretax_value = self.starting_value * (1+self.avg_ret)**horizon
        aftertax_value = pretax_value * (1-self.tax_rate_ord_inc)
        return aftertax_value
    def Taxable_value(self, horizon=30):
        curr_cost_basis = self.cost_basis
        curr_value = self.starting_value
        for year in range(1, horizon+1):
            taxes_div = self.payout_rate * curr_value * self.tax_rate_payout
            taxes_cap_gain = (self.turnover_rate * curr_value
                              * self.tax_rate_cap_gains)
            curr_cost_basis += ((self.payout_rate * curr_value)
                                + (self.turnover_rate * curr_value)
                                - (taxes_div + taxes_cap_gain))
            curr_value = (curr_value * (1+self.avg_ret)
                          - (taxes_div + taxes_cap_gain))
        aftertax_value = (curr_value
                          - (curr_value - curr_cost_basis)
                          * self.tax_rate_cap_gains)
        return aftertax_value
    def Taxable_minus_IRA(self, horizon=30):
        difference = (self.Taxable_value(horizon) - self.IRA_value(horizon)
                      - self.starting_value * self.tax_rate_ord_inc)
        return difference



    def Roth_value(self, horizon=30):
        aftertax_value = self.starting_value * (1+self.avg_ret)**horizon
        return aftertax_value
```

This method is called automatically when a new object is created to initialize the object's attributes.

For the taxable account, keeps track of the increase in the cost basis every year

The initial tax liability of the IRA is taken out to normalize the difference: an asset with zero returns will have zero difference between a taxable account and an IRA.

The `__init__()` method is called automatically when an object is created to initialize the object's attributes. For each attribute, we have default values that can be changed when an object is created. Let's create an object, or instance, of the `Asset()` class for a stock:

```
stock = Asset()
```

To simplify things, we assume the stock pays no dividend, the geometric average return is 8%, and the capital gains tax rate is 20%. Because these are the default values, we do not have to pass them as arguments when constructing an instance of the class.

We can do the same thing for a bond. Again, to simplify things, we assume the average return is 3%, which is all paid out as interest and taxed as ordinary income. To create the bond object, we pass the new parameters:

```
bond = Asset(avg_ret=0.03, payout_rate=0.03, tax_rate_payout=0.35)
```

In addition to the initialization method in listing 8.1, there are four other methods. We will discuss the first two now and the other two in the next two sections. The method `IRA_Value()` computes the after-tax value of an asset over a given time horizon if the asset is placed in an IRA. The method `Taxable_Value()` computes the after-tax value of an asset that is placed in a taxable account. Therefore, for a 30-year investment horizon, the after-tax value of a stock in a brokerage grows to

```
stock.Taxable_value()
> 4125063
```

and the after-tax value of a bond in an IRA grows to

```
bond.IRA_value()
> 788860
```

These results are shown in the first row of table 8.2 as the "good strategy." We can compute the after-tax value for the "bad strategy" of placing stocks in the IRA and bonds in the taxable account using the same methods, as shown in the second row of table 8.2. Placing stocks in the brokerage account and bonds in the taxable account results in an additional $751,104 of after-tax value. That's equivalent to an additional after-tax return of 0.55%/year. A "middle strategy" of a 50-50 allocation in each account falls exactly in the middle of the "good" and "bad" strategies.

Table 8.2   Example of value-added from asset location

	Value of stocks	Value of bonds	Total value
Good strategy: Stocks in taxable, bonds in IRA	4,125,063	788,860	4,913,923
Bad strategy: Stocks in IRA, bonds in taxable	3,270,363	892,456	4,162,819
Difference	854,700	−103,596	751,104

8.2 *The tax efficiency of various assets*

We used an extreme example to illustrate the benefits of asset location. But there are many different types of assets, and the taxation features of these assets usually mitigate, but could also increase, the benefits of asset location:

- *Turnover*—In the example, we assume stocks are held for 30 years with no turnover, so all capital gains are deferred. The earlier capital gains are realized, the less tax-efficient the asset is. There are several reasons capital gains may be realized early. For example, individual investors or an actively managed fund may sell winners and reinvest the proceeds. Corporate mergers could also lead to realized gains.

- *Dividends and interest*—In the example, we assume stocks pay no dividends. Incorporating dividends reduces the tax efficiency of stocks because some of the gains cannot be deferred. Dividends and interest have the same effect as turnover.

- *Tax treatment of dividends and interest*—Dividends on domestic companies, as well as some foreign companies, are classified as *qualified dividends* and are subject to the lower capital gains tax rates if holding period requirements are met. However, distributions from REITs and master limited partnerships (MLPs) are nonqualified dividends. These entities pass through their income to investors and often have higher yields. The dividends from a foreign company are considered qualified only if the company is readily tradable on a US stock market (for example, an American depository receipt [ADR]) or is located in a country that has a tax treaty with the United States.

- *Expected rate of return*—The expected rate of return of an asset also plays an important role in its tax efficiency. As an extreme example, consider a money market investment that pays close to zero interest, which was the case for many years until relatively recently. In that case, there are no gains and no dividends, so there is no advantage to placing it in an IRA or a taxable account. In contrast, for an asset with very high expected returns, the benefits of holding it in a particular type of account are magnified.

Some of these effects can have contradictory implications for asset location. Rather than qualitatively ranking different assets, we can quantitatively rank them using the functions we have developed in this chapter. As an example, consider the assets listed in table 8.3. We assume some typical attributes for these assets in terms of expected returns, payout rates, and tax treatment. Furthermore, we assume the investor is in the 20% capital gains tax bracket and the 35% ordinary income tax bracket. Note that we ignore state tax—for example, government bonds are free of state tax—but state taxes could be incorporated into the tax rate attributes of the various assets.

For each asset, we will compare its after-tax value in a taxable account relative to its after-tax value in an IRA to assess its tax efficiency, as shown in figure 8.1 (see the book's website at https://www.manning.com/books/build-a-robo-advisor-with-python-from-scratch or GitHub at https://github.com/robreider/robo-advisor-with-python/blob/main/chapter_08.ipynb for the code that generates the figure). The assets farthest to the right are inherently the most tax-efficient, and the assets farthest to the left are the most tax-inefficient. Note that the tax efficiency of various assets in figure 8.1 is investor-specific because different investors may be in different tax brackets.

Table 8.3 Typical attributes of various assets

Type of asset	Average return	Payout rate	Tax rate payout	Turnover rate
Large-cap stocks	8%	1.5%	0.2	0
High-growth stocks	9.5%	1.5%	0.2	0
International stocks	8%	1.5%	0.25	0
REITs	8%	4.5%	0.35	0
Money market fund	3%	3%	0.35	0
Government bonds	4%	4%	0.35	0
High-yield bonds	7.5%	5.5%	0.35	0
Municipal bonds	2.5%	2%	0	0
Large-cap, high-turnover stocks	8%	1.5%	0.2	0.2
High-growth, high-turnover stocks	9.5%	1.5%	0.2	0.2

Let's start with large-cap stocks, which are relatively tax-efficient, even with a 1.5% dividend yield, for the reasons we gave at the beginning of the chapter. International stocks in our example have the same attributes as large-cap stocks, except we assume that a third of the dividends are nonqualified, so they are taxed at ordinary income rates of 35% rather than 20%; therefore, international stocks fall a little to the left of US stocks in terms of tax efficiency. Our high-growth stock fund is assumed to be identical to the large-cap stocks but with 1.5% higher average returns (we realize that high-growth stocks typically have lower dividend yields, but we wanted to isolate the effects of expected returns), and even with that modest increase in expected returns, the tax efficiency is significantly higher. Municipal bonds, offering interest that is exempt from federal taxes, are more tax-efficient in a taxable account than an IRA. And the money market asset, which has a low rate of interest, is close to neutral in terms of tax efficiency. In fact, if money market interest rates were zero, as they were relatively recently, the asset would be completely neutral in terms of tax efficiency. Also noteworthy is that when we add a 20% turnover to the large-cap stock fund, it becomes tax-inefficient; and when we add a 20% turnover to the high-growth stock fund, it goes from the most tax-efficient asset to the most tax-inefficient asset.

Once the tax efficiency of the various assets is established, the optimal way to place assets into the taxable and IRA accounts becomes straightforward: either work from the far left toward the middle and place those assets in the IRA account until it is filled or, equivalently, start from the far right and place those assets in the taxable account until it is filled.

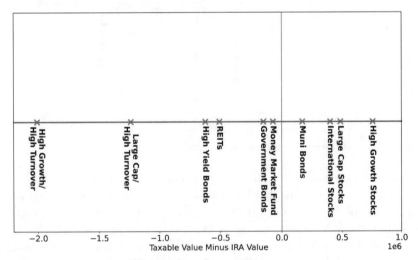

Figure 8.1   Range of tax efficiency for various assets

8.3   *Adding a Roth account*

So far, we have been comparing taxable and IRA accounts. Table 8.1 shows that investors may hold a third type of account: tax-exempt accounts like Roth IRAs and Roth 401(k)s, which differ from IRAs because an investor does not pay taxes even when the funds are distributed. The last method in listing 8.1 computes the after-tax value of a Roth, which is very simple because these accounts are not taxed at all. The accounts are compounded at the geometric average return, which is only one line of code. Now we are ready to go through an example that includes Roth accounts in addition to taxable and IRA accounts.

8.3.1   *A simple example with three types of accounts*

Is there an easy way to locate assets among three different account types, and can we still use the information from figure 8.1 for the tax efficiency of various assets? To gain some intuition, suppose an investor with $1.5 million in assets has three types of accounts: an IRA, a taxable account, and a Roth. For simplicity, assume that the investor has an equal amount of $500,000 in each type of account. Further, suppose the investor desires three asset types, each with a $500,000 allocation: a large-cap stock fund, a high-yield bond fund, and, say, a high-growth stock fund with a small, 4% turnover rate (the reason we add this third asset will become apparent soon). Figure 8.2 shows the tax efficiency of these three assets. The exercise is to match each of the three types of accounts with each of the three types of assets.

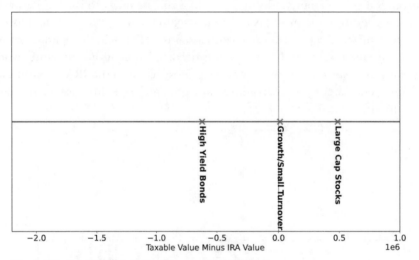

Figure 8.2   Tax efficiency in the three-asset example

You might argue that because Roth accounts are even more tax-favorable than IRAs, we should place the high-yield bond fund, which is farthest to the left on the tax-efficiency scale, in the Roth. Another argument is to place the large-cap stocks in the Roth because investors like to avoid capital gains taxes, and the stock fund, with higher returns than bonds, faces a larger future tax liability even at the lower capital gains tax rate. It turns out that in this case, the growth stocks with some turnover, in the middle of the tax-efficiency range, should be placed in the Roth. The high-growth stock fund is squarely in the center because, on the one hand, it has higher returns and low capital gains tax rates, but it is also tax-inefficient because there is some turnover. These two effects cancel out in terms of tax efficiency, but the greatest tax savings can be realized by placing the high-growth fund in the Roth (see the book's code for the details).

How do we know this is optimal? In this simple example, there are only six permutations of placing three assets in three accounts, and we can try each one. But we need a different approach when we have several assets, as we explore next.

8.3.2 An example with optimization

In general, we can't manually try every possible placement of assets into each possible account. We have to use some type of optimization, and fortunately, Python is very useful for performing these kinds of tasks.

The types of optimization we need to do have been solved in other contexts and are called *general assignment problems*, a branch of combinatorial optimization. In these problems, which have numerous applications, n agents have to perform m tasks; each agent has a profit associated with each task, and the goal is to assign each agent to a set of tasks to maximize profit. In our case, the "agents" are the three types of accounts, and the "tasks" are the potential investments placed in each account. The size of the three accounts is a budget constraint in the problem, and the profits are the after-tax value of each investment in each potential account, which we can compute using the functions we developed in this chapter. The details and coding of the optimization solution are a bit long, so we have relegated the details to the book's website and GitHub. Here is a worked example of asset location with three types of accounts and five types of investments. Table 8.4 shows an example of three accounts that hold $1 million and an asset allocation among five types of assets. The goal is to place the assets optimally in the best accounts.

Table 8.4 An example with three types of accounts and five types of assets

Account type	Assets		Asset type	Assets
IRA	$300,000		High-yield bonds	$200,000
Roth	$200,000		Government bonds	$100,000
Taxable	$500,000		REITs	$200,000
			Money market	$100,000
			High-growth stocks	$400,000

Even though we saw in the last section that the range of tax efficiencies cannot be relied on when placing assets in three accounts, it still offers some intuition about the optimal solution. The tax efficiency for the five assets is shown in figure 8.3.

The main input to the optimization, in addition to the budget constraints on the account sizes and the size of the assets, is a three-by-five matrix that shows the after-tax value for each of the three accounts and each of the five assets, using the functions described earlier in the chapter. That matrix looks like this:

```
value_matrix = array([[2845360,  788860, 3270363,  788860, 4946601],
                       [4377477, 1213631, 5031328, 1213631, 7610156],
                       [2398898,  892456, 2939715,  892456, 5876907]])
```

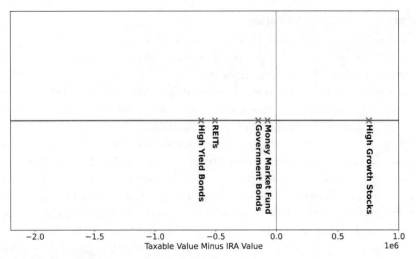

Figure 8.3   Tax efficiency among five assets

The optimization then gives the asset locations shown in figure 8.4.

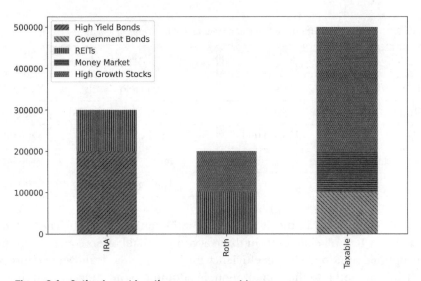

Figure 8.4   Optimal asset location across account types

Often, a good rule of thumb for placing assets among the three types of accounts is to fill the Roth with the assets that have the highest tax bill and then, once the Roth is out of the way, fill the IRA and taxable account based on the tax efficiency of the remaining assets in figure 8.3. In this example, this would mean the $200,000 Roth would contain high-growth stocks, but then the taxable account would be forced to hold some very tax-inefficient REITs. The optimizer instead has the Roth holding $100,000 of high-growth stocks and $100,000 of REITs so the taxable account can hold more tax-efficient assets. This example is designed to illustrate that the optimal asset location can't be performed in isolation, and each location depends on the alternatives for the other assets.

8.4 Additional considerations

Simplifying assumptions are always made when mathematically modeling complex systems, and this chapter is no exception. Here is a list of some other considerations when thinking about asset location:

- *Effect of asset location on asset allocation*—So far, we have assumed that the asset location decision is completely separate from the asset allocation decision, but that is not entirely true. To go back to our first example at the beginning of the chapter, an investor who wants a 50-50 asset allocation between stocks and bonds and places their bonds in an IRA and their stocks in a taxable account is really tilted more toward stocks. An investor in a 35% tax bracket, the argument goes, owns only $500,000 \times 0.65 = \$325,000$ of bonds in the IRA and $500,000 of stocks in the taxable account. A common analogy is that an IRA holder is in a partnership with the government, where the government owns 35% of the partnership. But we think this understanding is overly simple. It is true that in an IRA, the government is a partner with an ownership stake. And for a Roth account, the government is not a partner at all. But for a taxable account, the government takes part of the profits as well and therefore has "partnership" interest. To deal with this, some authors have tried to incorporate asset location into the asset allocation process.

- *Stepped-up cost basis on death*—We assume that investors in the taxable account will pay capital gains taxes at the end of the investment horizon. However, if we incorporate the stepped-up cost basis on death, which requires just a minor change to the method that computes the after-tax value of a taxable account, the optimal asset location will favor putting high-return stocks in the taxable account, even for a moderate turnover that would have favored putting stocks in an IRA.

- *Liquidity considerations*—An investor may need to keep some money in a checking or money market account as a cash reserve to meet unexpected needs like a medical bill or loss of a job. This should probably be placed in a taxable account, which can be preassigned in the optimization.

- *Tax-loss-harvesting opportunities*—Some authors have argued that placing higher-volatility assets like stocks in a taxable account provides more opportunities for tax-loss harvesting (we discuss tax-loss harvesting in chapter 14). However, over the longer investment horizons we are considering here, it is unlikely that higher-return stocks will offer many tax-loss-harvesting opportunities beyond the first few years, so this is a minor consideration.

- *HSAs and 529 accounts*—Health savings accounts and 529 plans also fall into this tax-exempt category, although they should probably be handled differently. A 529 account, for example, cannot be held indefinitely but must be used to pay for education expenses.
- *Non-deductible IRAs*—Even though there are three main types of accounts, there exist other, less-common types of accounts, like nondeductible IRAs, where contributions are not tax-deductible but gains are tax-deferred. Nonqualified annuities fall into this category as well. The optimization routine we use is flexible and can handle more than three types of accounts. However, for nondeductible IRAs, the IRA function can be modified slightly to handle nondeductible IRAs by using the cost basis attribute. Nondeductible IRAs can be treated as IRAs but with a cost basis of $500,000, whereas traditional IRAs essentially have a cost basis of zero.
- *Yield splitting*—There may be advantages to decomposing a stock fund into dividend-paying and non-dividend-paying stocks so the more tax-efficient non-dividend-paying stocks can be placed in the taxable account. It is easy to separate dividend-paying and non-dividend-paying stocks, but some funds can also be decomposed into higher- and lower-yielding components. For example, the S&P 500 ETF SPY has a value component, SPYV, with a current dividend yield of 2.10% and a growth component, SPYG, with a dividend yield of 0.66%.

Summary

- Asset location refers to the optimal placement of assets in different types of accounts.
- Asset location is close to a "free lunch" and, in some extreme cases, can add 50 basis points (bp) per year in additional performance.
- Each asset has an inherent tax efficiency based on factors like its expected return, dividend/interest rate, percent annual turnover, and tax rate on dividends, and is specific to an investor's tax brackets.
- Asset location between a taxable account and an IRA can be determined from the tax efficiencies of each asset by placing the most tax-efficient assets in the taxable account and the most tax-inefficient assets in the IRA.
- Adding a third type of account, a Roth, requires an optimization to determine the best asset location.

Tax-efficient withdrawal strategies

This chapter covers

- Understanding the principles of tax-efficient withdrawal strategies
- Comparing tax-withdrawal strategies and quantifying their benefits
- Incorporating RMDs, capital gains taxes, and state taxes into the analysis
- The role of inheritance in withdrawal strategies

During the decumulation phase of retirement, individuals must often draw down their savings to pay for expenses. There are several strategies for choosing which investment accounts to liquidate first. Choosing an optimal strategy can extend the life of your assets by years, and we will write some Python code to quantify the differences between several strategies.

9.1 The intuition behind tax-efficient strategies

Before we analyze various withdrawal strategies, it will be helpful to understand the intuition behind them. Two general principles can explain why some strategies perform better than others. Those principles have complications and exceptions, but we will discuss those later.

9.1.1   Principle 1: Deplete less tax-efficient accounts first

The conventional wisdom is to withdraw from taxable accounts first and then withdraw from IRA and Roth accounts after the taxable accounts are depleted to let the tax-advantaged accounts grow as long as possible. Taxable accounts, such as brokerage accounts, face a tax drag on returns when interest, dividends, and realized capital gains are taxed every year rather than growing tax-free.

If taxable accounts are depleted first, what should be depleted next, IRAs or Roth IRAs? Suppose we placed X of pretax income in an IRA, invested for T years at an average return r, and, at the end of the T years, paid taxes at a tax rate τ. The amount of money we would have at the end is

$$X(1+r)^T(1-\tau)$$

Now suppose we started with the same X of pretax income, paid taxes at a tax rate τ, and placed the $X(1-\tau)$ in a Roth IRA, earning the same average return r over T years. With a Roth IRA, no taxes are owed at the end of T years, so the amount of money at the end is

$$X(1+r)^T(1-\tau)$$

Notice that the IRA and Roth accounts have the exact same value at the end of time T. We made one simplification here: we assumed that the tax rate at year T when we cash out of the IRA is the same as the tax rate at time 0 when we pay tax on income used to fund the Roth IRA. Those tax rates do not have to be the same, so if we let the tax rate at time 0 be τ_0 and the tax rate at time T be τ_T, the IRA value becomes

$$X(1+r)^T(1-\tau_T)$$

and the value of the Roth IRA is

$$X(1+r)^T(1-\tau_0)$$

Therefore, if tax rates are expected to go down in the future, IRAs are preferred to Roth IRAs; and if tax rates are expected to go up in the future, either because federal tax rates are expected to go up or because income is expected to push you into a higher tax bracket, a Roth IRA is preferable to an IRA. If tax rates are not expected to change, the sequence of withdrawals between a Roth IRA and a traditional IRA will not make a difference. We are ignoring the tax rates of beneficiaries, which are covered later.

9.1.2   Principle 2: Keep tax brackets stable over time

The second goal to minimize taxes is to keep tax rates stable over time. This is easiest demonstrated with an example. We will assume that there are only two tax brackets, as shown in table 9.1. In the next section, we will use the actual tax brackets and rates, but to make our numerical example simpler, we assume there are only 12% and 22% brackets; to use round numbers, we further assume that the higher rate kicks in at incomes above $100,000 and stops at $300,000.

Table 9.1   Simplified tax brackets for our example

Tax rate	Income range
12%	0 – $100,000
22%	$100,000 – $300,000

In figure 9.1, we consider two scenarios. In the first scenario, the "unequal income" case, income jumps from $50,000 the first year to $150,000 the second year, and the total taxes owed over the two years is $29,000. In the second scenario, the "equal income" case, income is steady at $100,000 in both years, and the total taxes owed are reduced to $24,000. Even though the total income is the same in both cases, taxes are reduced in the second case because none of the income is taxed at the higher 22% tax rate.

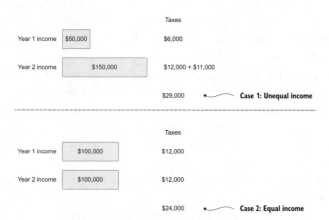

Figure 9.1   Taxes for stable and unstable tax brackets

For each of the examples that follow, we will indicate whether it achieves these two goals for reducing taxes.

9.2   *Examples of sequencing strategies*

Now that we have laid out these two principles that drive the optimal sequencing of withdrawals, it should be easier to understand the examples that follow and why some strategies outperform others. Before we go through the examples, we will make some simplifying assumptions.

9.2.1   *Starting assumptions*

To understand the intuition behind the various sequencing strategies and avoid getting bogged down in some of the tax code's practical details, we will make some simplifying assumptions to start the analysis (later we will relax many of these assumptions):

- An individual has $2 million in a taxable account and $1 million in an IRA. Spending is 4% of those total assets, or $120,000 per year, which grows with inflation. This is the common 4% spending rule that ensures you won't run out of money in retirement.
- An individual only faces federal taxes. Later, we will show that adding other taxes, like state taxes and taxes on Social Security income, is straightforward.
- Rather than increasing spending, tax brackets, and standard deductions by the inflation rate every year, we will keep these values constant over time. Therefore, everything we do will be in real terms or in today's dollars. Our assumptions about stock and bond returns will also be in real terms after inflation.
- One key simplifying assumption is that the after-tax return, after inflation, on the taxable account is 3%, and the returns on the IRA and Roth are 4%. That differential represents the tax drag from taxes owed on interest income and realized capital gains. The proper way to account for the tax drag is to keep track of the realized and unrealized capital gains, which we do later. We are also ignoring capital gains taxes for now and assuming that the tax drag on stocks comes from realized short-term gains.
- We are ignoring asset location, which we covered in chapter 8. Our goal here is to focus on the tax savings from optimal sequencing of withdrawals and not to conflate that with the tax savings from asset location. Similarly, we are ignoring the potential tax savings from tax-loss harvesting covered in chapter 14.
- For now, we are ignoring required minimum distributions (RMDs) for IRAs, but this will be addressed later in the chapter.
- We are ignoring considerations related to inheritance. Later, we will discuss the effects of the stepped-up cost basis for beneficiaries and how the tax rate of the beneficiaries can affect the withdrawal sequencing strategies.

The code for analyzing different sequencing strategies is much simpler with these assumptions. In the next section, we go through a few helper functions we'll use.

9.2.2 Tax-sequencing code

With the assumptions from the previous section, the code for computing how long an investor's money will last for any sequencing strategy is straightforward. We start by creating a DataFrame that contains the federal tax brackets and corresponding tax rates. The following listing creates the DataFrame, and table 9.2 shows the resulting DataFrame that represents the tax brackets and rates for a single filer in 2023.

> **Listing 9.1 Creating a DataFrame of tax brackets and rates**

```
import pandas as pd
import numpy as np
```

```
import matplotlib.pyplot as plt

rates = [0.1, 0.12, 0.22, 0.24, 0.32, 0.35, 0.37]
top_of_bracket = [11000, 44725, 95375, 182100, 231250, 578125, np.inf]
TaxTable = pd.DataFrame({'rate': rates,
                         'top_of_bracket': top_of_bracket,})
print(TaxTable)
```

Table 9.2   DataFrame of federal tax brackets for a single filer in 2023

	rate	top_of_bracket
0	0.10	11000
1	0.12	44725
2	0.22	95375
3	0.24	182100
4	0.32	231250
5	0.35	578125
6	0.37	inf

The function `calc_taxes()` takes the `TaxTable` DataFrame, as well as income and the federal deduction (either standard or itemized), and computes the federal taxes owed.

Listing 9.2   Computing taxes from income

```
def calc_taxes(income, TaxTable, deduction):
    taxable_income = income - deduction
    i = 0
    tax = 0
    bottom = 0
    while taxable_income > bottom:
        bracket_income = min(TaxTable.iloc[i]['top_of_bracket'],
                             taxable_income) - bottom
        tax += TaxTable.iloc[i]['rate'] * bracket_income
        bottom = TaxTable.iloc[i]['top_of_bracket']
        i += 1
    return tax
```

When we distribute money from an IRA, it is treated as ordinary income, and taxes must be paid on the amount withdrawn. So if we withdraw $120,000 from an IRA to meet our spending needs and take the standard deduction of $13,850, the function can be used to compute the taxes owed:

```
calc_taxes(120000, TaxTable, 13850)
```

The income taxes owed are $18,876, so additional money must be distributed from the IRA to cover them.

To solve for the pretax amount we need to withdraw from an IRA to meet the after-tax spending needs, we can use the root finding function `fsolve` in the `SciPy` library, which was described in chapter 7 when we were trying to find the internal rate of return of an investment. In listing 9.3, we create a two-line function `gross_up()` whose first argument is a suggested gross amount to withdraw from an IRA and whose second argument is the desired after-tax amount needed for spending. The `gross_up()` function computes the taxes on the gross amount and returns the difference between the after-tax IRA withdrawal and the desired spending. We use `fsolve` to find the gross amount of IRA withdrawal so that the after-tax amount equals spending. The arguments for `fsolve` are the function we want to set to zero, `gross_up()`, a starting estimate for the value of gross withdrawal that we are trying to solve for, and the parameters of `gross_up()`, which are the after-tax spending, the tax table, and the deduction. In the following example, the pretax amount we need to withdraw from the IRA to meet the spending needs of $120,000 is $144,836.84.

Listing 9.3   Solving for the required pretax withdrawal amount

```
from scipy.optimize import fsolve

def gross_up(gross, net, TaxTable, deduction):
    tax = calc_taxes(gross, TaxTable, deduction)
    return gross - tax - net

root = fsolve(gross_up, 0, args=(120000, TaxTable, 13850))
print('The pre-tax withdrawal amount is ', root.item())
```

We are now ready to compute how long savings will last for different orders of withdrawals. The DataFrame `df` keeps track of the year-end values of all three account types each year. For simplicity, the code assumes that all spending and account withdrawals occur at the beginning of the year rather than being spread throughout the year.

Listing 9.4   Computing how many years savings will last

```
ret = {'taxable':0.03, 'IRA':0.04, 'Roth':0.04}
starting_values = {'taxable':2000000, 'IRA':1000000, 'Roth':0}
spending = 120000
deduction = 13850
max_years = 55

def compute_years(order,
                  ret, starting_values, max_years,
                  spending, deduction, TaxTable):
    df = pd.DataFrame(0., columns=['taxable', 'IRA', 'Roth'],
                      index = range(max_years+1))    ← DataFrame that keeps track
                                                        of assets in each account
                                                        type by year
```

```
df.iloc[0] = starting_values
i = 0
while (df.iloc[i].sum() - calc_taxes(df.iloc[i]['IRA'],TaxTable,deduction)
        > spending) and i < max_years:
    spending_left = spending
    for acct_type in order:
        if acct_type != 'IRA':
            withdraw = min(df.iloc[i][acct_type], spending_left)
            spending_left -= withdraw
        else:    ← For an IRA, gross up the amount of money needed for spending
            withdraw = min(df.iloc[i][acct_type],
                           fsolve(gross_up, spending_left,
                           args=(spending_left, TaxTable, deduction)))
            spending_left -= (withdraw -
                             calc_taxes(withdraw,TaxTable,deduction))
        df.iloc[i+1][acct_type] = ((df.iloc[i][acct_type] - withdraw) *
                                   (1+ret[acct_type]))
    i = i + 1
frac = (df.iloc[i].sum() -
        calc_taxes(df.iloc[i]['IRA'],TaxTable,deduction))/spending
print(i+frac)
return df
```

Using this code, we can now compare different withdrawal strategies.

9.2.3 *Strategy 1: IRA first*

The first sequencing strategy we will look at is withdrawing from the IRA first and, when the IRA is depleted, withdrawing from the taxable account. This strategy violates both of our principles:

☒ *Principle 1*: Deplete less-tax-efficient accounts first.
☒ *Principle 2*: Keep tax brackets stable over time.

We are depleting the tax-advantaged account first. And to pay for our $120,000 of after-tax spending, we need to withdraw $144,836 from the IRA, with most of that money taxed at the 22% and 24% tax rates. To see how long the money will last, we assign a variable called order that contains the order of withdrawals, with the IRA first, and pass that variable into the compute_years() function we created in the last section:

```
order = ['IRA', 'taxable', 'Roth']
compute_years(order, ret, starting_values, max_years,
              spending, deduction, TaxTable)
```

We find that the money will last 40 years. In figure 9.2, we show the evolution of assets over time when the IRA is liquidated first. The assets in the IRA are completely depleted after eight years. Note that the total assets on the *y*-axis are the sum of the taxable and IRA accounts (pretax) rather than an alternative representation of summing the taxable account with the after-tax value of the IRA.

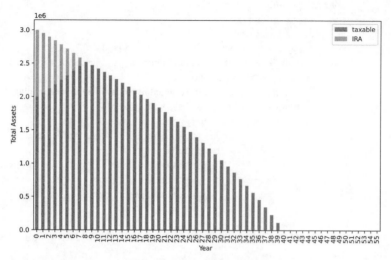

Figure 9.2   Total assets when liquidating the IRA first

9.2.4   *Strategy 2: Taxable first*

The second sequencing strategy is to liquidate the taxable account first and, when that account is depleted, liquidate the IRA account. In terms of the two principles, it satisfies the first goal but still fails the second:

- ☑ *Principle 1*: Deplete less-tax-efficient accounts first.
- ☒ *Principle 2*: Keep tax brackets stable over time.

To see how long the savings will last with this new withdrawal sequence, we can use the same code but change the order:

```
order = ['taxable', 'IRA', 'Roth']
compute_years(order, ret, starting_values, max_years,
              spending, deduction, TaxTable)
```

Table 9.3 compares the number of years the assets will last with these two sequencing strategies. By merely changing the sequence and depleting the less-tax-advantaged taxable account first, the assets will last an additional 8.7 years.

Table 9.3   Comparison of the first two sequencing strategies

Strategy	Number of years money lasts
IRA first, then taxable	40.0
Taxable first, then IRA	48.7

Figure 9.3 shows how the assets evolve over time. In this case, the IRA is allowed to grow, free of any tax drag, from an initial $1 million to over $2.5 million by the time the taxable account is depleted.

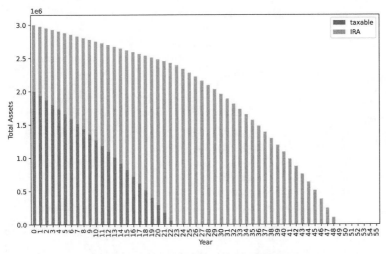

Figure 9.3 Total assets when liquidating the taxable account first

9.2.5 *Strategy 3: Fill lower tax brackets*

Neither of the first two strategies satisfies the second goal of keeping the tax brackets stable. In both cases, in the years when the IRA is liquidated to pay for spending, the income from large IRA withdrawals pushes tax brackets higher. One way to avoid that is to withdraw smaller amounts from the IRA every year, just up to the top of the 12% bracket, but never take out more than that. Therefore, this strategy satisfies the second goal, but it partially fails the first goal: taking some money out of the IRA every year does not allow the tax-advantaged account to grow as much as it does in the second strategy:

- ☒ *Principle 1*: Deplete less-tax-efficient accounts first.
- ☑ *Principle 2*: Keep tax brackets stable over time.

This strategy requires a slight modification of the code in listing 9.4. The modified code is shown in the following listing with the additional lines annotated in the code.

Listing 9.5 Years savings will last with bracket fills and Roth conversions

```
def compute_years_new(order, IRA_fill_amt, conversion_flag,
                      ret, starting_values, max_years,
                      spending, deduction, TaxTable):
    df = pd.DataFrame(0., columns=['taxable', 'IRA', 'Roth'],
                      index = range(max_years+1))
    df.iloc[0] = starting_values
    i = 0
```

```
    while (df.iloc[i].sum() - calc_taxes(df.iloc[i]['IRA'],TaxTable,deduction)
            > spending) and i < max_years:
        spending_left = spending

        if df.iloc[i]['taxable'] > spending:
            withdraw = min(df.iloc[i]['IRA'], IRA_fill_amt)
            if conversion_flag == 0:
                spending_left -= (withdraw -
                                    calc_taxes(withdraw,TaxTable,deduction))
                df.iloc[i]['IRA'] = (df.iloc[i]['IRA']-withdraw)

            else:
                df.iloc[i]['IRA'] = (df.iloc[i]['IRA']-withdraw)
                df.iloc[i]['Roth'] += (withdraw -
                                    calc_taxes(withdraw,TaxTable,deduction))

        for acct_type in order:
            if acct_type != 'IRA':
                withdraw = min(df.iloc[i][acct_type], spending_left)
                spending_left = spending_left - withdraw
            else:
                withdraw = min(df.iloc[i][acct_type],
                                fsolve(gross_up, spending_left,
                                args=(spending_left, TaxTable, deduction)))
                spending_left -= (withdraw -
                                    calc_taxes(withdraw,TaxTable,deduction))
            df.iloc[i+1][acct_type] = ((df.iloc[i][acct_type] - withdraw) *
                                    (1+ret[acct_type])  )
        i = i + 1
    frac = (df.iloc[i].sum() -
            calc_taxes(df.iloc[i]['IRA'],TaxTable,deduction))/spending
    print(i+frac)
    return df
```

Take out of IRA first up to IRA_fill_amt ← (annotation for `withdraw = min(df.iloc[i]['IRA'], IRA_fill_amt)`)

If no conversion, withdraws from the IRA account first (annotation for `df.iloc[i]['IRA'] = (df.iloc[i]['IRA']-withdraw)`)

If conversion, withdraws from the IRA account and places the net amount after taxes into the Roth (annotation for `df.iloc[i]['Roth'] +=`)

Table 9.4 compares the "Fill 12% bracket" strategy with the previous two strategies. As expected, this strategy does better than the naive first strategy of depleting the IRA first but does a little worse than the second strategy of depleting the taxable account first. As we said, the fill-bracket strategy has the advantage that it smooths tax brackets but has the disadvantage that it depletes the tax-advantaged accounts sooner. In this case, the principle of depleting less-tax-advantaged accounts first plays a bigger role in reducing taxes.

Table 9.4 Comparison including IRA bracket-fill strategy

Strategy	Number of years money lasts
IRA first, then taxable	40.0
Taxable first, then IRA	48.7
Fill 12% bracket first	**44.5**

Figure 9.4 shows how the IRA and taxable accounts evolve over time with the "Fill 12% bracket." By design, the IRA account is not depleted as quickly as in the IRA-first strategy in figure 9.2, but it is depleted more quickly than in the taxable-first strategy in figure 9.3

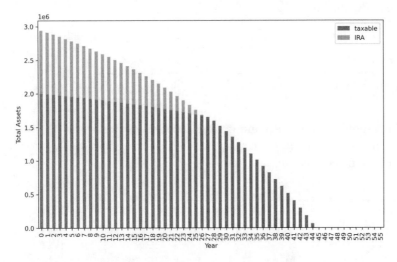

Figure 9.4   Total assets when filling the 12% tax bracket first

9.2.6   *Strategy 4: Roth conversions*

The fourth strategy is similar to the third one, except that when we take money out of the IRA every year up to the top of the 12% tax bracket, rather than using that money for spending, we keep the money in a tax-advantaged account by converting it to a Roth IRA and use the taxable account for spending until it is depleted. Therefore, this strategy satisfies both goals:

- ☑ *Principle 1*: Deplete less-tax-efficient accounts first.
- ☑ *Principle 2*: Keep tax brackets stable over time.

Anyone, regardless of income, can convert an unlimited amount of a traditional IRA into a Roth IRA. Taxes must be paid on the traditional IRA in the year you make the conversion. A "five-year rule" applies to each conversion: converted funds must remain in the Roth for five years. If you withdraw converted funds within five years of the conversion and before age 59½, you will generally owe a 10% penalty on the converted principal.

Table 9.5 shows the results of the Roth conversion strategy. This strategy is the best of the four, extending savings by 4.5 years more than the second-best strategy (the taxable-first strategy).

Table 9.5 Comparison including the Roth conversion strategy

Strategy	Number of years money lasts
IRA first, then taxable	40.0
Taxable first, then IRA	48.7
Fill 12% bracket first	44.5
Roth conversion	**53.2**

Figure 9.5 shows how the IRA and taxable accounts evolve over time with the Roth conversion strategy. The Roth account starts with zero and gradually grows to be the largest of the three accounts.

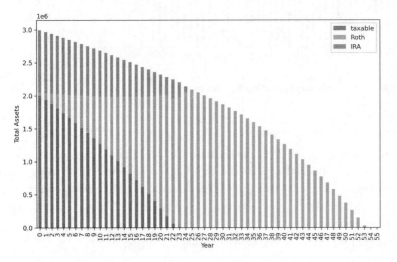

Figure 9.5   Total assets with the Roth conversion strategy

The differences between the strategies depend, of course, on the assumptions made. In particular, the results are very sensitive to the assumption we made about the drag that taxes have on taxable accounts. We assumed that tax-advantaged accounts have an expected real return of 4%, whereas taxable accounts have an expected real return of only 3% due to taxes that must be paid on investment income every year. If we lower that drag from 1% to 0.5%, for example, the first principle of depleting less-tax-advantaged accounts first becomes much less important. In fact, the difference in years between the first two sequencing strategies goes from 8.7 years to 6.6 years. Conversely, if the assumed tax drag is higher, the difference between the first two sequencing strategies grows. In the next section, we will relax some of the assumptions and compute taxes directly rather than assuming a tax drag.

9.3 Additional complications

We listed numerous simplifying assumptions that we made to focus on the strategies' intuition and keep the code simple. However, several complications creep in that can alter the previous ideas. We will go through several of those next.

9.3.1 Required minimum distributions

RMDs are the minimum amount that must be distributed from pretax retirement accounts like IRAs each year after reaching a certain age. As part of the Secure Act 2.0 of 2022, retirees now have to start taking RMDs in the year they turn 73. For those born in 1960 or later, the RMD starting age is 75.

The RMD is calculated by dividing the value of each retirement account on December 31 of the prior year by a life-expectancy factor that the IRS publishes. These life-expectancy factors were updated in 2022 to reflect a longer life expectancy (the tables were created prior to COVID-19, which has reduced life expectancy by about two years) and therefore slightly lowered RMDs. For most people, the Uniform Lifetime Table is the relevant table to use for RMDs, but other tables may apply: for example, if a spouse is the sole beneficiary of an IRA and is more than 10 years younger than the account owner.

How do RMDs affect withdrawal strategies? Intuitively, they can reduce the benefit of depleting less-tax-advantaged accounts first. Also, the Roth conversion strategy can potentially reduce the effect of RMDs. By converting IRAs to Roth IRAs, which are not subject to RMDs, the value of the IRAs declines, and therefore the RMDs decline as well. On the other hand, there are situations where RMDs have no effect on a withdrawal strategy. For example, if an RMD were less than a planned IRA withdrawal, the required distributions would not make any difference. Also, RMDs can't be converted to a Roth, so RMDs may reduce the desired amount of a Roth conversion.

We can look at a specific example to see how RMDs affect the longevity of different strategies. To incorporate RMDs, we must modify the code in listing 9.5. An additional input of age is required to compute the RMD, and the RMDs are calculated for each age. To avoid repeating large blocks of code, we include the RMD code on the book's website and GitHub (https://www.manning.com/books/build-a-robo-advisor-with-python-from-scratch and https://github.com/robreider/robo-advisor-with-python/blob/main/chapter_09.ipynb).

In table 9.6, for the four withdrawal strategies in the last section, we compare longevity without RMDs as in the last section with those same strategies but when an RMD is included for a 65-year-old retiree. The first strategy (withdrawals from IRA first) is not affected by RMDs. The IRA is depleted by the time RMDs would have kicked in. As expected, the second strategy (withdrawals from the taxable account first) is modestly hurt by RMDs. RMDs force the tax-advantaged account to be depleted slightly earlier than if there were no RMDs, but the effect is modest in this example. First, the RMDs are relatively small in the early years. In addition, the taxable-first strategy with RMDs is similar to the fill-bracket strategy (the third strategy earlier). In both cases, a small amount of the IRA is distributed in a lower tax bracket. In the tax bracket strategy, IRAs are withdrawn up to the top of the 12% bracket, and with the RMDs for a modest IRA account, IRAs are also withdrawn in a lower tax bracket, although not to the top of the bracket. So, as we expect, the second strategy (taxable first) with RMDs has results similar to the fill-bracket strategy in the third row.

The third strategy (the bracket-fill strategy) does not change with RMDs because the RMDs are smaller than the top of the bracket, so they do not constrain this strategy. Finally, the fourth strategy (Roth conversion) is slightly hurt by RMDs. Because RMD withdrawals cannot be converted to Roth IRAs, the presence of RMDs modestly reduces the amount that can be converted and maintained in tax-favorable accounts. Of course, this is just one example, and the results can be very different with different assumptions on age, IRA assets, spending, etc. This is why it's nice to have a program to customize advice to an individual's circumstances while still understanding the intuition behind the results.

Table 9.6   Comparison of strategies with and without RMDs

Strategy	Number of years money lasts	Years money lasts with RMDs
IRA first, then taxable	40.0	40.0
Taxable first, then IRA	48.7	47.3
Fill 12% bracket first	44.5	44.5
Roth conversion	53.2	52.1

There are also several less common situations where RMDs do not apply to retirement accounts. For example, the "still-working" exception allows RMDs to be delayed from your company plan, like a 401(k) (not an IRA), if you continue working past the age of 73. And, of course, there is an exception to this exception if you own more than 5% of the company for which you are still working. Another situation where different RMD rules apply is for inherited IRAs, which we cover in the next section on inheritance issues.

9.3.2   Inheritance

Inheritance is another important consideration for withdrawal strategies that we have not yet addressed. We touched on inheritance at the end of chapter 6 when we discussed incorporating a reward that represents the utility derived from passing down money to heirs. Even if you came up with an estimate of the trade-off between enjoying your money yourself and the enjoyment from passing money to heirs or charity, it can still be very complicated to find the best withdrawal strategy. Heirs can be in different tax situations. We don't attempt to incorporate inheritance here quantitatively, but we can intuitively discuss the issues involved. The two main areas that affect withdrawal strategies are the stepped-up cost basis upon death and the rules involved with inherited IRAs:

Stepped-up cost basis–When heirs inherit assets, the cost basis of those assets is reset to their value on the date of the original owner's death. And it's very common for older retirees to have some long-held assets with a very low cost basis. In the extreme, consider an older retiree with a terminal illness. If they need to raise cash and their only choice is between selling taxable assets with a low cost basis or selling from an IRA, the heirs may prefer that the owner sell from the IRA and pass down the taxable account with the stepped-up basis. This potentially goes against the principle that taxable accounts should be depleted first.

Inherited IRAs—The rules for inherited IRAs changed with the passage of the SECURE Act in 2019. Generally speaking (there are exceptions), if a nonspouse like a child inherits an IRA whose owner dies in 2020 or later, the beneficiary must distribute the entire amount of the IRA within 10 years. There has been some confusion over the 2019 law about whether RMDs must be taken in years 1 through 9. The IRS has issued guidance to clear up the confusion, and, as of this writing, the IRS says that RMDs must be taken in years 1 through 9 if the RMDs had already started when the original account owner died. For inherited Roth IRAs, the 10-year rule applies as well, but there are no RMDs in years 1 through 9. There are several implications for withdrawal-sequencing strategies, and the best strategy partially depends on whether the account owner is in a higher or lower tax bracket than the beneficiaries:

- If the account owner is in a lower bracket, it is better if the account owner depletes the IRA rather than passing it down. The Roth conversion strategy is a particularly good way to achieve that goal. Therefore, traditional IRAs should be depleted before Roth IRAs. It may even make sense to deplete IRAs before taxable accounts.

- If the account owner is in a higher tax bracket, it is better to pass down the IRA. Roth IRAs should be depleted before traditional IRAs. It may even be better to deplete a taxable account with an imminent stepped-up cost basis before depleting IRAs.

For the beneficiaries who inherit an IRA, the strategies are a little more straightforward. If the beneficiary inherits a Roth IRA, it is best to wait until the very end of the 10-year period to distribute the assets. If the beneficiary inherits a traditional IRA, and if the amount of the IRA is small, it still may make sense to wait 10 years to distribute the assets. But if the IRA is large, distributing the assets more evenly over the 10 years may be better to smooth tax brackets.

The next set of restrictive assumptions we want to relax relates to how we treat taxes. We will cover this topic in the next few sections.

9.3.3   *Capital gains taxes*

Purely to simplify the code, rather than explicitly calculating the tax drag of holding taxable assets, we made the critical assumption that the drag reduced returns by 1%. The reality is that tax drag depends on numerous factors, which we can model: the percentage of assets invested in bonds versus stocks, the percentage of capital gains realized each year, the mix between short-term and long-term capital gains, and the tax brackets for investment gains. Thus far we have only considered ordinary income from IRA withdrawals, so one place to start is how long-term gains are treated and how it affects the various withdrawal strategies we discussed earlier.

Capital gains have separate tax brackets and lower tax rates. A key concept to understand is that capital gains and qualified dividends are stacked on top of ordinary income. In other words, ordinary income is taxed first and capital gains are taxed second, so capital gains can't push ordinary income into a higher bracket, but ordinary income can push capital gains into a higher bracket. It's best shown with an example.

Assume that ordinary income is taxed at the simplified brackets used in table 9.2. We also create a simplified capital gains bracket in table 9.7. Again, these are not the actual capital gains rates and brackets—we are using simple, round numbers to simplify the example.

Table 9.7   Simplified capital gains tax brackets for the example

Tax rate	Income range
0%	0–$100,000
15%	$100,000–$500,000

Suppose an investor has $80,000 of ordinary income and $40,000 of long-term capital gains. Table 9.8 shows that, using the simplified tax brackets, the total taxes owed are $12,600. Notice that the capital gains taxes are stacked on top of the $80,000 of ordinary income. The first $20,000 of capital gains falls in the $0–$100,000 tax bracket and is taxed at 0%. But the next $20,000 of capital gains falls in the $100,000–$500,000 bracket and is taxed at 15%.

Table 9.8   Example of capital gains taxes stacked on top of ordinary income

Type of tax	Amount of tax
Ordinary income	$80,000 × 12% = $9,600
Long-term capital gains	$20,000 × 0% + $20,000 × 15% = $3,000
Total	$12,600

Suppose the ordinary income increases from \$80,000 to \$90,000, perhaps due to an extra \$10,000 withdrawn from an IRA. Table 9.9 shows that the taxes owed are now \$15,300. Only \$10,000 of the capital gains will be taxed at 0%, and an additional \$10,000 is pushed up into the higher 15% capital gains bracket. Because the \$10,000 of additional income results in \$2,700 of additional taxes, the marginal tax rate is 27%, not the 12% ordinary income rate you may expect.

Table 9.9 Capital gains tax example with an extra \$10,000 of income

Type of tax	Amount of tax
Ordinary income	**\$90,000** × 12% = \$10,800
Long-term capital gains	\$10,000 × 0% + **\$30,000** × 15% = \$4,500
Total	\$15,300

The higher potential marginal tax rates that arise when ordinary income pushes capital gains into a higher tax bracket can have several implications for tax-efficient withdrawal strategies. There is a similar effect with Social Security taxes. Higher income—say, through more IRA withdrawals—leads to more Social Security income that is taxable. And more taxable Social Security income can push more capital gains into a higher tax bracket. It turns out you can get a 50% marginal tax rate under some circumstances from an additional dollar of IRA withdrawals. The code we describe in the last section of the chapter can handle Social Security taxes and can answer questions like whether it is better to take IRA distributions early in retirement, before Social Security income starts, to avoid the taxation of Social Security benefits.

Higher income can also trigger tax phase-outs of several types of tax deductions and credits. In addition, Medicare premiums may be increased due to the income-related monthly adjustment amount (IRMAA) surcharge. The potential deduction for unreimbursed medical expenses may be curtailed. And contributions to traditional IRAs may not be fully deductible. As we saw with capital gains taxes and taxes on Social Security income, these indirect taxes increase the effective marginal tax rate. As a consequence, they can affect the optimal tax-efficient withdrawal strategies.

In listing 9.6, we modify the tax calculation from listing 9.2 to include long-term capital gains taxes and stack the capital gains on top of ordinary income. The capital gains tax bracket is assumed to be a DataFrame with the same format as the income tax bracket. The code also allows the tax brackets and deductions to increase with inflation. The listing includes a line at the end that computes the 3.8% Medicare surtax, known as the net investment income tax (NIIT). This tax is computed as the lesser of the net investment income or the amount that the modified adjusted gross income (MAGI) exceeds a threshold, which is \$200,000 for individual filers. For simplicity, we assume that MAGI is the same as gross income.

Listing 9.6   Computing income, capital gains, and state taxes

```python
def calc_taxes(income, TaxTable, deduction, State_TaxTable,
               state_deduction, LTCG_TaxTable, ST_gains, LT_gains, t):

    taxable_income = (income - state_deduction * (1+infl)**t
                      + ST_gains + LT_gains)
    i = 0
    tax = 0
    bottom = 0
    while taxable_income > bottom:
        bracket_income = min(State_TaxTable.iloc[i]['top_of_bracket'] *
                             (1+infl)**t, taxable_income) - bottom
        tax += State_TaxTable.iloc[i]['rate']*bracket_income
        bottom = State_TaxTable.iloc[i]['top_of_bracket'] * (1+infl)**t
        i += 1

    taxable_income = income - deduction*(1+infl)**t + ST_gains
    i = 0
    bottom = 0
    while taxable_income > bottom:
        bracket_income = min(TaxTable.iloc[i]['top_of_bracket'] *
                             (1+infl)**t, taxable_income) - bottom
        tax += TaxTable.iloc[i]['rate']*bracket_income
        bottom = TaxTable.iloc[i]['top_of_bracket']*(1+infl)**t
        i += 1

    i = (LTCG_TaxTable['top_of_bracket'] *
         (1+infl)**t).searchsorted(taxable_income).item()
    bottom = taxable_income
    while taxable_income + LT_gains > bottom:
        bracket_income = min(LTCG_TaxTable.iloc[i]['top_of_bracket'] *
                             (1+infl)**t,taxable_income+LT_gains) - bottom
        tax += LTCG_TaxTable.iloc[i]['rate'] * bracket_income
        bottom = LTCG_TaxTable.iloc[i]['top_of_bracket'] * (1+infl)**t
        i += 1

    NIIT = min(max(income+ST_gains+LT_gains-200000,0), LT_gains) * 0.038
    tax = tax + NIIT
    return tax
```

Labels in the left margin:
- **State taxes** (first while loop)
- **Federal taxes** (second while loop)
- **Capital gains taxes** (third while loop)
- **Medicare surtax** (NIIT section)

Annotation: **Finds the starting bracket for the stacked capital gains**

The code has a section that computes state taxes. In the next section, we discuss some concerns with state taxes.

9.3.4   State taxes

Up to this point in the book, we have only looked at federal taxes and have ignored state taxes. Part of the reason is that state taxes can be complicated. If it were just a matter of adding the tax brackets and rates for 50 states, it would be feasible. Free resources online, like www.taxfoundation.org, provide data on tax rates and brackets for every state and update the data every year. In listing 9.6, we added a section for state taxes, which is identical to the section for federal taxes for ordinary income.

Unfortunately, in addition to tax brackets, each state has additional tax policies that can vary wildly. Consider how various states treat Social Security income. Thirteen states tax Social Security benefits. Some states follow the federal rules for determining how much Social Security income is taxable; other states offer reductions based on age or income.

Some states partially or fully tax pensions, and others don't. Similarly, many states tax IRA distributions. Our home state of New York taxes IRA distributions but offers a $20,000 exemption. Some states have additional local taxes. For example, New York City imposes its own tax on city residents. Most states index their tax brackets to inflation, but a few states, like California, do not index the top bracket. We could go on. In our code, we have only incorporated state tax brackets and state deductions and ignored many of the other important provisions for now.

Earlier, we discussed how the tax drag can affect the performance of the different withdrawal strategies. Using the tax brackets for high-tax states like New York and California creates a larger tax drag on taxable accounts, and using the zero bracket for a state like Florida creates a smaller tax drag. In the next section, we discuss more sophisticated code that takes many more inputs, including these state tax brackets.

9.3.5 *Putting it all together*

On the book's website and GitHub, we have included code that computes the longevity for the four withdrawal strategies but makes many fewer assumptions and consequently takes more inputs. The assumptions for the expanded model are listed with the code.

The code we've posted is just a starting point—there are many areas for expansion. For example, throughout this chapter we have only considered single filers, but expanding to include other filing statuses is easy. Each individual's circumstances are different, and a program like the one we created can be used to customize a strategy for a particular set of inputs.

Summary

- During the decumulation phase of retirement, individuals must often draw down their savings.
- Two key principles provide guidance on optimal withdrawal strategies: deplete less tax-efficient accounts first, and keep tax brackets stable over time.
- It is better to deplete Roth IRAs before traditional IRAs if tax rates are expected to drop in the future and Roth last if tax rates are expected to rise.
- Strategy 1, depleting IRAs first, violates both principles and is generally the worst strategy.
- Strategy 2, depleting taxable accounts first, satisfies the first principle but violates the second.

- Strategy 3, filling lower tax brackets first with IRA withdrawals, followed by depleting taxable accounts, satisfies the first principle but violates the second.

- Strategy 4, converting the IRA withdrawals in strategy 3 to Roth IRAs, satisfies both principles and often performs the best.

- RMDs typically have no effect on strategies 1 and 3 and only a modest effect on strategies 2 and 4.

- The stepped-up cost basis in some cases can lead to depleting an IRA before taxable accounts when life expectancy is short.

- If heirs are in higher tax brackets, depleting IRAs first may reduce overall taxes.

- Capital gains taxes are stacked on top of ordinary income, so the tax bracket and Roth conversion strategies can push marginal tax rates much higher by pushing capital gains into higher brackets.

- High state taxes increase the tax drag, making strategies that satisfy the first principle more advantageous.

Part 3

Portfolio construction

In this part of the book, we'll discuss methods for determining "optimal" portfolio weights. Chapter 10 shows how to estimate expected returns and covariances, as well as other constraints or considerations, to build optimized portfolios using convex optimization. We'll also highlight some of the pitfalls associated with using optimization to build portfolios.

The next two chapters discuss methodologies designed to address these pitfalls. Chapter 12 covers the Black–Litterman model, which allows investors to express their opinions about the expected returns of various asset classes while anchoring their expectations to ones derived from the positions of other investors. Chapter 11 discusses an approach called *risk parity*, which dispenses with expected returns and allocates capital based solely on risk and correlations. In that chapter, we'll show how, under certain assumptions, risk parity and the canonical mean-variance optimization yield the same optimal portfolio.

Optimization and portfolio construction

10

This chapter covers

- Understanding the basics of convex functions and convex optimization
- Formulating and solving optimization problems in Python
- Modern portfolio theory and mean-variance portfolio optimization
- Pitfalls of portfolio optimization

Many problems in finance and asset management require the solution of optimization problems. Building portfolios with attractive risk and return trade-offs, determining trades to bring a portfolio that has drifted from its target allocation back on target without incurring painful taxes, and developing a tax-efficient withdrawal strategy are all examples of problems that can be solved using optimization. More importantly, optimization problems, once implemented, can solve these problems extremely quickly without the need for manual effort—a key requirement for robo-advisors.

This chapter will start with a refresher on optimization and some conditions that ensure that optimization problems are practically solvable. We'll also discuss some options for solving optimization problems with Python, as well as the strengths and weaknesses of each. We will show how to use Python libraries to formulate and solve portfolio optimization problems and how these problems can be used to generate target asset allocations similar to those employed by robo-advisors. Along the way, we will see examples of what can go wrong in portfolio optimization, which will motivate advanced portfolio construction techniques we'll cover in later chapters.

10.1 Convex optimization in Python

This section will start with a refresher on optimization and why it isn't always easy. We'll also discuss an important mathematical concept called *convexity*, which is an attractive property in optimization.

10.1.1 Basics of optimization

The basic idea of mathematical optimization is simple: a function, f, takes one or more variables as input and returns a single number as output. We want to find the choice of input variables that either minimize or maximize the function's value. You may remember from calculus that in the case where f takes a single input and there are no constraints, the minimum and maximum values occur at places where f's derivative is zero. The same idea extends to the case where f takes multiple inputs, as long as there are no constraints—optimal values occur at points where the gradient of f is 0. Numerical algorithms for solving unconstrained problems are essentially looking for points where this is true.

For example, let's consider the function $f(x) = x^2 - 6x + 10$. We want to find the value of x that minimizes this function. We take the derivative of f and equate it to 0, which gives us the equation $2x - 6 = 0$, or $x = 3$. Looking at the graph of f in figure 10.1, it is clear that this is the correct solution.

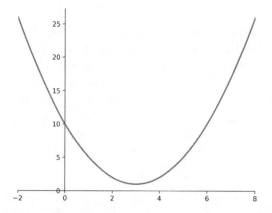

Figure 10.1   Plot of the function $x^2 - 6x + 10$

We can add complications to make the problem more interesting. Let's start with constraints. We can add the constraint that x has to take a value in the interval $[4, 7]$. Looking at the graph in figure 10.1, it's easy to see that the optimal solution occurs at the point $x = 4$; but our method of setting the derivative equal to 0 and solving the equation doesn't help us here because the solution of $x = 3$ doesn't satisfy the constraint.

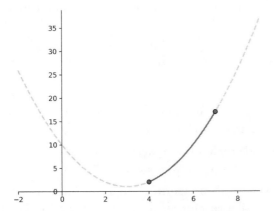

Figure 10.2 When minimizing over the interval $[4, 7]$, the minimum value occurs when $x = 4$.

Now let's look at another case where a derivative of 0 doesn't get us the right solution. This time, we'll change the constraints a bit to say that x has to be in the interval $[0, 5]$, but instead of minimizing f, we want to maximize it. In this case, the point $x = 3$, where the derivative is 0, satisfies the constraints, but we can easily see that this isn't right. The maximum value in the interval $[0, 5]$ happens at $x = 0$. Our derivative trick failed us again but for a different reason. In this case, the function f is not "concave down" where the derivative is 0—we have to check the endpoints of the interval defined by the constraints.

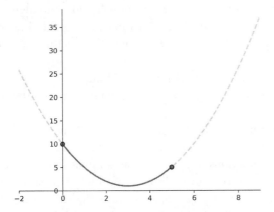

Figure 10.3 When maximizing over the interval $[0, 5]$, the maximum value occurs when $x = 0$.

The last two examples show that optimization problems can become nontrivial very quickly, even with only a single variable and simple constraints. In the following sections, we'll go over conditions that make optimization problems easy (but definitely still not trivial!) to solve. Before we move on, let's define a couple of terms:

- We'll refer to the function we are trying to minimize or maximize as the *objective function.*
- The set of points that satisfy all constraints in the problem is known as the *feasible set.*

Finally, because minimizing a function f is equivalent to maximizing the function $-f$, we can always assume that we'll be minimizing.

10.1.2 Convexity

Convexity is a term that can apply to both functions and sets of points. Generally, convexity in optimization guarantees two important things:

1. The problem can be solved efficiently or quickly.
2. We know for sure that the solution we've obtained is truly optimal.

Some optimization solvers work with nonconvex inputs, meaning the algorithm will try to solve the problem until it reaches some stopping condition. But without convexity, we won't know for sure that the solution obtained is truly the best one. There could be another, better, solution that the algorithm wasn't able to "find." Other solvers won't even allow nonconvex inputs.

In the next two sections, we'll demonstrate examples of convexity in functions and sets.

CONVEX FUNCTIONS

A function f is convex if, for any points x and y and any scalar λ between 0 and 1, the following holds:

$$f(\lambda x + (1 - \lambda)y) \leq \lambda f(x) + (1 - \lambda)f(y)$$

This inequality can be explained intuitively: take any points x and y and their function values $f(x)$ and $f(y)$. If f is convex, the function values along the line segment between x and y are always lower than the line segment connecting $(x, f(x))$ and $(y, f(y))$.

Figure 10.4 shows an example of a convex function. Notice that along the highlighted line segment, the function is always lower than the line between the function values at the endpoints.

Figure 10.5 shows a function that is not convex and an example of an interval where the convexity condition fails. This particular graph visualizes a problem with trying to optimize nonconvex functions. It has two local minima—one around $x = -1$ and another around $x = 2.5$—but only one global minimum. This shows another example of a globally optimal point that an optimization algorithm might not be able to locate, depending on how the algorithm was initialized.

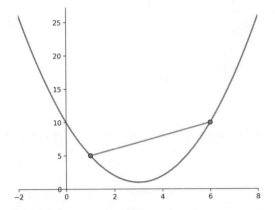

Figure 10.4   A convex function

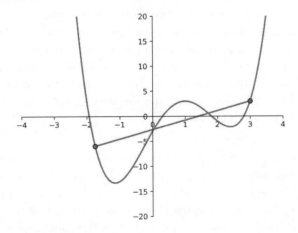

Figure 10.5   A nonconvex function

CONVEX SETS

A set S is convex if, for any two points x and y in the set S, every point on the line segment between x and y is also in the set. Practically, this means the set doesn't have any "holes" in it.

Figure 10.6 shows two examples of convex sets. Figure 10.7 shows two sets that are not convex, with line segments indicating where the convexity condition fails.

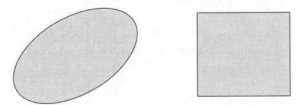

Figure 10.6   Two convex sets: an ellipse and a square

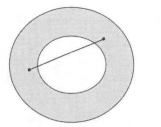 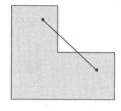

Figure 10.7   Two nonconvex sets. The line segments shown connect two points in each set but don't lie completely in the set.

Convex sets enter optimization when defining the feasible region for the optimization problem: the set of all points satisfying the constraints of the problem. Why is a convex feasible set preferable in optimization? Let's think about how an algorithm might solve an optimization problem. A common method works iteratively, starting with a point inside the feasible region. At each iteration, the algorithm identifies a direction in which the objective function is improving and then finds a new, improved solution by taking a small step in that direction. However, if the feasible region is not convex, meaning it has "holes," the algorithm may not be able to move in the improvement direction at all—it may run into a hole. There may be more feasible points beyond the hole, but the algorithm can't get to them.

CONVEX OPTIMIZATION

An optimization problem that has a convex objective function and a convex feasible set is known as a *convex optimization problem*. Efficient algorithms exist for solving convex optimization problems, so if we can make sure the problems we want to solve are convex (by only trying to minimize convex functions and avoiding constraints that result in nonconvex feasible sets), we can be sure we'll be able to solve them. Otherwise, if either the objective function or the feasible set is nonconvex, we don't have this guarantee.

Going back to our earlier examples with the function $f(x) = x^2 - 6x + 10$ (which is convex), we can see how convexity made some examples easy, and others hard. In the first example, we were minimizing the function without any constraints: this is a convex problem. In this case, finding the point where the derivative was zero got us the optimal solution. This is true in higher dimensions as well: when minimizing a convex function of multiple variables without any constraints, we can find an optimal solution just by finding a point where the gradient is zero (in this case, a vector of zeros).

On the other hand, the derivative trick failed when we tried to maximize the function; it gave us the minimum. In this case, the feasible region was a convex set, but the objective function wasn't convex.

EXAMPLES OF CONVEXITY

It would be impossible to list every convex function or every convex set. But we can start with a few common examples that will suffice for now and highlight more when we need to later:

- Any linear function of the form $f(x) = a^T x + b$ is convex.
- Quadratic functions of the form $f(x) = a \cdot x^T Q x + b^T x + c$, where a is nonnegative and the matrix Q is positive semidefinite, are convex.
- If f and g are two convex functions, any combination $a \cdot f + b \cdot g + c$ is convex as long as a and b are both nonnegative.
- If f is a convex function, the set $\{x \mid f(x) \leq 0\}$ is convex.
- The intersection of any two convex sets is convex.

10.1.3 Python libraries for optimization

This section will cover two ways to solve optimization problems in Python. The first uses functions in the `scipy` package that can be used on general problems but come with some pitfalls. The other relies on the `cvxpy` package, which requires some special conditions (convexity) but, as a result, can guarantee finding the right solution.

SCIPY FUNCTIONS

The `scipy.optimize` library provides several methods for optimizing arbitrary functions, including nonconvex ones. The methods in this library follow the naming convention `fmin_<algorithm>`, where the user can choose which algorithm should be used to solve the problem; the package also contains the interface `minimize`, which allows access to even more algorithms. Each algorithm has its own capabilities and requirements. Most algorithms only work with unconstrained problems, but some allow for simple constraints and others allow arbitrary constraints. Some methods require additional functions giving the gradient and Hessian matrix of the function being minimized.

One important requirement of all methods is that the user must input an initial guess for the point at which the function takes its minimum. If the problem has constraints, the initial guess must satisfy the constraints, and finding a point that does so can be a challenge in itself—sometimes just as challenging as solving the optimization problem. What's more, the solution returned by most methods can be highly dependent on the choice of the initial solution. Unless special conditions (such as convexity) are met, you can get an incorrect solution.

In practice, the need to provide an initial feasible solution makes these methods insufficient for most problems encountered by robo-advisors, which typically involve enough constraints to make finding an initial solution difficult. To avoid this requirement, we'll turn to a more robust optimization package.

THE CVXPY LIBRARY

`cvxpy` isn't an optimization algorithm. Rather, it is a modeling layer that allows users to specify optimization problems in a natural way. Once the problem is specified, `cvxpy` passes the problem to a solver. If the problem is nonconvex in any way (because of the objective or any of the constraints), `cvxpy` will give an error.

As a simple starting example, let's go back to one of the problems we looked at earlier: minimizing the function $f(x) = x^2 - 6x + 10$, with the added constraint that

x must be in the interval $[4, 10]$. The following code shows how to set up and solve this problem in cvxpy.

Listing 10.1 A simple problem in cvxpy

```
import cvxpy as cp

x = cp.Variable(1)
objective = cp.Minimize(x ** 2 - 6 * x + 10)
constraints = [x >= 4, x <= 10]
prob = cp.Problem(objective, constraints)
result = prob.solve()
x.value
```

Running this code should return the value 4.0.

Let's walk through what's happening here, line by line:

- The first line imports the cvxpy module.
- The next line defines x to be a decision variable. The value of 1 indicates that x is a one-dimensional variable.
- Next, we define the objective function: minimizing $x^2 - 6x + 10$. This step requires x to be defined—if it weren't, it would result in an error.
- After that, we define two constraints contained in a list.
- Then we define the "problem," which consists of an objective and constraints.
- Calling the solve() method passes the problem to the underlying solver.
- Calling x.value returns the optimal value of the variable x.

This problem contains only a single variable, x, of one dimension. If the problem involved two variables, say, x_1 and x_2, we could define x to be a two-dimensional variable by declaring x = cp.Variable(2) instead, or we could define two separate one-dimensional variables, such as x1 = cp.Variable(1) and x2 = cp.Variable(1). For problems with more variables, we can use a mix of both approaches.

This is an example of a convex optimization problem: the objective is a convex quadratic, and the constraints are linear. By specifying a nonconvex objective, we can get cvxpy to return an error.

Listing 10.2 Trying to solve a nonconvex problem with cvxpy

```
x = cp.Variable(1)
objective = cp.Maximize((x - 1) * (x + 1) * (x + 2) * (x - 3))
constraints = []

prob = cp.Problem(objective, constraints)
result = prob.solve()
```

If you run this code, you should get this error message: DCPError: Problem does not follow DCP rules. "DCP" here stands for Disciplined Convex Programming;

essentially, it means `cvxpy` has detected a nonconvex element to the problem and will not attempt to obtain a solution.

This is only scratching the surface of the capabilities of `cvxpy`. We will highlight more features as we address applications going forward.

10.2 Mean-variance optimization

Chapter 2 introduced one basic form of a mean-variance portfolio optimization problem: minimizing risk with an acceptable level of expected return. In this section, we'll show how this problem and some variants can be solved using `cvxpy`.

10.2.1 The basic problem

Remember that the version of the mean-variance problem we looked at before was

$$
\begin{aligned}
\text{minimize:} \quad & \tfrac{1}{2} w^T \Sigma w \\
\text{subject to:} \quad & \mu^T w \geq \mu_p \\
& \mathbb{1}^T \mu = 1
\end{aligned}
$$

The following listing shows how to formulate and solve this problem in `cvxpy`, with some sample data for the problem inputs.

> **Listing 10.3 Formulating the mean-variance problem**

```
import numpy as np
Sigma = np.matrix([[0.0225 , 0.0216 , 0.00075],
                   [0.0216 , 0.0324 , 0.00045],
                   [0.00075, 0.00045, 0.0025]])
mu = np.array([.06, .05, .03])
mu_p = .055
N = len(mu)
w = cp.Variable(N)
objective = cp.Minimize(cp.quad_form(w, Sigma))
constraints = [w.T @ mu >= mu_p, cp.sum(w) == 1]
prob = cp.Problem(objective, constraints)
result = prob.solve()
w.value
```

This code produces the optimal portfolio $[1.0798722, -0.36980831, 0.2899361]$.

Notice a couple of new pieces of `cvxpy` functionality used here:

- `cp.quad_form(w, Sigma)` represents the quadratic form $w^T \Sigma w$.
- `cp.sum(w)` represents the sum of all elements of the vector w.

Also, in this example we don't include the $\tfrac{1}{2}$ coefficient in the objective—this can be excluded because minimizing a function f is mathematically equivalent to minimizing any positive multiple of f. The optimal solution in this example contained negative values. In a setting where we don't want to allow short positions, we can add the constraint $w \geq 0$. With this constraint added, the optimal solution changes to [0.833333, 0, 0.166667].

A VARIANT: CONSTRAINING RISK

The mean-variance optimization problem we've looked at so far tries to find the portfolio with the least amount of risk that achieves a minimum acceptable return (and whose weights sum to 1). This is far from the only possible formulation of the problem incorporating notions of risk and return.

Suppose that instead of minimizing risk, you want to maximize your expected return according to a risk "budget." This is a convex problem as well. The mathematical formulation is

$$\text{maximize:} \quad \mu^T w$$

$$\text{subject to:} \quad w^T \Sigma w \leq \sigma_b^2$$

$$\mathbb{1}^T w = 1$$

where σ_b is the maximum volatility allowed for the portfolio. This version of the problem is useful for robo-advisors who wish to construct portfolios with varying levels of riskiness according to the risk appetite or tolerance of their clients. This code shows how to formulate this version of the problem in cvxpy.

Listing 10.4 Mean-variance problem with a risk constraint

```
Sigma = np.matrix([[0.0225 , 0.0216 , 0.00075],
                    [0.0216 , 0.0324 , 0.00045],
                    [0.00075, 0.00045, 0.0025]])
mu = np.array([.06, .05, .03])
sigma_b = .10
N = len(mu)
w = cp.Variable(N)
objective = cp.Maximize(mu.T @ w)
constraints = [cp.quad_form(w, Sigma) <= sigma_b ** 2, cp.sum(w) == 1]
prob = cp.Problem(objective, constraints)
result = prob.solve()
w.value
```

Running this gives the portfolio [0.88354577, −0.29400255, 0.41045678].

10.2.2 Adding more constraints

So far, we've used a few types of constraints in our portfolio-optimization problems. This section will highlight some additional constraints that are useful in practice and show how they can be added to a problem in cvxpy. In all the code snippets that follow, we assume that the problem data and variable w of portfolio weights have been defined. We also assume that we are constraining all weights to be nonnegative, which is standard for robo-advisors.

CONSTRAINING INDIVIDUAL POSITIONS

Constraints like this can help ensure diversification and reduce risk not captured by risk estimates created using historical data. Mathematically, a constraint bounding the size of a single position is written $w_i \leq u_i$. Adding a constraint like this in Python is similarly simple. Assuming a list of constraints called `constraints` already exists, and assuming we have an array u containing upper bounds for each weight, this line adds the upper bound on the ith weight:

```
constraints.append(w[i] <= u[i])
```

In a special case where we want to use the same upper bound for every variable—for example, no position can be larger than 0.5—cvxpy has some special syntax:

```
constraints.append(cp.norm_inf(w) <= 0.5)
```

This construction uses the so-called *infinity norm* of w, which is defined as the magnitude of the largest entry. This constraint ensures that every entry of w has a magnitude of 0.5 or less.

RELATIVE WEIGHTS

These types of constraints ensure that the weights of two assets aren't "too far" from one another. To motivate these constraints, consider the global equity market. The overall weighting is approximately 60% US, 30% foreign developed markets, and 10% emerging markets. If we are constructing an asset allocation that includes these three asset classes (among others), we may want to ensure that the equity portion of the portfolio doesn't deviate too much from the actual relative weighting. There are two possible formulations to achieve this goal. One uses the ratio of one weight to another. These constraints take the form $l_{ij} \leq (w_i/w_j) \leq u_{ij}$, which (because we have assumed all portfolio weights are nonnegative) is equivalent to $l_{ij}w_j \leq w_i \leq u_{ij}w_j$. Adding these constraints takes just two lines in Python:

```
constraints.append(l[i, j] * w[j] <= w[i])
constraints.append(w[i] <= u[i, j] * w[j])
```

Taking one pair from the equity example, the true ratio of US to emerging equities is 6.0. We may wish to constrain this ratio in our portfolio to be between 3.0 and 12.0 (half and twice the actual ratio).

Note that this could be extended beyond just pairs of assets. In our asset-allocation example, let's assume US, foreign developed, and emerging equities are assets 1, 2, and 3, respectively. We can constrain the relative weight of the US equities in this piece of the portfolio with constraints like $w_1 \leq \alpha(w_1 + w_2 + w_3)$, where α is a scalar value controlling how strict the constraint is.

An alternate formulation uses differences rather than ratios. These take the form $l_{ij} \leq (w_i - w_j) \leq u_{ij}$ and can be added to a set of constraints in Python like this:

```
constraints.append(l[i, j] <= w[i] - w[j])
constraints.append(w[i] - w[j] <= u[i, j])
```

The two formulations can be combined. Going back to the global equity example, the difference between the US weight and the foreign developed weight is 30% when expressed as a fraction of the global equity portfolio. We can add constraints saying that the difference in weights between US and foreign-developed stocks has to be between 20% and 40%. However, this may be too loose when trying to form a portfolio with a low-risk target that may consist of only 20% stocks—it would allow the possibility of not investing in foreign-developed stocks at all! If we want to constrain the difference to be between 20% and 40% as a fraction of the overall equity weighting, we can add the constraints

$$(w_1 - w_2) \le 0.4(w_1 + w_2 + w_3)$$

and

$$(w_1 - w_2) \ge 0.2(w_1 + w_2 + w_3)$$

This way, if the overall allocation to equities is small, the allowable gap between US and foreign developed equities will shrink as well. These constraints can be specified in Python via these two lines of code:

```
constraints.append((w[1] - w[2]) <= 0.4 * (w[1] + w[2] + w[3]))
constraints.append((w[1] - w[2]) >= 0.2 * (w[1] + w[2] + w[3]))
```

REFERENCE PORTFOLIOS

In section 10.2.1, we put a constraint on the overall volatility of the portfolio, formulated as $w^T \Sigma w \le \sigma_b^2$. Suppose that rather than constraining the overall volatility, we want to constrain the volatility of the difference in returns between our portfolio, w, and another reference portfolio, p. In this case, the relevant quantity to be constrained is $(w - p)^T \Sigma (w - p)$. The square root of this quantity is known as *tracking error*. In Python, adding a constraint on the tracking error takes almost exactly the same form as the previous volatility constraint (assuming a vector p containing the weights of the reference portfolio has been defined already):

```
constraints.append(cp.quad_form(w - p, Sigma) <= te_bound ** 2)
```

Along the same lines, we can constrain the sum of the total absolute deviations between w and p. cvxpy contains a built-in function norm1() that computes the sum of the absolute values of a vector, which is a convex function:

```
constraints.append(cp.norm1(w - p) <= dev_bound)
```

Expressions like these, comparing the portfolio being optimized to a reference portfolio, will be especially important later when we discuss rebalancing.

10.3 *Optimization-based asset allocation*

In this section, we will put the cvxpy package to work, creating diversified portfolios for a range of risk levels. We'll show how the addition of constraints can affect the weights obtained from the optimization to a significant degree.

We'll employ six asset classes in these examples: equities and bonds from US, foreign developed, and emerging markets. Throughout this section, we'll use expected returns and a covariance matrix that can be accessed using this function:

```
def get_default_inputs():
    tickers = ['VTI', 'VEA', 'VWO', 'AGG', 'BNDX', 'EMB']
    ers = pd.Series([.05, .05, .07, .03, .02, .04], tickers)
    sigma = np.array(
        [[0.0287, 0.0250, 0.0267, 0.0000, 0.0002, 0.0084],
         [0.0250, 0.0281, 0.0288, 0.0003, 0.0002, 0.0092],
         [0.0267, 0.0288, 0.0414, 0.0005, 0.0004, 0.0112],
         [0.0000, 0.0003, 0.0005, 0.0017, 0.0008, 0.0019],
         [0.0002, 0.0002, 0.0004, 0.0008, 0.0010, 0.0011],
         [0.0084, 0.0092, 0.0112, 0.0019, 0.0011, 0.0083]])
    sigma = pd.DataFrame(sigma, tickers, tickers)

    return ers, sigma
```

Table 10.1 shows the ETFs used in this section, along with the asset classes that each one represents.

Table 10.1 ETFs used in portfolio construction

Asset class	Ticker
US stocks	VTI
Foreign developed markets stocks	VEA
Emerging markets stocks	VWO
US bonds	AGG
Foreign developed markets bonds	BNDX
Emerging markets bonds	EMB

10.3.1 Minimal constraints

We'll start with an approach that is about as bare-bones as we can get. In this formulation, we maximize expected return subject only to the following three constraints:

- Long-only
- Full investment
- Bound on overall portfolio volatility

Every type of constraint we define will be its own class in our Python code. First, we'll define a generic `Constraint` class from which all other constraints will inherit:

```
from typing import Dict
class Constraint:
```

```
def generate_constraint(self, variables: Dict):
    """ Create the cvxpy Constraint

    :param variables: dictionary containing the cvxpy variables for the
      problem
    :return: A cvxpy Constraint object representing the constraint
    """
    pass
```

The long-only and full-investment constraints are simple. The following listing defines these two constraint types.

Listing 10.5 Basic constraints

```
class LongOnlyConstraint(Constraint):

    def __init__(self):
        """ Constrain all portfolio weights to be nonnegative """
        pass

    def generate_constraint(self, variables: Dict):
        return variables['w'] >= 0


class FullInvestmentConstraint(Constraint):

    def __init__(self):
        """ Constrain the sum of the portfolio weights to be one """
        pass

    def generate_constraint(self, variables: Dict):
        return cp.sum(variables['w']) == 1.0
```

The constraint on overall portfolio volatility isn't much more complicated than these, but we'll define a more general constraint type first. The `TrackingErrorConstraint` allows us to limit the tracking error of the portfolio being optimized, relative to another portfolio. The `VolatilityConstraint` is a special case where the reference portfolio is all zeros.

Listing 10.6 Tracking error constraints

```
from typing import Union, List
import pandas as pd
class TrackingErrorConstraint(Constraint):

    def __init__(self,
                 asset_names: Union[List[str], pd.Index],
                 reference_weights: pd.Series,
                 sigma: pd.DataFrame,
                 upper_bound: float):
        """ Constraint on the tracking error between a subset of the
        portfolio and a set of target weights
```

```
    :param asset_names: Names of all assets in the problem
    :param reference_weights: Vector of target weights. Index should be
      a subset of asset_names
    :param sigma: Covariance matrix, indexed by asset_names
    :param upper_bound: Upper bound for the constraint, in units of
      volatility (standard deviation)
    """
    self.reference_weights = \
        reference_weights.reindex(asset_names).fillna(0)
    self.sigma = sigma
    self.upper_bound = upper_bound ** 2

def generate_constraint(self, variables: Dict):
    w = variables['w']
    tv = cp.quad_form(w - self.reference_weights, self.sigma)
    return tv <= self.upper_bound


class VolatilityConstraint(TrackingErrorConstraint):

    def __init__(self,
                 asset_names: Union[List[str], pd.Index],
                 sigma: pd.DataFrame,
                 upper_bound: float):
        """ Constraint on the overall volatility of the portfolio

        :param asset_names: Names of all assets in the problem
        :param sigma: Covariance matrix, indexed by asset_names
        :param upper_bound: Upper bound for the constraint, in units of
          volatility (standard deviation)
        """

        zeros = pd.Series(np.zeros(len(asset_names)), asset_names)
        super(VolatilityConstraint, self).__init__(asset_names, zeros,
                                                   sigma, upper_bound)
```

Before we can create portfolios using optimization, we will create a class representing a problem instance where we maximize expected return, subject to arbitrary constraints that can be specified through the constructor. Before this, we'll define a parent class representing a generic mean-variance optimization problem. The parent is called a `MeanVarianceOpt`, and the child is called `MaxExpectedReturnOpt`.

Listing 10.7 Problem classes

```
class MeanVarianceOpt:

    def __init__(self):
        self.asset_names = []
        self.variables = None
        self.prob = None

    @staticmethod
```

```
    def _generate_constraints(variables: Dict,
                                constraints: List[Constraint]):
        return [c.generate_constraint(variables) for c in constraints]

    def solve(self):
        self.prob.solve()

    def get_var(self, var_name: str):
        return pd.Series(self.variables[var_name].value, self.asset_names)

class MaxExpectedReturnOpt(MeanVarianceOpt):

    def __init__(self,
                 asset_names: Union[List[str], pd.Index],
                 constraints: List[Constraint],
                 ers: pd.Series):
        super().__init__()
        self.asset_names = asset_names
        variables = dict('w': cp.Variable(len(ers)))

        cons = MeanVarianceOpt._generate_constraints(variables,
                                                     constraints)
        obj = cp.Maximize(ers.values.T @ variables['w'])
        self.variables = variables
        self.prob = cp.Problem(obj, cons)
```

Now we are ready to go. The next listing shows the setup and solution of a problem where we use 15% as the bound on expected annualized volatility.

Listing 10.8   Building an optimized portfolio

```
ers, sigma = get_default_inputs()
cons = [LongOnlyConstraint(), FullInvestmentConstraint(),
        VolatilityConstraint(ers.index, sigma, .15)]
o = MaxExpectedReturnOpt(ers.index, cons, ers)
o.solve()
weights = np.round(o.get_var('w'), 6)
print(weights)
```

This should produce these weights as output:

```
VTI     0.000000
VEA     0.000000
VWO     0.731976
AGG     0.268023
BNDX    0.000000
EMB     0.000000
```

Let's unpack this code. After retrieving the expected returns and covariance matrix, we define a list of constraints. In the source code, we define each constraint type as a subclass of a generic Constraint class. Each constraint object is initialized with any data specific to that constraint. The `LongOnlyConstraint` and `FullInvestment Constraint` types don't need any specific data—these constraints just make sure the weights are nonnegative and sum to 1. The volatility constraint does require arguments to initialize. Specifically, it takes three inputs:

- The names of all assets that will be included in the problem
- The covariance matrix
- The upper bound on portfolio volatility

Every constraint class implements a method called `generate_constraint()`. This method generates a `cvxpy` constraint that will be an input to the `cvxpy` problem. We also define a class called `MaxExpectedReturnOpt` as a subclass of a generic `MeanVarianceOpt` class. This class takes the asset names, a list of constraints, and a vector of expected returns to use in the objective function as inputs to its constructor. The constructor creates variables, generates the constraints and the objective, and creates a `cvxpy` `Problem` object. The optimization problem is solved by calling the `solve()` method, and the `get_var()` method can be used to retrieve the values of the optimal weights.

After running this code, you can easily check that the volatility constraint is binding: that is, the expected volatility of the portfolio is equal to the 15% bound. We also notice that the portfolio is very concentrated—the only positive weights are in VWO (emerging equities) and AGG (US bonds). This is actually a well-known deficiency of mean-variance optimization; it tends to produce portfolios that are concentrated or otherwise "unintuitive." To see another example of this, try running the following code. You'll find that by increasing the expected return for US stocks by 1% and decreasing the expected return for emerging markets stocks by 1%, you get a wildly different portfolio.

Listing 10.9 Perturbing inputs

```
ers, sigma = get_default_inputs()
ers['VWO'] -= .01   ← Modifying the expected returns for emerging markets and US stocks
ers['VTI'] += .01

cons = [LongOnlyConstraint(), FullInvestmentConstraint(),
        VolatilityConstraint(ers.index, sigma, .15)]
o = MaxExpectedReturnOpt(ers.index, cons, ers)
o.solve()
weights = np.round(o.get_var('w'), 6)
print(weights)
```

Here are the weights you should see:

```
VTI     0.763268
VEA     0.000000
VWO     0.072828
AGG     0.000001
BNDX    0.000000
EMB     0.163903
```

This motivates us to add more constraints to the problem to make the resulting portfolio more diversified, as well as to use some advanced portfolio construction techniques that we will discuss in later chapters.

10.3.2 *Enforcing diversification*

One way to avoid the concentrated portfolio we got in the last section is to add bounds on the maximum position size. Let's try this by setting a maximum weight of 25% on every asset. We can accomplish this via a new constraint class we call GlobalMaxWeightConstraint, which bounds the infinity norm of the weights vector (the *infinity norm* of a vector is the maximum of the absolute values of the vector's entries). The following listing shows the definition of this constraint.

Listing 10.10   Maximum position size constraint

```
class GlobalMaxWeightConstraint(Constraint):
    def __init__(self, upper_bound: float):
        """ Constraint to enforce an upper bound on the magnitude of every
        asset in the portfolio

        :param upper_bound: Magnitude of every position will be constrained
           to be at most this value
        """
        self.upper_bound = upper_bound

    def generate_constraint(self, variables: Dict):
        return cp.norm_inf(variables['w']) <= self.upper_bound
```

Let's reformulate the problem with the additional constraint that no asset's weight can be more than 0.25.

Listing 10.11   Optimizing with capped position sizes

```
cons = [LongOnlyConstraint(), FullInvestmentConstraint(),
        VolatilityConstraint(ers.index, sigma, .15),
        GlobalMaxWeightConstraint(0.25)]
o = MaxExpectedReturnOpt(ers.index, cons, ers)
o.solve()
weights = np.round(o.get_var('w'), 6)
print(weights)
```

This is what we get:

```
VTI     0.25
VEA     0.25
VWO     0.25
AGG     0.00
BNDX    0.00
EMB     0.25
```

As you may expect, adding the constraint pushes the weight on emerging market equities to the other equity asset classes. What is less expected is the weight on US bonds going to zero, while the weight on emerging markets bonds goes to 25%.

We can get behavior that is even worse if we change the volatility bound from 15% to 5% to get a less risky portfolio.

Listing 10.12 Tightening the volatility bound

```
cons = [LongOnlyConstraint(), FullInvestmentConstraint(),
        VolatilityConstraint(ers.index, sigma, .05),
        GlobalMaxWeightConstraint(0.25)]
o = MaxExpectedReturnOpt(ers.index, cons, ers)
o.solve()
weights = np.round(o.get_var('w'), 6)
print(weights)
```

What happened? Together, all the constraints make the feasible set empty. That is, there are no portfolios that can satisfy all the constraints simultaneously. In this situation, cvxpy returns a vector of NaN.

So although the constraint enforcing a maximum weight on every position can help enforce diversification, it doesn't work in all situations. In the next section, we'll show an approach that is more robust to different levels of target volatility.

BENCHMARK-RELATIVE CONSTRAINTS

The problem we're considering consists of both equities and bonds, each in three geographies. Let's imagine that the weights of the global equity portfolio are 60% US, 30% foreign developed, and 10% emerging markets. Similarly, we can imagine that the weights of global bond markets are 40% US, 40% foreign developed, and 20% emerging markets. In this section, we will show how to set constraints ensuring that the equity and fixed income portions of our portfolio don't stray too far from actual market weights.

Let's assume assets 1, 2, and 3 represent the three global equity asset classes (US, foreign developed, and emerging markets, respectively). If we let p denote the global equity portfolio, we have $p = [0.6, 0.3, 0.1]^T$. The weight of US stocks in the equity portion of the portfolio is $w_1/(w_1 + w_2 + w_3)$. We can set a constraint saying that US stocks have to be at least half of the equity portion of the portfolio as follows:

$$w_1 \geq 0.5(w_1 + w_2 + w_3)$$

If we bring all the variables over to one side, this can be rewritten as

$$(1 - 0.5)w_1 - 0.5w_2 - 0.5w_3 \geq 0$$

This is a simple linear constraint. The next listing shows the definition of a generic linear constraint in Python code. Notice that the definition of this constraint type includes a direction parameter. This allows us to easily set constraints as upper bounds, lower bounds, or equalities.

Listing 10.13   Generic linear constraint

```python
class LinearConstraint(Constraint):

    def __init__(self,
                 asset_names: List[str],
                 coefs: pd.Series,
                 rhs: float,
                 direction: str):
        """
        Generic linear constraint, of the form

            coefs * w [vs] rhs

        where [vs] can be <=, >=, or ==

        :param asset_names: Names of all assets in the problem
        :param coefs: Vector of coefficients, indexed by asset names. Can
          be a subset of all assets
        :param rhs: Right-hand side of the constraint
        :param direction: String starting with "<", ">", or "="
        """
        self.coefs = coefs.reindex(asset_names).fillna(0).values
        self.rhs = rhs
        self.direction = direction

    def generate_constraint(self, variables: Dict):
        w = variables['w']
        direction = self.direction
        if direction[0] == '<':
            return self.coefs.T @ w <= self.rhs
        elif direction[0] == '>':
            return self.coefs.T @ w >= self.rhs
        elif direction[0] == '=':
            return self.coefs.T @ w == self.rhs
```

To easily create constraints of the type we are discussing, we'll define a new class called `SubsetWeightConstraint`. Creating a constraint of this type requires a specific target asset (asset 1 in our example), a set of assets (assets 1, 2, and 3), and a right-hand side coefficient (0.5 in the example). The code does a little algebra and then creates a `LinearConstraint` with some newly calculated coefficients, which makes creating this type of constraint much more convenient.

Listing 10.14   Constraining asset weight relative to an asset subset

```python
class SubsetWeightConstraint(LinearConstraint):

    def __init__(self,
                 target_asset_name: str,
                 asset_names: List[str],
                 asset_subset_names: List[str],
```

```
            rhs: float,
            direction: str):
""" Create a constraint of the form

   w_k [vs] b * sum_I(w_i)

   where [vs] can be >=, <=, or ==.
   This constraints the weight of asset k as a fraction of the total
   weight of assets in the set I.

:param target_asset_name: Name of asset whose weight will be
   constrained
:param asset_names: All asset names in the problem
:param asset_subset_names: Target asset's weight will be constrained
   as a fraction of the total weight in this set
:param rhs: Bound for the constraint
:param direction: String starting with "<", ">", or "="
"""
coefs = pd.Series(-rhs, asset_subset_names)
coefs[target_asset_name] += 1
super(SubsetWeightConstraint, self).__init__(asset_names,
                                             coefs,
                                             0,
                                             direction)
```

Going back to our example, we can create the constraint we want using this code snippet:

```
con = SubsetWeightConstraint('VTI',
        ['VTI', 'VEA', 'VWO', 'AGG', 'BNDX', 'EMB'],
        ['VTI', 'VEA', 'VWO'], 0.5, '>')
```

Adding constraints like this for every asset could be a chore; to make it easier, we'll define a function that generates constraints for each asset in a subset in each direction (an upper bound and a lower bound) with specified reference weights.

Listing 10.15 Generating multiple constraints

```
def generate_subset_weight_constraints(asset_subset_names,
                                       all_asset_names,
                                       ref_weights,
                                       tolerance):

    ref_weights = ref_weights[asset_subset_names]
    ref_weights /= ref_weights.sum()
    cons = []
    for target_asset_name in asset_subset_names:
        ub = ref_weights[target_asset_name] + tolerance
        ub_con = SubsetWeightConstraint(target_asset_name,
                                        all_asset_names,
                                        asset_subset_names,
                                        ub,
                                        '<')
```

```
        lb = ref_weights[target_asset_name] - tolerance
        lb_con = SubsetWeightConstraint(target_asset_name,
                                        all_asset_names,
                                        asset_subset_names,
                                        lb,
                                        '>')
        cons.extend([ub_con, lb_con])

    return cons
```

As an example, to generate constraints enforcing that each of the three equity assets has to be within 10% (in an absolute sense) of its benchmark weight within global equities, we can do this:

```
con = generate_subset_weight_constraints(['VTI', 'VEA', 'VWO'],
        ['VTI', 'VEA', 'VWO', 'AGG', 'BNDX', 'EMB'], bmk, .10)
```

This creates a list of six linear constraints—an upper and lower bound for each asset in equities—that can be used in constructing an instance of an optimization problem.

Let's try a full example. The following code solves a problem with this type of constraint added for both equities and bonds.

Listing 10.16   Example with benchmark-relative constraints

```
ers, sigma = get_default_inputs()
cons = [LongOnlyConstraint(), FullInvestmentConstraint(),
        VolatilityConstraint(ers.index, sigma, .15)]
eq_bmk = pd.Series([.6, .3, .1], ['VTI', 'VEA', 'VWO'])
subset_cons_eq = generate_subset_weight_constraints(eq_bmk.index, ers.index,
                                                    eq_bmk, .20)
cons.extend(subset_cons_eq)
fi_bmk = pd.Series([.4, .4, .2], ['AGG', 'BNDX', 'EMB'])
subset_cons_fi = generate_subset_weight_constraints(fi_bmk.index, ers.index,
                                                    fi_bmk, .20)
cons.extend(subset_cons_fi)
o = MaxExpectedReturnOpt(ers.index, cons, ers)
o.solve()
weights = np.round(o.get_var('w'), 6)
print(weights)
```

This gives the following result:

```
VTI     0.366974
VEA     0.242718
VWO     0.261297
AGG     0.051605
BNDX    0.025802
EMB     0.051605
```

The portfolio that results from this approach is more balanced than the one we got using the maximum-position-size constraints and even has a slightly higher expected return (which is left to you to verify).

10.3.3 Creating an efficient frontier

Robo-advisors generally offer a selection of portfolios at varying levels of risk. To end this section, we'll construct a set of portfolios, each optimized to provide the highest level of expected return for a given level of risk. To ensure diversification, we will include constraints like the ones we used in the prior section. The next listing generates a table of the weights of each portfolio as well as the expected return and volatility of each. For some levels of target risk, we may not be able to find a portfolio that meets all the constraints and gets close to the desired level of volatility. If that happens, we'll exit the loop without recording any information about that portfolio.

Listing 10.17   Creating an efficient frontier

```
asset_vols = np.sqrt(np.diag(sigma))
target_vols = np.arange(np.min(np.floor(asset_vols * 100)) / 100,
                        np.max(asset_vols) + 0.005, 0.005)    ← Creates a range of
                                                                target volatilities
result = []
for target_vol in target_vols:
    cons = [LongOnlyConstraint(),
            FullInvestmentConstraint(),
            VolatilityConstraint(ers.index, sigma, target_vol)]

    # constraints on the equity part of the portfolio
    eq_bmk = pd.Series([.6, .3, .1], ['VTI', 'VEA', 'VWO'])
    subset_cons_eq = generate_subset_weight_constraints(eq_bmk.index,
                                                        ers.index,
                                                        eq_bmk, .20)

    cons.extend(subset_cons_eq)

    # constraints on the fixed income part
    fi_bmk = pd.Series([.4, .4, .2], ['AGG', 'BNDX', 'EMB']) #C
    subset_cons_fi = generate_subset_weight_constraints(fi_bmk.index,
                                                        ers.index,
                                                        fi_bmk, .20)

    cons.extend(subset_cons_fi)

    o = MaxExpectedReturnOpt(ers.index, cons, ers)
    o.solve()
    weights = np.round(o.get_var('w'), 6)
    if np.any(np.isnan(weights)):
        continue

    risk = np.sqrt(weights @ sigma @ weights)
    er = weights @ ers
    if risk < (target_vol - .005):    ← If volatility target isn't met, break.
        break
```

```
      info = pd.Series([risk, er], ['Risk', 'ER'])
      result.append(pd.concat((info, weights)))

pd.concat(result, axis=1).T
```

To end this chapter, we'll show a way to construct a portfolio that doesn't consider expected return at all but instead tries to maximize the overall ESG score while keeping tracking error to a benchmark portfolio small.

10.3.4 *Building an ESG portfolio*

In chapter 4, we discussed the rising popularity of socially responsible investing. Now we can show how to use optimization to build a portfolio with a higher overall ESG score. Table 10.2 shows the additional ETFs that we will introduce into the problem.

Table 10.2   ESG scores of ETFs

Asset class	Ticker	ESG quality score
US stocks (large cap)	ESGU	7.06
US stocks (small cap)	ESML	6.87
Foreign developed markets stocks	ESGD	9.05
Emerging markets stocks	ESGE	7.82
US bonds	EAGG	7.08
Global bonds	BGRN	7.70

The approach we will take to build the ESG portfolio is to maximize the average ESG score while constraining tracking error to a reference portfolio. Mathematically, the problem looks like this:

$$\text{maximize:} \quad \varepsilon^T w$$

$$\text{subject to:} \quad (w - p)^T \Sigma (w - p) \leq \sigma_b^2$$

$$\mathbb{1}^T w = 1$$

$$w \geq 0$$

where ε is a vector of the ESG scores for each ETF. The parameter σ_b controls how much tracking error we allow from the reference portfolio. The code in listing 10.18 generates portfolios for a range of values of σ_b and builds a table with the results. It starts by calculating a covariance matrix that includes both the ETFs we've used up to this point and the ESG-tilted ETFs from table 10.2. We then define a reference portfolio, which for this example is the 10% volatility portfolio from the efficient frontier we generated. Finally, we iterate over a series of tracking-error tolerances, solving the problem for each tolerance and building a DataFrame holding the output.

Listing 10.18   Building ESG portfolios

```
import yfinance as yf
tickers = ['VTI', 'VEA', 'VWO', 'AGG', 'BNDX', 'EMB',
           'ESGU', 'ESML', 'ESGD', 'ESGE', 'EAGG', 'BGRN']
rets = yf.download(tickers, period='max')['Adj Close'].pct_change()
rets = rets.dropna(axis=0, how='any')[tickers]

sigma = rets.cov() * 252

esg_scores = pd.Series([6.03, 8.01, 4.74, 6.63, 6.58, 2.99,
                        7.06, 6.87, 9.05, 7.82, 7.08, 7.70], tickers)
reference_port = pd.Series([.2492, .1362, .1652, .2696, .0899, .0899],
                           ['VTI', 'VEA', 'VWO', 'AGG', 'BNDX', 'EMB'])
reference_port = reference_port.reindex(tickers).fillna(0)
ref_risk = np.sqrt(reference_port @ sigma @ reference_port)
ref_esg = reference_port @ esg_scores
reference_info = pd.Series([0.00, ref_risk, ref_esg], ['TE', 'Risk', 'ESG'])
esg_frontier = [pd.Series([0.00, ref_risk, ref_esg], ['TE', 'Risk', 'ESG'])]

te_bounds = [0.0025, 0.005, 0.0075, 0.01, 0.0125, 0.015, 0.0175, 0.02, 0.0225,
0.025]
for te_bound in te_bounds:
    te_con = TrackingErrorConstraint(tickers, reference_port, sigma, te_bound)
    cons = [LongOnlyConstraint(), FullInvestmentConstraint(), te_con]
    o = MaxExpectedReturnOpt(tickers, cons, esg_scores)
    o.solve()
    weights = np.round(o.get_var('w'), 6)

    diffs = weights - reference_port
    te = np.sqrt(diffs @ sigma @ diffs)
    port_esg = esg_scores @ weights
    risk = np.sqrt(weights @ sigma @ weights)

    esg_frontier.append(pd.Series([te, risk, port_esg], ['TE', 'Risk', 'ESG']))

esg_frontier = pd.concat(esg_frontier, axis=1).T
```

The output is shown in table 10.3. Your results will vary somewhat because the amount of history available for the ETF returns gets longer each day, changing the exact values in the covariance matrix.

You can see how allowing more tracking error results in a higher overall ESG score for the portfolio—increasing from 6.02 for the reference portfolio to 8.13 when we allow 2.5% tracking error. On the other hand, the predicted volatility of the portfolio doesn't change much. Note that the volatility here is around 12.8% rather than the 10% we mentioned earlier. In this example, we use a covariance matrix estimated using a shorter returns history to accommodate the ESG-tilted ETFs, which launched much more recently than the standard ones. Ultimately, it is up to the advisor to decide the trade-off between tracking error and ESG score.

Table 10.3   Results from the ESG frontier

Tracking error	Volatility	ESG quality score
0.00%	12.87%	6.02
0.25%	12.84%	6.34
0.50%	12.83%	6.66
0.75%	12.80%	6.97
1.00%	12.78%	7.27
1.25%	12.75%	7.52
1.50%	12.74%	7.68
1.75%	12.75%	7.81
2.00%	12.76%	7.92
2.25%	12.77%	8.03
2.50%	12.82%	8.13

Summary

- Convexity is a property that applies to sets, functions, and optimization problems. Convexity is desirable in optimization because it ensures that the problem can be solved quickly and that the solution found is truly optimal.
- The optimization functions in `scipy` can be used for very lightweight optimization problems and will accept nonconvex inputs. However, you should be careful using these functions, because they can seemingly work but potentially give nonoptimal solutions when solving nonconvex problems.
- Naive portfolio optimization—without constraints—can be very sensitive to inputs and result in concentrated or otherwise nonintuitive portfolios. This can be mitigated by adding constraints to the portfolio-optimization problem.
- You can use standard optimization formulations to construct ESG-friendly portfolios.

Asset allocation by risk: Introduction to risk parity

This chapter covers

- Understanding risk contributions in investment portfolios
- Using different definitions of risk-parity portfolios and computing their weights

In chapter 10, we saw two pitfalls of mean-variance optimization:

- Without explicit constraints on diversification, mean-variance optimization can result in very concentrated portfolios.
- The weights of portfolios obtained using mean-variance optimization can be very sensitive to the inputs: expected returns, covariances, and constraints.

We'll start this chapter by revealing another unattractive property of portfolios that appear to be diversified and how this motivates us to allocate assets within a portfolio by risk rather than by capital—an approach known as *risk parity*. We'll cover several different risk-parity methods for constructing portfolios according to each approach and also discuss some practical implications of managing a risk-parity portfolio.

11.1   Decomposing portfolio risk

Let's start by thinking about the classic diversified portfolio, a 60/40 mix of stocks and bonds. On the surface, this portfolio certainly seems diversified—the amounts allocated to stocks and bonds aren't far from 50/50, after all. But what if we want to know how much of the portfolio's risk is allocated to stocks? Intuitively, it seems that the amount of risk would be more than 60%, because 60% of the portfolio's weight is in stocks, and stocks are riskier than bonds. But how much more? To answer this question, we'll first take a detour into some theory.

11.1.1 Risk contributions

Imagine that we have a portfolio, p, consisting of allocations to N assets, with p_i being the weight on the ith asset. Now suppose we can write the portfolio p as a sum of N subportfolios, p^1 through p^N, where each subportfolio contains only one asset. Specifically, each portfolio p^i is all zeros except for the value p_i in the ith slot. Expressed mathematically, this decomposition is

$$p = p^1 + p^2 + \ldots + p^N$$

If Σ is the covariance matrix associated with the N assets, the *risk contribution* of the ith asset to portfolio p is defined as $\left(p^T \Sigma p^i\right) / p^T \Sigma p$. In words, the risk contribution of the ith asset is the covariance of the ith asset with the full portfolio, divided by the variance of the full portfolio.

It is easy to check that for any decomposition, the risk contributions of the subportfolios add to 1. Thus, they can be thought of as the fraction of risk allocated to each subportfolio. In the specific case of our asset-based decomposition, the risk contributions are the fractions of risk coming from each asset. An important fact to note is that using this choice of decomposition, the risk contributions from each asset remain the same as the portfolio is scaled up or down. That is, we can multiply portfolio p by any real number, and the risk contributions stay the same, although the volatility of the resulting portfolio is different. This fact will be important later.

11.1.2 Risk concentration in a "diversified" portfolio

Now let's return to our example of the 60/40 portfolio. Using values from the covariance matrix from chapter 10, we can compute the risk contributions from stocks and bonds.

> Listing 11.1   Risk contributions of the 60/40 portfolio

```
import numpy as np
p = np.array([0.6, 0.4])
sigma = np.array([[0.0287, 0], [0, 0.0017]])
p_var = p @ sigma @ p
risk_contribs = np.diag(p) @ sigma @ p / (p @ sigma @ p)
risk_contribs
```

This code calculates both risk contributions in a single line, using the `diag()` function to create a matrix with the subportfolios for stocks and bonds as columns.

We find that almost all the risk in the portfolio—over 117%—comes from stocks! This agrees with our intuition that the value is more than 60%, but to many people, the fact that the risk contribution from stocks is so high comes as a surprise. Figure 11.1 shows the risk contribution from stocks as the weight on stocks varies from 0 to 1. The risk contributions are equal when the portfolio is about 20% stocks. Constructing a portfolio with equal risk contributions from each asset or asset class is the goal of risk parity.

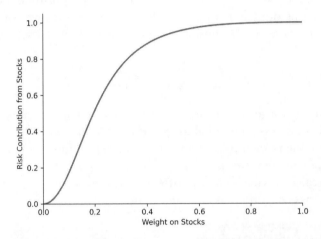

Figure 11.1   Risk contribution from stocks as a function of the weight on stocks

11.1.3 *Risk parity as an optimal portfolio*

We have previously mentioned the challenge of predicting expected returns. Suppose we decide to shy away from this challenge and make the simplifying assumption that the expected return of any asset is proportional to its volatility. Specifically, if μ_i and σ_i represent the expected return and volatility of the ith asset, we assume that there is some constant γ such that $\mu_i = \gamma \sigma_i$ for each i. Note that we don't need to know what γ is—we only assume that such a number exists. We'll also assume that the covariance matrix is diagonal.

Now let's solve a simple mean-variance optimization problem that trades off expected return and portfolio volatility, with no extra constraints. The mathematical formulation of the problem we'll solve is

$$\text{maximize: } \mu^T w - \frac{\lambda}{2} w^T \Sigma w,$$

where λ is a risk-aversion parameter. The optimal solution to this problem is

$$w^* = \frac{1}{\lambda} \Sigma^{-1} \mu$$

Because Σ is diagonal, the inverse Σ^{-1} can be calculated in closed form—it's also a diagonal matrix whose entries are $1/\sigma_1^2, \ldots, 1/\sigma_N^2$. Then, because we know $\mu_i = \gamma\sigma_i$ for each i, we get that

$$w_i^* = \frac{\gamma}{\lambda}\frac{1}{\sigma_i}$$

This holds no matter what the values of γ and λ are: regardless of the values we choose, the values of the optimal portfolio are always inversely proportional to the volatilities of the assets. Changing the values of γ and λ just scales the optimal portfolio up or down, changing its volatility but not the relative sizes of the portfolio weights.

Now let's compute the risk contribution of each asset in this portfolio. Because Σ is diagonal, this can be done in closed form. If we let e^i denote a vector whose entries are all 0 except for a 1 in the ith slot, the risk contribution of asset i is

$$\frac{\left(w_i^* e^i\right)^T \Sigma w^*}{(w^*)^T \Sigma w^*}$$

Plugging in the formula for w^* and using the fact that Σ is diagonal, we get that the numerator of this expression is equal to $(\gamma/\lambda)^2$ and the denominator is equal to $N(\gamma/\lambda)^2$, meaning the risk contribution from each asset is simply $1/N$. In other words, the optimal portfolio for this problem is a risk-parity portfolio.

This Python code calculates the optimal portfolio in the previous two-asset example and verifies that the risk contributions are indeed equal.

> ### Listing 11.2   Risk contributions of a two-asset risk-parity portfolio

```
lamb = 4.0
gamma = 0.3
sigma = np.array([[0.0287, 0], [0, 0.0017]])
mu = gamma * np.sqrt(np.diag(sigma))

w_star = 1.0 / lamb * np.matrix(sigma).I @ mu
w_star = np.asarray(w_star).flatten()

w_var = w_star @ sigma @ w_star
risk_contribs = np.diag(w_star) @ sigma @ w_star / w_var
risk_contribs
```

This produces the risk contributions [0.5, 0.5], as we expected.

If you take the values of the optimal solution and normalize them so that they sum to 1, you will see that the weight on stocks is about 19.57%, which agrees with what we saw in figure 11.1.

We do make a couple of simplifying assumptions in this derivation of risk parity as an optimal portfolio. We assume that the covariance matrix is diagonal and that expected returns are proportional to volatility. Looking at historical data from as far back as we can, the second assumption is fairly reasonable—risk-adjusted returns across asset classes are close to one another. On the other hand, the second assumption doesn't always hold. For example, the long-term correlation between stocks and bonds is close to zero, but stocks and commodities are positively correlated. However, we have shown that under these assumptions, the risk-parity portfolio is mean-variance optimal, giving some theoretical justification to the approach.

We will see in the following sections that calculating weights for risk-parity portfolios doesn't actually require a vector of expected returns. This is attractive from a practical standpoint because estimating expected returns is a notoriously difficult task.

11.2 Calculating risk-parity weights

Having defined the concepts of risk contributions and a risk-parity portfolio, we now turn to the task of actually computing the portfolio weights.

11.2.1 Naive risk parity

In the special case where the covariance matrix is diagonal, we already know how to compute the risk-parity weights. Any portfolio whose weights are inversely proportional to the asset volatilities is a risk-parity portfolio. Specifically, a portfolio whose ith value is $1/\sigma_i$ is a risk-parity portfolio. We only need to rescale this portfolio by the sum of its values to make the weights sum to 1. Such a portfolio is known as a *naive risk-parity* portfolio. Although the case of a diagonal covariance matrix is rare, the naive risk-parity portfolio can be a good starting point for iterative algorithms and a useful test case for algorithms designed to work in the general (nondiagonal) case.

11.2.2 General risk parity

General risk parity refers to the case when the covariance matrix is not assumed to be diagonal but we wish to have an equal risk contribution from each asset in the portfolio. In this section, we will show how to use convex optimization to find risk-parity portfolios.

Remember from earlier that the risk contribution from asset i in a portfolio w is equal to

$$\frac{\left(w_i e^i\right)^T \Sigma w}{w^T \Sigma w}$$

Risk parity requires that these values are equal for all i. Because the denominator of this expression is the same for all i, we can ignore it for simplicity. We can also simplify the numerator to $w_i (\Sigma w)_i$, where $(\Sigma w)_i$ is the ith element of the vector Σw. So the risk-parity constraint can be expressed as

$$w_i (\Sigma w)_i = w_j (\Sigma w)_j$$

which must hold true for every choice of i and j.

Now let's consider the following unconstrained optimization problem:

$$\text{minimize: } \frac{1}{2} w^T \Sigma w - \gamma \sum_{i=1}^{N} \ln w_i$$

In this problem, γ is a positive fixed constant. This is a convex optimization problem: the quadratic expression $w^T \Sigma w$ is convex, and the function $-\ln x$ is convex as well. Because the objective is convex and there are no constraints, we know the optimal solution will occur where the gradient of the function is equal to a vector of 0s. The ith element of the gradient of the objective function is $(\Sigma w)_i - \frac{\gamma}{w_i}$, so the gradient is equal to $\mathbf{0}$ only when $(\Sigma w)_i = \frac{\gamma}{w_i}$ for each i or (multiplying both sides by w_i), $w_i (\Sigma w)_i = \gamma$ for each i. This clearly implies the condition given earlier, so the optimal portfolio for the optimization problem will be a risk-parity portfolio.

Let's do an example in Python to verify that this works.

Listing 11.3   Risk contributions of a three-asset risk-parity portfolio

```
import cvxpy as cp
sigma = np.matrix([[0.0225 , 0.0216 , 0.00075],
                   [0.0216 , 0.0324 , 0.00045],
                   [0.00075, 0.00045, 0.0025]])
N = sigma.shape[0]
w = cp.Variable(N)
gamma = 1.0
objective = cp.Minimize(0.5 * cp.quad_form(w, sigma) - gamma * sum(cp.log(w)))
constraints = []
prob = cp.Problem(objective, constraints)
result = prob.solve()
p = w.value
risk_contribs = np.diag(p) @ sigma @ p / (p @ sigma @ p)
risk_contribs
```

The risk contributions are all equal to $1/3$ (at least, up to small numerical differences), as expected. In this example, we use a value of 10 for the parameter gamma (γ). In theory, any positive choice of γ should give the same solution, but in practice, different values may give very slightly different solutions. We recommend not using a value of γ that is extremely large or extremely small. In a situation where correctness is critical, it would be prudent to check that the risk contributions from the optimal portfolio are indeed close to equal and to potentially solve the problem multiple times with different values of γ until a satisfactory solution is found. Also note that this method will always give a solution where the portfolio weights are positive, as is typically desired.

11.2.3 *Weighted risk parity*

In the previous example, the optimization problem produced a portfolio with equal risk contributions coming from each asset included in the portfolio. In practice, the assets may be index-tracking instruments representing certain asset classes—for example, equities, bonds, and commodities. Let's complicate things a bit and suppose that we use multiple instruments to represent each asset class. For instance, we can break up equities or bonds by geography or market cap range (or both). Figure 11.2

shows one possible breakdown using stocks, bonds, and commodities. Within both equities and bonds, we divide the global market into US, foreign developed, and emerging markets; and with US stocks, we divide the market into large cap and small cap. The leaves of the tree are the ETF instruments we can use to represent the most granular divisions.

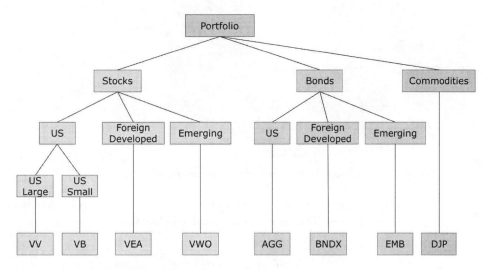

Figure 11.2 Tree of portfolio constituents, from asset classes to instruments

This gives us a total of eight instruments representing three top-level asset classes. We know how to form a risk-parity portfolio out of these eight instruments—all we need is an estimate of the covariance matrix. But what happens when we do this? Figure 11.3 shows the risk contributions we get from each of the most granular asset classes (or instruments) as well as the totals for each of the three top-level asset classes. We end up with much more risk coming from stocks: because four of the eight assets used in the portfolio fall into the stocks bucket, we end up with 50% of the total risk coming from stocks. Similarly, we get 3/8 of the total portfolio risk from bonds and only 1/8 from commodities.

Luckily, it turns out there is an easy solution to this problem. Let's look back to our original formulation of the risk-parity portfolio optimization problem:

$$\text{minimize: } \frac{1}{2}w^T \Sigma w - \gamma \sum_{i=1}^{N} \ln w_i$$

In this problem, the log of each asset weight gets a weight of γ in the objective, and we end up with equal risk contributions from each asset. This is no coincidence—it follows directly from the math we just did. To get equal risk contributions from each top-level asset class, we just need to make sure the total weight on instruments in each

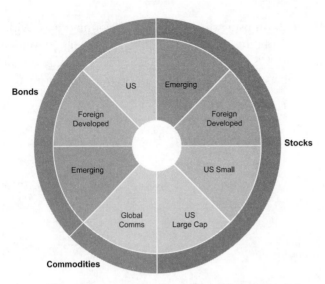

Figure 11.3   Risk contributions from top-level and most-granular asset classes

asset class is equal. To do this, we can change the formulation to have instrument-specific weightings. The new formulation looks like this:

$$\text{minimize: } \frac{1}{2} w^T \Sigma w - \sum_{i=1}^{N} \gamma_i \ln w_i$$

One way to assign the γ_i values is to set γ_i to be the inverse of the number of instruments representing the asset class of which the ith instrument is a member. Or, said another way, if an asset class is represented by m instruments in the strategy, each instrument gets a weight (or γ_i value) of $1/m$. This guarantees not only equal risk contributions from each top-level asset class but also equal risk contributions from each asset within an asset class.

Let's look at an example to help make this clear. This code calculates a weighted risk-parity portfolio using the asset classes and instruments from figure 11.2 .

Listing 11.4   Weighted risk parity in Python

```
import yfinance as yf

tickers = ['VV', 'VB', 'VEA', 'VWO', 'AGG', 'BNDX', 'EMB', 'DJP']
rets = yf.download(tickers, start='2014-01-01', end='2021-12-31')
rets = rets['Adj Close'].pct_change().dropna(axis=0, how='any')[tickers]
sigma = np.matrix(rets.cov().values) * 252

N = sigma.shape[0]
w = cp.Variable(N)
gamma = np.concatenate((np.ones(4) / 4, np.ones(3) / 3, np.ones(1) / 1))
objective = cp.Minimize(0.5 * cp.quad_form(w, sigma) - (gamma @ cp.log(w)))
constraints = []
```

```
prob = cp.Problem(objective, constraints)

result = prob.solve()
p = w.value
p_var = p @ sigma @ p
risk_contribs = np.diag(p) @ sigma @ p / (p @ sigma @ p)
risk_contribs
```

In this code, the equity assets occupy the first four indices. The next three are fixed income, and the last is commodities. As desired, each group of risk contributions adds to 1/3.

Figure 11.4 shows a chart of the risk contributions by instrument and by asset class from the weighted risk-parity portfolio. By weighting the instruments differently, we avoid the problem of imbalance risk across asset classes when the asset classes contain different numbers of instruments.

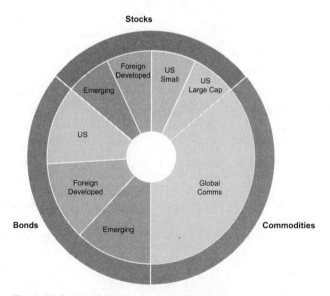

Figure 11.4 Weighted risk-parity portfolio with equal risk contributions from each asset class and from each instrument within each asset class

This approach works well but perhaps leaves something to be desired. Within the equities asset class, we have four instruments representing large cap and small cap, foreign developed markets, and emerging markets. The approach described ignores the middle layers of the classifications between the asset class and instrument level. Specifically, we end up with half the risk contribution within equities coming from US stocks—only because two instruments are used to represent this asset class. If we used a "total market" fund to represent US stocks, rather than breaking it into large cap and small cap, we would end up with 1/3 of the risk contribution within equities coming from US stocks.

This could easily become more extreme. For example, we could choose to represent large-cap US stocks using 11 separate funds, each covering a different sector of the large-cap market. In this case, we would have 12 instruments representing the US stocks asset class, compared to only 1 each for foreign developed and emerging markets. Then 12/14 of the risk within equities would come from the United States! This motivates us to use an approach that considers the entire structure of the instrument classification rather than only the top and bottom levels.

11.2.4 Hierarchical risk parity

This section focuses on using the full structure of the hierarchy, or *tree*, from top-level asset class down to instruments, in creating risk-parity portfolios. The approach we'll take won't require us to define the tree manually as we did in figure 11.2. Instead, we will "learn" the structure of the tree automatically using the correlation matrix of the assets we include in the portfolio. This approach, known as *hierarchical risk parity* (HRP) consists of three steps that we will cover separately:

1 Clustering the assets
2 Rearranging the covariance matrix according to the clusters
3 Applying recursive bisection to compute portfolio weights

This approach was first described in a 2016 paper by Marcos Lopez de Prado called "Building Diversified Portfolios that Outperform Out-of-Sample" (https://doi.org/10.3905/jpm.2016.42.4.059). The code in this section is based on code from that paper as well.

HIERARCHICAL CLUSTERING

The first step of HRP is to break the assets being included in the portfolio into clusters based on their pairwise correlations. Let's assume we have the correlation matrix and denote it with R, where R_{ij} represents the entry in the ith row and the jth column. We begin by transforming the correlation matrix into a distance matrix, D, using the formula

$$D_{ij} = \sqrt{\frac{1}{2}(1 - R_{ij})}$$

Notice that the diagonal entries of this matrix are 0 (each asset has a distance of zero from itself), and pairs of assets that have higher correlation have lower distance values.

Next, we compute a second distance matrix, denoted by $\bar{D}$. Each entry of this matrix is the Euclidean distance between the corresponding columns of D. The formula for calculating each entry of $\bar{D}$ is

$$\bar{D}_{ij} = \sqrt{\sum_{k=1}^{N} \left(D_{ki} - D_{kj} \right)^2}$$

Whereas D captures how far apart pairs of assets are from each other in terms of their returns, $\bar{D}$ captures the distance between pairs of assets in terms of the similarity of their distances from all other assets. Put another way, the value of $\bar{D}_{ij}$ is small when the ith and jth assets have similar correlations to other assets. The following code shows the calculations so far, starting with downloading returns using the `yfinance` package.

Listing 11.5   Calculating the distance matrix

```
import itertools

tickers = ['VV', 'VB', 'AGG', 'VEA', 'BNDX', 'VWO', 'EMB', 'DJP']
rets = yf.download(tickers, start='2014-01-01', end='2021-12-31')['Adj Close']
rets = rets.pct_change().dropna(axis=0, how='any')[tickers]
cov, corr = rets.cov() * 252, rets.corr()

dist = ((1 - corr) / 2.) ** .5

d_bar = dist * 0
for i, j in itertools.permutations(dist.columns, 2):
    d_bar[i][j] = np.linalg.norm(dist[i] - dist[j])
```

This is the result you should see from running this code:

```
round(d_bar, 4)
          VV      VB     AGG     VEA    BNDX     VWO     EMB     DJP
VV    0.0000  0.2951  1.3087  0.3691  1.2905  0.5024  0.7878  0.9158
VB    0.2951  0.0000  1.2862  0.4083  1.2736  0.5327  0.7740  0.8929
AGG   1.3087  1.2862  0.0000  1.2948  0.6043  1.2355  0.9080  1.0853
VEA   0.3691  0.4083  1.2948  0.0000  1.2888  0.4091  0.7450  0.8790
BNDX  1.2905  1.2736  0.6043  1.2888  0.0000  1.2281  0.9455  1.1005
VWO   0.5024  0.5327  1.2355  0.4091  1.2281  0.0000  0.7039  0.8300
EMB   0.7878  0.7740  0.9080  0.7450  0.9455  0.7039  0.0000  0.8383
DJP   0.9158  0.8929  1.0853  0.8790  1.1005  0.8300  0.8383  0.0000
```

The next part of the clustering process is a little more complicated. It consists of actually computing the clusters of assets. The first cluster will contain two assets—the two "closest" assets according to the matrix $\bar{D}$—and the final cluster will contain all assets. However, the clusters are not "nested," meaning some clusters between the first and last may contain assets that are not part of a previous cluster.

We'll describe what the algorithm does before showing the code. Let's start by defining each of the N assets as its own cluster. This will help avoid confusion between assets and clusters. We can think of $\bar{D}$ as a matrix giving distances between clusters labeled 1 to N. $\bar{D}$ will be modified at each step of the algorithm, but this fact will remain true. At each iteration of the algorithm, we do the following:

1 Find the smallest nondiagonal entry of $\bar{D}$. Assume i and j give the labels of this minimum value.

2 Create a new cluster from clusters i and j.

3 Calculate the distance of every asset other than i and j to the new cluster. The distance for a particular cluster is defined as the minimum of the distance to cluster i and the distance to cluster j.

4 Update $\bar{D}$. This consists of two steps:

    a Remove the rows and columns corresponding to i and j.

    b Augment $\bar{D}$ by adding a row and a column with the distances from the new cluster to each existing cluster.

The algorithm decreases the size of $\bar{D}$ at each iteration and terminates when only one cluster is left, containing all the assets.

    Listing 11.6 shows this algorithm implemented in Python. It assumes that matrix $\bar{D}$ (denoted `d_bar`) is a pandas DataFrame. The output of this code is a matrix `link_mat` that provides information about each new cluster created as the algorithm progresses. The code contains some additional steps not mentioned in the textual description where this information is updated. Notice that we use the numpy method `tril_indices()`. This is a convenient way to get the row and column indices of the below-diagonal elements of a matrix—which is exactly what we need to find the smallest off-diagonal element of $\bar{D}$ (we only need the bottom half because $\bar{D}$ is symmetric).

Listing 11.6 Calculating the link matrix

```
import pandas as pd
n = d_bar.shape[0]
link_mat = np.zeros((n-1, 4))                           To start, each asset is
cluster_sizes = _: 1 for _ in d_bar.columns     ◄──    its own cluster of size 1.
cluster_indices = dict(zip(d_bar.columns, range(n)))  ◄──
                                                             Maps column labels
                                                             (asset names) to
for it in range(n - 1):                                      numerical indices
    col_names = d_bar.columns
    idx = np.tril_indices(d_bar.shape[0], -1)
    min_idx = np.argmin(d_bar.values[idx])     ◄── Finds the two closest clusters
    i_int, j_int = idx[1][min_idx], idx[0][min_idx]
    i, j = col_names[i_int], col_names[j_int]
    min_val = d_bar[i][j]
                                             Calculates the distance
    new_name = f"(i, j)"                     from the new cluster
    new_col = d_bar[[i, j]].min(axis=1)  ◄── to the others
    d_bar[new_name] = new_col
    new_col[new_name] = 0                                    Augments D̄ with
    d_bar = d_bar.append(pd.DataFrame({new_name: new_col}).T)  the distances
    d_bar.drop([i, j], axis=0, inplace=True)
    d_bar.drop([i, j], axis=1, inplace=True)

    cluster_sizes[new_name] = cluster_sizes[i] + cluster_sizes[j]
    cluster_indices[new_name] = n + it
    link_mat[it, :] = [cluster_indices[i], cluster_indices[j],
                       min_val, cluster_sizes[new_name]]
```

As we mentioned, the output of this algorithm is a matrix with $(N-1)$ rows encoding information about the clusters. Each row of this matrix contains three pieces of information:

- The labels of the two closest clusters found in the current iteration
- The distance between these two clusters
- The size of the cluster created in this step, meaning the number of underlying assets it contains

If we run the code from listing 11.6 on the matrix d_bar calculated in listing 11.5, we get the following output:

```
link_mat
array([[ 0.      , 1.  , 0.29511716, 2. ],
       [ 3.     , 8.  , 0.36912864, 3. ],
       [ 5.     , 9.  , 0.40906463, 4. ],
       [ 2.     , 4.  , 0.60430531, 2. ],
       [ 6.     , 10. , 0.70386939, 5. ],
       [ 7.     , 12. , 0.83002921, 6. ],
       [11.     , 13. , 0.90802712, 8. ]])
```

Let's examine the first few rows of this matrix:

1. In iteration 1, the algorithm finds that clusters 0 and 1 are the closest. The distance between them is 0.29511716. These two clusters are put into a new cluster (labeled 8). This cluster contains two of the original assets because clusters 0 and 1 both corresponded to single assets.
2. In iteration 2, clusters 3 and 8 are the closest. In this case, cluster 3 corresponds to a single asset, and cluster 8 was created in iteration 1. Together, these two clusters contain three original assets.
3. Iteration 3 is very similar to iteration 2. Clusters 5 and 9 are closest, and together they contain four original assets.
4. Iteration 4 finds that clusters 2 and 4 are closest. These two are placed in cluster 10, which contains two assets.

The progress of this algorithm can also be displayed visually: in figure 11.5, each row represents an iteration of the algorithm. The table starts with clusters (assets) 0 through 7. Each subsequent row sees the addition of a new cluster, which consists of the clusters highlighted in the row above. We also remove the clusters that were chosen in each iteration in the rows following. In all rows past the first, the rightmost value is the label of the newest cluster.

Looking at the first few rows of this diagram, we see that it matches the written description of the algorithm's progress. In the first row, assets 0 and 1 are chosen to create cluster 8. In the second, asset 3 and cluster 8 are chosen to create cluster 9, and so on. In the final iteration, clusters 11 and 13 are placed together to create the final cluster, which contains all assets. This general clustering technique, in which

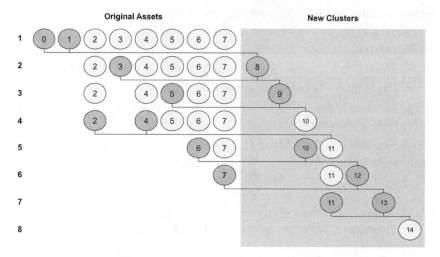

Figure 11.5   **Clustering visualized**

each object starts as a single-item cluster and proceeds by successively combining clusters at each iteration, is known as *agglomerative clustering*.

The Python files for this chapter contain all the code shown, placed into functions:

- `calc_d()` computes the matrix D using the correlation matrix as input.
- `calc_d_bar()` computes the matrix $\bar{D}$.
- `calc_link_matrix()` computes the linkage matrix.

Note that our method for computing the linkage matrix is inefficient. We chose a suboptimal algorithm to make the code easier to understand and to align with the textual description of the algorithm. The `scipy` package contains a far more efficient algorithm. Using this code will give the same clustering as our function, but will work much more quickly for larger sets of assets:

```
import scipy.cluster.hierarchy as sch
link_mat = sch.linkage(d_bar)
```

COVARIANCE MATRIX ORDERING

The second step of HRP isn't nearly as complicated. It consists of reordering the rows and columns of the covariance matrix so that assets close to one another (in terms of the matrix $\bar{D}$) are close to one another in the covariance matrix. This step is also known as *seriation* or *quasi-diagonalization*; you'll see why after we show the methodology and example output. The sorting in this step relies on the linkage matrix that we calculated in the previous clustering step. It essentially looks at the table in the previous section from the bottom up, expanding each cluster into its members until only the original assets, and no clusters, remain.

Figure 11.6 visualizes the process for our example. The process starts with a single cluster in the top row, labeled 14, which contains all the underlying assets. In the second row, we break cluster 14 into its constituents, clusters 11 and 13. We know from figure 11.5 that cluster 11 contains clusters 2 and 4 and cluster 13 contains clusters 7 and 12, so the next row breaks these out. At this point, cluster 12 is the only one that contains more than one asset. Row 4 breaks cluster 12 out into 6 and 10, the next row breaks 10 into 9 and 5, then 9 is broken into 3 and 8, and finally, 8 is broken into 0 and 1, and we are done. The final row gives us an ordering of the assets that will bring similar assets close to one another. In the figure, all the clusters that contain multiple underlying assets are shaded more darkly, while the ones that represent single assets are left lighter.

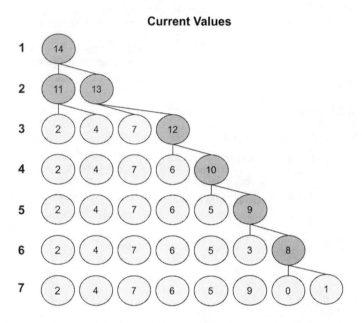

Figure 11.6 Visual depiction of the cluster-splitting process, resulting in reordered assets

This is great, but how do we do this process in code? Listing 11.7 shows an implementation in Python. The algorithm may look a little slick, but this is for practical reasons. In figure 11.6, which visualized the process, when we expanded a cluster at each step by replacing the cluster labels with their two components, we just pushed entries of the table to the right. In Python, this is harder to do. The algorithm first replaces the cluster labels with the label of one of their components, then appends the other components to the end, and finally rearranges the list to put the components next to each other.

Listing 11.7 Reordering the assets

```
# convert link matrix values to integers, since we will use them as indices
link_mat = link_mat.astype(int)
```
←┐ Converts link matrix values
  │ to integers because we
  │ will use them as indices

```
ordering = pd.Series([link_mat[-1, 0], link_mat[-1, 1]])        ← Starts the ordering
                                                                  with the last
                                                                  two clusters
n = link_mat[-1, 3]   ← Finds the number of assets in the problem

while ordering.max() >= n:

    ordering.index = range(0, len(ordering) * 2, 2)   ← Gives us space to
    clusters = ordering[ordering >= n]                  insert the contents of
                                                        any clusters in the list

    indices = clusters.index   ← Gets the locations of the clusters

    rows = clusters.values - n   ← Gives us the iterations of the clustering
                                   algorithm where these clusters were formed

    ordering[indices] = link_mat[rows, 0]   ← Replaces the clusters with
                                              one of their components

    clusters = pd.Series(link_mat[rows, 1], index=indices + 1)

    ordering = ordering.append(clusters)   ← Combines the two series

    ordering = ordering.sort_index()   ←────────── Puts the components of
                                                    each cluster next
ordering = pd.Series(tickers)[ordering.values]      to one another
```

Finds which of the current entries are clusters, not individual assets

Creates a series to hold the second component of each cluster

When we run this code on the linkage matrix we computed earlier, we get this ordering:

```
2       AGG
4       BNDX
7       DJP
6       EMB
5       VWO
3       VEA
0       VV
1       VB
```

We can visualize the effect of the reordering via a heatmap of the correlation matrix. The seaborn package makes this easy:

```
import seaborn as sns
import matplotlib.pyplot as plt

heatmap = sns.heatmap(np.round(corr, 2),
                      vmin=-1, vmax=1, annot=True,
                      cmap='viridis')
plt.show()
```

Figure 11.7 shows the plot that results from this code.

When we rearrange the correlation matrix according to the new ordering, we get a different picture:

```
heatmap = sns.heatmap(np.round(corr.loc[ordering ordering], 2),
                      vmin=-1, vmax=1, annot=True, cmap='viridis')
plt.show()
```

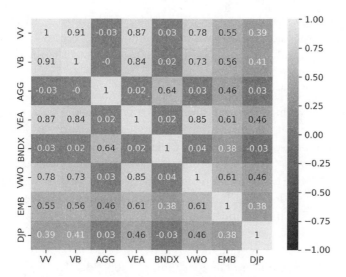

Figure 11.7   A heatmap of the correlation matrix for the individual assets

Figure 11.8 shows the result of this code. Notice that the matrix now looks a lot more orderly. The equity funds—VWO, VEA, VV, and WB, which are all highly correlated with each other—are placed together. Similarly, AGG and BNDX are placed together. The commodities and emerging markets bond funds are in between. We can now also see the reasoning for the term *quasi-diagonalization*. The reordered matrix isn't diagonal, but it is much closer to being *block-diagonal*. For example, the four equity funds form one block of large correlation values, as do AGG and BNDX. DJP isn't especially highly correlated with anything else—it is basically its own block.

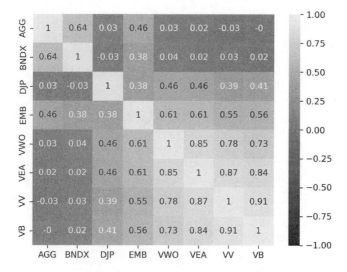

Figure 11.8   Heatmap of the reordered correlation matrix

In the Python source files on the book's website and GitHub (https://www.manning
.com/books/build-a-robo-advisor-with-python-from-scratch and https://github.com/
robreider/robo-advisor-with-python), the algorithm used to calculate the reordering
vector is in the function `calc_ordering_index()`.

RECURSIVE BISECTION

The final step of constructing the hierarchical risk-parity portfolio is known as *recursive
bisection*. This step relies on the observation that the naive risk-parity approach is optimal in the case when the covariance matrix is diagonal and applies that observation
to the now quasi-diagonal (after the reordering step) covariance matrix.

To begin, we will define two helper functions that the recursive bisection algorithm
will use. These are shown in listing 11.8. The first function, `split_indices()`, takes
as input a list of arrays of integer index values. It iterates over each array in the list,
and if the array has at least two elements, that array is split into a left half and a right
half. If the length of the array is even, the two halves will be equal in size. Otherwise,
the right side will have one more element than the left side. The output is a list
containing all the "left" and "right" arrays. The second function takes the covariance
matrix and a set of assets and calculates the variance of the naive risk-parity portfolio
formed from those assets.

Listing 11.8   Helper functions for recursive bisection

```python
def split_indices(indices):
    splits = []
    for i in indices:
        if len(i) <= 1:
            continue
        splits.extend([i[0:(len(i) // 2)], i[(len(i) // 2):len(i)]])

    return splits

def calc_cluster_variance(cov, assets):
    sub_cov = cov.loc[assets, assets]
    w = (1. / np.diag(sub_cov)).reshape(-1, 1)
    w /= w.sum()
    return (w.T @ sub_cov @ w)[0][0]
```

This code snippet shows the application of the first function:

```python
indices = [np.array([0, 1, 2, 3]),np.array([5]), np.array([6, 7, 8])]
split_indices(indices)
```

This gives

```python
[(array([0, 1]), array([2, 3])), (array([6]), array([7, 8]))]
```

The first array of indices (containing 0, 1, 2, 3) is split into [0, 1] and [2, 3]. The second, which has only one element, is skipped. The third (containing [6, 7, 8]) is split into [6] and [7, 8]. The algorithm begins with two initial values:

- A list containing an array of index values computed in the recording step
- A vector of initial weights in which each asset has a weight of 1.0

Each iteration of the algorithm splits the current array of indices by applying the split_indices() function. It then considers each left/right pair in the list of split indices. Remember, each element of a left/right pair is an array of indices corresponding to individual assets. The algorithm updates the current weights of the assets covered by each left/right pair with a function of the variances of the naive risk-parity portfolio corresponding to each half. The algorithm stops when each element of the current list of indices contains only one asset, and can't be split anymore. The following listing shows the full algorithm.

Listing 11.9   Recursive bisection algorithm

```
weights = pd.Series(1, index=ordering)
indices = [ordering.index]
while len(indices) > 0:                                    Calculates the variance of
                                                            the naive risk-parity
    indices = split_indices(indices)               portfolio corresponding to the
    for i in range(0, len(indices), 2):                 assets in the left half
        i_left, i_right = indices[i], indices[i + 1]
        left_var = calc_cluster_variance(cov, ordering[i_left])  ←
        right_var = calc_cluster_variance(cov, ordering[i_right])

                                                         Alpha is the weight
                                                         adjustment factor.
        alpha = left_var / (left_var + right_var)  ←
        weights[ordering[i_left]] *= 1 - alpha     ← Updates the current weights
        weights[ordering[i_right]] *= alpha
```

Splits the index arrays into left/right pairs → (annotation)

Does the same thing for the right half → (annotation)

In essence, the algorithm treats each left/right pair like two uncorrelated assets. The "assets" are naive risk-parity portfolios. The adjustment factors multiply the two portfolios by their naive risk-parity weights.

These are the weights we get when we apply this algorithm using inputs we have previously computed:

```
weights
AGG      0.302460
BNDX     0.555113
DJP      0.027373
EMB      0.080985
VWO      0.007208
VEA      0.010242
VV       0.009530
VB       0.007088
```

To calculate the risk contributions, we can do the following:

```
weights = weights[tickers]
port_var = weights @ cov @ weights
risk_contribs = np.diag(weights) @ cov @ weights / port_var
risk_contribs = pd.Series(risk_contribs.values, index=weights.index)
risk_contribs
```

Here are the results:

```
VV      0.016722
VB      0.014747
AGG     0.307062
VEA     0.019443
BNDX    0.429784
VWO     0.016622
EMB     0.159982
DJP     0.035638
```

Notice that the bond funds (BNDX, AGG, and EMB) get a lot of weight—about 94% of the total—and the total risk contribution from these assets is nearly as large, at about 90%. Figure 11.9 shows the risk contributions visually, with asset classes grouped as in figures 11.3 and 11.4.

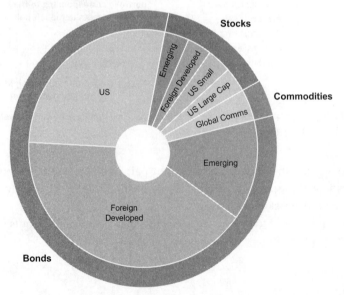

Figure 11.9   **Risk contributions in the portfolio computed using the hierarchical risk-parity approach.**

Why do bonds end up with such a large risk contribution? The main reason is that the HRP approach has no concept of asset classes. It simply sees assets and their correlations and volatilities. In this example, the emerging markets bonds fund is actually more correlated with the stock funds than with the other bond funds. In the weighted risk-parity approach, we specifically dictated that the risk contribution from bonds had to be exactly 33%. The second reason is that risk contributions are sensitive to weights. We saw that in the HRP portfolio, the three bond funds account for about 94% of the total weight and 90% of the risk. If we look at the portfolio we obtained using the weighted risk-parity approach, these three funds add up to 72% of the weight but only 33% of the risk. A difference in weight of roughly 22% leads to a difference in risk contribution of almost 60%. This echoes what we saw in figure 11.1 when considering only stocks and bonds. The risk contribution from stocks increases rapidly as the weight on stocks increases, before leveling off near 100%.

So although the chart in figure 11.9 may be unexpected, we don't consider it a shortfall of the HRP approach. After all, categorizations of assets are artificial. If a bond fund behaves like a stock fund, why should we force it into the bond category?

11.3 Implementation of risk-parity portfolios

Although we have been talking about contributions to risk in portfolios and ways to create portfolios with balanced risk contributions, we haven't looked at the riskiness of the portfolios we've constructed. What we find may come as a bit of a surprise. Let's see what we get when we calculate the volatility of the risk-parity portfolio we constructed using only two assets. Looking back at section 11.1.2, this portfolio consists of 19.57% stocks and 80.43% bonds:

```
sigma = np.array([[0.0287, 0], [0, 0.0017]])
w_rp = np.array([0.1957, 1 - 0.1957])
np.sqrt(w_rp @ sigma @ w_rp)
```

This should result in a value of about 4.69%. Let's compare that to the volatility of the 60/40 portfolio:

```
w = np.array([0.60, 0.40])
np.sqrt(w @ sigma @ w)
```

This gives a value of 10.3%—the volatility of the risk-parity portfolio is less than half that of the 60/40 portfolio. This may not be that surprising, considering that the risk-parity portfolio is 80% bonds. Is it a problem? It depends. Let's continue to assume the same expected returns from section 11.1.3, which were proportional to the volatilities of the assets, and compute the expected returns of the 60/40 portfolio and the risk-parity portfolio:

```
gamma = 0.3
mu = gamma * np.sqrt(np.diag(sigma))
w = np.array([0.60, 0.40])
w @ mu, w_rp @ mu
```

The expected return of the 60/40 portfolio is much higher than the expected return of the risk-parity portfolio: about 3.5% versus about 2%. But we said risk parity is optimal when expected returns are proportional to volatilities and assets are uncorrelated—what happened?

The key here is our definition of *optimal*. Remember that the problem we solved had two terms in its objective function: one for return and one for risk. The risk-parity portfolio gets the portfolio that maximizes the combination of the two terms—the risk-adjusted return. Also, remember that we rescaled the risk-parity portfolio so the weights summed to 1. Before we rescaled, the weights summed to about 2.26. So what's the problem? Well, high risk-adjusted returns are great, but you can't spend them in retirement. A portfolio that earns a return of 1% per year with 1% volatility is better in a risk-adjusted sense than a portfolio that earns 6% per year with 12% volatility, but only one of those portfolios will realistically help an investor achieve their goals later in life. In this section, we'll discuss how risk-parity portfolios are implemented (or traded) to provide an acceptable level of absolute return while maintaining the attractive risk-balanced quality.

11.3.1 Applying leverage

Clearly, the risk-parity portfolio with weights summing to 1 isn't attractive from a total return standpoint. But what if the weights don't have to sum to 1? If we can do away with this constraint, the risk-parity portfolio may look more attractive. We just saw that the simple 60/40 portfolio has a volatility of about 10.3% versus only 4.7% for the risk-parity portfolio. So let's say we scale up the risk-parity portfolio to have the same level of risk as the 60/40 portfolio. This is a simple calculation:

```
w_rp_scaled = w_rp * 10.3 / 4.7
```

Let's check the expected return of the scaled portfolio:

```
w_rp_scaled @ mu
```

This gives a value of 4.36%. Now we have a portfolio with not only a better risk-adjusted return than the 60/40 portfolio but also a higher level of expected return. This "scaling up" of the portfolio weights so that the sum is more than 1 is called taking *leverage*.

OBTAINING LEVERAGE

Unfortunately, we can't just scale up a portfolio—we can't buy $220 worth of stocks and bonds if we have only $100 to invest. To obtain more than $100 in exposure, we need to purchase securities on margin—this essentially means borrowing money to buy the securities. Most brokerages offer this feature to individuals. You can buy some securities and borrow to purchase more, with the purchased securities acting as collateral in case the value of those purchased on margin declines. The brokerage will limit how much can be purchased on margin relative to the amount that has been paid for. Additionally, if the value of the portfolio drops enough, the brokerage may require a cash deposit into the account or may sell the securities you've purchased to limit its potential losses.

Borrowing comes at a cost as well. Brokerages typically charge an interest rate of 2% to 3% above the current risk-free rate. As such, the cost of borrowing must be carefully considered. Institutional managers can access leverage more cheaply using derivatives contracts, but these are beyond the scope of this book.

HOW MUCH LEVERAGE IS NEEDED?

As we saw, the volatility and expected return of an unlevered risk-parity portfolio are typically low, and leverage is applied to reach a higher level of expected return. But how much leverage should be applied? There is no "right" answer to this question, but risk-parity funds tend to target a fixed level of volatility, usually between 10% and 15% annually—levels of risk comparable to a portfolio of around 60% stocks or higher. A risk-parity portfolio targeting these levels of risk may require around 2 to 3× leverage, on average, but it will fluctuate. In particularly calm times, it may take a lot of leverage to reach a set volatility target—up to the point where a brokerage's limits on margin may restrict the implementation of the portfolio.

Summary

- Higher-volatility assets can dominate the risk of seemingly diversified portfolios.
- Risk parity is a method for constructing portfolios with balanced risk contributions from the assets it contains.
- Risk-parity portfolio weights can be calculated using simple convex optimization problems with target contributions from each asset.
- Alternatively, hierarchical risk parity uses machine learning to group assets into clusters and calculate weights based on these clusters.
- Risk-parity portfolios are well-diversified but require leverage to achieve a level of expected return comparable to traditional portfolios.
- Leverage can be obtained in different ways. Each way has costs, and no one way is necessarily always the most efficient.

The Black–Litterman model

In chapter 10, we learned how to use convex optimization to build portfolios. The key inputs to these optimization problems are the expected returns of the assets and the covariance matrix of asset returns. We saw that portfolios obtained via optimization can be very sensitive to the expected returns inputs.

The Black–Litterman model, developed by Fischer Black and Robert Litterman while working at Goldman Sachs in the early 1990s, aims to accomplish two goals:

- Address the sensitivity of portfolio optimization to its inputs
- Allow the user the flexibility to express opinions about the future returns of the assets in the portfolio.

In this chapter, we'll cover both the theory and implementation of the Black–Litterman model.

12.1 *Equilibrium returns*

Chapter 3 showed multiple ways of estimating expected returns. Of course, each method results in different values. Then, in chapter 10, we saw that portfolio optimization can be highly sensitive to expected returns—portfolios built using different methods of estimating expected returns can be wildly different. We then showed that we can use constraints to keep the optimized portfolio "close" to a reference portfolio.

The Black–Litterman model starts with a similar idea. But instead of using constraints around a reference portfolio, the model finds expected returns that result in the reference portfolio as an optimal solution when they are used in a mean-variance optimization problem.

That may sound a bit strange and hard to understand at first. The rest of this chapter will walk through what it means and how we can obtain the expected returns with this special property.

12.1.1 *Reverse optimization*

In the appendix of chapter 2, we learned how to obtain closed-form solutions to portfolio optimization problems of this form:

$$\min_{w} \quad w^T \Sigma w$$
$$\text{subject to} \quad \mu^T w = \mu_p$$
$$\mathbb{1}^T w = 1$$

Here's a reminder about notation:

- w is our vector of decision variables: the portfolio's weights.
- Σ and μ are the covariance matrix and vector of expected returns, respectively.
- μ_p is the target expected return.
- $\mathbb{1}$ (in bold) is a vector consisting of all 1s. Multiplying this vector by any other simply sums the entries of the other.

This is an example of a constrained formulation. The objective is to minimize risk, but we impose the constraints that the expected return of the portfolio has to be equal to a specified value and that the portfolio weights must sum to 1.

We can also formulate portfolio optimization problems without constraints. In particular, we'll use this formulation in this chapter:

$$\max_{w} \quad \mu^T w - \frac{\lambda}{2} w^T \Sigma w$$

In this problem, λ is a value controlling the relative importance of expected return and risk. Using the same techniques as in chapter 2, we can show that the optimal solution to this problem, denoted w^*, is given by this expression:

$$w^* = \frac{1}{\lambda} \Sigma^{-1} \mu$$

Now, suppose we have a reference portfolio, p. This portfolio can be anything, but in practical usage of the Black–Litterman model, p is generally taken to be the market portfolio. That is, the weights of p are just the market capitalizations of the assets in the universe, scaled to sum to 1 or to the desired level of risk. If we assume that p is the optimal solution to the problem, that is,

$$p = \frac{1}{\lambda}\Sigma^{-1}\mu$$

we can solve for μ by multiplying by λ and the covariance matrix Σ to give

$$\mu = \lambda\Sigma p$$

It's not hard to check that using this value for μ will result in p as the optimal solution in the unconstrained problem. We can do this for any portfolio p. This trick is sometimes referred to as *reverse optimization*, although in reality it doesn't require any optimization—we're just multiplying by the covariance matrix and the risk-aversion parameter λ.

We can also formulate the objective slightly differently and obtain a similar result. Instead of using an unconstrained formulation with an objective balancing expected return and risk, we use this constrained formulation:

$$\max_{w} \quad \mu^T w$$
$$\text{subject to} \quad w^T \Sigma w \le \sigma^2$$

We can show using similar techniques that as long as μ is proportional to Σp, the optimal solution will be proportional to p. In the case where p has the desired volatility σ, the optimal solution will be exactly p.

This result means if we have a reference portfolio p and a covariance matrix Σ, we can easily find a vector of expected returns μ so that the optimal solution to a basic mean-variance optimization problem will turn out to be p. It's so easy that the Python code to do so is a one-liner:

```
def compute_equilibrium_ers(weights, sigma, risk_aversion):
    return risk_aversion * sigma @ weights
```

The risk aversion parameter was denoted by λ earlier.

Intuitively, if we think the portfolio p is attractive or reasonable in some sense, we know that the reverse-optimized expected returns μ lead to a solution that we find reasonable, at least when solving a lightly constrained mean-variance problem. Of course, we may want to add constraints to the problem; but by using μ for the expected returns, we know we are at least pointing the optimizer in a reasonable direction.

As mentioned, the reference portfolio used in practice is typically the market portfolio. In the next section, we'll explain the rationale for referring to the derived expected returns μ as *equilibrium* returns when this convention is used and discuss some other possible choices for the reference portfolio.

12.1.2 *Understanding equilibrium*

We can think of "the market" as the aggregation of the portfolios of every single investor on Earth. Now let's assume that everyone agrees on Σ, the covariance matrix for asset returns. Assume that, as a whole, investors construct portfolios that are mean-variance efficient. You can imagine this as the aggregation of all investors solving a problem like this one:

$$\max_{w} \quad \mu^T w - \frac{\lambda}{2} w^T \Sigma w$$

for some values of μ and λ, which in this case are the aggregate expected returns and risk aversions of all investors.

Because we can observe what the market portfolio p is, we know the solution to this problem: it's p. Then, using the results from the last section, we know what μ is: it must be equal to $\lambda \Sigma p$! Again, referring to the previous section, we don't even really need to know what λ is—anything proportional to Σp is sufficient. This explains why the expected returns derived from the market portfolio this way are referred to as *equilibrium* returns—they represent the aggregate expectations and aversions of the entire universe of investors.

ALTERNATIVE CHOICES FOR THE REFERENCE PORTFOLIO

The label *equilibrium* makes the most sense when the reference portfolio p is the market portfolio—the portfolio chosen in aggregate by all investors. However, the Black–Litterman model doesn't require p to be the market portfolio. If we have a different portfolio that we think is reasonable or attractive in some sense, we can use that instead. Alternative choices for the reference portfolio include the following:

- Float-adjusted market capitalization weights (*float-adjusted* market capitalization is simply the market capitalization multiplied by the fraction of readily tradable shares).
- The portfolio of a certain subset of investors. For example, investors in the United States may use the aggregate portfolio of all US-based investors as their reference portfolio.
- A risk-parity portfolio, such as a portfolio with equal risk contributions from every asset, or a weighted risk-parity portfolio as covered in chapter 11.

The equilibrium returns serve as a starting point in the Black–Litterman model. They tell us what the universe of investors believes expected returns to be, in aggregate. However, the model allows the incorporation of investor-specific beliefs (or *views*) to produce investor-specific expected returns. The model incorporates the views, together with the equilibrium expected returns, through a Bayesian update. Before we get into detail on this step, the next section will review what Bayes' rule is and some examples of Bayesian updates in simple settings.

12.2   *Conditional probability and Bayes' rule*

We'll start with a little notation. If A represents the occurrence of some random event, $P(A)$ represents the probability of A happening. For example, if A represents seeing a total value of five from rolling two fair six-sided dice, $P(A)$ is $1/9$. If A represents seeing tails when flipping a fair coin, $P(A)$ is $1/2$.

If B is another event that can influence whether A occurs, $P(A|B)$ means the probability that event A happens, *conditional* on the fact that event B happens. As an example, let's imagine that someone has selected a person at random out of the US population. Event A is "the person is more than six feet tall," and event B is "the person is a professional basketball player." In this case, $P(A)$ is small—only a small fraction of the US population is more than six feet tall (the actual number is about 7%, ignoring gender and age for simplicity). But $P(A|B)$ is much larger: if we know the person chosen plays professional basketball, the chance that the person is over six feet tall is very high (about 99%). So knowing whether B is true makes a huge difference.

Generally, $P(A|B)$ is called a *conditional* probability, and $P(A)$ is called an *unconditional* probability. Bayes' rule is a theorem about conditional probabilities. The exact mathematical statement is

$$P(A|B) = \frac{P(B|A)P(A)}{P(B)}$$

In this equation, $P(A)$ and $P(B)$ are unconditional probabilities, whereas $P(A|B)$ and $P(B|A)$ are conditional probabilities. Bayes' rule is usually used when $P(A|B)$ is more difficult to calculate than the other quantities in the equation. What if we swap the definitions of A and B in our previous example? A is now "the person plays professional basketball," and B is "the person is more than six feet tall." We want to calculate $P(A|B)$, or the probability that the person plays professional basketball, given that the person is over six feet tall. This probability is certainly not obvious, but it can be calculated easily using Bayes' rule. These are the ingredients:

- $P(A)$—The number of professional basketball players in the United States is about 450, in a population of about 330 million. So

$$P(A) = \frac{450}{330,000,000} = 0.0000013636$$

- $P(B)$—The fraction of the US population over six feet tall is about 0.07.
- $P(B|A)$—The fraction of professional US basketball players over six feet tall is about .99.

Plugging these quantities into the formula, we get $P(A|B) = 0.0000193$. This is still a small number, but it is about 14 times higher than the unconditional probability that the person is over six feet tall. Said another way, the unconditional probability that a random US person plays in the NBA is about 1 in 733,000. But if we know the person is over six feet tall, the chance increases to about 1 in 52,000.

In the language of conditional probability (and in the statement of Bayes' rule), $P(A)$ is known as the *prior* probability—it's the probability of A being true prior to any other information. $P(B|A)$ is known as the *likelihood*, and $P(B)$ is the probability of the *evidence* (or data). The conditional probability $P(A|B)$ is called the *posterior* probability.

These definitions make intuitive sense in the context of our example. Prior to any other knowledge about the randomly chosen person, the probability that they are over six feet tall is 0.0000013636. Knowing that the person plays pro basketball provides information, or evidence. *Likelihood* is just another way of saying *probability*, so $P(B|A)$ is certainly a likelihood. Finally, $P(A|B)$ is the probability of the person being over six feet tall *after* learning about the evidence that the person plays professional basketball (*posterior* means "coming after").

In this example, we use binary observations about a person as the events for which we calculated probabilities. Bayes' rule applies more generally and can be used to calculate posterior probability distribution functions in addition to single probabilities. Let's say we have a probability distribution function, f, which takes a parameter, θ. For concrete examples, θ may represent the rate parameter for an exponential distribution or the mean parameter for a normal distribution. In the framework of Bayesian statistics, the parameter θ is treated as a random variable subject to uncertainty. Before seeing data, we have a belief about the distribution of θ—this is the prior distribution. After observing data, or evidence, we use Bayes' rule to update our belief about the distribution of θ. The updated distribution is the posterior. If we let π denote the distribution for θ, the formula for Bayes' rule in this context is written as

$$\pi(\theta|x) = \frac{\pi(\theta)f(x|\theta)}{f(x)}$$

Here, x represents the data (or evidence). The posterior distribution $\pi(\theta|x)$ is the distribution of the parameter, θ, conditional on the data, x.

An example will help here as well. Let's imagine you have a coin, but you aren't sure if it's a fair coin. We'll let θ denote the probability of seeing heads when we flip the coin. Of course, we know θ has to be in the interval $[0, 1]$, but we don't know anything else. Our prior distribution $\pi(\theta)$ is a uniform distribution on the interval $[0, 1]$. This means before seeing the results of any coin flips (in other words, collecting data), we think any possible value of θ is equally likely. Now suppose we flip the coin once and see heads. This gives us everything we need to compute the posterior distribution of θ. We'll go through each piece of the formula to find this distribution:

- $\pi(\theta) = 1$. Because the prior distribution is uniform, the density function doesn't even include θ—its value is 1 everywhere in the interval $[0, 1]$.
- $f(x|\theta) = \theta$. Our data, x, is the observation that the coin toss came up heads. If we are given the value of θ, we know the probability of seeing heads when flipping

the coin once is simply θ. If instead we did N flips and saw heads come up h times, the probability would be

$$\binom{N}{h}\theta^h (1-\theta)^{N-h}$$

which comes directly from the Binomial distribution formula.

- The last part, $f(x)$, is the most complicated. In words, $f(x)$ is the probability that we observed that the coin showed heads when we flipped it, without knowing what the true probability was prior to the flip. To calculate this value, we need to integrate over all possible values of that probability. In general, this is the integral we need to compute:

$$\int f(x|\theta)\pi(\theta)d\theta$$

In our specific case, this integral is

$$\int_0^1 \theta d\theta$$

which evaluates to $1/2$.

Putting all this together, the posterior distribution is $\pi(\theta|x) = 2\theta$. Looking at some values on this distribution can provide some insight. First, $\pi(0|x) = 0$. This means there is no chance that θ is 0, which makes sense—we just observed that the coin showed heads, so the probability of that happening can't be zero. Next, we notice that the distribution increases linearly as θ increases from 0 to 1. This also matches intuition. Given that all we've observed is heads, it makes sense that the most likely value for θ is 1, and larger values are less likely than smaller values.

We can apply this process repeatedly and obtain a new posterior distribution each time. With each iteration, we use the last calculated posterior as the new prior and then incorporate new evidence. The math just becomes a bit more complicated.

In this example, the calculation of the posterior distribution is relatively easy, and we can obtain a closed-form solution for the posterior distribution. This won't always be the case—it's true only for special combinations of prior and data distributions. In other cases, we need to rely on computational methods to evaluate the distribution. Those methods are beyond the scope of this book and unnecessary for our current application—the distributions assumed in the Black–Litterman model luckily fall into the special cases where the posterior is easily computable—but they are the basis for a simulation technique called Markov-chain Monte Carlo, used for sampling values from complicated distributions.

12.3 *Incorporating investor views*

The second step of the Black–Litterman model combines the equilibrium expected returns with a set of investor "views"—forecasts about future performance—to produce a final vector of expected returns. The model requires us to think of both the equilibrium returns and the investor's views as random.

12.3.1 *Expected returns as random variables*

The Black–Litterman model takes a probabilistic approach to describing expected asset returns. To say this another way, the asset returns are of course assumed to be random, but the estimates of expected returns are assumed to be subject to uncertainty (randomness) as well. The investor's views are also expressed as probabilistic statements, with uncertainty associated with each prediction. In this section, we'll cover the various types of randomness and uncertainty in the quantities used in the model and how they fit together.

UNCERTAINTY IN EXPECTED RETURNS

Going forward, we will let R denote the vector of random returns, which we assume follows a multivariate normal distribution. Let's assume we've arrived at a vector of equilibrium expected returns, μ, for the assets. The Black–Litterman model treats μ as the vector of means of a vector of normally distributed random variables with a certain covariance matrix. Specifically, the model assumes that returns are distributed with mean μ and covariance Σ, but that μ is itself a random variable with mean m and covariance C.

Another way of writing this is $\mu = m + \varepsilon$, where ε follows a multivariate normal distribution with mean 0 and covariance C. Clearly $E[\mu] = m$, because ε has mean 0. Then accounting for the uncertainty in μ, the covariance of the returns is given by $\Sigma + C$. In the language of probability, $\Sigma + C$ is the *unconditional* covariance—the covariance assuming the true value of μ is not known—and Σ is the *conditional* covariance.

In practice, it is typical to assume that C is proportional to Σ, meaning the correlation of the uncertainty in μ is the same as the correlation in the returns themselves. The constant of proportionality is often denoted as τ. Following this convention, the unconditional covariance of returns is $(1 + \tau)\Sigma$.

In Bayesian terms, the unconditional distribution of returns is the prior. The data (or evidence) is described in the model as a set of views, or the investor's beliefs about future returns.

12.3.2 *Expressing views*

The Black–Litterman model allows a very flexible specification of beliefs about future returns. Any linear function of the assets' expected returns can be used in a model. That is, any expression of the form $\alpha^T R = \beta$ can be put into the model, where α is a set of coefficients and β is a scalar (both chosen by the investor). Some specific examples include the following:

- *Performance of a single asset*—If we have a view about how a specific asset (say, asset i) will perform, we can express this as $R_i = \beta$, where β is the return we expect.
- *Spread between two assets*—Let's say we have two assets, i and j. The assets may be stocks and bonds, or US stocks versus non-US stocks. We aren't sure about the exact return of each, but we have a view about the relative performance. If we

believe that asset i will outperform asset j by some amount β, we can express this view as $R_i - R_j = \beta$.

- *Spread between portfolios*—Let's say we have two different portfolios, x and y. As an example, x may represent the portfolio of global stocks, with weights on US stocks, non-US developed markets stocks, and emerging markets stocks, and y may be an analogous portfolio representing global bonds. As in the previous example, we may not have any assumptions about the expected returns of the portfolios x and y but may have an expectation about their relative performance. We can express this view as $(x - y)^T R = \beta$, which says we expect portfolio x to outperform portfolio y by a specific amount β.

The key feature of the model is that, as with the equilibrium returns, the views are thought of as probabilistic statements. When we specify views, we also need to express the amount of uncertainty in these views. In the model, the uncertainty is expressed via a covariance matrix Ω. We'll discuss common methods for choosing Ω and τ later in this chapter.

All the views, with their corresponding uncertainty, can be combined into matrices: A, b, and Ω. A is a matrix with N columns, where N is the number of assets. The number of rows of A is the number of views the investor has. Each row contains one of the coefficient vectors α. b is a column matrix, with each value corresponding to a β value from a single view. Finally, Ω is a square matrix giving the uncertainty and correlation between the views.

Mathematically, the views are expressed in the following way. If R is the vector of random returns, in aggregate the views mean AR is normally distributed with mean b and covariance Ω. Another way of expressing this is to write $AR = \beta + \eta$, where η follows a multivariate normal distribution with mean zero and covariance Ω.

Returning to the language of Bayes' rule, we now have both the prior distribution of returns as well as evidence (expressed as investor views). This setting is a little different than the examples we discussed earlier in that the data contains uncertainty as well. In the previous examples, the data was simple observations—a person's height or the result of a coin flip. Here, the data is a set of probabilistic statements about future returns. However, as we will see, the model is capable of handling uncertainty in the views to produce the posterior distribution of returns.

12.3.3 *Updating equilibrium returns*

The last step of the Black–Litterman model updates the equilibrium returns with the information contained in the views to produce a set of expected returns that incorporate both the equilibrium data and the investor views. Our prior distribution on the expected returns is a multivariate normal distribution with mean μ and covariance $\Sigma + C$. Our data comes from the views, which say that AR follows a multivariate normal distribution with mean b and covariance Ω. We update the prior distribution with the data to form the posterior distribution. Under the assumptions of normality, the posterior distribution is also normal. Its mean and covariance are given by

$$\left(C^{-1}+A^{T}\Omega^{-1}A\right)^{-1}\left(C^{-1}\mu+A^{T}\Omega^{-1}b\right)$$

and

$$\Sigma+\left(C^{-1}+A^{T}\Omega^{-1}A\right)^{-1}$$

respectively. If we are following the convention where the covariance of the uncertainty in μ is assumed to be $\tau\Sigma$, we can simply replace C with $\tau\Sigma$ in these expressions.

The mathematics required to derive these expressions is involved and beyond the scope of our book. For readers who are curious and mathematically inclined, we recommend the 2017 paper "On the Bayesian Interpretation of Black–Litterman" by Petter Kolm and Gordon Ritter (https://doi.org/10.1016/j.ejor.2016.10.027).

The Python code required to calculate these quantities, however, is very straightforward. The following listing shows two functions that compute the posterior mean and covariance.

Listing 12.1 Posterior mean and covariance

```python
import numpy as np
import pandas as pd

def compute_posterior_mean(mu, C, A, b, omega):
    c_inv = np.linalg.inv(C)
    a_t_oinv = A.T @ np.linalg.inv(omega)   # Compute these first because they
                                            # are used multiple times.
    er = np.linalg.inv(c_inv + a_t_oinv @ A) @ (c_inv @ mu + a_t_oinv @ b)

    return pd.Series(er, index=mu.index)

def compute_posterior_cov(sigma, C, A, omega):
    return sigma + np.linalg.inv((np.linalg.inv(C) + A.T @ omega @ A))
```

Note that this implementation is fully general—it doesn't assume that $C=\tau\Sigma$, for example, or that Ω is diagonal.

With these quantities calculated, we can proceed with the standard optimization problems used to construct our asset allocations, using the posterior mean and covariance rather than the prior. Portfolio optimization has been covered in prior chapters, so we won't cover it again in this one; however, before some examples, we'll discuss some approaches to choosing the parameters involved in the model.

12.3.4 Assumptions and parameters

The model uses several parameters or assumptions in addition to the repeated assumption of normality. First, the uncertainty of the estimate of expected returns is assumed to be normal with a covariance of C—but how do we choose the matrix C? Even with the common and simplifying assumption that $C=\tau\Sigma$, we still need to choose the parameter τ. This question has spawned a large volume of research, with entire papers dedicated to estimating τ. In a paper co-authored with Guangliang

He, Litterman suggests setting τ to 0.05, because this is the value that corresponds to the level of uncertainty if the mean returns were estimated empirically with 20 years of historical data. More generally, several authors recommend values of $1/T$ or $1/(T - N)$, where T is the number of years of historical data used to estimate mean returns and N is the number of assets in the portfolio.

To use the Black–Litterman model, we must also specify the matrix Ω, which represents uncertainty in the views. One method is to make Ω a diagonal matrix based on the investor's confidence in each view. For example, if the investor believes the expected return of the combination of assets expressed in one particular view has a mean of 2% and a standard deviation of 1%, the investor sets the corresponding diagonal entry of Ω to $0.01^2 = 0.0001$. Another method is to make Ω proportional to the variance of the prior estimate for the mean returns. If the views are represented by the matrix equation $AR = b$, this method is implemented by first calculating the matrix $A(\tau\Sigma)A^T$ and then setting Ω to be the diagonalized version of this matrix (in other words, the matrix obtained by setting all nondiagonal elements to 0).

At this point, we have all we need to use the model. In the next section, we'll cover the implementation of the model in Python, with some examples.

12.4　Examples

Although the math behind the Black–Litterman model is a bit complex, we've seen that the implementation is straightforward—each calculation requires only a few lines of Python. This section will use that code to show how the model works through two numerical examples.

12.4.1　Example: Sector selection

In this example, pretend we're a manager of a US equity portfolio running a sector-selection strategy—actively choosing weights on each sector of the overall market to try to improve returns. Table 12.1 shows the 11 sectors of the US market along with their current market-cap weights and the tickers of ETFs that we'll use to represent each sector.

Listing 12.2 gets historical returns for each of these ETFs; estimates the covariance matrix, denoted by Σ in the model; and then calculates the equilibrium returns. We'll use a risk aversion of 1.4: with this value, the resulting equilibrium expected returns imply an expected return of about 7% for the overall US market (this value is obtained by multiplying expected returns, mu, by the vector of sector weights).

> **Listing 12.2　Computing equilibrium expected returns for US sectors**

```
import yfinance as yf

tickers = ['VOX', 'VCR', 'VDC', 'VDE', 'VFH', 'VHT', 'VIS', 'VGT',
           'VAW', 'VNQ', 'VPU']
prices = yf.download(tickers, start='2018-01-01', end='2022-12-31')
rets = prices['Adj Close'].pct_change()
rets = rets.dropna(axis=0, how='any')[tickers]
sigma = rets.cov() * 252
```

```
weights = [.077, .107, .067, .048, .117, .143, .085, .273, .028, .027, .028]
weights = pd.Series(weights, index=tickers)
mu = compute_equilibrium_ers(weights, sigma, 1.4)
```

Table 12.1 Sector weights of the US equity market

Sector	Weight	ETF ticker
Communication services	7.7%	VOX
Consumer discretionary	10.7%	VCR
Consumer staples	6.7%	VDC
Energy	4.8%	VDE
Financials	11.7%	VFH
Health care	14.3%	VHT
Industrials	18.5%	VIS
Information technology	27.3%	VGT
Materials	2.8%	VAW
Real estate	2.7%	VNQ
Utilities	2.8%	VPU

Now we have to express our views about the future performance of the sectors. Suppose we think the economy is headed into a downturn and the defensive sectors (consumer staples, health care, and utilities) will outperform cyclical sectors (consumer discretionary, energy, financials, industrials, technology, and materials). One way to express this view is through two portfolios: one containing the defensive sectors at their market weights, and another containing the cyclical sectors at their market weights (in both cases, the weights are normalized to sum to 1). The view is expressed as the performance spread between the two portfolios.

We'll start by defining the portfolios and then two views:

- The defensive portfolio will outperform the cyclical portfolio by 1%, contrary to the equilibrium expectation that the cyclical portfolio will outperform the defensive one by about 2.6%.
- Real estate will perform very poorly: 2% compared to the equilibrium value of 6.1%.

This listing shows how to define the portfolios and then encode the views into two matrices, A and b.

Listing 12.3   Constructing views

```python
defensive = ['VDC', 'VHT', 'VPU']
cyclical = ['VCR', 'VDE', 'VFH', 'VIS', 'VGT', 'VAW']

defensive_port = weights[defensive] / weights[defensive].sum()
cyclical_port = weights[cyclical] / weights[cyclical].sum()

spread_port = pd.concat((defensive_port, -cyclical_port))
real_estate_port = pd.Series([1], index = ['VNQ'])

A = pd.DataFrame([spread_port, real_estate_port])
A = A.T.reindex(tickers).fillna(0).T

b = pd.Series([.01, .02])
```

The last steps are to calculate the view uncertainty matrix, $\boldsymbol{\Omega}$, and then calculate the posterior means and covariances. We'll use one of the recommended methods we mentioned earlier, with $\boldsymbol{\Omega} = diag\left(\boldsymbol{A}(\tau\boldsymbol{\Sigma})\boldsymbol{A}^T\right)$ and $\tau = 0.05$. Listing 12.4 shows how this is done in Python. Notice the repeated calls to `np.diag()` in calculating $\boldsymbol{\Omega}$—these may look strange at first glance. The inner call returns the diagonal of the matrix $\boldsymbol{A}(\tau\boldsymbol{\Sigma})\boldsymbol{A}^T$ as a vector. The outer call turns that vector into a diagonal matrix.

Listing 12.4   Calculating posteriors

```python
tau = 0.05
omega = np.diag(np.diag(A @ (tau * sigma) @ A.T))
post_mean = compute_posterior_mean(mu, tau * sigma, A, b, omega)
post_cov = compute_posterior_cov(sigma, tau * sigma, A, omega)
```

We're done! Figure 12.1 shows the prior (equilibrium) and posterior expected returns for each sector side by side.

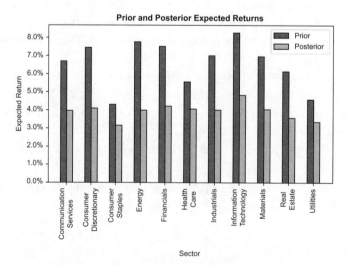

Figure 12.1   Prior and posterior expected returns

We can go one step further and compute an optimal portfolio using the posterior expected returns. We do this using an optimization problem like the ones we solved in chapter 10. Our objective will be to maximize the expected return of the portfolio, with constraints that the portfolio weights must be nonnegative and sum to 1 and that the volatility of the portfolio must be less than or equal to the volatility of the market portfolio. The next listing shows how to formulate and solve this problem.

Listing 12.5 Building an optimized sector portfolio

```
import cvxpy as cp

w = cp.Variable(len(mu))
market_vol = np.sqrt(weights @ sigma @ weights)

objective = cp.Maximize(post_mean.values @ w)
constraints = [cp.quad_form(w, sigma) <= market_vol ** 2,
               cp.sum(w) == 1,
               w >= 0]
prob = cp.Problem(objective, constraints)
result = prob.solve()
w = pd.Series(w.value, index=mu.index)
```

Table 12.2 shows optimized weights from this problem next to the market weights. The result is rather concentrated, with most of the weight in the health care and technology sectors. Other cyclical sectors whose weights in the market portfolio were already fairly low now receive zero (or nearly zero) weight.

Table 12.2 Sector weights in the market and optimized portfolios

Sector	Market weight	Optimized weight
Communication services	7.7%	0.0%
Consumer discretionary	10.7%	0.0%
Consumer staples	6.7%	0.0%
Energy	4.8%	0.0%
Financials	11.7%	0.4%
Health care	14.3%	58.1%
Industrials	18.5%	0.0%
Information technology	27.3%	41.5%
Materials	2.8%	0.0%
Real estate	2.7%	0.0%
Utilities	2.8%	0.0%

These results will change if we vary the inputs. If we specify higher uncertainty in the views via the matrix Ω, the optimized portfolio will look more similar to the market. In the limit, where the diagonal matrices Ω approaches infinity, the optimized portfolio will converge to the market portfolio.

For the next example, we'll use the Black–Litterman model again, but we'll incorporate an asset class that has become increasingly notable in recent years: cryptocurrency.

12.4.2 *Example: Global allocation with cryptocurrencies*

In this section, we'll use the Black–Litterman model to construct a portfolio containing global equities (US, non-US developed markets, and emerging markets), US bonds, and two of the largest (by market capitalization) cryptocurrencies: Bitcoin and Ethereum. To begin, we'll download prices, calculate returns, and build the covariance matrix. This step has one small difference compared to the previous example. Because cryptocurrencies trade 24/7, if we download daily prices, we'll end up with crypto prices on weekends and holidays, but the other assets will only have prices for market days. To avoid any complications due to this, we just download weekly prices, which can be accomplished by setting `interval='1wk'` in the call to the `yf.download()` method. Then, because the returns are weekly instead of daily, we multiply by 52 instead of 252 when calculating the annualized covariance matrix. Here's the code:

```
tickers = ['VTI', 'VEA', 'VWO', 'AGG', 'BTC-USD', 'ETH-USD']
prices = yf.download(tickers, start='2018-01-01', end='2022-12-31',
                     interval='1wk')
prices = prices['Adj Close'].dropna(axis=0, how='any')[tickers]
rets = prices.pct_change()
sigma = rets.cov() * 52
```

For simplicity, we'll put the rest of the code needed to get to the posterior quantities in a single listing.

For the market weights, we have taken the current market capitalizations of all assets (as of the time of writing) and normalized them so that they sum to 1. The resulting equilibrium weights on Bitcoin and Ethereum are 0.45% and 0.18%, respectively.

In this example, we'll take a bullish view on crypto and assume that Bitcoin will return 10% and Ethereum will return 15%. We won't have views on the traditional assets. We'll specify the uncertainty in the crypto views simply as confidence intervals, specifically assuming that each view has a standard deviation of 5%. After all the calculations of the various quantities involved in the process, we will inspect and comment on their exact numerical values.

Listing 12.6   Applying Black–Litterman with cryptocurrency

```
weights = [.3401, .1559, .0708, .4269, .0045, .0018]
weights = pd.Series(weights, index=tickers)
mu = compute_equilibrium_ers(weights, sigma, 2.8)

btc_port = pd.Series([1], index = ['BTC-USD'])
eth_port = pd.Series([1], index = ['ETH-USD'])
A = pd.DataFrame([btc_port, eth_port])
A = A.T.reindex(tickers).fillna(0).T
b = pd.Series([.10, .15])
omega = np.diag([.05 ** 2, .05 ** 2])

tau = 0.05
post_mean = compute_posterior_mean(mu, tau * sigma, A, b, omega)
post_cov = compute_posterior_cov(sigma, tau * sigma, A, omega)
```

Let's look at some of the quantities calculated in this code. Table 12.3 shows the prior and posterior estimates for the expected return and volatility of each asset.

Table 12.3   Prior and posterior returns statistics

Asset class	Prior expected return	Prior volatility	Posterior expected return	Posterior volatility
US stocks	7.0%	21.2%	7.3%	21.7%
Foreign developed stocks	6.5%	19.7%	6.7%	20.2%
Emerging markets stocks	5.5%	19.8%	5.8%	20.3%
US bonds	1.0%	5.6%	1.0%	5.7%
Bitcoin	7.0%	72.2%	9.8%	74.0%
Ethereum	11.2%	96.9%	14.9%	99.3%

It may seem surprising that the expected return for emerging markets stocks is lower than the expected return for US stocks in both the prior and posterior values. After all, emerging markets are usually more volatile than US markets. This is a function of the relatively short time window used for estimating the covariance matrix. Over the five-year period we used, emerging markets happened to be less volatile than US stocks, but this isn't something we would expect going forward (nor is it something we observe if we look over longer periods).

The volatilities of the cryptocurrencies we included are very high—about 72% and 97% for Bitcoin and Ethereum, respectively. Their equilibrium expected returns are commensurately high. The intuitive explanation is that given their very high volatility, the expected returns must be high to justify their inclusion in the market portfolio, even at their relatively low weights.

With the posterior means and covariance calculated, we can construct an optimized portfolio using the posterior parameters. We'll do this the same way as in the last example—a long-only, fully invested portfolio that maximizes expected return subject to having the same volatility as the market portfolio:

```
w = cp.Variable(len(mu))
objective = cp.Maximize(post_mean.values @ w)
market_vol = np.sqrt(weights @ post_cov @ weights)

constraints = [cp.quad_form(w, post_cov) <= market_vol ** 2,
               cp.sum(w) == 1,
               w >= 0]
prob = cp.Problem(objective, constraints)
result = prob.solve()
w = pd.Series(w.value, index=mu.index)
```

Table 12.4 shows the weights of the market portfolio and the optimized portfolio.

Table 12.4   Sector weights in the market and optimized portfolios

Asset class	Market weight	Optimized weight
US stocks	34.01%	32.5%
Foreign developed stocks	15.59%	14.4%
Emerging markets stocks	7.08%	7.1%
US bonds	42.69%	43.6%
Bitcoin	0.45%	1.63%
Ethereum	0.18%	0.81%

The optimized portfolio does have a larger allocation to the cryptocurrencies than the market portfolio, but not by much: about 2.44% compared to 0.63%. This shouldn't be too surprising—our optimization problem constrained the volatility of the portfolio to be no more than about 12.3%. The portfolio can hold only so much crypto without exceeding that level of volatility.

Summary

- The Black–Litterman model uses Bayesian statistics to combine an investor's views about returns with the expected returns implied by a reference portfolio.
- The model helps to anchor optimized portfolios to the reference portfolio and combat the sensitivity of portfolio optimization to its inputs.
- The amount of anchoring can be controlled by the level of uncertainty the user assigns to their views.
- The model requires several parameters, each of which can be specified fairly intuitively.

Part 4

Portfolio management

A robo-advisor's work doesn't stop once they've designed an optimal portfolio, or even once they've purchased the securities they want to hold. They need to monitor the portfolio to ensure that its weights stay on track (close to the target weights) and make trades to correct deviations—a process called *rebalancing*.

Some robo-advisors go beyond rebalancing by doing tax-loss harvesting. Tax *harvesting* refers to selling assets that have declined in value to create realized losses in the investor's portfolio, which can then offset realized gains (from the same portfolio or from elsewhere) and even some ordinary income.

Although simple to describe, both rebalancing and tax-loss harvesting require some care to ensure that the costs of the trades don't outweigh the benefits. In these final two chapters, we discuss several approaches to rebalancing (including building a backtester to compare different approaches using historical data) and how to implement a tax-loss harvesting strategy using ETFs.

Rebalancing: Tracking a target portfolio

13

This chapter covers

- Rebalancing portfolios with defined target weights, and the pitfalls of not rebalancing
- Simple rebalancing rules based on fixed time schedules or deviation thresholds
- Optimization-based rebalancing incorporating transaction costs and taxes

Over time, a portfolio may naturally drift away from its target weights due to differing changes in asset prices. *Rebalancing* refers to the process of periodically correcting the drift to bring the portfolio closer to its target weights. In this chapter, we'll show why rebalancing is important and cover various methods for rebalancing, starting with the simplest and ending with the most sophisticated.

13.1 Rebalancing basics

Earlier chapters have discussed ways of constructing portfolios that are "optimal" in some sense. They optimized an objective function—for example, maximum expected return or minimum tracking error—with some constraints on the portfolio weights.

Given the goals and constraints or concerns of the investor, these portfolios are the best possible. However, once a portfolio is implemented (purchased), it won't stay optimal for long. The assets held by the portfolio will experience differing returns, and the portfolio's weights will drift from its targets. Generally, this can mean the portfolio no longer satisfies the constraints specified at the time the target weights were determined or that the objective function is no longer optimized. Some specific examples of consequences of drift are as follows:

- The portfolio is riskier than intended.
- The portfolio has higher (or lower) weight than intended in a particular asset or set of assets.
- The portfolio is no longer tracking a benchmark as closely as it could.
- The expected return of the portfolio is no longer maximized.

13.1.1 The need for rebalancing

Of these four examples, the first may be the easiest to understand. Let's think about the classic 60/40 stocks/bonds portfolio, designed for a moderate level of risk. Over time, we expect that stocks will have higher returns than bonds. This will tend to make the portfolio's weights drift toward stocks, which makes the portfolio riskier than intended. This is the opposite of what we typically want, which is a portfolio that becomes less risky as the investor ages.

This code calculates portfolio weights over 30 years, starting with the 60/40 portfolio and assuming constant returns of 6% and 2% annually for stocks and bonds. It also calculates the volatility of the portfolio as it drifts over time.

Listing 13.1   Growing portfolio weights through time

```python
import numpy as np
n_years = 30
yearly_rets = np.array([.06, .02])
sigma = np.array([[0.0287, 0], [0, 0.0017]])
start_weights = [.6, .4]

portfolios = np.zeros((n_years + 1, 2))
portfolios[0,:] = start_weights
vols = np.zeros(n_years + 1)
vols[0] = np.sqrt(portfolios[0,:] @ sigma @ portfolios[0,:])

for year in range(n_years):
    last_weights = portfolios[year,:]
    grown_weights = last_weights * (1 + yearly_rets)
    grown_weights /= np.sum(grown_weights)
    grown_vol = np.sqrt(grown_weights @ sigma @ grown_weights)
    portfolios[year + 1, :] = grown_weights
    vols[year + 1] = grown_vol
```

Figure 13.1 shows how both the weight on stocks and the portfolio's volatility increase over time.

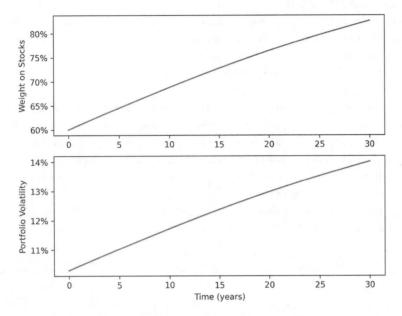

Figure 13.1 Weight and volatility drift through time

By the end of 30 years, the portfolio has drifted from 60% stocks to about 83% stocks! Volatility increases from about 10% to about 14%. Again, this is the opposite of what most investors want, motivating the need to rebalance the portfolio periodically.

13.1.2 *Downsides of rebalancing*

The need to rebalance arises from the dispersion in returns across assets. Unfortunately, this usually means rebalancing requires selling the assets that have appreciated the most (in a case where everything is down, it can mean selling the assets that have depreciated the least, but that is unfortunate for a different reason). Selling appreciated assets means realizing capital gains and paying taxes (unless the account is tax-advantaged like a 401(k)). Therefore, when designing a rebalancing policy, we want to consider the potential tax consequences.

The other downside of rebalancing is that by definition, it requires trading, and trading is not free. Because the cost of trading liquid ETFs typically employed by robo-advisors is low, this effect is generally less important than the taxes but should be considered nonetheless.

13.1.3 *Dividends and deposits*

Nearly all equity and fixed-income ETFs pay regular dividends. Quarterly is typical for equity funds, and monthly (or even more frequently in some cases) is typical for fixed-income funds. When you hear quotes about long-run stock market performance, they often include the phrase "with dividends reinvested," meaning it is assumed that all dividends are used to repurchase stocks immediately. In fact, many retail brokerages offer dividend reinvestment programs that automatically use dividend proceeds from a stock or ETF to purchase additional shares of that stock or ETF as soon as possible. However, it is not necessary to reinvest a dividend into the same security that paid it. This can make dividends a useful tool for rebalancing without the need for realizing gains and paying taxes. To better understand this, let's look at the mechanics of a dividend payment.

In rebalancing, dividends paid by higher-returning assets work to our advantage. They decrease the value of the higher-return assets (thus reducing their weight in the portfolio) and provide cash that can be reinvested into the lower-returning assets. Listing 13.2 is a variant of listing 13.1, except we assume that both stocks and bonds have dividend yields of 2% (for the purposes of this example, this means each $100 invested at the beginning of the year yields $2 in cash at the end). The code never does any selling but invests the dividends paid at the end of each year in a way that brings the portfolio back to its 60/40 target at the end of each year.

Listing 13.2   **Growing portfolio weights with dividends**

```
n_years = 30
yearly_rets = np.array([.06, .02])
div_rates = np.array([.02, .02])
sigma = np.array([[0.0287, 0], [0, 0.0017]])
start_weights = [.6, .4]

portfolios = np.zeros((n_years + 1, 2))
portfolios[0,:] = start_weights
vols = np.zeros(n_years + 1)
vols[0] = np.sqrt(portfolios[0,:] @ sigma @ portfolios[0,:])

for year in range(n_years):
    last_weights = portfolios[year,:]
    grown_values = last_weights * (1 + yearly_rets)
    divs = last_weights * div_rates
    ex_div_values = grown_values - divs
    # calculate how to split the dividends between stocks and bonds
    frac = (start_weights[0] * grown_values.sum() - ex_div_values[0]) \
            / divs.sum()
    trades = np.array([frac, 1 - frac]) * divs.sum()
    new_values = ex_div_values + trades
    new_weights = new_values / new_values.sum()
    new_vol = np.sqrt(new_weights @ sigma @ new_weights)
    portfolios[year + 1, :] = new_weights
    vols[year + 1] = new_vol
```

This is great, but it won't work all the time: the returns of stocks and bonds vary from year to year, and sometimes dividends won't be enough to bring the portfolio back to its targets. Deposits help—they are similar to dividends in that they provide an opportunity for rebalancing without selling anything and potentially realizing gains. But, unfortunately, we can't always count on regular deposits either. The rest of the chapter will cover various ways to rebalance the portfolio through buying and selling.

13.2 Simple rebalancing strategies

Ideally, dividends and deposits would be large and frequent enough that selling assets to rebalance would be unnecessary. Unfortunately, we can't be sure this will be the case. This section will cover two of the simplest rebalancing strategies (other than not rebalancing at all). These strategies have the benefit of being simple to understand and implement, and they can be made relatively tax-friendly through the use of some simple rules.

13.2.1 Fixed-interval rebalancing

The idea of this strategy is extremely simple: pick a time interval (for example, one week or one quarter), and trade the portfolio back to its target at the end of each interval. That's it. In the interim, the portfolio drifts. Because this rule is so simple, there isn't much more to say.

A natural question to ask is how the interval should be chosen. Rebalancing frequently reduces the potential drift from the targets but also results in more trading because drift is being corrected more often. Remember that asset prices are volatile, and drift can "self-correct" to some degree as prices move up and down. Trading very frequently is usually unnecessary. On the other hand, we don't want to wait too long between rebalances and allow the portfolio to drift far from its targets, potentially exposing us to unwanted risk.

13.2.2 Threshold-based rebalancing

Whereas interval-based rebalancing rebalances the period at fixed time intervals, the basic idea of threshold-based rebalancing is to rebalance the portfolio only when it needs to be rebalanced. The portfolio is checked periodically (say, every day or every week) and rebalanced if it has deviated too far from the target. We can use any number of measurements and thresholds to decide when to rebalance the portfolio. For example

- *Weight deviation*—Rebalance when any asset's weight has drifted away from its target by a predetermined amount.
- *Tracking error*—Rebalance when the tracking error against the target portfolio is large.
- *Volatility-based deviation*—Rebalance when the product of an asset's deviation from its target weight and the asset's volatility exceeds a threshold.

You can imagine countless other measures or combinations of measures to use in determining whether a portfolio should be rebalanced.

Threshold-based rebalancing is slightly more complicated than interval-based—we need to decide which measurement and thresholds to use, and it involves inspecting the portfolio more frequently to determine whether it should be rebalanced. However, we think that it makes more intuitive sense than rebalancing at fixed intervals. With more frequent inspections of the portfolio, there is less opportunity for drift. Also, rebalancing the portfolio only when it drifts significantly can reduce unnecessary trading.

13.2.3 Other considerations

The naive rebalancing strategies discussed so far don't make any decisions about which assets to sell, or how much—they simply trade all the way back to the target portfolio. Before we talk about more advanced strategies involving optimization, we should point out a few ways that naive strategies can be made "smarter" without much additional complexity.

TAX LOTS

In the previous examples, we've determined how much of each asset to buy or sell—specifically, how many shares. However, not all shares are equal when selling. Different shares may have been acquired at different times and at different prices, and when we sell shares, we need to specify exactly which ones.

The main consideration for selecting which shares to sell is taxes. Both the amount of appreciation (or depreciation) a share has experienced since its purchase and the amount of time the share has been held affect the effective tax rate on a sale. All else equal, we generally prefer paying less in current taxes.

A group of shares purchased at the same time is referred to as a *tax lot*. The shares all have a single shared purchase price associated with them and are equivalent for tax purposes. A simple rule is to sell the shares with the lowest effective tax rate first.

The following listing calculates tax rates for a set of tax lots held in an example portfolio. The code assumes a short-term capital gains rate of 40% and a long-term rate of 20%. The boundary between short-term and long-term gains is 365 days.

Listing 13.3   Calculating tax exposure

```
import datetime as dt

lt_gains_rate = 0.20
income_rate = .40
current_price = 110
current_date = dt.date(2022, 5, 11)

lots = pd.DataFrame({'price': [80, 85, 105, 115],
                     'quantity': [25, 30, 20, 10],
                     'purchase_date': ['2021-02-10', '2021-07-21',
                                       '2021-11-23', '2022-03-25']})

tax_info = {}
for i in lots.index:
```

```
lot_info = lots.iloc[i]
purchase_date = dt.date.fromisoformat(lot_info['purchase_date'])
holding_period = (current_date - purchase_date).days
if holding_period <= 365:
        lot_rate = income_rate
else:
lot_rate = lt_gains_rate

purchase_price = lot_info['price']
gain = (current_price / purchase_price - 1)
effective_rate = gain * lot_rate

tax_info[i] = pd.Series({'holding_period': holding_period,
                  'applicable_rate': lot_rate,
                  'pct_gain': gain,
                  'effective_rate': effective_rate})

tax_info = pd.DataFrame(tax_info).T
```

We get this output:

	holding_period	applicable_rate	pct_gain	effective_rate
0	455.0	0.2	0.375000	0.075000
1	294.0	0.4	0.294118	0.117647
2	169.0	0.4	0.047619	0.019048
3	47.0	0.4	-0.043478	-0.017391

NOTE Notice that we use Python's default indexing, which starts at 0. Although it may sound a bit odd to say something like "lot zero contains 10 shares," we think the ease of following Python's convention outweighs the potential verbal awkwardness.

With the effective tax rates calculated, and given a desired number of shares to sell, we can decide which lots to sell from. Listing 13.4 orders the lots by effective tax rate and then works through each lot until we have found enough shares to satisfy the trade. When inspecting each lot, we need to check the number of shares it contains against the number of shares left to complete the desired sale. If the lot doesn't contain enough shares, we set its quantity to 0 and move to the next. Otherwise, we deduct the number of shares we need, and the algorithm concludes. For this example, we'll assume that we want to sell 35 shares of this asset.

Listing 13.4 Simple tax lot selection

```
shares_to_sell = 35
order = tax_info['effective_rate'].argsort().values    ←── Orders the tax lots
shares_available = lots['quantity'].copy()

sells = shares_available * 0
while shares_to_sell > 0:
```

> This means there aren't enough shares in the lot to sell.

```
current_best_lot = order[0]
if shares_available[current_best_lot] < shares_to_sell:    ◄─┐
    sells[current_best_lot] = shares_available[current_best_lot]
    shares_to_sell -= shares_available[current_best_lot]
    shares_available[current_best_lot] = 0
    order = order[1:]
else:
    shares_available[current_best_lot] -= shares_to_sell
    sells[current_best_lot] = shares_to_sell
    shares_to_sell = 0
```

After running this code, we get the following trades:

```
sells
0      5
1      0
2     20
3     10
```

The algorithm tells us to sell 5 shares from lot 0, 20 from lot 2, and 10 from lot 3. Notice that the shares in lot 0 are at a larger gain than the shares in lot 1, but because lot 0 has been held for over 365 days, the long-term capital gains tax applies and the effective tax rate is lower.

INCOMPLETE TRADING

We mentioned how threshold-based rebalancing results in trading only when the portfolio deviates from the target. But we also assumed that when we rebalance, we trade all the way back to the target portfolio. This isn't necessary. For example, let's say we rebalance the portfolio any time an asset deviates more than 1% from its target weight. If an asset has drifted to 3% above its target, we can only sell enough shares to get back within the 1% tolerance. This is most relevant when the trades required to get all the way back to the target would require realizing gains and paying taxes. If overweight assets are at large short-term gains and would result in large tax bills, we may prefer to let some deviations persist.

MORE TAX HEURISTICS

In general, we know that realizing a long-term gain is preferable to realizing a short-term gain (assuming the sizes of the gains are the same) because of the difference in tax rates applied to each. But there are differences within the short-term bucket as well. Imagine that you bought an ETF once 360 days ago and again 10 days ago. You paid $10 both times, and the price is now $12. Selling one share from each tax lot will result in the same tax bill because both lots are short-term gains. But selling from the newer lot is preferable in this case. Both lots are short-term at the moment, but the older lot will become long-term in just 5 days, and the other will take 355 days to become long-term and get the favorable tax treatment. Even if the newer lot were at a slightly higher gain, you may prefer selling from it rather than the older lot.

The exact holding periods of short-term lots can be used in deciding which tax lots to sell from, or we can even disallow selling from lots that are very close to becoming long-term. The opposite is true for lots trading at losses: realizing a loss in a lot that's about to become long-term is preferable to realizing a loss in an older lot because the higher short-term tax rate works to our advantage when realizing losses.

13.2.4 Final thoughts

Everything in section 13.2.3 is an example of something that can be implemented simply and added to a rebalancing process on its own. But the more rules we add, the more complicated the implementation becomes. Also, trade-offs may be difficult to express through rules. Think of the example of gains close to the one-year holding period. It's unlikely we'd ever want to realize a gain from a tax lot with a holding period of 364 days—all we need to do is wait a day to get better tax treatment. What if the lot had a holding period of 355 days? Or 345 days? The "right" answer isn't a strict cutoff at a particular holding period but rather something continuous. This serves as motivation for the next section, where we'll cover formulating rebalancing as an optimization problem. Using optimization, we can express trade-offs like the holding period by adding constraints or terms to the objective function.

13.3 Optimizing rebalancing

In this section, we'll show how to formulate rebalancing as an optimization problem. We'll draw from a lot of what we saw in chapter 10 on portfolio optimization. After all, rebalancing is a generalization of the portfolio construction problem. We are still trying to find the "best" portfolio, but beyond just identifying the optimal target, we have other considerations—most importantly taxes, but trading costs as well.

This section is rather code-heavy. As usual, all the relevant code can be found on the book's website and in the GitHub repo (https://www.manning.com/books/build-a-robo-advisor-with-python-from-scratch and https://github.com/robreider/robo-advisor-with-python, respectively). In this section, we'll define a class called `RebalancingOpt` piece by piece. When we're done, we'll be able to use instances of this class to formulate and solve rebalancing problems with various objectives and constraints.

13.3.1 Variables

In the optimization problems we solved in chapter 10, we had one variable for each asset's weight in the portfolio. That suffices for finding an optimal target portfolio but isn't enough when we're formulating a rebalancing problem. First, we'll need separate variables for both buys and sells. But even that isn't enough. In section 13.2.3, we discussed how not all holdings are equivalent, as well as some considerations for choosing which tax lots to sell from. We can express the nonequivalence in an optimization problem by using multiple variables for each asset. Specifically, we define a variable for every tax lot in the current portfolio.

In our rebalancing problem, we'll identify the "buy" variables with the tickers of the assets they correspond to. For the "sell" variables, we'll use the tickers and the purchase dates. We'll also define a third set of quantities called *positions*, representing the actual positions of the portfolio. We'll call these variables in our problem, although they technically are not cvxpy Variable objects—they are linear combinations of input values and other variables. Specifically, the position variable for each asset is just the starting value of the portfolio's holdings in that asset, plus the trades (buys and sells) in that asset that the optimizer chooses. Simple functions of variables such as these are known as *expressions* in cvxpy, and they simplify the formulation of optimization problems.

We'll show how the variables are defined a bit later. Before that, you'll see them used in the sections covering objectives and constraints.

13.3.2 *Inputs*

The RebalancingOpt class needs the following data to set up and solve a rebalancing problem:

- The current date (for calculating tax rates)
- The target portfolio
- The current portfolio
- Constraints to enforce in the optimization
- The objective to use in the optimization

The first three items are fairly straightforward. The current date is simply a datetime.date object, for example:

```
import datetime as dt
current_date = dt.date(2022, 8, 1)
```

The target portfolio is given as a pandas Series indexed by asset names. The value for each asset is the amount the target portfolio should invest in, in dollars. For example, if our target portfolio is 60% in VTI and 40% in AGG, and we have $10,000 to invest, we can create the target portfolio like this:

```
target_port = pd.Series({'VTI':0.60, 'AGG':0.40}) * 10_000
```

Finally, the current portfolio should detail the portfolio's current holdings at the level of tax lots. This is necessary for calculating the tax effect of selling particular lots. Here is an example that creates a pandas DataFrame holding information about current holdings:

```
tickers = ['VTI', 'VTI', 'VTI',
           'AGG', 'AGG']
purchase_prices = [60.78, 65.63, 90.04,
                   28.48, 26.28]
quantities = [40, 10, 20,
```

```
                75, 55]
purchase_dates = ['2021-02-18', '2021-07-21', '2021-11-23',
                  '2021-02-18', '2021-07-21']
lots = pd.DataFrame({'ticker': tickers,
                     'purchase_price': purchase_prices,
                     'quantity': quantities,
                     'purchase_date': purchase_dates})

prices = pd.Series({'VTI': 88.35, 'AGG': 31.59})
lots['current_price'] = prices[lots['ticker']].values
lots['value'] = lots['quantity'] * lots['current_price']
```

If you run this code, this should be what you see for the variable `lots`:

	ticker	purchase_price	quantity	purchase_date	current_price	value
0	VTI	60.78	40	2021-02-18	88.35	3534.00
1	VTI	65.63	10	2021-07-21	88.35	883.50
2	VTI	90.04	20	2021-11-23	88.35	1767.00
3	AGG	28.48	75	2021-02-18	31.59	2369.25
4	AGG	26.28	55	2021-07-21	31.59	1737.45

This portfolio currently holds 70 shares of VTI with a market value of $6,184.50 and a cost basis (total amount spent to purchase) of $4,888.30. It also holds 130 shares of AGG with a total value of $4,106.70 and a cost basis of $3,581.40.

Constructing inputs for the objective function and the constraints is a little more complicated. We'll cover those in their own sections.

CONSTRAINTS

In chapter 10, we defined classes corresponding to certain types of constraints. For example, we used a `LongOnlyConstraint` class to ensure that all the portfolio weights were nonnegative. For rebalancing, we'll define analogous classes. Like before, each constraint class will have a method called `generate_constraint()`. The only difference will be that the constraints in this chapter require more input data to generate the constraint. Each type will require the following:

- Current date
- Current holdings
- Problem variables
- Extra relevant information, like the amount of money to be invested

The following snippet shows the generic `Constraint` class, where the `generate_constraint()` method is left unimplemented. Every subclass of `Constraint` will implement this method differently:

```
class Constraint:
    def generate_constraint(self,
                            date: dt.date,
                            holdings: pd.DataFrame,
                            variables: Dict,
                            port_info: Dict) -> List:
        pass
```

For rebalancing, the constraints we use will overlap the ones we used for asset allocation, but we will define a few new ones as well. For example, the rebalancing optimization will have constraints enforcing nonnegativity of all positions (LongOnlyConstraint) and a constraint forcing the total amount invested to be equal to the desired amount (FullInvestmentConstraint). New constraints that we'll define include the following:

- MaxDeviationConstraint—This simply bounds each optimized position to be within an interval centered at the target position. The width of the interval is expressed as a fraction of the total invested amount. For example, let's say we want to invest $10,000, and the target portfolio has a $4,000 position in AGG. Using a tolerance value of 0.05, the optimized position in AGG would need to be between $3,500 and $4,500.

- VolBasedDeviationConstraint—This is similar to MaxDeviationConstraint, except it takes the volatility of each asset into account. It allows for larger deviations in lower-volatility assets.

- DoNotIncreaseDeviationConstraint—This constraint means optimized positions can't be any further from the targets than they already are. As an example, the target portfolio has a $4,000 position in AGG, and the current portfolio holds $3,800 in AGG. This constraint will stop the optimizer from selling any AGG, effectively putting a lower bound of $3,800 on the AGG position.

- DoNotTradePastTargetConstraint—This constraint makes sure we don't trade past the target position. If the position in a particular asset is overweight, the constraint says the asset can't be underweight in the optimized portfolio; and if the asset is underweight, it can't be overweight in the optimized portfolio. Using the previous example where the incoming AGG position is below the target of $4,000, the constraint will enforce a maximum value of $4,000 on AGG.

The following listing shows the definitions of two very basic constraints: FullInvestmentConstraint and LongOnlyConstraint. These should look very familiar after reading chapter 10.

Listing 13.5 Basic constraints

```python
class FullInvestmentConstraint(Constraint):

    def __init__(self):
        """ Enforce full investment """
        pass

    def generate_constraint(self, date, holdings, variables, port_info):
        positions = variables['positions']
        total_invested = sum(list(positions.values()))

        return [total_invested == port_info['investment_value']]


class LongOnlyConstraint(Constraint):
```

```
def __init__(self):
    """ Enforce all portfolio holdings are non-negative """
    pass

def generate_constraint(self, date, holdings, variables, port_info):
    return [v >= 0 for v in variables['positions'].values()]
```

Next we show the implementation of DoNotIncreaseDeviationConstraint. This constraint works by first calculating the weight of each asset in the current portfolio. Then it sets a constraint on the position in each asset, depending on whether the asset is currently above or below its target weight.

Listing 13.6   DoNotIncreaseDeviationConstraint

```
class DoNotIncreaseDeviationConstraint(Constraint):

    def __init__(self,
                 target_weights: pd.Series):
        """ Constraint that prohibits buying in currently overweight
        assets and selling in currently underweight assets """
        self.target_weights = target_weights

    def generate_constraint(self, date, holdings, variables, port_info):
        all_assets = variables['buys'].keys()
        current_port = holdings[['ticker', 'value']]. \
            groupby(['ticker']). \                          ◀─┐ Calculates the
            sum()['value']. \                                 │ current portfolio's
            reindex(list(all_assets)). \                      │ holdings by asset
            fillna(0.0)

        target_port = self.target_weights * port_info['investment_value']
        cons = []
        for asset in all_assets:
            if current_port[asset] >= target_port[asset]:
                cons.append(variables['buys'][asset] == 0)

            if asset not in variables['sells']:
                continue

            if current_port[asset] <= target_port[asset]:
                for sell in variables['sells'][asset].values():
                    cons.append(sell == 0)

        return cons
```

Moving on, the next listing shows DoNotTradePastTargetConstraint. It is similar to the last one in the way it works: a constraint is set on each asset depending on its weight in the current portfolio.

Listing 13.7   DoNotTradePastTargetConstraint

```
def __init__(self,
             target_weights: pd.Series):
    """ Prevent trading past the target weight.
    Constrain positions of currently overweight assets to not be less
    than the target, and positions of currently underweight assets
    to not be more than the target. """
    self.target_weights = target_weights

def generate_constraint(self, date, holdings, variables, port_info):

    positions = variables['positions']
    all_assets = variables['buys'].keys()
    current_port = holdings[['ticker', 'value']]. \
        groupby(['ticker']). \
        sum()['value']. \
        reindex(list(all_assets)). \
        fillna(0.0)

    target_port = self.target_weights * port_info['investment_value']
    cons = []
    for asset in all_assets:
        target_position = target_port[asset]
        if current_port[asset] >= target_position:
            cons.append(positions[asset] >= target_position)

        if current_port[asset] <= target_position:
            cons.append(positions[asset] <= target_position)

    return cons
```

Asset is above target. Constrain it so it can't go below.

Asset is below target. Constrain it so it can't go above.

Finally, the following listing shows MaxDeviationConstraint. This one is fairly straightforward: it sets both lower and upper bounds on each asset's position according to
the bounds parameter.

Listing 13.8   MaxDeviationConstraint

```
class MaxDeviationConstraint(Constraint):

    def __init__(self,
                 target_weights: pd.Series,
                 bounds: Union[float, pd.Series]):
        """ Constrain each asset to be within a given tolerance of the
        target """

        self.target_weights = target_weights
        self.bounds = bounds

    def generate_constraint(self, date, holdings, variables, port_info):

        positions = variables['positions']
```

```
all_assets = variables['buys'].keys()
investment_value = port_info['investment_value']
target_port = self.target_weights * investment_value

bounds = self.bounds
if not isinstance(bounds, pd.Series):
    bounds = pd.Series(bounds, list(all_assets))

cons = []
for asset in all_assets:
    lhs = cp.abs(positions[asset]: target_port[asset])
    rhs = bounds[asset] * investment_value
    cons.append(lhs <= rhs)

return cons
```

> **If only a single bound is specified, use it for all assets.**

The only constraint we discussed but have not shown implemented is `VolBased-DeviationConstraint`. The code for this constraint can be found on the book's website and GitHub.

OBJECTIVE

Similar to the `Constraint` class, we'll define a generic `Objective` class and multiple subclasses that can be used to optimize the portfolio in different ways. Similar to the constraint classes, each `Objective` subclass will implement a method called `generate_objective()`. The arguments for this method are exactly the same as the arguments for `generate_constraint()`. Here is what the generic `Objective` class looks like:

```
class Objective:
    def generate_objective(self,
                           date: dt.date,
                           holdings: pd.DataFrame,
                           variables: Dict,
                           port_info: Dict):
        pass
```

We can define the objective function in various ways. Two objective functions that we define in the source code on the book's website and GitHub are

- `MinTaxObjective`—Minimizes the total tax consequence from sales. This includes sales on assets that are held at a loss, in which case the tax is negative. Strategically realizing losses to save money on taxes is something we'll cover in chapter 14.

- `MinTrackingErrorObjective`—Minimizes the tracking error between the optimized portfolio and the target. This objective doesn't consider taxes at all.

The next listing shows `MinTaxObjective` implemented in Python. Some of the code should look familiar—it uses information from the portfolio's holdings to compute effective tax rates for sales.

Listing 13.9 Tax-minimization objective

```python
class MinTaxObjective(Objective):

    def __init__(self, lt_gains_rate: float, income_rate: float,
                 lt_cutoff_days=365):
        self.lt_gains_rate = lt_gains_rate
        self.income_rate = income_rate
        self.lt_cutoff_days = lt_cutoff_days

    def generate_objective(self, date: dt.date, holdings: pd.DataFrame,
                           variables: Dict, port_info: Dict):

        current_date = date
        lt_cutoff_days = self.lt_cutoff_days
        st_rate, lt_rate = self.income_rate, self.lt_gains_rate

        sells = variables['sells']
        tax = 0
        for i in holdings.index:
            lot_info = holdings.loc[i]
            asset, date = lot_info['ticker'], lot_info['purchase_date']
            purchase_date = dt.date.fromisoformat(date)
            holding_period = (current_date - purchase_date).days
            if holding_period <= lt_cutoff_days:
                lot_rate = st_rate
            else:
                lot_rate = lt_rate
            gain = lot_info['current_price'] / lot_info['purchase_price']
            effective_rate = (gain - 1) * lot_rate
            tax += sells[asset][date] * effective_rate

        objective = cp.Minimize(tax)

        return objective
```

Finally, here is the implementation of `MinTrackingErrorObjective`.

Listing 13.10 Tracking error minimization objective

```python
class MinTrackingErrorObjective(Objective):

    def __init__(self, target_weights: pd.Series, sigma: pd.DataFrame):
        self.target_weights = target_weights
        self.sigma = sigma

    def generate_objective(self, date: dt.date, holdings: pd.DataFrame,
                           variables: Dict, port_info: Dict):

        target_weights = self.target_weights
        assets = target_weights.index
        weights = pd.Series(variables['positions'])[assets] \
                  / port_info['investment_value']
```

```
sigma = self.sigma.loc[assets][assets]
diffs = weights - target_weights

objective = cp.Minimize(sum((sp.linalg.sqrtm(sigma) @ diffs) ** 2))

return objective
```

13.3.3 Formulating the problem

Now that we know how to create all the necessary inputs, we can build and solve the rebalancing problem. Our optimization problems will be instances of a class called RebalancingOpt. This class will contain methods that do the following:

- Set up the cvxpy optimization problem using the given inputs.
- Solve the problem.
- Extract the trades chosen by the optimizer.

The next few code listings walk through the implementation of the RebalancingOpt class. Keep in mind that each method shown is part of this class.

We'll start by showing the constructor inside the class definition. The constructor calls three other methods, which we'll show separately.

Listing 13.11   The RebalancingOpt class

```
class RebalancingOpt:
    def __init__(self, date: dt.date, target_port: pd.Series,
                 holdings: pd.DataFrame,
                 constraints: List[Constraint],
                 objective: Objective):
        """ Create an instance of an optimization problem to rebalance a
        portfolio """

        self.date = date
        self.target_port = target_port
        all_assets = target_port.index.values
        if holdings.shape[0]:
            all_assets = np.concatenate((all_assets,
                                         holdings['ticker'].values))

        self.assets = np.unique(all_assets)
        self.holdings = holdings
        self.variables = self._generate_variables(holdings)
        cons = self._generate_constraints(constraints)
        obj = self._generate_objective(objective)
        self.prob = cp.Problem(obj, cons)
```

The _generate_variables() method is shown in listing 13.12. This method returns a dictionary that holds the buy, sell, and position variables. Notice that each of these three sets of variables is a dictionary. Buys and positions are keyed by asset, and sells are keyed by asset and purchase date.

Listing 13.12 Generating problem variables

```
def _generate_variables(self, holdings):
    all_assets = self.assets
    variables = {'buys': {}, 'sells': {}, 'positions': {}}

    asset_holdings = holdings[['ticker', 'value']]. \       ← Calculates current
        groupby(['ticker']). \                                 portfolio holdings
        sum()['value']. \                                      by asset
        reindex(all_assets). \
        fillna(0.0)
                                                    Buys and sells must
    for asset in all_assets:                            be nonnegative.
        variables['buys'][asset] = cp.Variable(nonneg=True)   ←┘

    for i in holdings.index:
        lot_info = holdings.loc[i]
        asset, date = lot_info['ticker'], lot_info['purchase_date']
        if asset not in variables['sells']:    ← Adds the asset to "sells"
            variables['sells'][asset] = {}       if not there already
        variables['sells'][asset][date] = cp.Variable(nonneg=True)

    for asset in all_assets:
        variables['positions'][asset] = asset_holdings[asset] + \
                                        variables['buys'][asset]
        if asset in variables['sells']:
            asset_sell = \
                sum([x for x in variables['sells'][asset].values()])
            variables['positions'][asset] -= asset_sell

    return variables
```

Positions are current holdings plus buys and minus sells. →

Next, we show the `_generate_constraints()` method. It works by calling the `generate_constraint()` method of each constraint provided. It also sets upper bounds on the size of each sell variable so the optimizer can't try to sell more from each lot than the lot contains.

Listing 13.13 Generating constraints

```
def _generate_constraints(self, constraints):
    target_port = self.target_port
    port_info = 'investment_value': target_port.sum()
    cons = [c.generate_constraint(self.date, self.holdings,
                                  self.variables, port_info)
            for c in constraints]

    sell_size_cons = []
    sells = self.variables['sells']
    holdings = self.holdings
    for i in holdings.index:
        lot_info = holdings.loc[i]
```

```
        asset, date = lot_info['ticker'], lot_info['purchase_date']
        sell_size_cons.append(sells[asset][date] <= lot_info['value'])

    cons = list(itertools.chain.from_iterable(cons))
    cons.extend(sell_size_cons)

    return cons
```

⟵ Collapses a list of lists into a single list

Finally, three more simple methods complete the class. The _generate_objective() method works similarly to _generate_constraints() by calling the generate_objective() method of the provided Objective object. The solve() method solves the underlying cvxpy problem instance, and get_trades() returns the values of the optimized trades.

Listing 13.14   Generating the objective and solving the problem

```
def _generate_objective(self, objective):
    target_port = self.target_port
    port_info = {'investment_value': target_port.sum()}
    return objective.generate_objective(self.date, self.holdings,
                                        self.variables, port_info)

def solve(self):
    self.prob.solve()

def get_trades(self):
    variables = self.variables

    buys = {a: v.value for a, v in variables['buys'].items()}
    buys = np.round(pd.Series(buys), 2)
    sells = variables['sells']
    sell_values = {}
    for asset, asset_sells in sells.items():
        asset_sells = {d: v.value for d, v in asset_sells.items()}
        asset_sells = np.round(pd.Series(asset_sells), 2)
        sell_values[asset] = asset_sells

    return {'buys': buys, 'sells': sell_values}
```

The sells for each asset are keyed by the purchase date. ⟵

13.3.4 *Running an example*

We can now run an end-to-end example where we start with an existing portfolio, define an optimization problem for rebalancing, and generate optimal trades. Note that the code assumes that many of the classes described are already defined.

Listing 13.15   A sample rebalancing

```
assets = pd.Index(['VTI', 'VEA', 'VWO', 'AGG', 'BNDX', 'EMB'])
target_weights = pd.Series([0.4, 0.24, 0.16, 0.1, 0.06, 0.04], assets)
prices = pd.Series([69.75, 23.12, 29.54, 7.87, 35.33, 40.22], assets)

tickers = ['VTI', 'VTI', 'VTI', 'VEA', 'VEA', 'VWO', 'VWO',
           'AGG', 'AGG', 'BNDX', 'BNDX','EMB']
```

```
purchase_prices = [40.78, 45.63, 50.04, 14.18, 15.99, 25.64, 31.77,
                   10.19, 8.45, 40.33, 48.28, 30.12]
quantities = [40, 10, 20, 35, 90, 20, 30,
              75, 55, 7, 5, 2]
purchase_dates = ['2021-02-18', '2021-07-21', '2021-11-23',
                  '2021-02-18', '2021-07-21', '2021-02-18', '2021-11-23',
                  '2021-02-18', '2021-07-21', '2021-02-18', '2021-07-21',
                  '2021-02-18']
lots = pd.DataFrame({'ticker': tickers,
                     'purchase_price': purchase_prices,
                     'quantity': quantities,
                     'purchase_date': purchase_dates})

lots['current_price'] = prices[lots['ticker']].values
lots['value'] = lots['quantity'] * lots['current_price']

investment_value = lots['value'].sum()
target_port = target_weights * investment_value

cons = [FullInvestmentConstraint(),
        LongOnlyConstraint(),
        DoNotIncreaseDeviationConstraint(target_weights),
        MaxDeviationConstraint(target_weights, 0.01)]
obj = MinTaxObjective(.15, .4, 365)

date = dt.date(2022, 6, 1)
opt = RebalancingOpt(date, target_port, lots, cons, obj)
opt.solve()
trades = opt.get_trades()
```

If you run this code, you should get these buys:

```
AGG       33.26
BNDX     160.03
EMB      286.27
VEA        0.00
VTI        0.00
VWO      180.12
dtype: float64
```

Sells for all assets except for VEA and VTI are zero. These are the optimal sells for VTI

```
2021-02-18     463.93
2021-07-21       0.00
2021-11-23       0.00
dtype: float64
```

and for VEA:

```
2021-02-18     195.75
2021-07-21       0.00
dtype: float64
```

Notice that for both VTI and VEA, the sales came from the lots purchased on February 18, 2021. This is despite the fact that these lots have a lower purchase price than later lots. Because the newer lots are less than a year old, the higher short-term tax rate applies, making the older lots more tax-efficient to sell.

This code snippet calculates the weights of the optimized portfolio and compares them to the weights of the existing and target portfolios:

```
current_weights = lots[['ticker', 'value']] \
                         .groupby(['ticker']). \
                         sum()['value'] \
                     / lots['value'].sum()

sells_by_asset = pd.Series({a:trades['sells'][a].sum()
                                for a in trades['sells']})
trades_by_asset = trades['buys'] - sells_by_asset
optimized = (current_weights * lots['value'].sum() + trades_by_asset) \
                  / lots['value'].sum()
comparison = pd.DataFrame({'starting': current_weights,
                             'optimized': optimized,
                             'target': target_weights})
```

This is what you should see for the comparison DataFrame:

```
        starting   optimized   target
AGG     0.094934    0.098020     0.10
BNDX    0.039339    0.054189     0.06
EMB     0.007464    0.034027     0.04
VEA     0.268164    0.250000     0.24
VTI     0.453048    0.410000     0.40
VWO     0.137051    0.153764     0.16
```

As we expect, the optimization brings each weight closer to its target. We can see the effect of some of the constraints in the optimized weights. Notice that the optimized weights for VEA and VTI are exactly 1% above their targets. This is because we constrained each asset's weight to be within 1% of its target. The optimizer must obey this constraint, but it doesn't sell more VTI or VEA to get closer to the target because selling more of either asset would increase the total tax cost of the trades. If we had instead minimized tracking error with the same constraints, we would have ended up with the optimized weights being exactly equal to the targets. You can try this on your own by defining a covariance matrix for the six assets and then swapping out the `MinTaxObjective` for a `MinTrackingErrorObjective` in listing 13.15.

Now that we have covered several approaches to rebalancing, let's look at how we can use historical data to see how they stack up.

13.4   Comparing rebalancing approaches

We've discussed a few different ways of rebalancing. Which is best? The truthful answer is that we don't know—it depends on the strategy you are following and what you care about. If you are managing a portfolio in a tax-advantaged account like an IRA, a simple threshold-based or time-based rebalancing policy may suffice because realizing gains doesn't result in any tax consequences. Always rebalancing all the way back to the target portfolio may result in more trading than optimization-based rebalancing, but if the assets in the portfolio are liquid and cheap to trade, this may be fine.

This section shows how we can build a backtesting tool to test different rebalancing strategies by applying them historically. At a high level, the backtest will step forward one day at a time and on each day potentially generate trades to rebalance the portfolio back toward its target. We use historical asset prices to "grow" the portfolio each day and also account for dividends paid by the portfolio's holdings along the way. The results from the backtest—taxes, trading costs, deviations from the target portfolio—can help decide which rebalancing strategy makes the most sense.

The next few sections go through the details of the backtester. As usual, all the code for this section can be found on the book's website and in the GitHub repo.

13.4.1   Implementing rebalancers

The first key component of running the backtest will be an object called the rebalancer. On each day of the backtest, the rebalancer evaluates the current portfolio and possibly generates trades. We'll start by defining a generic `Rebalancer` class. This class has a single method called `rebalance()`, which takes three inputs:

- The current date.
- The portfolio's current holdings. These are just like the holdings used in the `RebalancingOpt` class.
- An investment value for the portfolio: the amount of money the portfolio should hold in investments (as opposed to cash).

Every subclass of `Rebalancer` will implement this method differently. This snippet shows the generic `Rebalancer` class:

```
class Rebalancer:

    def rebalance(self,
                  date: dt.date,
                  holdings: pd.DataFrame,
                  investment_value: float):
        pass
```

In the rest of this section, we'll go through the implementation of subclasses of `Rebalancer` that correspond to the different rebalancing strategies we discussed earlier.

SIMPLE REBALANCERS

For simple rebalancing strategies like threshold-based or interval-based, which trade all the way to the target portfolio, we'll start with a class called `SimpleRebalancer`. This class still doesn't implement the `rebalance()` method, but it adds some functionality for calculating the trades needed to bring the portfolio back to its target and choosing which tax lots to sell from to minimize taxes. Let's go through the code for `SimpleRebalancer`.

The following listing shows two methods that provide trades. `generate_complete_trades()` gives trades that would return the current portfolio to its target weights, and `_empty_trades()` gives a dictionary with the correct formatting but no actual trades.

Listing 13.16 A simple rebalancer

```python
class SimpleRebalancer(Rebalancer):

    def generate_complete_trades(self,
                                 date: dt.date,
                                 holdings: pd.DataFrame,
                                 investment_value: float):
        """ Calculate trades that would take the invested portfolio all
        the way back to the target weights, then select tax-optimized
        lots for sells. Trades are returned as dollar values. """
        asset_holdings = holdings[['ticker', 'value']]. \
            groupby(['ticker']). \
            sum()['value']. \
            fillna(0.0)
        target_values = self.target_weights * investment_value
        full_index = asset_holdings.index.union(target_values.index)
        trade_values = target_values.reindex(full_index).fillna(0) - \
            asset_holdings.reindex(full_index).fillna(0)
        buys = trade_values.where(trade_values > 0).dropna()
        sells = trade_values.where(trade_values < 0).dropna().to_dict()

        holdings = self.add_tax_info(holdings, date, self.tax_params)
        for asset, asset_sale in sells.items():
            asset_holdings = holdings[holdings['ticker'] == asset]
            shares_to_sell = -1 * asset_sale / \
                asset_holdings['current_price'].values[0]
            sells_by_lot = self.select_lots_for_sale(shares_to_sell,
                                                     asset_holdings)
            sells[asset] = sells_by_lot

        return 'buys': buys, 'sells': sells

    @staticmethod
    def _empty_trades():
        """ Gives empty trades in the right format """
        return {'buys': pd.Series(), 'sells': {}}
```

The next listing shows two methods whose functionality we've covered already. One adds information about effective tax rates to the tax lots in the current portfolio, and the other selects which lots to sell from to minimize taxes.

Listing 13.17   Simple tax functionality

```python
@staticmethod
def add_tax_info(lots: pd.DataFrame, current_date: dt.date,
                 tax_params: Dict) -> pd.DataFrame:

    tax_info = {}
    for i in lots.index:
        lot_info = lots.loc[i]
        purchase_date = dt.date.fromisoformat(lot_info['purchase_date'])
        holding_period = (current_date - purchase_date).days
        if holding_period <= tax_params['lt_cutoff']:
            lot_rate = tax_params['income_rate']
        else:
            lot_rate = tax_params['lt_gains_rate']

        purchase_price = lot_info['purchase_price']
        gain = (lot_info['current_price'] / purchase_price - 1)
        effective_rate = gain * lot_rate

        tax_info[i] = pd.Series({'holding_period': holding_period,
                                 'applicable_rate': lot_rate,
                                 'pct_gain': gain,
                                 'effective_rate': effective_rate})

    tax_info = pd.DataFrame(tax_info).T

    return lots.join(tax_info)

@staticmethod
def select_lots_for_sale(shares_to_sell: float,
                         holdings: pd.DataFrame) -> Dict:
    """ Choose which lots to sell from based on tax """

    holdings = holdings.reset_index(drop=True)
    order = holdings['effective_rate'].argsort().values
    shares_available = holdings['quantity'].copy()

    sells = {}
    while shares_to_sell > 0:
        current_best_lot = order[0]
        best_lot_date = holdings['purchase_date'][current_best_lot]
        if shares_available.iloc[current_best_lot] < shares_to_sell:
            sell_value = shares_available[current_best_lot] \
                * holdings['current_price'][current_best_lot]
            shares_to_sell -= shares_available[current_best_lot]
            shares_available[current_best_lot] = 0
            order = order[1:]
```

```
        else:
            shares_available[current_best_lot] -= shares_to_sell
            sell_value = shares_to_sell \
                * holdings['current_price'][current_best_lot]
            shares_to_sell = 0
        sells[best_lot_date] = sell_value

    return sells
```

The `select_lots_for_sale()` method should look familiar: it's largely copied from listing 13.4.

With this functionality defined, there isn't much left to do to define classes representing interval-based and threshold-based rebalancing. They share the functionality inherited from the `SimpleRebalancer` but differ slightly in the inputs they take and the exact implementation of the `rebalance()` method. Here are the definitions of `IntervalBasedRebalancer` and `ThresholdBasedRebalancer`.

Listing 13.18 Two naive rebalancers

```
class IntervalBasedRebalancer(SimpleRebalancer):

    def __init__(self,
                 target_weights: pd.Series,
                 rebalance_dates: List[dt.date],
                 tax_params: Dict):
        """ Rebalancer that trades all the way to the target
        on a fixed set of dates """

        self.target_weights = target_weights
        self.rebalance_dates = set(rebalance_dates)
        self.tax_params = tax_params

    def rebalance(self, date, holdings, investment_value):
        if date not in self.rebalance_dates:
            return self._empty_trades()

        return self.generate_complete_trades(date, holdings,
                                             investment_value)


class ThresholdBasedRebalancer(SimpleRebalancer):

    def __init__(self,
                 target_weights: pd.Series,
                 threshold_function: Callable,
                 tax_params: Dict):
        """ Rebalancer that trades all the way to the target when a
        trigger is satisfied """

        self.target_weights = target_weights
        self.threshold_function = threshold_function
        self.tax_params = tax_params
```

```
def rebalance(self, date, holdings, investment_value):
    current_weights = holdings[['ticker', 'value']] \
                          .groupby(['ticker']) \
                          .sum()['value'] \
                          / investment_value

    if not self.threshold_function(current_weights,
                                   self.target_weights):
        return self._empty_trades()

    return self.generate_complete_trades(date, holdings,
                                         investment_value)
```

Let's take a look at the constructors and the `rebalance()` method for each of these classes. Both take the weights of the target portfolio and the parameters needed to calculate the tax costs of asset sales. But each has one input that is specific to that class. The `IntervalBasedRebalancer` takes a list of dates as input. Its `rebalance()` method looks for the current date in that list and generates rebalancing trades if it's found. Otherwise, no trading happens. The `ThresholdBasedRebalancer` takes an input called `threshold_function`. This should be a function that takes both the current portfolio weights and target portfolio weights as input and returns a `True` or `False` value indicating whether the portfolio should be rebalanced. This snippet shows an example of a possible threshold function that returns `True` if any asset deviates by more than 0.50% from its target weight or `False` otherwise:

```
def threshold_fun(current, target):
    full_index = target.index.union(current.index)
    diffs = current.reindex(full_index).fillna(0) - \
            target.reindex(full_index).fillna(0)

    return diffs.abs().max() > 0.005
```

That does it for the simpler rebalancing types. Next, we'll cover how to implement a rebalancer that uses the optimization tools we built earlier.

OPTIMIZING REBALANCER

Defining a rebalancer that generates trades using optimization is actually very quick, thanks to the work we've already done. We just need to tell the class what to use for an objective and which constraints to set. The `rebalance()` method consists of passing these inputs to `RebalancingOpt`, solving the optimization problem, and then passing back the results. Here is the implementation of the `OptimizationBasedRebalancer`.

Listing 13.19   Rebalancer using optimization

```
class OptimizationBasedRebalancer(Rebalancer):

    def __init__(self,
                 target_weights: pd.Series,
                 objective: Objective,
                 constraints: List[Constraint]):
```

```
        self.target_weights = target_weights
        self.objective = objective
        self.constraints = constraints

    def rebalance(self, date, holdings, investment_value):
        target_port = self.target_weights * investment_value
        opt = RebalancingOpt(date,
                             target_port,
                             holdings,
                             self.constraints,
                             self.objective)
        opt.solve()
        trades = opt.get_trades()

        return trades
```

These are all the rebalancer classes we'll try in the backtests. With these defined, we can proceed with building the backtester.

13.4.2 Building the backtester

At its core, the backtester is just a big `for` loop. It iterates through time by the day, and each day it does the following:

1 Update the portfolio's holdings to reflect current prices.
2 Account for any income from dividends.
3 Evaluate the current portfolio against the target, and generate rebalancing trades if needed.
4 Update the portfolio's holdings using these trades.

HISTORICAL DATA

Once again, we'll use the `yfinance` package to retrieve historical data. For the back-tester, we need both prices and dividends. Listing 13.20 shows two functions that retrieve these items and format them nicely. Importantly, we use the "Close" price, not the "Adjusted Close." The former actually *is* adjusted in one sense—it corrects for stock splits—but it doesn't adjust for dividends. For the backtester, this is what we want. In real life, when we hold a stock or an ETF, dividends are paid as cash and not automatically reinvested into the security that paid them. Using the nonadjusted prices captures this correctly. The dividend values from finance are also adjusted for splits, meaning we don't need to worry about anything split-related in the backtester.

Listing 13.20   Retrieving prices and dividends

```
def get_dividends(assets: List[str]) -> Dict:
    """ Get all the historical dividends for a set of assets """
    div_dict = {}
    for ticker in assets:
        t = yf.Ticker(ticker)
        divs = t.dividends
```

```
        divs.index = pd.Index(map(lambda x: x.date(), divs.index))
        div_dict[ticker] = divs                    Converts datetime
                                                   objects to dates
    return div_dict

def get_prices(assets: List[str],
               start_date: str,
               end_date: str) -> pd.DataFrame:
    """ Retrieve historical prices for given assets """
    prices = yf.download(assets, start_date, end_date)['Close']
    prices.index = pd.Index(map(lambda x: x.date(), prices.index))
    if isinstance(prices, pd.Series):          Handles the odd case
        prices = pd.DataFrame(prices)          where we only ask for
        prices.columns = assets                prices for a single ticker

    return prices
```

Together, these two functions give us all the historical data we need. This data will be the same no matter what kind of rebalancing strategy we are using in the backtest. The next set of inputs, however, will not.

CONFIGURING THE STRATEGY

The next set of inputs we'll provide for the backtester tell the backtester what to do. They include parameters like these:

- The target weights for the portfolio
- The initial investment amount
- Tax rates
- How to rebalance the portfolio

To hold all the necessary parameters, we define a simple class called BacktestParams. This class has only one method—its constructor—and doesn't do anything except store the values provided as attributes.

Listing 13.21   Backtest parameters

```
class BacktestParams:

    def __init__(self,
                 target_weights: pd.Series,
                 start_date: str,
                 end_date: str,
                 starting_investment: float,
                 cash_buffer: float,
                 tax_params: Dict,
                 spreads: Union[pd.Series, float],
                 rebalancer: Rebalancer):
        self.target_weights = target_weights
        self.start_date = start_date
        self.end_date = end_date
        self.starting_investment = starting_investment
```

```
self.cash_buffer = cash_buffer
self.rebalancer = rebalancer
self.spreads = spreads
self.tax_params = tax_params
```

Later, when we run a backtest, we'll show sample inputs for all these values. Note that the constructor requires a `Rebalancer` as input—this is where we provide an instance of a `Rebalancer` from section 13.4.1. A couple of other parameters may require some explanation:

- `cash_buffer`—The fraction of the portfolio to be held in cash. (The rest is invested.) This will typically be a small amount. A little cash is helpful when buying and selling assets because prices can move adversely.
- `spreads`—Assumed values for bid–ask spreads of the assets being traded. We discussed how to find average spreads in chapter 4. This parameter should be provided as a fraction of the share price, not as a dollar value.

Now that we know how to define all the inputs, let's get to the actual backtester.

CORE BACKTEST FUNCTIONALITY

It's time to show the details of the backtester: exactly what happens inside the big loop. The next several code listings show the definition of the `Backtest` class and the methods it uses. We'll start by showing the constructor, which doesn't do anything important, and the `run()` method, which does. The `run()` method is the main loop where everything happens. This method calls almost every other method in the class on each day of the backtest. The details of what happens in each will be explained with its definition.

Listing 13.22   Basic backtest functionality

```
class Backtest:

    def __init__(self, params: BacktestParams,
                 prices: pd.DataFrame, dividends: Dict):
        self.assets = list(params.target_weights.index.values)
        self.prices = prices      ◄──── Output of get_prices()
        self.dividends = dividends  ◄──── Output of get_dividends()
        self.params = params

    def run(self):

        params = self.params
        cash = params.starting_investment
        holdings = pd.DataFrame({'ticker': [],
                                 'value': [],
                                 'quantity': []})
        rebalancer = params.rebalancer
        prices = self.prices
        dividends = self.dividends
        daily_info, weights_df, in_weights_df = {}, {}, {}
```

```
for date in self.prices.index:
    current_prices = prices.loc[date]
    holdings = self.mark_to_market(holdings, current_prices)
    divs = self.calc_dividend_income(date, holdings, dividends)
    cash += divs
    portfolio_value = holdings['value'].sum() + cash
    in_weights_df[date] = \
        self.weights_from_holdings(holdings,
                                   portfolio_value,
                                   self.assets)

    investment_value = portfolio_value * (1 - params.cash_buffer)
    trades = rebalancer.rebalance(date, holdings,
                                  investment_value)
    trade_prices = self.calc_trade_prices(current_prices,
                                           params.spreads)
    holdings, weights, info = \
        self.get_current_data(date, holdings, cash, current_prices,
                              trades, trade_prices,
                              params.tax_params)
    info['dividends'] = divs / info['portfolio_value']
    daily_info[date] = info
    weights_df[date] = weights
    cash = info['cash']

weights_df = pd.DataFrame(weights_df).fillna(0.0).T
in_weights_df = pd.DataFrame(in_weights_df).fillna(0.0).T
daily_info = pd.DataFrame(daily_info).T

return daily_info, weights_df, in_weights_df
```

The following listing shows the mark_to_market() method. It simply uses current
prices to update the value of each portfolio's tax lots.

```
@staticmethod
def mark_to_market(holdings: pd.DataFrame,
                   current_prices: pd.Series) -> pd.DataFrame:
    """ Update holdings values with current prices

    :param holdings: holdings information, including share quantity,
        price, ticker
    :param current_prices: current asset prices
    :return: DataFrame of the same shape as the input, with the
        price per share and total value updated to reflect the current
        asset prices
    """
    holdings['current_price'] = \
        current_prices[holdings['ticker']].values
    holdings['value'] = holdings['current_price'] * holdings['quantity']

    return holdings
```

The calc_dividend_income() method looks for any holdings paying dividends on the current date and computes the total amount of cash coming from dividends. This is added to the current cash balance of the portfolio to be invested in the day's rebalance.

Listing 13.24 Calculating dividend income

```
@staticmethod
def calc_dividend_income(date: dt.date, holdings: pd.DataFrame,
                         dividends: Dict) -> float:
    """ Calculate how much dividend cash the portfolio earned today"""
    if not holdings.shape[0]:     ←— Checks to make sure the portfolio has holdings
        return 0.0

    shares_by_asset = holdings[['ticker', 'quantity']]. \
        groupby(['ticker']). \
        sum()['quantity']

    div_income = 0.0
    assets = set(dividends.keys()). \
        intersection(set(shares_by_asset.index))
    for asset in assets:
        try:
            asset_div = dividends[asset][date]
        except KeyError:
            asset_div = 0.0
        div_income += shares_by_asset[asset] * asset_div

    return div_income
```

The next method, calc_trade_prices(), calculates the prices at which we assume trades will happen, accounting for bid–ask spreads. We assume that the price paid for buys will be higher than the quoted price and the price received for sells will be lower.

Listing 13.25 Calculating assumed trade prices

```
@staticmethod
def calc_trade_prices(current_prices: pd.Series,
                      spreads: Union[float, pd.Series]):
    """ Calculate prices for buys and sells, accounting for bid/ask
    spreads """
                                           If only one spread
    assets = current_prices.index          is provided, use it
    if not isinstance(spreads, pd.Series):  ←—┘ for all assets.
        spreads = pd.Series(spreads, assets)
    spreads = (spreads[assets] * current_prices).clip(lower=0.01)
    buy_prices = current_prices + spreads / 2
    sell_prices = current_prices - spreads / 2

    return 'buy': buy_prices, 'sell': sell_prices
```

The next listing shows a method called `calculate_tax()` that calculates the amount of tax incurred through a sale from a single tax lot. It's applied to all tax lots the optimizer decides to sell from, and the backtester keeps track of the total tax generated at each rebalance.

Listing 13.26   Calculating tax from a sale

```python
@staticmethod
def calculate_tax(purchase_price: float,
                  sell_price: float,
                  quantity: float,
                  purchase_date: dt.date,
                  sell_date: dt.date,
                  tax_params: Dict) -> float:
    """ Calculate tax due to a sale """

    holding_period = (sell_date - purchase_date).days
    if holding_period <= tax_params['lt_cutoff']:
        tax_rate = tax_params['lt_gains_rate']
    else:
        tax_rate = tax_params['income_rate']

    return (sell_price - purchase_price) * quantity * tax_rate
```

The next method, `get_current_data()`, mostly does bookkeeping. It calculates some summary information about the current portfolio, including the weights before and after trading, cash balance, amount traded, taxes, and trading costs. We'll use the data calculated here to compare rebalancing strategies.

Listing 13.27   Calculating daily portfolio information

```python
@staticmethod
def get_current_data(date: dt.date, holdings: pd.DataFrame,
                     cash: float, prices: pd.Series,
                     trades: Dict, trade_prices: Dict,
                     tax_params: Dict) -> tuple:
    """ Current portfolio info after applying trades """

    buys = trades['buys'].where(trades['buys'] > 0)
    buy_shares = buys / prices[buys.index]
    buy_prices = trade_prices['buy'][buys.index]

    buys = pd.DataFrame(\{'ticker': buys.index,
                         'purchase_price': buy_prices,
                         'current_price': prices[buys.index],
                         'quantity': buy_shares.values}\)
    buys['purchase_date'] = date.isoformat()
    buys['value'] = buys['quantity'] * buys['current_price']
    spread_costs = (buy_prices * buy_shares).sum() - buys['value'].sum()
    total_buy = (buys['quantity'] * buys['purchase_price']).sum()
```

```
        sells = trades['sells']
        total_sell, total_tax = 0, 0
        for i in holdings.index:
            asset = holdings['ticker'][i]
            purchase_date = holdings['purchase_date'][i]
            asset_sells = sells.get(asset, \{\})
            lot_sale = asset_sells.get(purchase_date, 0)
            if lot_sale == 0:
                continue
            shares_sold = lot_sale / prices[asset]
            holdings.loc[i, 'quantity'] -= shares_sold
            purchase_date = dt.date.fromisoformat(purchase_date)
            sell_price = trade_prices['sell'][asset]
            spread_costs += shares_sold * (prices[asset] - sell_price)
            tax = Backtest.calculate_tax(holdings['purchase_price'][i],
                                      sell_price, shares_sold,
                                      purchase_date, date,
                                      tax_params)
            total_sell += sell_price * shares_sold
            total_tax += tax
        holdings = pd.concat([holdings, buys], ignore_index=True)
        holdings = holdings[holdings['quantity'] > 0]
        holdings['value'] = holdings['quantity'] * holdings['current_price']

        cash += (total_sell - total_buy)
        portfolio_value = holdings['value'].sum() + cash
        assets = list(prices.index)
        current_weights = Backtest.weights_from_holdings(holdings,
                                                      portfolio_value,
                                                      assets)
        turnover = (total_sell + total_buy) / portfolio_value
        current_info = \{'portfolio_value': portfolio_value,
                      'cash': cash,
                      'turnover': turnover,
                      'tax': total_tax / portfolio_value,
                      'spread_costs': spread_costs / portfolio_value\}

        return holdings, current_weights, pd.Series(current_info)
```

The very last method is a helper function: it takes the entire DataFrame of portfolio holdings (which are maintained at the level of tax lots) and calculates asset weights.

Listing 13.28 Calculating portfolio weights from holdings

```
    @staticmethod
    def weights_from_holdings(holdings: pd.DataFrame,
                            portfolio_value: float,
                            assets: List[str]) -> pd.Series:
        """ Calculate weights of a portfolio """
        weights = holdings[['ticker', 'value']]. \
```

```
                          groupby(['ticker']). \
                          sum()['value']. \
                          reindex(assets). \
                          fillna(0.0) / \
                          portfolio_value

              return weights
```

13.4.3 *Running backtests*

In this section, we'll run backtests for the same target portfolio using three different rebalancing strategies and examine the output from each to compare them. First, let's define some basic settings that will apply to each of the three backtests we'll run. These include the target weights, the period to run the backtests over, and basic inputs like prices, dividends, and tax rates. We also specify a target cash level of 0.2% and a starting portfolio value of $10,000.

```
assets = pd.Index(['VTI', 'VEA', 'VWO', 'AGG', 'BNDX', 'EMB'])
target_weights = pd.Series([0.4, 0.24, 0.16, 0.1, 0.06, 0.04], assets)
start_date = '2013-08-01'
end_date = '2022-07-31'
starting_investment = 10_000
target_cash = 0.0020

prices = get_prices(list(assets.values), start_date, end_date)
dividends = get_dividends(assets)

tax_params = \{'lt_cutoff': 365,
              'lt_gains_rate': 0.20,
              'income_rate': 0.40\}
spreads = .0003
```

The first backtest we'll run is the simplest. We simply rebalance once every five market days, or approximately once per week.

Listing 13.29   Running an interval-based backtest

```
rebal_dates = list(prices.index[range(0, len(prices), 5)])
rebalancer = IntervalBasedRebalancer(target_weights, rebal_dates,
                                     tax_params)
interval_params = BacktestParams(target_weights, start_date, end_date,
                                 starting_investment, target_cash,
                                 tax_params, spreads, rebalancer)

interval_backtest = Backtest(interval_params, prices, dividends)
interval_results = interval_backtest.run()
```

Next, we'll run a version that checks the portfolio's deviations from its targets every day. If the weight of any asset deviates by 0.50% or more, we trade all the way back to the target.

Listing 13.30   Running a threshold-based backtest

This function checks the size of the largest weight deviation.

```
def threshold_fun(current, target):     ◄
    full_index = target.index.union(current.index)
    diffs = current.reindex(full_index).fillna(0) - \
            target.reindex(full_index).fillna(0)

    return diffs.abs().max() > 0.005

rebalancer = ThresholdBasedRebalancer(target_weights, threshold_fun,
                                      tax_params)
threshold_params = BacktestParams(target_weights, start_date, end_date,
                                  starting_investment, target_cash,
                                  tax_params, spreads, rebalancer)
threshold_backtest = Backtest(params, prices, dividends)
threshold_results = threshold_backtest.run()
```

Finally, we'll run a backtest that uses optimization. Although we solve an optimization problem every day, we may not necessarily trade anything. The constraints allow a deviation of 1% in every asset, so if all assets are within 1% of their targets, the optimizer may choose not to trade at all.

Listing 13.31   Running an optimization-based backtest

```
cons = [FullInvestmentConstraint(),
        LongOnlyConstraint(),
        DoNotIncreaseDeviationConstraint(target_weights),
        DoNotTradePastTargetConstraint(target_weights),
        MaxDeviationConstraint(target_weights, 0.01)]
obj = MinTaxObjective(tax_params['lt_gains_rate'],
                      tax_params['income_rate'],
                      tax_params['lt_cutoff'])
rebalancer = OptimizationBasedRebalancer(target_weights, obj, cons)
opt_params = BacktestParams(target_weights, start_date, end_date,
                            starting_investment, target_cash, tax_params,
                            spreads, rebalancer)

opt_backtest = Backtest(params, prices, dividends)
opt_results = opt_backtest.run()
```

The first thing you'll notice when you try this code is that the last backtest takes a long time to run. This makes sense—it's doing a lot more work each day than the others are. Depending on your use cases, it can make sense to combine rebalancing approaches: for example, use optimization but include a threshold as well so you won't need to formulate and solve an optimization problem every day. An extension such as this should be straightforward, given what you've learned so far.

In the final section of this chapter, we'll look at the results from these backtests.

13.4.4 Evaluating results

Now that the backtests are complete, we can look at summaries of the results under each method of rebalancing and see how they performed.

SUMMARIZING BACKTESTS

Compared to defining the rebalancing strategies and the backtester functionality, summarizing the results is a breeze. We'll use three functions to summarize the results of any backtest completed using the code we have written in this chapter. The first, `summarize_performance()`, calculates summary statistics related to the performance and trading of the portfolio over the backtest period. All values calculated by this function are in annualized terms, and, except for the "rebalance frequency" measure, all values from this function are expressed as percentages of the portfolio value. For example, daily turnover is defined as the total value of trades made (buys plus sells) divided by the portfolio value that day. The summary turnover measure is the aggregation of the daily values, annualized. Notice that for some measures, like turnover and spread costs, we omit the value from the very first day: the turnover and spread costs on this day will be anomalously high because the portfolio is starting from cash.

The second function, `summarize_deviations()`, shows some results for how closely the actual traded portfolio followed the target weights. The two metrics shown are the average mean absolute deviation in weights and the average maximum deviation in weights. These are just two of many possible measures of "closeness." Using the covariance matrix of the instruments in our portfolio, we can also measure the predicted tracking error between the actual portfolio and the target portfolio, or the tracking error between the returns of the traded portfolio and those of a hypothetical portfolio that holds the target weights every day. Finally, the following listing also contains a function called `summarize_backtest()` that calls the prior two functions and sticks the results together.

Listing 13.32 Summarizing a completed backtest

```
def summarize_performance(daily_info: pd.DataFrame, params: BacktestParams):
    starting_nav = params.starting_investment
    start_date = daily_info.index.min()
    end_date = daily_info.index.max()              Length of the
    n_years = (end_date - start_date).days / 365.25    backtest in years
    ending_nav = daily_info.loc[end_date, 'portfolio_value']

    mean_return = (ending_nav / starting_nav) ** (1 / n_years) - 1
    daily_rets = daily_info['portfolio_value']
    vol = daily_rets.pct_change().std() * np.sqrt(252)
    turnover = np.sum(daily_info['turnover'].values[1:]) / n_years
    spread_cost = np.sum(daily_info['spread_costs'].values[1:]) / n_years
    tax_cost = np.sum(daily_info['tax'].values[1:]) / n_years
    rebal_freq = np.sum(daily_info['turnover'] > 0) / n_years

                                          Days per year with
                                          nonzero trading
```

```
    return pd.Series({'Mean Return': mean_return, 'Volatility': vol,
                      'Turnover': turnover, 'Spread Cost': spread_cost,
                      'Tax Cost': tax_cost, 'Rebal Frequency': rebal_freq})

def summarize_deviations(weights_df: pd.DataFrame, params: BacktestParams):

    target_weights = params.target_weights
    devs = weights_df - target_weights
    mean_mean = devs.abs().apply(np.mean, axis=1).mean()
    mean_max = devs.abs().apply(np.max, axis=1).mean()

    return pd.Series({'Mean Avg Dev': mean_mean, 'Mean Max Dev': mean_max})

def summarize_backtest(bt_result: list, bt_params: BacktestParams):

    perf_summary = summarize_performance(bt_result[0], bt_params)
    dev_summary = summarize_deviations(bt_result[1], bt_params)

    return pd.concat((perf_summary, dev_summary))
```

Next, let's apply the summarization functions to each of our three backtests. The code is here, and table 13.1 shows the results.

```
interval_summary = summarize_backtest(interval_results, interval_params)
threshold_summary = summarize_backtest(threshold_results, threshold_params)
opt_summary = summarize_backtest(opt_results, opt_params)
result = pd.DataFrame({'Interval': interval_summary,
                       'Threshold': threshold_summary,
                       'Optimized': opt_summary})
```

Table 13.1 Summary of backtest results

	Interval	Threshold	Optimized
Mean return	7.00%	7.04%	7.04%
Volatility	13.9%	13.9%	13.9%
Turnover	39.8%	31.9%	17.6%
Bid/Ask spread cost	0.01%	0.00%	0.00%
Tax cost	0.19%	0.20%	0.16%
Rebalances per year	50.4	22.1	158.4
Mean average deviation	0.09%	0.12%	0.27%
Mean maximum deviation	0.21%	0.26%	0.60%

Looking at these summaries, the first thing you'll probably notice is that they aren't a whole lot different. The average returns and volatility are nearly identical. The optimized strategy saves a bit on taxes (as it should, considering taxes are in the objective function) and does somewhat less turnover. The largest differences are in the rebalance frequency and the deviations. Not surprisingly, the optimized strategy rebalances more often (although much of the trading is very small). It also has large deviations from the target weights on average. This shouldn't come as a surprise, either—the optimized strategy just tries to minimize taxes while imposing a bound of 1% on deviations from the target. The other two strategies trade all the way to the targets whenever a rebalance occurs.

This doesn't mean these rebalancing strategies will produce such similar results for all target portfolios. Portfolios including higher-volatility assets (for example, cryptocurrency, narrowly focused ETFs, or individual stocks) may have results with more differences between strategies. You will want to test various rebalancing strategies for any target portfolio you define, to see what's best for your use case.

Summary

- You can reduce taxes when selling assets to rebalance a portfolio by selling lots with the least tax exposure first.
- You can define naive rebalancers that trade all the way to the target portfolio based on simple triggers: the passage of time, or deviations from the target.
- You can formulate a rebalance as an optimization problem and define different constraints and objectives for that problem using cvxpy.
- You can build a backtester to simulate the process of portfolio management using historical data and compare the results of different rebalancing strategies.

Tax-loss harvesting:
Improving after-tax returns

This chapter covers

- Understanding tax-loss harvesting and its potential benefits
- The "wash-sale" rule and its implications for tax-loss harvesting
- Implementing a tax-loss harvesting system for ETFs

Investors hold assets that are expected to increase in value over time. However, the increases are never straight lines—there are always downturns along the way. As a result, investors sometimes hold assets at a loss. Tax-loss harvesting (TLH) is the process of selectively selling assets currently trading at a loss. Selling depreciated assets creates realized losses that can then be used to offset realized gains or ordinary income. The proceeds from the sales of depreciated assets can be reinvested in similar (but not identical!) assets to maintain the investor's desired exposures.

TLH is a fairly common feature among robo-advisors—half of the robo-advisors surveyed in chapter 1 include TLH as a feature. This chapter explains the mechanics and benefits of TLH and shows what an implementation using ETFs might look like. The exact tax rules used in this chapter are specific to US-based investors, but the concepts apply to all taxable investors.

14.1 The economics of tax-loss harvesting

TLH benefits investors in two ways:

- Delaying tax payments from the present to the future, known as *tax deferral*
- Achieving a lower tax rate on realized gains or income

Both benefits are important, and the differences can be somewhat subtle. Let's go into some more detail about each.

14.1.1 Tax deferral

The first way TLH provides economic benefit to investors is through the core tenet of finance called the *time value of money*. You may have heard this concept expressed colloquially as "a dollar today is better than a dollar tomorrow." What this means is, all else equal, an investor should prefer receiving a dollar today rather than at a future date. The dollar today can be invested (for example, in extremely safe government bonds, but also in stocks or other assets) and grow to a larger value in the future. Of course, if the dollar is invested in risky assets, growth isn't guaranteed—receiving the dollar earlier is only a "free lunch" if it's invested in an effectively riskless asset like an FDIC-insured savings account or government bonds with an appropriate maturity.

With TLH, the concept can be rephrased as "a dollar tax tomorrow is better than a dollar tax today." The idea is the same: given the option between paying $1 in tax today or at a future date, we should prefer the future date. Today's dollar can be invested and grow in value until the tax is due. At that time, the $1 tax can be paid, leaving any earnings from the investment to be spent or invested further.

Let's look at an example of tax deferral in action. We'll assume that we have a tax of $1,000 due from the sale of some assets and $1,000 in cash ready to pay the tax bill. If we simply pay the tax today, we're left with no cash, but the tax bill is settled. However, let's imagine we have an investment portfolio containing assets trading at losses large enough to generate $1,000 in negative tax. This could occur, for example, if we purchased $100,000 in an ETF that is now worth $95,000, and the tax rate applicable to that lot was 20%. The 20% tax rate multiplied by the $5,000 in depreciation gives $1,000 in tax benefit. By realizing this loss, we can "cancel out" the $1,000 owed. So we won't need to pay any tax currently, and we still have the $1,000 in cash available to invest. If we use the $95,000 in proceeds from selling the depreciated ETF to buy another similar ETF, the overall exposure of the portfolio hasn't changed drastically.

This may seem too good to be true—that's because we're not done yet. By selling the first ETF and buying the second, we have decreased the cost basis in this investment from $100,000 to $95,000. This means when we eventually sell the second ETF, we'll have to pay more tax than we otherwise would have. Going back to the example in the previous paragraph, let's imagine that after doing the TLH trade, we hold the second ETF until it appreciates to $150,000. When we sell, we now have $55,000 in realized gains and a tax bill of $11,000. If we had held the first until this point, the gain would be $50,0000, and the tax bill would be only $10,000. But the word *eventually* is key here—the sale of the second ETF could be many years away. Going back to our colloquial phrase about the time value of money, the distant tax payment is better than one today (and more distant is even better).

How much value does the deferral of the tax bill add? By using the losses to cancel out the tax owed, we get to keep the $1,000 in cash that we already had. But we also decreased our cost basis in the ETF position, so when we eventually sell the ETF, our gain (and therefore the tax owed) will be higher than it otherwise would have been. For simplicity, let's assume that the future tax rate is the same as the current one, so that the future tax owed will be the same $1,000. Then the economic benefit of deferring the tax payment depends on two things:

- How far in the future the payment is deferred for. Denote this by T.
- The discount rate between now and this time. Call this r. This can be subjective but should represent an expected rate of return between now and time T.

If we let x denote the size of the tax liability ($1,000 in our example), the current economic value of the tax deferral is given by

$$x \left(1 - (1+r)^{-T}\right)$$

Let's look at our example. If we assume that we'll hold the position for 20 years ($T = 20$), and the discount rate is 2% ($r = 0.02$), the current economic value of the tax deferral is about $327.03. The intuition here is this: by harvesting the loss, we have postponed our tax bill of $1,000 from today until 20 years in the future. If we can earn a 2% return for the next 20 years, to satisfy the tax liability, we can invest $672.97 now, and it will grow to $1,000 by then. This leaves us with the remaining $327.03, which we can use however we wish.

This calculation uses two quantities whose values aren't as straightforward as the amount of tax owed. In the next sections, we will discuss these quantities and how they affect the benefit of tax-rate deferral.

CHOOSING A DISCOUNT RATE

In the example, we use 2% for the discount rate. This seems reasonable—2% is about average for a "risk-free" rate that you can earn by just depositing money in a savings account. However, you can choose a different rate if you invest the tax savings in an asset with higher expected returns. On the other hand, assets with higher rates of return are usually riskier as well—you may expect a 6% to 7% return from the stock market, but it certainly isn't guaranteed. The choice of discount rate should reflect a value that the investor feels reasonably confident can be achieved (on average) over their investment horizon.

INVESTMENT HORIZON

TLH generally provides more value when your investment horizon is longer. This is plainly true from the formula provided for the economic benefit. If T is near zero, the benefit is as well. In practice, the benefit isn't exactly a continuous function of T:

if you harvest a loss but then liquidate your portfolio within the same tax year, the benefit will be exactly zero (because taxes are generally due at the end of the year).

A longer investment horizon is also helpful when deciding a discount rate. For instance, 6% may be a reasonable rate of return to expect from stocks over a long period (say, 30 years), but over a shorter period, the average can be significantly lower. A longer time horizon provides more confidence in the choice of discount rate.

14.1.2 *Rate conversion*

In the United States, capital gains are taxed at different rates depending on how long the asset was held. At the moment, federal tax rates on long-term capital gains are 0%, 15%, or 20%. Short-term capital gains are taxed at the same rate as ordinary income, which can be significantly higher. The second way that TLH can create economic benefit is by "converting" short-term gains into long-term gains and reducing the tax rate as a result.

Rate conversion works by offsetting short-term capital gains with harvested losses. As an example, let's assume our marginal federal tax rate is 35%, our long-term capital gains rate is 15%, and we've realized $1,000 in short-term capital gains. Ordinarily, this would result in a tax bill of $350. But suppose we can harvest $1,000 in short-term losses by selling an ETF currently trading at a loss and then buying a similar one. The harvested losses cancel out the gains, and the net tax bill becomes zero. As we saw in the last section, harvesting the loss now creates a tax liability in the future, when we eventually sell the replacement ETF. But as long as we hold the replacement ETF for at least a year, the future sale will be subject to the lower long-term gains rate. If the eventual gain on the replacement ETF is $1,000, the tax bill decreases from $350 to $150.

The rate-conversion case does have some flavor of deferral as well: you need to hold the replacement asset for at least a year, meaning you are delaying a tax bill for at least a year as well. But the benefit comes primarily from the differential in tax rates on short-term and long-term gains. In extreme cases—for example, if you retire and can keep your taxable income low enough—the future tax rate could actually be 0%, meaning you eliminate the original tax entirely.

Note that this discussion only applies to federal taxes. Most states charge tax on capital gains at the same rate as ordinary income no matter what the holding period is. This means rate conversion generally doesn't help to reduce state taxes.

What if we don't have any realized capital gains? Many younger investors won't, because they're generally buying investments rather than selling. It turns out we can still get some benefit from TLH. The IRS allows using realized losses to offset up to $3,000 of ordinary income each year. If we have excess losses (beyond $3,000), we can carry them forward and use them in later years. The only catch is that losses have to be used to offset any capital gains before they're used to offset ordinary income.

Of course, this isn't to say that everyone should use TLH. In the next section, we'll discuss situations where TLH probably doesn't make sense.

14.1.3 *When harvesting doesn't help*

Both ways in which TLH adds benefit have an element of delaying taxes. The implicit assumption is that the value of the taxes avoided today is higher than the present value of the increased tax burden that will be paid later. However, this may not always be the case.

The assumption can fail in one of two ways. First, our investment horizon may be very short—specifically, less than a year. If this is the case, rate conversion isn't possible: the benefit comes from holding on to the replacement assets for at least a year to get long-term tax treatment on the eventual gains. If we don't wait at least a year, the tax rate won't "convert" from short-term to long-term. There is still some element of deferral, but practically speaking, the benefit is zero because taxes are generally paid at the end of the year and not as gains are realized.

Second, our future tax rate could be higher than the one we currently face. For example, a young person (or married couple) with a low income may face a 0% federal capital gains tax rate, meaning there is no tax benefit at the federal level for harvesting losses today. In such a case, the state rate will likely be low as well (for states with graduated tax rates). By harvesting a loss now, the young investor reduces their current tax burden by a small amount. But suppose that 10 years later the investor wants to sell assets to make a large purchase. By this point, they may be significantly further along in their career with a higher income and consequently higher tax rates. The tax incurred at this point will be considerably higher.

So, generally, TLH provides the most benefit to investors with long investment horizons and whose tax rates are expected to either stay relatively flat or decrease until the time they wish to liquidate their portfolio. Now that we have established when and how TLH can benefit investors (and when it won't), the next section will discuss a specific regulatory limitation on TLH known as the *wash-sale rule*.

14.2 *The wash-sale rule*

Here's an example of a potential tax-reduction strategy. We buy some shares of an ETF for $100 per share. If the price dips below $100, we sell the shares and then immediately buy new ones. We repeat this any time the share price decreases to below our latest purchase price. Each time, we realize losses that we can use to decrease our current taxes.

This probably sounds too good to be true, and it is. Selling and repurchasing the same asset creates what is called a *wash sale*, and the losses are disallowed. The rule is intended to prevent investors from realizing losses (and avoiding taxes) without actually changing the economic exposure in their portfolio. This section explains the application of the wash-sale rule and how to handle it in an automated investing process.

14.2.1 *Wash-sale basics*

The wash-sale rule applies more generally than the example: it applies when "new" shares are purchased within 30 days of the sale of "old" ones—either before or after. The new and old shares don't have to be the same asset; the rule only states that the assets need to be "substantially identical." Unfortunately, this term isn't given a clear definition, and opinions differ as to what it means. For TLH with ETFs, a rule of thumb used by several robo-advisors is that two ETFs that seek to track different indices will not be considered substantially identical. Under this assumption, we can realize a loss in the VTI ETF (which tracks the CRSP US Total Market Index) and then immediately buy the ITOT ETF (which tracks the S&P Total Market Index) without triggering the wash-sale rule. We'll use the same convention later in this chapter.

It's obviously important to know exactly when the wash-sale rule applies. However, even aside from the definition of "substantially identical," this isn't always obvious. The next two sections look at examples to help understand when the wash-sale rule applies and what happens when it does.

WASH-SALE RULE EXAMPLES

In this section, we'll go through several examples of buying and selling patterns and show whether the wash-sale rule applies. In each example, we assume that there are no other transactions other than the ones shown and that all the transactions are in the same instrument. If some of the examples seem repetitive, we apologize— we will err to this side to help ensure understanding. For another great resource, we recommend Fairmark's guide to the wash-sale rule at https://fairmark.com/investment-taxation/capital-gain/wash/.

Let's start with an example where the wash-sale rule doesn't apply. If we buy some shares and then sell them at a loss, the wash-sale rule doesn't apply. This makes sense; the purchase wasn't made to maintain an exposure after selling to harvest the loss. Figure 14.1 shows an example in which nine days pass between the purchase and the sale, but it's important to note that the wash-sale rule never applies in this case, no matter how quickly the sale follows the purchase.

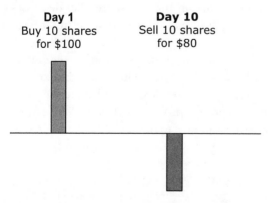

Day 1
Buy 10 shares
for $100

Day 10
Sell 10 shares
for $80

The wash-sale rule does not apply here.

Figure 14.1   The wash-sale rule does not apply when a sale follows a single purchase.

The simplest example of when the wash-sale rule does apply is the strategy described at the beginning of this section. If we have sold a security at a loss, we can't buy that security until 30 days have passed without triggering the wash-sale rule. Figure 14.2 shows an example of this case. This scenario can arise when making deposits into a portfolio. Suppose we've harvested a loss in VTI and purchased ITOT as a replacement. Ten days later, we'd like to invest some more money into US stocks. Buying VTI would trigger the wash-sale rule, so we have to buy ITOT instead. If we've harvested losses in both VTI and ITOT, we can't buy either one. We either need to wait until 30 days have passed or find a third ETF to buy.

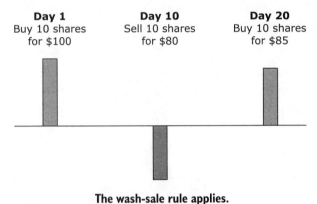

The wash-sale rule applies.

Figure 14.2   The wash-sale rule applies when a second purchase follows a sale, all within 30 days.

The next three examples all follow the pattern of two purchases followed by a sale. The factors that determine whether the wash-sale rule applies are the timing of the transactions and which lot shares are sold from.

First, let's consider the case where the first purchase comes more than 30 days before the sale (see figure 14.3). If the shares sold come from the second purchase, the wash-sale rule won't apply. This seems reasonable; it's actually similar to the very first case, except there was an additional lot in the portfolio.

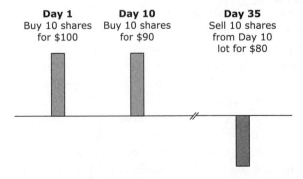

The wash-sale rule does not apply: more than 30 days have passed since the first purchase.

Figure 14.3   The wash-sale rule does not apply when a sale when selling newer shares.

What if the timeline is compressed, and all three transactions take place within 30 days? In this case, the wash-sale rule applies, no matter which lot the shares are sold from. This may seem counterintuitive in the case where shares from the second lot are sold—when we purchase the second set of shares, we don't know that we'll be able to sell them at a loss in the future. But the IRS considers this a wash sale nonetheless. This scenario can be summarized succinctly: if we have purchased more than one lot of substantially identical securities within the past 30 days, we can't harvest losses in any of the lots without triggering the wash-sale rule.

If the lots sold are from the first lot, the application of the wash-sale rule makes more sense. The situation is essentially the same as the second case, except the order of the second and third transactions is reversed. Figure 14.4 depicts this situation.

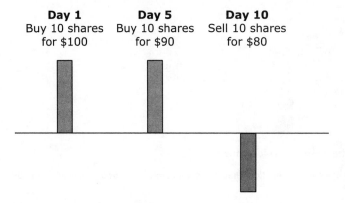

Day 1 **Day 5** **Day 10**
Buy 10 shares Buy 10 shares Sell 10 shares
for $100 for $90 for $80

The wash-sale rule applies.

Figure 14.4   The wash-sale rule does apply with "new" shares in the portfolio.

What happens if we make a trade that creates a wash sale? The next section will cover the details of what it really means when the wash-sale rule is applied.

APPLYING THE WASH-SALE RULE

First, creating wash sales isn't illegal. We just can't use the losses generated by harvested losses to reduce current taxes. Second, a wash sale doesn't necessarily negate all the losses realized. If the purchases are smaller than the sales, only part of the losses gets negated. For example, if we sell 100 shares of VTI for a total loss of $1,000 and then buy 10 shares within the next 30 days, we only "lose" the losses from 10 of the shares sold. We still get to keep $900 in losses to use in lowering our current taxes.

So where do the "washed" losses go? They don't disappear—the cost basis of the shares to which the rule was applied is added to the cost basis of the new shares. Going back to the example, let's say the first shares of VTI cost $250 each and are sold for $240 each, and the new shares are purchased at $275. The cost basis of the 10 shares to which the rule applies is added to the cost basis of the new shares. After applying the rule, the cost basis of the new 10-share lot is $5,250, which is $2,750 from the purchase price and \$2,500 from the shares that were sold. If those shares are sold later (say, after more than 30 days have passed), the gain or loss is calculated based on the new \$5,250 cost basis. The same accounting applies if the buys come before the sells—the cost basis of the sold shares is added to the cost basis of the shares that stay in the portfolio.

Now that we've described what triggers the wash-sale rule and how it works, let's see how we can implement the rule in Python.

14.2.2 Wash sales with Python

Determining when the wash-sale rule applies is very formulaic, so it's not a surprise that it's straightforward to implement in Python. We'll start by implementing checks on tax lots to determine whether the wash-sale rule will apply before any more trading happens; then we'll show how to perform the necessary accounting when a wash sale happens.

DETERMINING ELIGIBILITY

As in previous chapters, we'll represent tax lots using a pandas DataFrame object. The difference in this chapter is that we need to keep track of positions that no longer exist because they've been sold. So, in addition to the usual information, we'll include the sell date and sell price of closed lots in the DataFrame. Here's an example of such a DataFrame, which contains some open lots as well as one that's been closed:

```
import datetime as dt
import numpy as np
import pandas as pd

lots = \
    pd.DataFrame({'ticker': ['VTI', 'VTI', 'VTI'],
                  'purchase_price': [90, 85, 105],
                  'quantity': [25, 30, 20],
                  'purchase_date': ['2021-02-10', '2021-07-21',
                                    '2022-03-15'],
                  'sell_price': [75, np.NaN, np.NaN],
                  'sell_date': ['2022-04-01', np.NaN, np.NaN],
                  })
```

To determine whether the wash-sale rule should apply, we also need to know the current price of the asset (in this case, VTI) and the current date. This is what we'll use for this example:

```
current_date = dt.date.fromisoformat('2022-04-08')
current_price = 90
```

We'll need to check trading eligibility in two ways:

- For each lot, determine whether selling from the lot would create a wash sale.
- Check whether we can buy the asset without washing previously realized losses.

Listing 14.1 shows two functions that perform these checks. Note that both functions look for information from columns that aren't (yet) present in the tax lots. We'll show how to add that information when we implement the function that will call these two helpers. The names of the new columns are very intuitive logical values:

- is_sold is a flag noting whether the lot has been sold already.
- is_new is true when the lot has been held for 30 days or less.
- is_at_loss is true when the purchase price of the lot is more than the current price.

Listing 14.1   Determining TLH eligibility

```
def sellable(lot: pd.Series, new_lots: pd.Series) -> pd.Series:
    """ Check whether a lot can be sold without
    creating a wash sale """

    idx = ['sellable', 'blocking_lots']
    if not lot['still_held']:
        return pd.Series([False, []], idx)        ◄─┐ Can't sell from a lot
                                                     │ that's already closed

    if not lot['is_at_loss']:
        return pd.Series([True, []], idx)   ◄── Selling at a gain is fine.

    if lot['is_new'] and len(new_lots) > 1:
        blocking_lots = new_lots[new_lots != lot.purchase_date]
        return pd.Series([False, blocking_lots], idx)

    if not lot['is_new'] and len(new_lots) > 0:
        return pd.Series([False, new_lots], idx)

    return pd.Series([True, []], idx)


def blocks_buying(lot: pd.Series, current_date: dt.date) -> bool:
    """ Check whether a lot prevents us from buying an
    asset because it was recently sold at a loss """

    if lot['still_held']:
        return False
    how_long = (current_date - dt.date.fromisoformat(lot['sell_date'])).days

    return how_long <= 30 and lot['sell_price'] < lot['purchase_price']
```

Next we'll show a function that will calculate the new information and call these two functions to determine which lots can be sold and whether the asset can be purchased. The function calculates when the wash-sale period starts (30 days before the current date), calculates the three new flags mentioned, and counts the number of recently purchased open lots. It then applies the two previously defined functions to each tax lot. The function adds a new column to the DataFrame, indicating sellability for each lot, and also returns a flag indicating whether the asset can be purchased without creating wash sales.

Listing 14.2 Checking assets for buying and selling restrictions

```
def check_asset_for_restrictions(lots: pd.DataFrame,
                                 current_price: float,
                                 current_date: dt.date) -> pd.DataFrame:
    """ Check buying and selling eligibility for an asset """

    lots = lots.copy()                              Calculates the start of
    ws_start = \                                     the wash-sale period
        (current_date - dt.timedelta(days=30)).strftime('%Y-%m-%d')  ◄─┘
    lots['is_new'] = list(map(lambda x: x >= ws_start,
                              lots['purchase_date']))
    lots['is_at_loss'] = list(map(lambda x: current_price < x,
                                  lots['purchase_price']))
    lots['still_held'] = list(map(lambda x: x != x, lots['sell_date']))
    new_lots = lots[lots['is_new'] & lots['still_held']]['purchase_date']

    sellability = \                          Checks the sellability of each lot
        {i: sellable(lots.loc[i], new_lots) for i in lots.index}  ◄─┘
    lots = lots.join(pd.DataFrame(sellability).T)
    buy_blocks = list(map(lambda x: blocks_buying(x[1], current_date),
                          lots.iterrows()))  ◄─────────┐ Checks if each lot prevents
    buy_blocks = pd.Series(buy_blocks, lots.index)     │ buying the asset it holds
    lots['blocks_buy'] = buy_blocks
    lots.drop(['is_new', 'is_at_loss', 'still_held'], axis=1, inplace=True)

    return lots
```

Before we apply this function to our sample lots, let's think about what we expect to see. There are two open lots: one was purchased more than 30 days before the current date, and the other was purchased within the past 30 days. So we shouldn't be able to harvest losses in the old lot. But the old lot is also held at a gain, so we don't need to worry. Because there is only one "new" lot, we're free to sell it. There's also one closed lot, which was closed only seven days before the current date at a loss of $15 per share. Because of this recent sale, we can't buy VTI without "washing" this loss.

Now let's see if the function's output matches this reasoning:

```
lots = check_asset_for_restrictions(lots, current_price, current_date)
```

After running this code, you should have this for the value of the blocks_buy column:

```
0    True
1    False
2    False
```

This indicates that we can't purchase VTI without creating a wash sale, because of the recent sale of the first lot. The function also added a sellable column, which should look like this:

```
0    False
1    True
2    True
```

This is what we expect as well. The first lot can't be sold because it's closed already. The second can be sold, but only because it's not at a loss. The third can also be sold because it's the only recently purchased lot.

Applying this logic for each instrument in a portfolio's holdings is straightforward—we simply need to iterate over each instrument. Or, if our portfolio contains instruments with different tickers but that should be considered substantially identical, we iterate over each set of instruments considered substantially identical (these sets should be disjoint). The following listing shows code that can be used in the simpler case, although extending the functionality to handle sets of substantially identical instruments isn't hard.

Listing 14.3   Determining TLH eligibility for all assets

```
def check_all_assets_for_restrictions(lots: pd.DataFrame,
                                      current_prices: pd.Series,
                                      current_date: dt.date):
    """ Check buying and selling eligibility for an asset """
    tickers = lots['ticker'].unique()
    results = []
    for ticker in tickers:
        asset_lots = lots[lots['ticker'] == ticker].copy()
        asset_res =              check_asset_for_restrictions(asset_lots,
                                      current_prices[ticker],
                                      current_date)
        results.append(asset_res)

    results = pd.concat(results)
    return results
```

We can try running this code on tax lots containing multiple different instruments:

```
current_prices = pd.Series([90, 34], ['VTI', 'AGG'])
lots = \
    pd.DataFrame({'ticker': ['VTI', 'VTI', 'VTI', 'AGG', 'AGG'],
                  'purchase_price': [90, 85, 105, 40, 35],
                  'quantity': [25, 30, 20, 10, 10],
                  'purchase_date': ['2021-02-10', '2021-07-21', '2022-03-15',
                                    '2022-01-15', '2022-04-07'],
                  'sell_price': [75, np.NaN, np.NaN, np.NaN, np.NaN],
                  'sell_date': ['2022-04-01', np.NaN, np.NaN, np.NaN, np.NaN],
                  })

lots = check_all_assets_for_restrictions(lots, current_prices, current_date)
```

In this case, we can't sell the older lot of AGG because we purchased a brand-new lot the prior day. This is indicated in the `sellable` and `blocking_lots` columns. The latter column tells us exactly which lots prevent the sale. We can sell the newer AGG lot without creating a wash sale. The buying and selling eligibility for VTI remains the same, as expected.

We now have code that allows us to determine which lots we can sell, and whether an asset can be purchased, without triggering the wash-sale rule. Sometimes, however, creating a wash sale may be unavoidable, or even desired. Perhaps we harvested a small loss in some asset but have cash to invest and want to buy the asset again. We may prefer to buy the asset and wash the previously realized loss rather than hold cash until the wash-sale period ends. In the next section, we'll show how to perform the tax-lot adjustments necessitated by wash sales.

Tax-lot adjustments

As described, wash sales can be created both by purchases (buying something that's been recently sold at a loss) and by sales (selling something at a loss when new shares have been purchased recently). This section shows code for the adjustments that need to be made to tax lots as a result of wash sales.

We'll start with buys. When we buy shares, we need to update our tax lots in two ways. The first is adding to our existing lots the new lots representing the purchases—essentially, creating new rows in the DataFrame holding tax lots. The next listing shows a function, create_new_lots(), that creates a row with all the relevant data for each new purchase and returns the result in a DataFrame.

Listing 14.4 Creating new lots for purchases

```
def create_new_lots(buys: Dict, current_date: dt.date,
                    current_prices: pd.Series):
    """ Create new tax lots from buy trades """

    new_lots = []
    for ticker, buy_amount in buys.items():
        idx = ['ticker', 'purchase_price', 'quantity', 'purchase_date',
               'sell_price', 'sell_date', 'wash_sale']
        new_lot = pd.Series([ticker, current_prices[ticker],
                            buy_amount / current_prices[ticker],
                            current_date.strftime('%Y-%m-%d'),
                            np.NaN, np.NaN, False],
                            index=idx)
        new_lots.append(new_lot)

    return pd.DataFrame(new_lots)
```

The second step is a little more involved. We need to

1 Find which (if any) of the new purchases created wash sales.
2 Mark the closed lots that, in combination with new purchases, created wash sales.
3 Add the cost basis of any "washed" losses to the cost basis of the new lots.

Listing 14.5 performs these three steps. The function takes tax lots as one of its inputs and assumes that all the lots have been through the check_all_assets_for_ restrictions() function so they show which assets would create wash sales if purchased. The `adjust_lots_with_buys()` function starts by creating new lots for the purchases using the function we just saw. After that, it iterates through the new lots. For each purchase, the code finds old lots where the asset being purchased was recently sold at a loss and calculates the extent of the adjustment needed (if any). The code then begins iterating through each of these closed lots and performs adjustments until the washed sales are fully adjusted for. In each iteration, the adjustments include steps 2 and 3 of the previous list: marking an old closed lot as a wash sale and adding to the cost basis of the new purchase.

It's important to note that the size of a new purchase can be larger or smaller than the total size of recently closed lots. If the new purchase is smaller, the losses from the closed lots are only partially washed. If the new purchase is bigger, the previous losses are completely washed. This is seen in the `shares_to_wash` variable in the code. The value of this variable decreases every time an old lot is adjusted, and the loop breaks when the value reaches 0. In cases where the number of shares left to wash is less than the number of shares in a closed lot, we split the closed lot into two pieces—one marked as a wash sale, and one not.

Listing 14.5   Adjusts lots for wash sales caused by buys

```
def adjust_lots_with_buys(lots: pd.DataFrame,
                          buys: Dict,
                          current_date: dt.date,
                          current_prices: pd.Series) -> Tuple:
    """ Update existing lots with buys, adjusting cost basis for wash sales
    where necessary """

    new_lots = create_new_lots(buys, current_date, current_prices)
    leftover_lots = []
    for new_idx, new_lot in new_lots.iterrows():
        ticker_lots = lots[lots['ticker'] == new_lot['ticker']]
        blocking_lots = ticker_lots[ticker_lots['blocks_buy']] \
            .sort_values(by='purchase_date')          ←──┐ Finds any old sales blocking
                                                          │ buys in this asset
        shares_to_wash = min(new_lot['quantity'],
                             blocking_lots['quantity'].sum())  ←──┐
        for i in blocking_lots.index:                              How many shares
            lot = lots.loc[i].copy()                               should be washed?
            lot['wash_sale'] = True
            if shares_to_wash < lot['quantity']:
                leftover_lot = lots.loc[i].copy()
                leftover_lot['quantity'] -= shares_to_wash
                lot['quantity'] = shares_to_wash
                shares_to_wash = 0
                leftover_lots.append(leftover_lot)
            else:
                shares_to_wash -= lot['quantity']

            washed_loss = lot['quantity'] * (lot['purchase_price'] -
                                             lot['sell_price'])
```

```
        new_lots.loc[new_idx, 'purchase_price'] += washed_loss / \
            new_lot['quantity']
        lots.loc[i] = lot

        if shares_to_wash == 0:
            break
    leftover_lots = pd.DataFrame(leftover_lots) \
        .drop(['sellable', 'blocking_lots', 'blocks_buy'],
            axis=1, errors='ignore')

    return new_lots, leftover_lots, lots
```

To help understand the last point about washing only part of a closed lot, let's walk through an example. We'll assume that we recently sold two lots of VTI at a loss: one lot of 10 shares and another of 5 shares. We buy 12 shares of VTI today, which means 12 of the 15 shares we recently sold should be marked as wash sales. Because the 10-share lot is older, it is adjusted first, and the full lot is marked as a wash sale. This leaves two more shares. Because the second lot had more than two shares, we split it into two parts: one with two shares, which is marked as a wash sale, and one with three shares, which is not a wash sale.

The following snippet of code prepares the inputs and performs the adjustments for this specific example:

```
current_prices = pd.Series([90], ['VTI'])
current_date = dt.date.fromisoformat('2022-04-08')
lots = \
    pd.DataFrame({'ticker': ['VTI', 'VTI'],
                  'purchase_price': [100, 105],
                  'quantity': [10, 5],
                  'purchase_date': ['2022-01-01', '2022-01-08'],
                  'sell_price': [75, 85],
                  'sell_date': ['2022-04-01', '2022-04-05'],
                  'wash_sale': [False, False]})
lots = check_asset_for_restrictions(lots, current_price, current_date)
buys = {'VTI': current_prices['VTI'] * 12}
new_lots, leftover_lots, adj_lots = adjust_lots_with_buys(lots, buys,
    current_date, current_prices)
```

After running the code, the value of new_lots looks like this (some columns omitted to save space):

```
  ticker  purchase_price  quantity purchase_date
0    VTI       114.166667      12.0    2022-04-08
```

This lot represents the 12 just-purchased shares. However, notice that the purchase price of $114.17 is higher than the current price of $90. This is because the cost bases from the washed sales were added to this new lot. The value of leftover_lots holds the three-share remainder:

	ticker	purchase_price	quantity	purchase_date	sell_price	sell_date	wash_sale
1	VTI	105	3.0	2022-01-08	85	2022-04-05	False

Notice that this lot is not marked as a wash sale.

Finally, the value of `adj_lots` shows the old closed VTI lots, with the wash-sale flag now set to True (some columns also omitted here):

	ticker	purchase_price	quantity	purchase_date	sell_price	sell_date	wash_sale
0	VTI	100	10.0	2022-01-01	75	2022-04-01	True
1	VTI	105	2.0	2022-01-08	85	2022-04-05	True

Let's move on to updating lots for sales. This requires a few steps as well. The first and most straightforward is to make the updates to sales of assets that don't cause any wash sales; those don't necessitate any cost-basis adjustments. In this step and later ones, we'll use a helper function shown in the following code snippet. This function helps us create a new tax lot by modifying an existing one. It's called by passing in an existing lot, an index, and new values to place into that index:

```
def update_lot(lot: pd.Series, idx: List[str], values: List):
    """ Helper function to create a new lot by updating
    an existing one """
    new_lot = lot.copy()
    new_lot[idx] = values
    return new_lot
```

Listing 14.6 closes lots that don't create wash sales. The code works in a loop through each ticker and the sale from each lot. If the lot being sold from would create a wash sale (has at least one value in the `blocking_lots` position), we skip it but store that sale to be handled later. Otherwise, the code creates a new closed lot for the portion that was sold and, if anything is left (in other words, if the sale was smaller than the total lot size), creates a lot representing the leftover amount. The code returns three things:

- Fully closed lots resulting from sales
- The still-held lots
- The sells left to be processed

Listing 14.6   Closes unblocked lots

```
def close_unblocked_lots(lots: pd.DataFrame, sells: Dict,
                         current_date: dt.date, current_prices: pd.Series):
    """ Update tax lots for sales that don't create any wash sales """
    lots = lots.copy()
    closed_lots = []
    remaining_sells = {k:{} for k in sells}
    for ticker, ticker_sells in sells.items():
        ticker_lots = lots[np.isnan(lots['sell_price']) *
                      lots['ticker'] == ticker]
        for purchase_date, sell_value in ticker_sells.items():
```

```
        i = ticker_lots['purchase_date'].tolist().index(purchase_date)
        i = ticker_lots.index[i]
        sold_lot = lots.loc[i]
        if len(sold_lot['blocking_lots']):
            remaining_sells[ticker][sold_lot['purchase_date']] = \
                sell_value
            continue
        sold_shares = sell_value / current_prices[ticker]
        idx = ['quantity', 'sell_date', 'sell_price', 'wash_sale']
        val = [sold_shares, current_date.strftime('%Y-%m-%d'),
                current_prices[ticker], not sold_lot['sellable']]
        closed_lot = update_lot(sold_lot, idx, val)        ◁── A new closed lot
        closed_lots.append(closed_lot)                         represents the
                                                               portion sold.
        remaining_shares = sold_lot['quantity'] - sold_shares
        if remaining_shares > 0:      ◁───────────── If we didn't sell the whole lot, we
            remainder_lot = sold_lot.copy()           need a new lot for the amount left.
            remainder_lot['quantity'] = remaining_shares
            lots.loc[i] = remainder_lot
        else:
            lots = lots.drop(i)
    closed_lots = pd.DataFrame(closed_lots, columns=lots.columns)

    return closed_lots, lots, remaining_sells
```

The next part isn't too bad either. We need a short helper function that will append a column to our current tax lots. The column is called remaining_quantity, and it holds the number of shares that will remain in the lot after any sales. The code loops through each lot, looks for any sales from this lot, and subtracts the quantity sold from the quantity originally held. It returns a copy of the lots object with the new column appended.

Listing 14.7 Calculating remaining shares after sales

```
def calculate_remaining_quantities(lots: pd.DataFrame, sells: Dict,
                                   current_prices: pd.Series):
    """ Calculate the number of shares remaining in tax lots after any
    sales """

    lots = lots.copy()
    remaining_quantities = pd.Series(0, lots.index)
    for (i, lot) in lots.iterrows():
        if not np.isnan(lot['sell_date']):    ◁── Has this lot been sold?
            continue
        ticker = lot['ticker']
        ticker_sells = sells.get(ticker, )               Subtracts the
        purchase_date = lot['purchase_date']            shares sold from
        lot_sale = ticker_sells.get(purchase_date, 0)    the original
        remaining_quantities[i] = \                       quantity
            lot['quantity'] - lot_sale / current_prices[ticker]  ◁─┘
```

```
lots['remaining_quantity'] = remaining_quantities

return lots
```

The next part is where things get a little tricky. The reason for the trickiness is that we can potentially sell from multiple lots that cause wash sales—perhaps even wash sales with each other. This would apply in the somewhat unintuitive case we discussed earlier, where we sell from lots that have both been purchased in the last 30 days.

Let's walk through an example to understand the need for this somewhat complicated step. Assume that we bought 10 shares of VTI for $100 each 10 days ago and another 15 shares for $95 each 5 days later. Today, we sell 8 shares from the early lot and 12 shares from the later lot. These trades both create wash sales, so we need to do a cost-basis adjustment. Ordinarily, we would add the cost basis of the eight shares sold from the early lot to the cost basis of the later lot. But the later lot has only three shares remaining in it—so we should consider only those three shares washed. Then, focusing on the later lot, we would normally add the cost basis of the 12 shares sold from this lot to the cost basis of the earlier lot. However, the earlier lot didn't have 12 shares in the first place. Even if we hadn't sold from it, we would need to wash the losses from only 10 of the 12 shares sold from the later lot. Of course, we did sell from the earlier lot, and only two shares remain. So only the losses from 2 of the 12 shares sold should be washed.

Another case can arise if we hold two old lots (more than 30 days old) and one lot purchased within the last 30 days. If we realize losses from the old lots, we need to adjust the cost basis of the new lot. But we have to be careful not to double-count. For example, if we sold 10 shares from each of the old lots, but the new lot only contains 5 shares, only 5 shares' worth of losses should be washed.

Because of the potential for situations like this, we need to be careful with our adjustments for sales that create wash sales. Listing 14.8 shows the code that does the adjusting. Note that this function operates on lots from a single asset. Later we'll loop over the assets and apply this function to each. The function is long, so let's look at a few of the key steps:

1 For a given sale, find which other lots cause a wash sale. That's what the object `blocks_idx` is—essentially, a list of all the lots that cause the sale to be considered a wash sale.

2 Calculate the number of shares to wash. This isn't necessarily the same as the number of shares sold from the lot being examined, for the reasons we just discussed.

3 If there are shares to wash, create a new closed lot marked as a wash sale. Store the adjustments that need to be made to the "blocking" lots, and deduct the number of shares washed from these lots.

4 If the number of shares sold is greater than the number that needed to be washed, create another closed lot that isn't marked as a wash sale.

5 If the size of the lot we sold from was larger than the number of shares sold, modify the original lot with the new remaining quantity.

6 Loop through the lots that had blocked sales and perform the necessary cost-basis adjustments.

Listing 14.8   Updating lots for wash sales caused by sells

```
def update_ticker_lots_with_wash_sells(lots, sells, current_date,
                                       current_price):
    """ Adjust lots for a single ticker for sales that
    could create washes """
    lots = lots.copy()
    closed_lots, adjustments = [], []
    blocking_lots = lots['blocking_lots']
    idx = np.unique(np.concatenate([x.index.values for x in blocking_lots]))
    blocking_shares = lots.loc[pd.Index(idx), 'remaining_quantity']
    date_str = current_date.strftime('%Y-%m-%d')

    for purchase_date, sell_value in sells.items():
        i = lots.index[lots['purchase_date'].tolist().index(purchase_date)]
        sold_lot = lots.loc[i]
        shares_sold = sell_value / current_price
        blocking_lots = sold_lot['blocking_lots'].sort_values()
        blocks_idx = blocking_lots.index
        shares_washed = \
            min(shares_sold, blocking_shares[blocks_idx].sum())
        loss_to_wash = shares_washed * \
            (sold_lot['purchase_price'] - current_price)

        idx = ['quantity', 'sell_date', 'sell_price', 'wash_sale']
        if shares_washed > 0:
            val = [shares_washed, date_str, current_price, True]
            closed_lots.append(update_lot(sold_lot, idx, val))
            adjustments.append((blocking_lots, loss_to_wash))
            shares = blocking_shares[blocks_idx].cumsum() - shares_washed
            blocking_shares[blocks_idx] = np.clip(shares, 0, np.Inf)

        if shares_sold > shares_washed:
            val = [shares_sold - shares_washed, date_str, current_price,
                   False]
            closed_lots.append(update_lot(sold_lot, idx, val))

        if sold_lot['quantity'] > shares_sold:
            remainder_lot = sold_lot.copy()
            remainder_lot['quantity'] -= shares_sold
            lots.loc[i] = remainder_lot
        else:
            lots.drop(i, axis='index', inplace=True)

    for blocking_lots, wash_amount in adjustments:
        for purchase_date in blocking_lots.values:
            idx = lots[lots['purchase_date'] == purchase_date].index
```

Finds the lot sold from by its purchase date → (points to `i = lots.index[lots['purchase_date'].tolist().index(purchase_date)]`)

Creates a nonwash closed lot ← (points to `if shares_sold > shares_washed:`)

Creates the remainder lot, if necessary → (points to `if sold_lot['quantity'] > shares_sold:`)

Cost-basis adjustments ← (points to `for blocking_lots, wash_amount in adjustments:`)

```
        if len(idx) == 0:
            continue
        adj_per_share = wash_amount / lots.loc[idx[0], 'quantity']
        lots.loc[idx[0], 'purchase_price'] += adj_per_share

    return pd.DataFrame(closed_lots), lots
```

To perform the adjustments for all the assets in the portfolio, we call this function once for each asset.

Listing 14.9   Updating all lots for sales

```
def update_with_wash_sells(lots, sells, current_date, current_prices):
    """ Adjust lots for sales """
    lots = calculate_remaining_quantities(lots, sells, current_prices)
    closed_lots, open_lots = [], []
    for ticker, ticker_sells in sells.items():
        ticker_lots = lots[lots['ticker'] == ticker]
        price = current_prices[ticker]
        ticker_res = \
            update_ticker_lots_with_wash_sells(ticker_lots, ticker_sells,
                                               current_date, price)
        closed_lots.append(ticker_res[0])
        open_lots.append(ticker_res[1])

    return pd.concat(closed_lots), pd.concat(open_lots)
```

Finally, we define two more functions, update_lots_for_sells() and update_lots_with_trades(), that sit above everything we've shown so far. The first takes care of all adjustments due to selling. This function is called by the second one, which also calls the function that performs the updates due to buys. There isn't much to say about either of these, because they're simply calling the more complicated functions we looked at already.

Listing 14.10   Updating all lots for sales

```
def update_lots_for_sells(lots: pd.DataFrame,
                          sells: Dict,
                          current_date: dt.date,
                          current_prices: pd.Series):      Creates closed
    """ Adjust lots for sells """                          lots for sells
    unblocked_res = \                                      that didn't
        close_unblocked_lots(lots, sells, current_date, current_prices)  ◄── cause washes
    updates = update_with_wash_sells(unblocked_res[1], unblocked_res[2],
                                     current_date, current_prices)  ◄───────
                                                           Performs any
    closed_lots = pd.concat((unblocked_res[0], updates[0]))  needed wash-sale
                                                           adjustments
    return updates[1], closed_lots

def update_lots_with_trades(lots: pd.DataFrame,
```

```
                              buys: Dict,
                              sells: Dict,
                              current_date: dt.date,
                              current_prices: pd.Series) -> pd.DataFrame:
    """ Modify tax lots to reflect buys and sells, with any necessary
        adjustments for wash sales """
```

This includes adjustments for wash sales caused by buys.

```
    lots, closed_lots = update_lots_for_sells(lots, sells, current_date,
                                              current_prices)
    new_lots, leftover_lots, lots = update_lots_with_buys(lots, buys,
                                              current_date,
                                              current_prices)

    updated_lots = pd.concat((closed_lots, lots, leftover_lots, new_lots),
                             ignore_index=True)
    updated_lots.drop(['sellable', 'blocking_lots', 'blocks_buy',
                       'remaining_quantity'], axis=1, inplace=True)

    return updated_lots
```

That's it for wash sales! We know how to identify trades that would create wash sales ahead of time and how to make any necessary cost-basis adjustments to account for wash sales after they happen. But the point of TLH is to make trades that help save on taxes without causing wash sales. In the next section, we'll cover how to decide when to make these more valuable TLH trades.

14.3 Deciding when to harvest

Assuming we are holding an asset at an unrealized loss, should we sell the asset to realize the loss? The answer depends on more than just the current price being below the purchase price. Trading does have costs, after all, whether through explicit commissions or bid–ask spreads. But there are more subtle "costs" that should be considered as well. This section goes over the multiple factors that should be taken into account when considering harvesting a loss.

Throughout this chapter, we'll compare various costs to the benefit of harvesting a loss. In each case, the benefit will be assumed to be the amount of taxes that can be offset using the losses. Specifically, this is the size of the loss multiplied by the appropriate tax rate for the lot: either the long-term gains rate or the ordinary income rate at the federal level, plus additional state or local tax rates.

We'll also assume that we'll be replacing whatever asset (or assets) we sell with new purchases of other assets so the portfolio remains fully invested. That is, every TLH event has two parts: selling to realize losses and buying to replace the sold assets.

14.3.1 Trading costs

The comparison of trading costs to tax benefits is fairly simple. Commissions are generally fixed and known in advance (and often nonexistent for retail investors), and typical bid–ask spreads are available online.

The following listing shows a function called `evaluate_tcost()`, which computes the net benefit of a trade after considering the costs of trading. The function allows the possibility that the bid–ask spreads on the asset being sold and the asset being purchased are different.

Listing 14.11   Measuring benefit of harvesting a loss, net of trading cost

```
def evaluate_tcost(lot: pd.Series, current_price: float,
                   sell_spread: float, buy_spread: float,
                   commission_rate: float = 0):
    """ Evaluate a loss harvest based on the cost to execute it """
    trade_size = lot['quantity'] * current_price

    spread_cost = (buy_spread + sell_spread) * trade_size
    commission_cost = 2 * commission_rate * trade_size

    return lot['tax_benefit'] - (spread_cost + commission_cost)
```

Note that we haven't included any notion of fixed commissions in this calculation. These are per-trade charges that don't change with the size of the trade. Once common, most online brokerages have stopped charging these fees, so we don't worry about how to incorporate them into trading cost calculations here.

Trading costs are fairly straightforward and intuitive—if we're making a trade, we want the tax benefit to outweigh the cost. In the next section, we'll look at a "cost" that is somewhat more subtle.

14.3.2 *Opportunity cost*

For this section, we'll assume that the asset we're considering harvesting is an ETF and that we plan to replace the ETF we sell with a similar ETF to stay fully invested. This is how robo-advisors, including Wealthfront, Betterment, and Charles Schwab, perform TLH in their ETF-based portfolios: each ETF has an assigned "alternate" that is purchased as a replacement when the "primary" ETF is sold for TLH purposes. Losses in the alternate ETF may be harvested as well if they are held at a loss. In such an event, the alternate is replaced with the primary after the sale of the alternate.

Let's start with an example, using VTI and ITOT as our primary and alternate ETFs to represent the US stock market. Assume that we bought 10 shares of VTI for $200 each, and the current share price is $190 (a 5% loss). The $10 per share loss is large enough to overcome the costs of trading, so we sell the VTI shares and purchase shares to ITOT to stay fully invested. For simplicity, we can assume that the ITOT shares cost $190 each as well.

A week later, the prices of VTI and ITOT drop again—they each now trade at $170. This is an even better harvesting opportunity than the first one. Unfortunately, we can't take advantage of it. If we sold the shares of ITOT, we'd need to replace them with shares of VTI. But we can't buy VTI, because we harvested losses in VTI a week ago, and buying it now would create a wash sale. We have to wait until 30 days have passed, at which point we can buy VTI without triggering a wash sale. By that time, there is a chance that the market will recover and the harvesting opportunity may be gone—we've missed out on additional benefit because harvesting when we did locked us into holding ITOT for at least 30 days.

Figure 14.5 shows a plot of the additional tax benefit we miss out on as a function of the primary ETF price during the 30-day period for which we are locked into holding that ETF. When the price is above the harvest price, the additional benefit is zero. However, when the price is below the harvest price, the additional benefit increases linearly with the distance between the two.

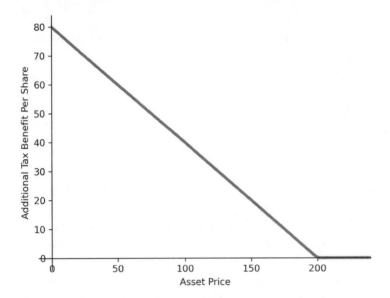

Figure 14.5 Potential additional tax benefit as a function of VTI's price

The line in figure 14.5 has the same shape as the payout curve for a put option. For those unfamiliar with this concept, a *put option* gives the holder the right, but not the obligation, to sell an underlying instrument at a previously agreed price—called the *strike price*—any time before a preset expiration date. For example, a put option may give its holder the right to sell a share of AAPL (currently trading at about $150) for $130 at any time in the next six months. Anyone familiar with options may recognize that this describes an American put option. A European put option is largely similar, except that the sale can only be done on the expiration date.

A put option has value because if the price of the underlying security drops below the strike price, the option holder can buy the stock at the market price and then sell it at a strike price for a profit. Of course, the stock price may never drop below the strike price during the life of the option. In this scenario, the option expires worthless. The value of the option comes from the *possibility* that it can be exercised for a profit, although there is no guarantee of that occurring.

COMPUTING THE OPPORTUNITY COST

The theory of options pricing is fascinating but far too deep to cover in this book. Certain types of options (under certain assumptions about the random movement of stock prices) can be priced using the Black–Scholes formula. For other types of options, or for different models of stock price movement, there is no simple formula, and options need to be priced using numerical methods or Monte-Carlo simulations. American put options fall into the latter category. Luckily, there is a Python package that has the pricing solutions coded for easy use. The package is called `option-price`, and it can be installed via the command line by running `pip install option-price`.

To use the package to price an option, we first instantiate an `Option` object with the necessary parameters:

- `european`—`True` for European options and `False` for American; we want `False`.
- `kind`—Must be either `put` or `call`; we want `put`.
- `s0`—Current price of the asset.
- `k`—Strike price for the option.
- `t`—Length of the option life in days.
- `sigma`—Annualized volatility of the asset.
- `r`—Risk-free rate of return.
- `dv`—Dividend yield of the asset.

Once the `Option` object is instantiated, we can obtain a price by calling its `getPrice()` method. This method requires two parameters:

- `method`—For American put options, this must be `BT` (for binomial tree). For other option types, specifying `BSM` will price the option using the Black–Scholes formula, and `MC` will price the option using Monte-Carlo simulations.
- `iteration`—For pricing options with binomial trees or simulations, this specifies the number of iterations to do: either the depth of the tree or the number of simulations.

Here's an example usage, pricing an American put:

```
from optionprice import Option

x = Option(european=False, kind='put', s0=150, k=140, t=30,
           sigma=.45, r=.03, dv=.01)
p = x.getPrice('BT', iteration=1000)
```

Running this code should result in a price of about $3.4284. Note that specifying an invalid pricing method (for example `BSM` for an American put) won't result in an error—the price returned will simply be `None`. Now let's use this knowledge to evaluate a harvesting opportunity in light of the opportunity cost.

There is one small detail that we need to incorporate. Tax rates, and thus the benefit of harvesting a loss, aren't fixed. They typically decrease as time passes. For instance, an investor's tax rate for short-term gains and losses may be 40%, whereas the long-term rate is only 20%. This of course affects the current benefit of harvesting a loss, but it should affect the opportunity-cost calculation as well. If the 30-day holding period for avoiding wash sales doesn't straddle the point at which a lot goes from short-term to long-term, this doesn't really matter—we just need to be sure to apply the correct tax rate to both the tax-benefit calculator and the option-value calculation. However, if the tax rate changes during the 30-day waiting period, we need to account for the change.

To see why this matters, let's go back to the example with VTI where we introduced the concept of the opportunity cost. In that example, the price dropped from $200 at the time of purchase to $190 at the time of harvesting to $175 a week later. We missed out on harvesting an additional $15 worth of losses per share. If the date of the harvest is (for example) only a few days after the initial purchase, the $10 loss and the additional $15 loss are equally valuable in terms of taxes—the short-term rate applies to both. But if the harvest is 364 days after the initial purchase, the additional $15 loss isn't worth as much, because the lower long-term tax rate applies. If the tax rates are 40% and 20%, the $10 harvested loss is worth $4 in tax benefit, whereas the $15 loss we missed out on is worth only $3.

We can account for the decreasing tax rate (and hence the decreasing value of harvesting) by breaking the 30-day waiting period into two parts:

- From the current date until the tax lot becomes long-term
- From the time the tax lot becomes long-term until the end of the 30-day waiting period

Then we can break the option value into two components, each corresponding to one of these time segments. The value corresponding to the first segment can be computed by simply changing the t parameter in the definition of the Option object to be the time at which the tax rate changes. For example, if we're considering a lot that has been held for 355 days, we use $t = 10$ to calculate the option value for the first time segment. The value for the second time segment is the option value over the whole 30-day period less the option value for the first time segment. We'll show the exact calculations in the next section.

DECIDING TO HARVEST

The framework for deciding whether harvesting a loss is worth the opportunity cost is the same as deciding whether it's worth the trading costs: we compute the benefit of the harvest and compare it to the option value that we give up by harvesting the loss and starting the 30-day waiting period when we can't harvest again. Listing 14.12 shows a function that computes both the tax benefit and opportunity cost and returns the difference.

The code handles an interesting possibility where the 30-day wash-sale period crosses the point at which the lot we are considering selling goes from a short-term to a long-term holding (usually 365 days). If this happens, we price two options: one that covers the entire 30-day period and another that only covers the period from now until the holding period becomes long-term and the tax rate changes. We then decompose the value of the first option into two parts corresponding to before and after the tax-rate switch. The opportunity cost is obtained by applying the appropriate tax rate to each part: short-term rate for the first part and long-term rate for the second. In cases where the wash-sale period doesn't cross over a tax-rate switch, we can use one rate.

Listing 14.12   Calculating TLH benefit after opportunity cost

```
def evaluate_opp_cost(lot: pd.Series, price: float, current_date: dt.date,
                      tax_params: Dict, sigma: float, risk_free: float,
                      div_yield: float):
    """ Evaluate a loss harvest based on the opportunity cost
    vs the tax benefit """

    purchase_date = dt.date.fromisoformat(lot['purchase_date'])
    holding_period = (current_date - purchase_date).days
    if holding_period >= tax_params['lt_cutoff']:          ◄─────┐ Finds the applicable
        rate_now = rate_later = tax_params['lt_rate']            │ tax rates
    else:
        rate_now = tax_params['st_rate']
        rate_later = tax_params['lt_rate']
    price = float(price)

    o_full = Option(european=False, kind='put', s0=price, k=price,
                    t=30, sigma=sigma, r=risk_free, dv=div_yield)
    p_full = o_full.getPrice('BT')    ◄── Option price over the full time period

    days_to_switch = tax_params['lt_cutoff'] - holding_period
    if 0 < days_to_switch <= 30:
        o_pre_switch = Option(european=False, kind='put', s0=price,
                              k=price, t=days_to_switch, sigma=sigma,
                              r=risk_free, dv=div_yield)
        p_til_switch = o_pre_switch.getPrice('BT')
        p_after_switch = p_full - p_til_switch    ◄── Decomposes the option value

        opp_cost = rate_now * p_til_switch + rate_later * p_after_switch
    else:
        opp_cost = rate_now * p_full

    benefit = rate_now * (lot['purchase_price'] - price)

    return benefit - opp_cost
```

Option price for the period until the tax-rate change (annotation pointing to `p_til_switch = o_pre_switch.getPrice('BT')`)

Remember that we have been assuming that the harvests under consideration are being done by selling one ETF and buying a similar ETF as a replacement, and that the wash-sale rule creates an opportunity cost because we won't be able to harvest any additional losses in the alternate ETF for 30 days. It is possible to relax this assumption and partially avoid the opportunity cost by using additional ETFs. Let's say that in addition to VTI and ITOT, we can also employ SCHB and SPTM—two additional ETFs covering nearly the entire US stock market. Then, assuming we've already harvested a loss in VTI and bought ITOT, we can harvest an additional loss in ITOT and replace it with SCHB. This means we don't need to consider the opportunity cost when considering harvesting a loss in VTI or even if we're considering harvesting a loss in ITOT. However, if we get to the point of holding SCHB and are considering harvesting a loss in that ETF, we do need to consider the opportunity cost. If we sell SCHB, we can buy SPTM as a replacement, but then we're out of options—harvesting a loss in SPTM would require buying back one of the other three ETFs, which (assuming this all happens within 30 days of the VTI harvest) would create a wash sale.

Such a scenario is possible with certain asset classes (US stocks are a good example) but may not be for others. In the case of foreign bonds, for example, the number of ETFs that are similar enough to be considered replacements for each other may be smaller. For generality, the next section will assume that each asset class can contain any number of ETFs considered exchangeable for investment purposes but not "substantially identical."

14.3.3 End-to-end evaluation

We've covered several criteria when considering harvesting an unrealized loss. In this section, we'll put all these considerations together in code. In doing so, we'll assume that each ETF we consider harvesting is a member of a predefined set of ETFs that are considered exchangeable. For the examples we'll run, we can use the following:

```
etf_sets = (('VTI', 'ITOT', 'SCHB', 'SPTM'),
            ('VEA', 'IEFA', 'SCHF'))
```

Note that there is no concept of ordering in the ETF sets. When we look at specific instances of harvesting, we'll consider previous transactions to determine which ETF looks most attractive to use as a replacement.

Before we start, let's consider a somewhat pathological case. Imagine we have a set of ETFs that we consider exchangeable, we have come to hold all ETFs in the set, and they are all currently at a large loss. We may want to harvest losses by selling each of the lots, but we can't. If we sell all the lots and replace the holdings from each lot with a different ETF from the set, we'll end up buying and selling the same ETF and creating a wash sale. To avoid this, we'll need to keep track of which ETFs we are buying and selling as part of TLH trades and make sure we don't buy anything we're planning on selling. Because we may not be able to harvest all our losses, we will order the lots by their tax benefit to make sure we harvest the most valuable losses first. As we said, this case is somewhat pathological, but it could happen if the portfolio has had frequent deposits and has experienced lots of volatility.

The first function considers a single lot with a known replacement ETF. The function simply calculates the net benefit considering trading costs and the net benefit considering the opportunity cost and produces a trade if the net benefit is positive for both.

Listing 14.13   Full evaluation of a TLH opportunity

```
def evaluate_harvest(lot: pd.Series, replacement: str,
                     current_date: dt.date, prices: pd.Series,
                     tax_params: Dict, sigma: float, risk_free: float,
```

```
                     div_yield: float, spreads: pd.Series):
""" Given a lot trading at a loss, decide whether the lot
should be harvested """

ticker = lot['ticker']
benefit_net_tcosts = evaluate_tcost(lot, prices[ticker],
                                    spreads[ticker],
                                    spreads[replacement])
benefit_net_oppcost = evaluate_opp_cost(lot, prices[ticker],
                                        current_date,
                                        tax_params,
                                        sigma, risk_free, div_yield)
if min(benefit_net_tcosts, benefit_net_oppcost) < 0:
    return None

value = lot['quantity'] * prices[ticker]
return pd.Series([ticker, lot['purchase_date'], value, replacement],
                 ['ticker', 'purchase_date', 'amount', 'replacement'])
```

Now let's go one level higher: listing 14.14 shows a function that decides about harvesting trades for all ETFs in a particular set. For example, this function can be used to decide about harvesting trades for all holdings of VTI, ITOT, SCHB, and SPTM.

The code starts by calling the `check_all_assets_for_restrictions()` function we defined before and filters out lots that we can't sell because they would create a wash sale. It then orders the lots by the amount of tax benefit from selling (this is the applicable tax rate multiplied by the size of the loss, which we have seen previously as well). Next, it orders the set of potential replacement ETFs. The ones that come first are any that

- Can be purchased without creating a wash sale
- Aren't found in the lots being considered for harvesting

These are followed by ETFs in the lots being considered for harvesting that have the *opposite* ordering of the lots. This is because we don't want to commit to using a particular ETF as a replacement if we're holding a lot of that ETF with a large potential tax benefit. We can only buy or sell the ETF—doing both would create a wash sale.

Finally, the code iterates through each lot. When considering a particular lot, the code looks at the list of potential replacements and chooses the first suitable one. At this point, the harvesting trade is evaluated using the `evaluate_harvest()` function. If the outcome is to harvest the loss, we add the ETF being sold and the ETF being purchased as a replacement to lists of ETFs being sold and purchased, respectively. These lists are used in later iterations to find suitable replacements.

Here is the code:

Listing 14.14 Full evaluation of a TLH opportunity

```
def evaluate_harvests_for_etf_set(lots, current_date, prices, tax_params,
                                  sigmas, risk_free, div_yields,
                                  spreads, etf_set):
    """ Decide whether to harvest eligible lots from holdings
    belonging to one set of exchangeable ETFs """
    all_lots = check_all_assets_for_restrictions(lots, prices,
                                                 current_date)
    lots = all_lots[all_lots['sellable']]
    gains = (prices[lots['ticker']].values - lots['purchase_price'])
    lots['gain'] = lots['quantity'] * gains
    lots = lots[lots['gain'] < 0]
    lots['hp'] = \
        list(map(lambda d: (current_date - dt.date.fromisoformat(d)).days,
                 lots['purchase_date']))        # Calculates holding periods,
    lots['tax_rate'] = tax_params['st_rate']    # then tax rates
    lt_lots = lots['hp'][lots['hp'] >= tax_params['lt_cutoff']].index
    lots.loc[lt_lots, 'tax_rate'] = tax_params['lt_rate']    # Orders lots by
    lots['tax_benefit'] = -lots['gain'] * lots['tax_rate']   # tax benefit
    lots = lots.sort_values(by='tax_benefit', ascending=False)

    tickers_by_benefit = lots.groupby('ticker')['tax_benefit'] \
        .sum().sort_values().index.values
    non_buyable = all_lots[all_lots['blocks_buy']]['ticker'].values
    replacements = [_ for _ in etf_set if _ not in tickers_by_benefit
                    and _ not in non_buyable]    # Finds potential replacement ETFs
    replacements.extend(tickers_by_benefit)
    harvests, buying, selling = {}, [], []
    for i, lot in lots.iterrows():
        ticker = lot['ticker']
        lot_replacements = [_ for _ in replacements if _ != ticker
                            and _ not in selling]
        if ticker in buying or len(lot_replacements) == 0:    # Can't sell this lot;
            continue                                          # move to the next
        replacement = lot_replacements[0]
        result = evaluate_harvest(lot, replacement, current_date,
                                  prices, tax_params, sigmas[ticker],
                                  risk_free, div_yields[ticker], spreads)
        if result is not None:
            harvests[i] = result
            buying.append(replacement)    # Adds the replacement
            selling.append(ticker)        # ETF to the list of ETFs
                                          # we're buying
    return pd.DataFrame(harvests).T
```

The final piece of code goes up one more level. It breaks the portfolio's holdings into sets of ETFs, applies the previous function to each set, and returns all the harvesting trades.

Listing 14.15   Evaluating TLH opportunities for all assets

```
def evaluate_all_harvests(lots: pd.DataFrame, current_date: dt.date,
                          prices: pd.Series, tax_params: Dict,
                          sigmas: pd.Series, risk_free: float,
                          div_yields: pd.Series, spreads: pd.Series,
                          etf_sets: Union[Tuple, List]):
    """ Generate harvesting trades for all currently held assets """
    harvests = []
    for etf_set in etf_sets:
        set_lots = lots[lots['ticker'].isin(etf_set)]
        if len(set_lots) == 0:
            continue
        set_harvests = \
            evaluate_harvests_for_etf_set(set_lots, current_date, prices,
                                          tax_params, sigmas, risk_free,
                                          div_yields, spreads, etf_set)
        if len(set_harvests) > 0:
            harvests.append(set_harvests)

    return pd.concat(harvests, ignore_index=True)
```

These three functions aren't extremely complicated, but they aren't exactly trivial. Let's walk through two examples and make sure the results match our expectations.

EXAMPLES

For the first example, we'll consider a pathological case where we hold lots of multiple assets that are all part of one TLH set. This snippet of code gives all the inputs for this example:

```
lots =      pd.DataFrame(\{'ticker': ['VTI', 'ITOT', 'SCHB', 'SPTM', 'VTI'],
                'purchase_price': [90, 91, 92, 93, 94],
                'quantity': [10, 10, 10, 10, 10],
                'purchase_date': ['2021-02-01', '2021-02-02', '2021-02-03',
                                  '2021-02-04', '2021-02-05'],
                'sell_price': [np.NaN, np.NaN, np.NaN, np.NaN, np.NaN],
                'sell_date': [np.NaN, np.NaN, np.NaN, np.NaN, np.NaN],
                'wash_sale': [False, False, False, False, False],
                \})
prices = pd.Series([80, 80, 80, 80], ['VTI', 'ITOT', 'SPTM', 'SCHB'])
spreads = pd.Series([.0001, .0001, .0001, .0001], ['VTI', 'SCHB',
                                                   'SPTM', 'ITOT'])
current_date = dt.date(2021, 4, 1)
tax_params = \{'st_rate': .40, 'lt_rate': .20, 'lt_cutoff': 365\}
sigmas = pd.Series([.18, .18, .18, .18], ['VTI', 'ITOT', 'SPTM', 'SCHB'])
div_yields = pd.Series([.02, .02, .02, .02], ['VTI', 'ITOT',
                                              'SPTM', 'SCHB'])
risk_free = .03
```

Looking at the inputs, we have five 10-share lots of four different ETFs, all falling into the same set of ETFs for TLH purposes. The losses are fairly large (with purchase prices between $90 and $94 against a current price of $80 for all four ETFs) and short-term. The bid–ask spread for each ETF is very small, so the tax benefit outweighs both the opportunity and trading costs for each lot. However, we can't harvest every lot because doing so would require buying and selling the same instrument, creating a wash sale. So which lot or lots may we expect not to harvest? The first lot (VTI purchased at $90) has the smallest loss, so we may expect to skip this one. But we hold another lot of VTI that we purchased at $94, so the tax benefit we can get by harvesting both VTI lots is bigger than the tax benefit of harvesting any other ETF. Of what remains, the ITOT lot has the smallest loss and least tax benefit, so this is the one we should expect not to sell. To get the results, we call the `evaluate_all_harvest()` function:

```
tlh_trades = evaluate_all_harvests(lots, current_date, prices,
                                   tax_params, sigmas, risk_free,
                                   div_yields, spreads, etf_sets)
```

We get this result for `tlh_trades`:

	ticker	purchase_date	amount	replacement
0	VTI	2021-02-05	800	ITOT
1	SPTM	2021-02-04	800	ITOT
2	SCHB	2021-02-03	800	ITOT
3	VTI	2021-02-01	800	ITOT

As expected, we sell all lots except the ITOT lot, and we use ITOT as the replacement ETF for all sales. This choice of lots maximizes the tax benefit for this example.

Let's try one more. It is similar, but we assume that we hold five lots of the same instrument, all purchased at different prices. The current price is now assumed to be just below the price of the cheapest lot. Here are the new lots and prices:

```
lots = \
    pd.DataFrame({'ticker': ['VTI', 'VTI', 'VTI', 'VTI', 'VTI'],
                  'purchase_price': [90, 91, 92, 93, 94],
                  'quantity': [10, 10, 10, 10, 10],
                  'purchase_date': ['2021-02-01', '2021-02-02', '2021-02-03',
                                    '2021-02-04', '2021-02-05'],
                  'sell_price': [np.NaN, np.NaN, np.NaN, np.NaN, np.NaN],
                  'sell_date': [np.NaN, np.NaN, np.NaN, np.NaN, np.NaN],
                  'wash_sale': [False, False, False, False, False],
                  })
prices = pd.Series([89, 89, 89, 89], ['VTI', 'ITOT', 'SPTM', 'SCHB'])
```

When we evaluate these lots, we get the following result:

	ticker	purchase_date	amount	replacement
0	VTI	2021-02-05	890	ITOT

1	VTI	2021-02-04	890	ITOT
2	VTI	2021-02-03	890	ITOT
3	VTI	2021-02-02	890	ITOT

We choose to sell all but the first lot, where the loss is very small. For this lot, the tax benefit isn't worth the opportunity cost. For each sale, we replace VTI with ITOT.

14.4 Testing a TLH strategy

How much value can TLH add? As we've discussed, this answer depends on many variables, including tax rates, deposit size and frequency, and, of course, market conditions. It can also depend on the implementation details of the strategy: the size of the sets of exchangeable ETFs, or how often tax lots are evaluated for harvesting opportunities.

Luckily, the backtest code from chapter 11 gives us nearly all the machinery we need to run a historical backtest of a TLH strategy. We won't show all the modifications required to incorporate harvesting into the backtest, but we can give some pointers about things to consider.

14.4.1 Backtester modifications

The first and most obvious change needed in the backtester is the retention of closed lots. The original backtester discarded any lots with a quantity of zero shares after each rebalance. This is an easy change.

Next, we need to insert a harvesting evaluation step into the loop in the backtester's `run()` method. Moreover, any harvesting trades need to be combined with trades made for the purposes of rebalancing. Luckily, this isn't too difficult. When we generate a harvesting trade, we choose a lot to sell and a replacement ETF to buy. So far, we have assumed that we buy exactly as much as we sell, leaving the total position size the same before and after harvesting. However, if we wish to either purchase or sell a certain asset (or asset class) for rebalancing, we can simply change the size of the "replacement" purchase in a TLH trade.

As an example of this, let's assume we have a portfolio of $100,000 with a target of $60,000 in US stocks. We're currently holding $50,000 in VTI. We can generate a harvesting trade for US stocks to sell $50,000 of VTI and buy $50,000 of ITOT. Then we can also generate a rebalancing trade to buy $10,000 worth of VTI to bring the portfolio back to its 60% target. Of course, we can't harvest a loss in VTI and purchase it on the same day, so we add the $10,000 to the purchase of ITOT. The same principle applies with more ETFs in the mix. If rebalancing calls for purchasing any asset in the same ETF set as one being purchased as part of a harvesting trade, it makes sense to make the "replacement" purchase larger.

Finally, there is the question of wash sales. We know how to check whether assets can be bought or sold without creating wash sales, and we know how to do an after-the-fact adjustment to tax lots if we happen to create a wash sale. We can do one of two things:

- Add constraints to the rebalancing optimization to make sure the trades generated by the rebalancing process don't create any wash sales
- Allow wash sales, but penalize them through an objective term

Each has its merits. The downside to hard constraints in the first option is that we can potentially run into cases where we've harvested losses in every ETF recently and can't buy anything without creating wash sales. This can be a problem if there is a deposit coming into the portfolio or the portfolio is far below its target weight in the unbuyable asset class. We've mentioned this case before—we'd need to wait until 30 days have passed since the last harvest trade before we can make new purchases. Allowing wash sales gets around this problem but introduces another parameter into the optimization: the weight on the wash-sale term. Which option makes more sense depends on the strategy and specifics of the investor.

14.4.2 *Choosing ETFs*

Earlier we showed some examples of sets of ETFs that can be used to represent the same asset class, but we didn't say how we chose them. Generally, if you have a primary ETF in mind, it isn't difficult to find potential replacements by going online. Commercial robo-advisers show the ETFs they use to represent asset classes, and multiple sites show suggested comparisons. For example, the etf.com page for VTI lists ITOT, SCHB, SPTM, IWV, and PBUS as comparisons.

However, we don't suggest taking all these suggested comparisons blindly. Although they are generally similar, there can be differences. In the example in the previous paragraph, PBUS is a much smaller and more thinly traded fund than VTI. The cost of trading is significantly higher, with a typical bid–ask spread of $0.09 versus $0.03 for VTI. Moreover, PBUS tracks a narrower index, holding under 1,000 stocks, compared to over 4,000 for VTI. The code we wrote in chapter 3 can pull realized historical returns to help with comparisons. Ultimately, the question of "how similar is enough" is up to the investor.

We should also point out that comparisons found online can suggest funds that are "too similar"—meaning they track the same index and can be considered substantially identical by the IRS. The etf.com page for SPY lists IVV and VOO as potential comparisons, but all three funds track the S&P 500.

Summary

- Tax-loss harvesting is a method for reducing current taxes, but it also creates future liabilities.
- TLH creates economic benefits by delaying taxes into the future, taking advantage of the time value of money and the differential between short-term and long-term capital gains tax rates.
- The wash-sale rule limits the applicability of TLH and needs to be considered when making trading decisions.

- Wash sales aren't illegal, but they effectively disallow current tax benefits. Wash sales require adjusting the cost basis of any still-held lots that were involved in the washed transaction.
- TLH has costs: both monetary trading costs and more conceptual opportunity costs.
- Harvesting trades should be required to provide more tax benefit than either of the costs.
- The exact amount of value that can be achieved through TLH depends on several variables. As with rebalancing, the benefit can be estimated and optimized through backtesting.

index

The Manning Early Access Program

Don't wait to start learning! In MEAP, the Manning Early Access Program, you can read books as they're being created and long before they're available in stores.

Here's how MEAP works.

- **Start now.** Buy a MEAP and you'll get all available chapters in PDF, ePub, Kindle, and liveBook formats.

- **Regular updates.** New chapters are released as soon as they're written. We'll let you know when fresh content is available.

- **Finish faster.** MEAP customers are the first to get final versions of all books! Pre-order the print book, and it'll ship as soon as it's off the press.

- **Contribute to the process.** The feedback you share with authors makes the end product better.

- **No risk.** You get a full refund or exchange if we ever have to cancel a MEAP.

Explore dozens of titles in MEAP at www.manning.com.